# WILLIAM BLAKE AND THE DAUGHTERS OF ALBION

# William Blake and the Daughters of Albion

Helen P. Bruder

PR
4148
.W6
B78
1997
copy 2

First published in Great Britain 1997 by
**MACMILLAN PRESS LTD**
Houndmills, Basingstoke, Hampshire RG21 6XS and London
Companies and representatives throughout the world

A catalogue record for this book is available from the British Library.

ISBN 0–333–64036–5

First published in the United States of America 1997 by
**ST. MARTIN'S PRESS, INC.,**
Scholarly and Reference Division,
175 Fifth Avenue, New York, N.Y. 10010

ISBN 0–312–17481–0

Library of Congress Cataloging-in-Publication Data
Bruder, Helen P.
William Blake and the daughters of Albion / Helen P. Bruder.
p.   cm.
Includes bibliographical references and index.
ISBN 0–312–17481–0 (cloth)
1. Blake, William, 1757–1827—Characters—Women.   2. Blake,
William, 1757–1827—Political and social views.   3. Feminism and
literature—England—History—18th century.   4. Women and
literature—England—History—18th century.   5. Patriarchy in
literature.   6. Sex role in literature.   I. Title.
PR4148.W6B78  1997
821'.7—dc21                                          97–7119
                                                         CIP

This book is printed on paper suitable for recycling and made from fully managed and
sustained forest sources.

10   9   8   7   6   5   4   3   2   1
06   05   04   03   02   01   00   99   98   97

Printed and bound in Great Britain by
Antony Rowe Ltd, Chippenham, Wiltshire

For Charlie,
'and they sang soft thro' Lambeth's vales,
In a sweet moony night & silence they had created'

# Contents

# List of Plates

The references given at the end of captions for Plates 4–7 inclusive are those given in the William Blake Illuminated Books: *The Early Illuminated Books*, Volume 3 and *The Continental Prophecies*, Volume 4, published by the William Blake Trust and the Tate Gallery.

# Acknowledgements

I am grateful to the staff of the Bodleian Library and Oxford Brookes University Library. In particular I want to thank Brookes Inter-Library loan librarians for the speed and generosity with which they have dealt with my endless stream of pink and blue forms. Thanks also go to Charmian Hearne at Macmillan and to the supervisors of my postgraduate research: Susan Matthews, Paul O'Flinn, Colin Pedley and Nicolas Shrimpton. Judith Barbour and David Worrall provided great encouragement and inspiration; as did all the students whom I have been privileged to teach over the last five years.

My friends have also helped me immeasurably. In particular I want to thank Sam Mace, for always listening (and only occasionally laughing) and Vicki Bertram, because she has almost proved Blake right in his observation that 'Opposition is true Friendship'. I also want to thank the following people for their wisdom, indulgence and (most importantly) for their refreshing company: Michele Allen Miles, Paula Booth, Jenni Cockram, June Davies, the Gaines girls of Cardiff, Darren 'Mr Pastry' Green, Maria Hardy, Christen Lemieux, Caroline Morrell, Ann Ross and Roz Tallett. Great thanks also to 'The Kicking Daffodils' (the *best* women's football team in Oxford), for the many occasions on which they have given me something other than myself to kick.

Finally, and most profoundly, I wish to thank my family. Jane made this book possible. Her love and support over the past six years have convinced me beyond doubt that 'there is no friend like a sister'. I also want to thank my Mum and Dad for their faith in me. Without this encouragement I doubt I'd ever have put pen to paper. Lastly, I dedicate this work to Charlie Wakeham, the woman who once rescued me.

# List of Abbreviations

All quotations are from *The Complete Poetry and Prose of William Blake*, ed. David V. Erdman (New York: Anchor Press/Doubleday, 1982). Plate references in brackets are from David Erdman, *The Illuminated Blake* (New York: Anchor Press/Doubleday, 1974), unless otherwise stated.

## POEMS, PROSE WORKS AND ANNOTATIONS

| | |
|---|---|
| All Religions | *All Religions are One* |
| NNR | *There is No Natural Religion* |
| Thel | *The Book of Thel* |
| FR | *The French Revolution* |
| Lav | Annotations to Lavater's *Aphorisms on Man* |
| Songs | *Songs of Innocence and of Experience* |
| LGL | 'A Little GIRL Lost' |
| MHH | *The Marriage of Heaven and Hell* |
| VDA | *Visions of the Daughters of Albion* |
| Am | *America: A Prophecy* |
| Europe | *Europe – A Prophecy* |
| SL | *The Song of Los* |
| Urizen | *The Book of Urizen* |
| Ahania | *The Book of Ahania* |
| FZ | *The Four Zoas* |
| Milton | *Milton a Poem in 2 Books* |
| Jerusalem | *Jerusalem: The Emanation of the Giant Albion* |
| DC | *A Descriptive Catalogue* |

## JOURNALS

| | |
|---|---|
| BJECS | *British Journal for Eighteenth Century Studies* |
| BN | *The Blake Newsletter* |
| BNYPL | *Bulletin of the New York Public Library* |
| BRH | *Bulletin of Research in the Humanities* |

| | |
|---|---|
| BS | *Blake Studies* |
| BQ | *Blake: An Illustrated Quarterly* |
| CLQ | *Colby Library Quarterly* |
| ECS | *Eighteenth Century Studies* |
| ELN | *English Language Notes* |
| MLQ | *Modern Languages Quarterly* |
| PMLA | *Publications of the Modern Languages Association of America* |
| PQ | *Philological Quarterly* |
| SiR | *Studies in Romanticism* |
| SP | *Studies in Philology* |
| WC | *The Wordsworth Circle* |

# 1

# Blake Studies: A Critical Survey

> Nothing is absolutely dead: every meaning will have its home-coming festival.
>
> Mikhail Bakhtin[1]

This book aims to bring home a whole set of Blake's meanings, politically important and historically specific meanings which have been submerged by the distorting procedures central to the process of institutional canonization. Specifically, canonization requires that a writer's works be framed by 'literary' texts; these are to form the primary interpretative context, and whilst many have joined T.S. Eliot in his lamentation that Blake demonstrated a 'certain meanness of culture'[2] many more have busied themselves to show that Blake was not really that culturally impoverished. It was Northrop Frye's now classic *Fearful Symmetry* (1947) which in the postwar period established Blake as a great English writer, diligently working with the myths and archetypes central to Western culture, and from here his journey into the academy was irresistible. Before long the often unemployed Cockney engraver William Blake became a Romantic Poet, a producer of that most elite form of discourse in the well-established hierarchy of literary genres.

It is my argument that this cultured Blake is now a somewhat redundant construction, and that what is needed is the recontextualization of his works in a number of neglected historical and discursive contexts. Furthermore, it is my conviction that whilst many aspects of late eighteenth-century radical and popular culture have been significantly understudied,[3] the most seriously neglected contemporary discourses ignored by Blake scholars are those concerned with women, sexuality, gender and sexual difference. It can be no accident that this particular

1

intertextual material has been disregarded, for even the most cursory contextual explorations reveal a myriad of diverse discourses in which these issues are addressed. Theologians, mystics, doctors, politicians, journalists, artists, moralists, midwives, pornographers and many more of Blake's contemporaries offered earnest and often polemical sexual speculation and it is their voices which I seek to restore. As Mikhail Bakhtin reminds us, there are 'immense boundless masses of forgotten contextual meanings' which at certain moments in the great dialogue of history 'are recalled and invigorated in renewed form (in a new context)'.[4] Before I begin this recontextualizing task I shall, however, spend this first chapter offering a detailed explanation of both my commitment to a feminist-historicist methodology and my contention that the Blake establishment has been deeply negligent in its treatment of Blake's engagement with the late eighteenth-century debate about the nature, rights and role of women.[5]

The rest of this book consists of four chapters in which a small selection of Blake's verbal and visual texts are subjected to rigorous close readings. This 'minute particulars' approach is not especially new in Blake studies but the theory of language underlying it differs markedly from the new critical underpinnings of many of its predecessors. Fundamentally, my focus will not be narrowly fixed on the words on the page but, following Bakhtin, on the 'social life of the verbal sign'.[6] Blake's words will be seen as part of that social dialogue in which they cannot help but participate. Sadly many writers on Blake, like Peter Ackroyd, have seen him as a man who 'withdrew from the world of common discourse [. . .] He worked for himself, and he listened only to himself'[7] but throughout this study I will rely heavily upon Bakhtin's view that language only exists in use, in motivated and reciprocal social utterances. Over the years Bakhtin came to believe that, 'A word is the purest and most sensitive medium of social existence', a view which is elaborated in a passage which is central to my work:

> Countless ideological threads running through all areas of social intercourse register effect in the word. It stands to reason, then, that the word is the most sensitive *index of social changes, and what is more, of changes still in the process of growth*, still without definitive shape and not as yet accommodated into already regularized and fully defined ideological systems. The word is the

medium in which occur the slow quantitative accretions of those changes which have not yet achieved the status of a new ideological quality, not yet produced a new and fully-fledged ideological form. The word has the capacity to register all the transitory, delicate, momentary phases of social change.[8]

By paying close attention to the life of certain ideologically loaded signs, the struggle of emergent ideas can be identified and the words central to this study are: female, woman, virgin, maid, harlot, nymph and queen. Within these signs many threads of meaning coexist, and by developing a sensitivity to the significance of verbal nuance, to the 'double-voicedness'[9] of Blake's texts, we can begin to see the ways in which he enters the sexual debate mentioned above. From the outset, however, we need to conceptualize this internal dialogue correctly, for meanings do not stand neatly beside each other but rather are in conflict. Bakhtin himself was extremely expansive on this subject, but I think the following comments are sufficient to make his meaning clear, 'Each word, [. . .] is a little arena for the clash and criss-crossing of differently orientated social accents. A word in the mouth of a particular individual person is a product of the living interaction of social forces [. . .] The word, directed towards its object, enters a dialogically agitated and tension-filled environment of alien words, value judgements and accents, weaves in and out of complex interrelationships, merges with some, recoils from others'; and in a more succinct and politically explicit form, 'differently orientated accents intersect in every ideological sign. Sign becomes an arena of the class struggle'.[10] Bakhtin's priorities led him to focus only on the issue of dialogic class struggle, but many feminists (in recent years especially those working on Romantic Gothic) have successfully appropriated and extended his ideas to incorporate an element of sexual dialogism and in this study I shall follow their example.[11]

There is, however, a price to be paid for the acknowledgement that language is a shared and socially specific medium and this is the recognition that working with 'the social stock of available signs'[12] placed restraints upon what Blake could actually do with language. He was not free to say or even think whatever he wanted, hence perhaps all the fury and repetition in his works, because he could not empty words of other people's intentions and meanings: 'The word in language is half someone else's [. . .]

Each word tastes of the contexts in which it has lived its socially charged life'.[13] This issue of words being already occupied and not submitting easily to new significations will come into especially clear focus in my third chapter, where I examine the difficulties Blake had in writing about women's sexuality, although the issue of what was discursively possible at this particular historical moment is one which I will return to repeatedly.

Bakhtin's ideas also contribute to our understanding of the formal aspects, and perhaps even generic classification, of Blake's works, for Bakhtin was a great celebrator of prose writing and an equally harsh critic of various tendencies which he found manifest in poetic discourse.[14] For Bakhtin the ideal verbal artist was the novelist Dostoevsky who he believed had created a new type of artistic thinking: polyphonic thinking which involved the writer placing 'himself' in an entirely new relationship with his created world. Characters in Dostoevsky's novels were not 'voiceless slaves', but distinct consciousnesses capable of entering into genuine dialogue and not at the mercy of an all-knowing authorial presence who retained a surplus of knowledge with which to manipulate them as the plot unfolded.[15] Polyphony, the dynamic interaction of socially distinct voices, came for Bakhtin to characterize the novel, but this quality was not restricted to prose discourse, and the idea of 'novelization' adds much to our understanding of Blake's texts (even those we know as his 'epics'). The salient features of novelized writing have been summarized thus:

> They become more free and flexible, their language renews itself by incorporating extraliterary heteroglossia and the 'novelistic' layers of literary language, they become dialogized, permeated with laughter, irony, humor, elements of self-parody and finally – this is the most important thing – the novel inserts into these other genres an indeterminacy, a certain semantic openendedness, a living contact with unfinished, still-evolving contemporary reality (the openended present).[16]

This passage describes the aspect of Blake's work which I shall make explicit: its vibrant and responsive contemporaneity, its historically specific polyphonic abundance, and it is the lack of precisely these qualities which led to Bakhtin's hostility towards poetry. What he objected to in this form of discourse was what he called its 'monological steadfastness [. . .] Everything that enters the work must immerse itself in Lethe, and forget its previous life in any other contexts: language may remember only its life in poetic contexts'.[17] Bakhtin disliked the way poetry (or at least its theorists) desired to set itself apart from the heteroglot languages of social life; he found poetry, 'stripping all aspects of language of the intentions and accents of other people, destroying all traces of social heteroglossia and diversity of language'.[18] And for Blake – who as I will show shared Bakhtin's faith that 'A single voice ends nothing and resolves nothing. Two voices is the minimum for life, the minimum for existence'[19] – only a Urizen, 'Self-clos'd, all repelling [. . .] That solitary one in immensity', would attempt to write in this way. He was also equally clear about what the nature of this monologic gospel would be,

> Let each chuse one habitation . . .
> One command, one joy, one desire,
> One curse, one weight, one measure,
> One King, one God, one Law.
> (*Urizen*, 4:36, 38–40; E.72)

## BLAKE'S LANGUAGE

It would be inaccurate to suggest that mine is the first engaged study of Blake's language. The stress many modern critical theories lay upon textuality has had an impact upon the Blake industry, and we need briefly to look at what past critics have had to say on this subject. In the last decade or so the most prolific writer on Blake's language was Nelson Hilton, whose *Literal Imagination* (1983) advertises itself as a book concerned with 'Blake's vision of words' – all of which Hilton tells us, 'can be appreciated in their aural, graphic, contemporary, historical-etymological associations'.[20] Hilton is admirably comprehensive in his tracing of the manifold layers of meaning contained within a selection of words central to Blake's thought, but the theory which underlies this practice is somewhat problematic.[21]

Fundamentally Hilton, like generations of critics before him, believes that Blake's value lies in what is unique about him, and this urge to say why Blake is so special is focused in this study upon his understanding and use of language: 'Blake had a relationship with words in their literal being that is unique in literature

[. . .] Blake participated in, and manifested, a vision of the word as object, as other, and as divine [. . .] The word becomes more than the mark of an idea; it becomes an eternal living form with its own personality, family, and destiny' (pp. 2–3). This idealization, indeed spiritualization, of Blake's words reaches grand proportions and leads Hilton to a conclusion about the social function of language which is, at least from a Bakhtinian perspective, highly unproductive:

> Every word is a parable about linguistic structure as incarnate human imagination [. . .] Every word has unlimited potential [. . .] The word has a spirit of its own more expansive than the individual mind through which it speaks or is read. Like Jesus – the Divine Imagination, Blake would say – the word is the reality in the midst of us sent to reintegrate our fallen and disparate identities (pp. 7–8).

Rather than acknowledging language as the site of various human struggles Hilton grants it its own life and gives it a suspiciously consensual and conservative function, it is 'the medium of communication and communion, in which we are all one'.[22] Hilton characterizes Blake's words and texts not as dialogic or polyphonic but as 'polysemous' and multidimensional (p. 10). He hears not voices in debate and conflict but self-generating linguistic playfulness and an almost supernatural discursive abundance which miraculously heals divisions rather than being the locus of their annunciation.

Interestingly Hilton was hailed by established Blake critics as a scholar able to incorporate post-structuralism in ways which generated new insights into Blake's work, but he was, I think, the subject of their approbation precisely because he restated a number of critical orthodoxies in a fashionable new tongue. Hilton, like so many before him, trivialized the messages and politics embodied in Blake's texts, openly admitting that the 'Literal imagination might image the text as a game board', and promising the 'player-reader' that his method 'returns to the concept of allusion its original pleasures'.[23] Reading Blake, yet again, becomes synonymous with the gentlemanly pastime of allusion spotting (usually literary, often biblical). Moreover, Hilton also subscribes to the oldest of Blake-ist maxims: Blake's essential subject is his role as a poetic user of language, Blake's work being, 'an exploration of what it is possible to say, of how directly the poetic genius/Imagination/Los can speak through a language that is itself his creation' (p. 9). This is an internalized conception of Blake's efforts which is very much in tune with the more conventional linguistic understanding expressed by one of Hilton's establishment predecessors, Robert Gleckner: 'everything he says about anything – is translatable into a comment upon language, words, the poet's task, poetry'.[24]

I have dealt with Hilton's theories in a little detail because of the influential role he has had as the editor of a number of direction-charting collections of essays; collections which gather together works that focus in various ways upon 'Blake's verbal thought and practice'.[25] The most significant of these is the volume *Unnam'd Forms: Blake and Textuality* (1986) which is an important work because it not only addresses in highly self-conscious ways questions of discourse and power, and of the materiality of the sign, but also because it does this through an engagement with the ideas of practically every 'major' modern thinker with the single exception of Mikhail Bakhtin.[26] Later on I shall suggest that this omission was in no sense accidental. At present it is sufficient to note that all this work is unsatisfactory largely because its various writers refuse to address, or engage with, the fundamental materialist premise that, 'language [...] is a purely historical phenomenon'.[27] Certainly it set in motion a train of depoliticized writing about Blake's language which has continued into the 1990s. One might expect that this decade would witness the production of critical material willing to engage with politicized variants of post-structuralist theory, especially feminist ones. Yet this has not been the case. For example, Angela Esterhammer opted to continue a rather tired comparative tradition in her, *Creating States: Studies in the Performative Language of John Milton and William Blake* (1994) and the theorists centred in her dialogue with post-structuralism about visionary language and the power of logos are J.L. Austin and John R. Searle. Her aim in the book is to reach a point of 'compromise', or at least beneficial co-existence'[28] and questions of politics, including sexual politics, have no place on this agenda. Even more disappointing is Molly Anne Rothenberg's stab at *Rethinking Blake's Textuality* (1993). Her claim is to demonstrate 'that Blake arrives at some recognizably post-structuralist positions because he is responding to the same epistemological crises' by historicizing 'the links among philosophical discourses of the late eighteenth century, twentieth century Blake criticism, and current post-structuralist thought'.[29] Yet her refusal to grant feminist post-structuralism more than a sentence or two leaves a suspicious and substantial gap in this self-proclaimed argument. In Rothenberg's account of Blake's critique of Kantian deterministic reason and transcendental subjectivity all conflict is textual, rarely literal, and never sexual. As this Introduction continues it will become clear how recurrent such priorities are in Blake Studies.

In concluding this section on language-based studies of Blake, I am happy to note, however, that the critical landscape is not entirely barren. David Aers has begun to explain how Blake's works 'contribute a major critique of monologism', and is a vital antecedent to this study in his insistence that 'Any attempt to understand a text should include an attempt to re-place it in the web of discourses and social practice where it was made'.[30] Moreover a number of other left-wing writers have drawn upon Bakhtin's theories in significant though hardly sustained ways.[31] The one group of critics who, sadly, have not utilized any of his ideas (excepting a single reference to the concepts of monologic and dialogic discourse) are feminist Blakeans,[32] and, again, I shall describe later the consequences of their critical decisions.


As the preceding critique makes clear, I think it is very important to trace the contours of the critical establishment, for it is their impoverished Blake who has become the best known. I shall continue this critical review by offering brief accounts of three specific aspects of the Blake establishment. By looking at the Blake Industry, at the tradition of left-wing scholarship on Blake and at feminist studies of his work I hope to illuminate a number of serious deficiencies in past understandings and constructions, and thereby illustrate the need for a historically sensitive feminist reading of Blake's texts.


## THE BLAKE INDUSTRY

A vast amount has, of course, been written about Blake[33] and whilst I see the need for a comprehensive examination of this

critical heritage my own focus is firmly fixed upon writing produced in the last two decades. The reason for this is very simple:
my desire is to illustrate the reluctance of Blakeans to take feminist concerns seriously, and whilst it is clear that chauvinist priorities have always existed in Blake studies[34] there seemed little
excuse for their maintenance in the 1980s and 1990s. For a scholar
to articulate sexist sentiments at the middle of this century was
a matter of academic custom but after the impact of feminist
criticisms it became a matter of choice, with much greater political implications. To speak plainly, the feminist revolutions of the
past four decades should have revolutionized the study of Blake
(as they did the study of Milton, for instance) and it is my concern to describe the critical consequences of feminism's failure
to achieve this vital re-visioning of our subject. Each chapter of
my book returns to this issue, as I look at the criticism surrounding
a number of individual poems, but a more general introductory
map is, I feel, also needed.

Like any effective intellectual power structure the Blake establishment has always urbanely denied its potency, a practice much
in evidence in the early 1980s, when a *Studies in Romanticism*
special issue promised to take us 'Inside the Blake Industry' (1982).
This feature, which took the form of a chain prophecy, was opened
by an angry Morris Eaves, who lambasted the 'many . . . loose
tongued author(s)' who have 'tossed off complaints about a "Blake
industry" or a "Blake establishment"'. Eaves tells them quite
bluntly that they are 'wrong' and 'melodramatic' in their characterization of what he deprecatingly calls 'the little homemade,
bumptious, and entirely unintimidating world of high Blake scholarship'. Yet all his homely talk of a welcoming and responsive
'cottage industry' begins to look extremely unconvincing when
we note who his chosen intellectual seers are: we find Blake in
the possession of an elite of institutionally ensconced North-
American critics, all of whom are male.[35]

This enterprise would not, of course, be beyond redemption if
these individuals had shown themselves to be aware of their
privileged and problematic position, but none does. On the few
occasions when feminism is mentioned the remarks are cursory
and complacent[36] and this negligence is even more striking when
we note that the event was staged as an act of 'homage' to David
Erdman. Again and again writers lament the failure of Blakeans
to build on Erdman's sociopolitical work, yet even as they opine

'the relative lack of development in the treatment of him as part of his social and intellectual climate'[37] none mentions the late eighteenth-century debate about women's rights, nature and role which I noted at the outset of this Introduction.

In fact, feminism does not figure as a theoretical perspective at all. Most of the writers are suspicious about theory of any kind but when forced to detail which variants they feel are insurgent or valuable, all agree with Morton Paley's (significantly insular) assessment: 'In literary criticism the question before the house is whether structuralist and post-structuralist theory will have anything to contribute to the study of our subject.'[38] The 1980s did indeed see some assimilation of these theories, starting with Steven Shapiro's article 'Striving with Systems' which appeared in 1982, and continuing through Hilton's work up to the collection *Critical Paths: Blake and the Argument of Method* (1987) which addressed the question of Blake and deconstructive theories openly and at some length; yet for all the ink expended in this kind of work it contributed very little to our understanding, for as W.J.T. Mitchell pertinently notes, Blake 'anticipates so many of the strategies of deconstruction, and offers [. . .] a powerful antidote to its skeptical and nihilistic tendencies'.[39] Blake's world is, after all, one of redeemable Los, not existential lack. Moreover, as I have already shown, none of these engagements with deconstructionist theory drew the next generation of Blake critics towards the various feminist adaptations and elaborations of post-modern thought. In terms of sensitivity to issues of gender it was very much a case of, 'the same dull round over again' (*NR* b:VII, E.3).

The lack of interest in feminism shown by Eaves' selected seers was fairly prophetic, as we can see if we look at the contents of some of the collections of essays about Blake published later in the decade. Harold Bloom's collection, *William Blake: Modern Critical Views* (1985) is probably the most negligent, and not only because it reprints some very aged articles but also because it includes Diana Hume George's 'spirited defense of Blake against some recent feminist attacks' whilst largely failing to represent these allegedly hostile studies.[40] Nelson Hilton's *Essential Articles for the Study of William Blake*, which appeared the following year, partially redressed this omission by including the ground-breaking essays of both Susan Fox and Alicia Ostriker.[41] They were, however, robbed of some of their revisionary power because the only paradigm-shift addressed in Hilton's introduction was a linguistic one, which formed the frame of the collection. Indeed, Nelson Hilton continued to be instrumental in the marginalizing of feminist contributions in his role as co-editor of that other volume which appeared in the same year. *Unnam'd Forms: Blake and Textuality* grew out of the conference 'Blake and Criticism' which had taken place at the University of California in 1982. This conference was addressed by a number of leading Blakean feminists (including Margaret Storch, Alicia Ostriker, Jackie Di Salvo and Anne Mellor) yet when the editorial selections were made none of these women found a place in the collection, which was again an all-male affair and which interestingly did have room for Hilton's own pseudo-feminist article on *Visions*.[42] The only collection published in the 1980s that did do justice to various feminist voices was *Critical Paths* (1987) which allowed genuine dialogue to develop amongst a wide range of theoretical perspectives (although no woman made it onto the editorial staff). This, however, may prove to be an enlightened aberration, as the first collection of the 1990s – Hazard Adams, *Critical Essays on William Blake* (1991) – gave feminist writers only the scantiest, and most misfocused, of representation.[43]

By the end of the 1980s then, there were some slight signs that the Blake establishment was beginning to acknowledge feminism's existence. These are signs, however, that it would be foolish to exaggerate, for most Blakean writing is, quite simply, about other things and critics have developed various strategies for keeping it this way. One of the oldest techniques is to subsume Blake's treatment of gender and sexuality within discussions of other (tacitly more important) topics. For example, Leopold Damrosch's comprehensive enveloping of the subject within his exhaustive, if problematic, discussion of dualism is a classic instance and Steven Cox's, *Love and Logic: The Evolution of Blake's Thought* (1992) shows this displacement activity continuing in the new decade.[44] Another technique is adopted by David Fuller in his *Blake's Heroic Argument* (1988) which moves into the confessional mode in an attempt to be honest about the problems of masculine sexuality and male attempts to write about gender. In the end though his rather lengthy exercise in soul-baring has very little impact upon the body of the text and is more likely to embarrass than illuminate the reader.[45] But by far the most common strategy is that employed in Peter Otto's, *Constructive*

*Vision and Visionary Deconstruction* (1991) which relegates the topic to a number of decidedly guilty yet nonetheless decisive foot-notes.[46] The point I am trying to make, then, is a simple one: the main (largely male) stream of Blake studies simply has not con-sidered gender a topic worthy of serious consideration. Other issues (albeit potentially suggestive ones) ranging from Blake's treatment of insects to his relationship with Goethe, Kierkegaard and Spenser, are all considered more important and it is this kind of intellectualized logic which needs to be exposed and discarded.[47]

In fact the need to scrutinize the strategies of the Blake estab-lishment is now, in the mid-1990s, even more pressing as the current decade has seen various critics actively respond to the threat feminists present to their orthodox assessments of Blake's work. Most noteworthy here is an article by Robert Essick en-titled 'William Blake's "Female Will" and Its Biographical Con-text' (1991). Essick begins his argument by greatly exaggerating the number of those who have been interested in Blake's com-plex attitudes towards women, claiming indeed that the subject has 'received considerable attention from his legion of modern critics'.[48] Strangely, though, he is able (without mentioning any particular writers or publications) to summarize all their argu-ments in just one footnote and as the article unfolds his motives become clear. Essick, whilst urbanely noting that 'debate will no doubt continue' (p. 617), wants to give us a few clues about how future feminist studies should be conducted and as the article's title suggests he recommends (following the lead not of any fem-inist Blakean but of the Freudian Morris Dickstein) that we should take a biographical tack if we want to understand what he sees as the later Blake's 'misogyny' (p. 616). And what he produces is an undeniably interesting argument which pivots upon Blake's response to the professional success of the artist Caroline Watson and her sponsorship by the queen. The problem, however, is that this focus enables Essick to marginalize the significance of con-temporary feminists like Mary Wollstonecraft (who has appar-ently also 'been granted considerable attention by modern scholars and need[s] no further treatment here' (p. 620) and offers a very distorted sense of Blake's historical context. Indeed there are simi-larities between the beginning of the article, which found Blake studies besieged by 'legions' of feminists and the end, which talks about Blake's sense of female threat. In his conclusion Essick explains how, 'the two women joined a sense of professional domination by a female with the more public dangers of matri-archy, and both in turn contributed to Blake's delineation of the Female Will as a universal enemy of the male self and its cul-tural ideas' (p. 626). Quite clearly this is an inaccurate assess-ment of each woman's power, but it is also an ingenius shift of focus which elides the significance of patriarchy in both the pro-fessional and political worlds which Blake inhabited. Not a very productive lead for feminist Blakeans to follow in the 1990s, but one which would certainly dissipate the disruptive impact of our arguments should we pursue it.

It must also be noted that Essick is not alone in this desire to offer feminists 'help' with our studies. Morris Eaves in his *The Counter-Arts Conspiracy: Art and Industry in the Age of Blake* (1992) likewise suggests that we take note of a clue from the artistic world. This time the focus is on the feminization of harmony and Blake's comments in the *Descriptive Catalogue*, and Eaves' insistence is that 'the technological discourse of harmony in the English school should become a more important touchstone in arguments over the gender bias of Blakean mythology than it has been to date'.[49] This may be a fine, if limited, idea but what is interesting is that Eaves too has a sense that Blake is under threat from feminists, adding as a cautionary reminder the com-ment that whilst Blake's 'bias is, unsurprisingly, masculine [. . .] biases should not be mistaken for seamless garments' (p. 255). It is a shame that Eaves believes feminists want only to produce critiques of Blake (as I will show later in this Introduction such has hardly been the case) and it is an even greater shame that this view prevented Eaves developing his earlier, very interest-ing, arguments about Blake's unorthodox definition of beauty in suggestively linear terms. Indeed what seems to motivate these defences of Blake is a sense of insecurity not about *his* ability to withstand feminist scrutiny but rather whether they themselves, Blake's interpreters, can. Comments made by G.E. Bentley in the main forum of discussion about the man, *Blake: An Illustrated Quarterly*, suggest that this is precisely the case.

For the last few years, Bentley has been editing the annual checklist of Blake Studies publications and in 1993 he made a rather weary first acknowledgement of feminist studies of Blake, commenting on the 'predictable number of essays concerning "gen-der" and attitudes towards sexuality'.[50] Feminism, in this context, is seen as nothing more than a 'North American fashion' (p. 6) which has yet to be adopted by the great many Japanese and Korean writers who were amongst the most productive new contributors. And rather interestingly (or predictably?) listings of their work filled the subsequent 1994 list – a list which I have to confess has personal significance for me, as it is here that we find the Blake establishment directly responding to the kind of work this book argues the need for and obviously contains. Bentley generally found the year's work rather disappointing but nonetheless found space to consign my article on patriarchal readings of *The Book of Thel* (a version of which is Chapter 2 in the present study) to 'the wilder shores of Blake speculation and assertion'.[51] Nothing is said about the content of my piece, which Bentley clearly did not believe worthy of the status of criticism or scholarship, and he ended his assessment with the relieved comment that at least I was the only 'rabid' (p. 144) writer he had encountered in 1994. These comments may seem self-indulgent (they are) but much more important is how indicative they are of resistance to, or even a denial of, the importance of sexual politics in writing about Blake in the 1990s.

Let me explain. This study grows out of my PhD thesis which was completed in 1993. I returned to work on the present text in 1994/5 with the, perhaps rather vain, hope that things in Blake Studies might have changed; that I might find at least some amenability to feminist readings of his work. This has not been the case. Everywhere I've turned I've found yet more attempts to marginalize our concerns, and Peter Ackroyd's *Blake* (1995) is especially noteworthy is this regard. The glowing pre-publication reviews of his biography gave the impression that sexuality and sexual politics would be extensively explored[52] and hence I picked up the book with great interest, yet what I found was that Ackroyd is not at all keen to address what are for feminists the central questions. Biographically, the text has nothing new to say about Blake's wife Catherine, it has nothing at all to say about Blake's sister and there is no interest whatsoever in the professional women so vehemently flagged by Robert Essick. Ackroyd's discussions of eroticism, again centred in the reviews, are also disappointing. His comments about eighteenth-century sexual magic are not elaborated and we are asked to believe that 'all the repressed or unacknowledged erotic potentialities of his period' just passively 'gather' (p. 82) in Blake's work. Another troubling aspect of the book's assessment of Blake is the repeated assertion that his alleged emphasis on 'huge phalli' is part of his 'sexual radicalism' (p. 351) without being told how or why this might be a radical gesture. Generally Ackroyd provides very poor analysis of Blake's work. He has nothing more to say about things like the images of homosexual fellatio in *Milton* than that they add 'a quality of strangeness to Blake's association' (p. 313) with his great mentor – which is surely a weak conclusion? Yet it is characteristic of the text. Sexuality and sexual politics must be kept on the sidelines if we are to be convinced by Ackroyd's portrait of Blake as a great English patriarch, one who expressed 'apparent misogyny' (p. 22) and who 'held relatively orthodox views of the status of men and women' (p. 83).

After reading a book like *Blake*, feminist critics might well feel that their attempts at re-visioning the poet have been entirely pointless. To find any interest in the kind of Blake who concerns us we seem to have to turn outside the academy and the mainstream and towards the kind of enthusiasts who thankfully still abound. To places like The House of William Blake which recently put on an exhibition celebrating his proverbial wisdom that 'The Genitals are Beauty' or to publications like *The Journal of the Blake Society at St James*, which in its first edition (Spring 1995) was happy to speculate on whether Blake's famous *The Tyger* might be 'about sex in the middle of the night'.[53] This, though, is a rather frustrated and hasty judgement. Much more does need to be said about critical writing on Blake, even if disappointment is the depressing keynote.


## 'RADICAL' STUDIES OF BLAKE'S POETRY

One group of writers who might be expected to join in the task I've been describing are the various left-wing critics who have worked on Blake. In the corpus of radical scholarship a feminist might reasonably hope to find some sensitivity to issues of sexual power and exploitation, to the historically specific ways in which ideology constructs gender and maintains its naturalized illusions. On examination, however, this hope turns out to be largely misplaced.

Before I offer a few details about left-wing scholarship on Blake it is necessary to make one framing comment about radical treatments of the poet, which is that despite the promising mid-century leads given by Mark Schorer, Jacob Bronowski, David Erdman and E.P. Thompson, Marxist critics have never really made Blake their own.[54] Terry Eagleton may confidently tell us that 'Milton, Blake and Shelley/Will smash the ruling class yet'[55] but he, and many other radical writers, would be better employed focusing their attention upon who has obtained intellectual possession of this revolutionary trinity. Much rebuttal is certainly needed of Peter Ackroyd's 1995 Blake, who 'believed only in the efficacy of individual virtue or enlightenment' and who further, 'displays not the slightest interest in any particular political or social philosophy'.[56]

From the perspective of this study, however, the most problematic aspect of this tradition of scholarship is not its uneven development but rather its practitioners' almost wholesale refusal to acknowledge that Blake's sensitivity to issues of gender is an important facet of the radicalism which they have long explicated and enjoyed. The implications of this have been serious for those writers who want to offer us Blake 'as a man in the world'[57] rather than a mystic in the clouds, as their gender-blind conceptions of this world have radically impoverished their historical and material understanding. Take for example the great (and much reprinted) work of David Erdman, who explains that the aim of his 'historical approach is to [. . .] locate, as nearly as we can, the moment and place in which he stood, to discover what he saw and heard in London's Streets – what loomed on the horizon and what sounds filled the air'.[58] Yet Erdman's rightly classic *William Blake: Prophet against Empire* (1954, 1969, 1977), which is so painstaking in its presentation of Blake's sociopolitical context, includes women as at best bit-part actors, and this after Blake's own confession that what he 'most' hears through *London*'s midnight streets is 'the youthful Harlots curse', not the cries of the Gordon rioters. Erdman's is quite literally 'a land of men', which not only ignores the particularities of women's history but also drastically neglects the productions of women writers: Mary Wollstonecraft's first *Vindication* (1790) is given preference and the works of such contemporaries as Catherine Macaulay Graham, Mary Hays, Mary Robinson, Priscilla Wakefield and Helen Maria Williams  are not even glanced at. And to compound the problem, Erdman is further handicapped by his debt to Northrop Frye, whose relentless association of women with an ensnaring natural world leads Erdman to a rather reductive understanding of the roles performed by Blake's female characters, whom he describes as 'not so much people as states of nature'.[59]

Radical writers of the present generation, then, do not have a particularly promising heritage, and though some efforts have been made to assimilate feminist concerns into assorted Marxist/materialist studies few attempts have been either sustained or convincing. In most cases other concerns and priorities tend to stifle the nascent feminism of these writers. This is certainly true of the work of Erdman's most direct descendant, Stewart Crehan, whose *Blake in Context* (1984) populates its historical landscape with quite a few more women (prostitutes and female labourers especially) and also engages in discussions of changes in familial and sexual mores, and in speculation about the sexual politics of rococo and neoclassical art.[60] Crehan's study is, however, ultimately unsatisfactory because its author shows no awareness of the vast amount of historical context which is almost daily being revealed. In an article written after the publication of his book Crehan spoke of his earlier suspicion that the older generation of radical scholars had 'closed the case on the context issue'[61] – a comment which bespeaks an ignorance of the work of late twentieth-century feminist and socialist historians that is painfully evident in his book.

More theoretically sophisticated writers have submerged their embryonic feminist awareness in other ways. For example, Edward Larrissy's suggestive asides about Blake's insights into sexual oppression remain undeveloped in his study, *William Blake* (1985) because of the author's single-minded desire to demonstrate the ambiguity of form and boundary in Blake's works.[62] Larrissy's overarching argument concerns the complexity of Blake's ideological formation, and the way in which this necessitates the self-conscious grafting and splicing of discourse; and the style of address required to advance this kind of theoretical argument tends to exclude the discussion of more straightforward political issues. The problem of obfuscating theoretical language is evident in an even starker form in the extensive writings of David Punter. Punter's work contains many valuable comments on the problematic yet profound nature of Blake's treatment of sexuality, gender and patriarchy. He also offers a timely warning against the tendency to 'settle for Blake's texts as applicable commodities rather than as themselves participants in the vicissitudes of history, politics, patriarchy' – yet most readers are denied access to Punter's insights by the bizarre and singular mix of post-structuralist jargon and assertive psycho-babble in which these ideas are conveyed.[63]

The worst example of an inadequate 'radical' discussion of Blake's treatment of gender is, however, offered by a writer who superficially appears to grant the subject a good deal of attention. Michael Ferber's *The Social Vision of William Blake* (1985) devotes a whole chapter to the topic, yet this section is entitled 'Nature and the Female' and Ferber's decision to follow Frye leads him into apologistic contortions for a stereotypical association of women with nature which is more the work of the author of *Fearful Symmetry* (1947) than it is of Blake himself. And it is the nature of Ferber's apologism which is a cause of concern, for in the course of his argument he trivializes the one strategy that would in fact produce a genuine advance in knowledge: Ferber suggests that we need to place Blake's sexual thinking in its historical context, asking the key question 'Against the background of prevalent assumptions in 1790, with respect even to the few feminist thinkers of the time, how advanced or liberatory can Blake's world of argument and imagery be said to be?'[64] Yet the great problem is that though Ferber claims 'careful study' (p. 112) is needed to gain an answer to this question he nowhere attempts to offer such detailed historicist work. Rather he settles for an impoverished sense of context (only Mary Wollstonecraft is mentioned as a feminist contemporary) accompanied by a 'guess' at what might be revealed by more diligent research, ultimately reaching the stereotypical decision that while Wollstonecraft 'was the braver soul [. . .] Blake was the more profound and revolutionary thinker, whatever his unsound tendencies' (p. 112).[65]

And as if this sloppy scholarship wasn't enough Ferber goes on to flaunt his supposed historical wisdom, as he chastises feminist critics of Blake whilst colonizing our struggle:

> A sense of Blake's historical moment ought to lead feminists to forgive the disturbing connotations of imagery, the contamination of tenor by vehicle, and find Blake's total vision an inspiration in our struggle against the tyranny of patriarchy – a tyranny strong enough in 1790 to infect the most liberated soul of the time, and still strong enough today to forbid the luxury of dispensing with imperfect spiritual allies. (pp. 112–13)

Clearly Ferber considers himself to be one of these imperfect allies, but I think there is very little to salvage from his work because his positing of a monolithically sexist social context makes it impossible for us to hear the many voices of the great sexual dialogue that Blake was part of. It also enables the utterance of valueless generalized pronouncements: 'he was not exactly a male supremacist, just the child of his time making use of traditional symbolism' – but what exactly were those 'male-supremacist assumptions Blake shared with nearly everyone else in his day'? (pp. 92; 111). This question certainly needs answering for many writers, like for example Stephen Behrendt, still present Blake as one 'whose life and work embody a measure of the sexism that was the inevitable baggage of his culture' without looking in any detail at what else that culture contained.[66]

My general assessment of 'radical' treatments of Blake's interest in gender and feminism is that their development has been erratic, their depth and scope of enquiry unimpressive and their level of commitment extremely disappointing. Why, we might ask, hasn't Terry Eagleton (who clearly fancies himself as something of a critical cross-dresser after his brushes with the Brontes and Clarissa) developed his comments on Blake beyond the level of a few suggestive sentences about the poet's 'revolutionary ambiguity'?[67] Or perhaps more to the point, why hasn't David Erdman supplemented his work in the light of the revolutionary impact of feminism on both historical and literary studies?[68] The only honourable exception to this catalogue of missed opportunity and academic inarticulacy has been David Aers, whose lucid and principled account of Blake's engagement with the 'dialectic of sex' is discussed in the following section of this critical review.

Furthermore, the 1990s have yet to produce any work which would necessitate a revision of my judgements. Despite the publication of a couple of important studies of Blake's radical context (both like this one focused upon the 1790s) there seems to be very little change in 'radical' priorities. Jon Mee's *Dangerous Enthusiasm: William Blake and the Culture of Radicalism in the 1790s* (1992) is an initially promising book as it argues for a view of Blake as a *bricoleur*: a writer immersed in and using the discourses central to a variety of dangerous and popular cultures. Yet sexual politics seem to have very little relevance in any of the heated political debates which Mee excavates and explains. This is a strange historical view to entertain, especially when, for example, Mee discusses Radical Millenarianism, as the popular enthusiasm of the 1790s touched women as well as men and gave female prophets a role in the public sphere which was rarely accorded to women in this period.[69] Sadly Mee has inherited the values of his predecessors and when the issue of feminism is directly addressed it appears only as something Blake got wrong, his works being found to 'reflect a perennial tendency among male prophets of women's liberation to limit that liberation to the sexual sphere' (p. 144). A good point but one which needed to be pursued if justice were to be done and Mee's interest is elsewhere, hence this brief discussion shifts its focus onto a variety of other male writers and their interest in the sexual basis of religion. In friendly conversation Jon Mee is only too ready to admit the serious omissions which mark his text, but perhaps this makes even more disheartening the fact that gaps do indeed remain.

The other important radical work of the early 1990s was E.P. Thompson's long-awaited *Witness against the Beast: William Blake and the Moral Law* (1993). This is a fascinating study of the antinomian culture of the 1790s and every page demonstrates the truth of Thompson's initial claim: 'it is Blake's unique notation of christian belief, and not his 'Jacobin' political sympathies, which still stands in need of examination'.[70] And yet, as ever, it is a work full of leads which are not pursued, full of promise which is not grasped. For example, Thompson shows how many of the sexually radical ideas of the ranters were still alive in the 1790s yet these are not substantially related to Blake's work; he explains a host of Muggletonian heresies concerned with original sin and the role of Eve yet he largely avoids any discussion of Blake's view of these things – opting instead for a brief chastisement of the poet: 'It should be said, and sharply, that Blake, who is supposed to have transcended gender prejudices, often was willing to employ anti-feminine imagery.' (pp. 80–81) This is hardly a full, or indeed fair, comment and is a wholly dismal one to find in a work like *Witness*. When reading the book one gets the sense of a culture pregnant with possibility for women. The Muggletonian heresies Thompson so poignantly retells have direct and often stark feminist relevance but this is something which, quite simply, does not interest the author – which is surely a great shame. The moral law which the Muggletonians so forcefully rejected most often had in its sights women and their sexuality; Blake apprehended this and joined passionately in their critique and yet Thompson scarcely mentions such things. Jean Moskal's *Blake, Ethics, and Forgiveness* (1994)[71] goes some way towards gendering antinomian ideas, but is no substitute for the kind of meticulous work a social historian of Thompson's calibre could have produced. But didn't. Above all his *Witness against the Beast* sadly shows that radical Blake studies have yet to be feminized in the 1990s.

Moreover, activities beyond the pages of print reinforce my gloomy observations. The main events (in the UK, that is) of this decade were the two 'Historicizing Blake' conferences (1990/94) which took place at St Mary's University College, Twickenham. The conference co-ordinators David Worrall and Steve Clark were only too keen to encourage new scholars interested in questions of gender and sexual power (I am personally very grateful for their interest and support) but these issues still remained firmly marginal at both events and engaging the interest of established critics was no easy task. I have already noted G.E. Bentley's assessment of the paper I presented, and the volume of essays produced from the first conference underscores the attitudes and nature of the establishment. *Historicizing Blake* (1994) contains the work of two women/eight men, only one work with any kind of feminist orientation and an article by John Beer which is astonishingly blithe in its treatment of Blake's troubling erotic illustrations to The Book of Enoch.[72] Again, one can only be sad to see the organizer's/editor's efforts result in such a disappointing volume. In his role as chair of the Blake Society, Worrall has constantly given feminists a lively forum and Clark's 'Blake and Female Reason' is one of the best comparative essays on Wollstonecraft and Blake in print to date,[73] but even they could do little more than crack the edifice.

## FEMINIST STUDIES OF BLAKE

Although the disinterest of the critics discussed earlier suggests otherwise, there has, in fact, been a sizable body of scholarship produced by various feminist Blakeans. Whilst much of this material is of only dubious value I think it is important to offer a general map of the field, if for no other reason than that this will bring into especially clear focus the calculated indifference of other more institutionally influential Blake scholars. Also, by tracing the contours of previous studies I hope to further illustrate the quite pressing need for a work like this one, which marries a discursively sensitive historicist methodology to a politically engaged feminist critique.

Before the mid-1970s there were no explicitly feminist treatments of Blake's work, and those writers who did wish to comment on questions of gender or sexual conflict usually had to do so in covert ways. A good example of this kind of work is Irene Chayes' article 'The Presence of Cupid and Psyche' (1970) which was the first attempt to offer an even-handed account of Blake's treatment of sexual love and sexual violence. It was something of an exception as Blake critics have, on the whole, managed to discuss sexuality and the body in surprisingly gender-blind ways.[74] The first self-proclaimed feminist account of Blake's treatment of women was Irene Tayler's 'The Woman Scaly' (1973), which is a classic piece of anti-essentialist feminism. Tayler takes up the distinction she finds in Blake's work between negative feminine characteristics (such as the 'female will') and the individual women who may or may not exhibit such attributes.[75] By gesturing at social and economic circumstances, Tayler suggests that women behave in cruel and manipulative ways as a response to patriarchy's treatment of them – thereby rejecting Northrop Frye's archetypal rumblings and offering us a Blake who favoured nurture over nature.

The next significant feminist contribution came from Susan Fox, an author who had already signalled her interest in the subject in an earlier book on Milton. In 'The Female as Metaphor in William Blake's Poetry' (1977), Fox took the important step of arguing that the nature of Blake's depiction of the female was not a peripheral issue but one central to the interpretation of his poetry. Furthermore, she warned gender-blind critics that their past refusal to acknowledge this meant that 'images of females [...] have been so little defined that they have clouded full understanding of his work'.[76] Fox's belief was that 'A study of Blake's use of females as metaphors should not only identify his complicated attitudes towards women but also reveal a serious self-contradiction in his vision of the universe', and it is not necessary to agree with her claim that stereotypical metaphors of femaleness undermine Blake's philosophy of mutuality to see that Fox is right in observing that the female gave Blake unique problems: 'In no other issue do abstraction and particularity seem so seriously to contradict each other.' (pp. 507; 509) Her focus on the problems caused for critics by Blake's complex use of female metaphors was much needed, and her insistence that such issues are 'not minor in our conception of the poet Blake' (p. 519) is a valuable legacy.

Once these foundations were laid, feminist criticism went in a number of directions and took various forms. One of the most popular was the survey article, whose primary aim was to adjudicate on the issue of whether or not Blake should be termed a sexist. Probably the best of these often reductive productions was Alicia Ostriker's 'Desire Gratified and Ungratified: William Blake and Sexuality' (1982/3) which offered us four different Blakes, and which came to the conclusion that antagonism between views is the life of his poetry, poetry in which she found 'both a richly developed anti-patriarchal and proto-feminist sensibility [. . .] and its opposite, a homocentric gynophobia'.[77] Most writers of surveys came to similar conclusions, for example see Karleen Middleton Murphy's '"All the Lovely Sex": Blake and the Woman Question' (1982), although Anne Mellor has remained unwavering in her account of 'Blake's constantly sexist portrayal of women'.[78]

At the other end of the scale were a clutch of articles which focused not on the corpus of Blake's work, but on a number of individual poems. I will return to such essays later but it is worth just noting here that *The Four Zoas* in particular attracted the attention of a number of writers concerned with feminist issues – including, among others, Michael Ackland and Judith Lee who both discussed the poem in the light of Mary Wollstonecraft's writings.[79] Judith Lee's 'Ways of Their Own: The Emanations of Blake's *Vala, or the Four Zoas*' (1983) was the most extensive and interesting application of Wollstonecraft's ideas, although it is hard to concur with her assessment that the Emanations ultimately 'grow toward the state of self-affirming interdependence she [Wollstonecraft] espoused as a social ideal' (p. 132). The claim that 'women are not mere witnesses but active participants in the cosmic revolution' (p. 150) is hardly borne out by the poem. The feminist Catherine Haigney also wrote on *The Four Zoas*, although in a very different way. Her, 'Vala's Garden in Night the Ninth: Paradise Regained or Woman Bound?' (1987) is an exemplary close textual exposition of one of the most perplexing

sequences of the poem.[80] Haigney both problematizes the commonplace view that the pastoral passage is a positive movement
and anatomizes the prejudices of those critics who have propounded such an assessment.

Two other articles also deserve mention here, for the sophisticated contributions of Elizabeth Langland and Catherine
McClenahan have advanced the understanding and increased the
possibilities of feminist Blake studies immensely. Langland's,
'Blake's Feminist Revision of Literary Tradition in "The Sick Rose"'
(1987) is a critically self-conscious article, which takes the reader
through the three interrelated moments of the feminist critique
and culminates in a revolutionizing of our view of the poem,
the critical community and the traditions with which Blake was
working. Each aspect of Langland's article is impressive but her
demonstration of how 'the feminist critique has the power to
uncover the politics of interpretation'[81] is perhaps the most valuable. She questions 'the ways meaning has been foreclosed within
a certain reading community' and shows how 'certain interpretations, as well as texts, have been canonized to support patriarchy' (pp. 231–2). Langland shows what an active and resisting
reader can achieve and we must hope that many will follow her
example.[82]

Catherine McClenahan's contribution, 'No Face Like the Human Divine?: Women and Gender in Blake's Pickering Manuscript' (1990) is a very different piece of writing, although it shares
the virtue of exemplary close reading – indeed her detailed analysis
is doubly valuable as the poems in the Pickering Manuscript have
been strangely neglected by critics, especially feminist ones. The
difference lies in McClenahan's rigorous historicizing of the poems,
both in the context provided by historians of eighteenth-century
women and also, more narrowly, with regard to the fortunes of
the feminist movement in the 1790s. This latter concern involves
a sensitive discussion of Mary Wollstonecraft's writings and generates what will probably be the definitive reading of that auto-
biographically baffling yet historically fascinating poem 'Mary'
(c. 1803). The cumulative effect of the article is to reveal a mid-
dle-aged Blake much less patriarchal in his sympathies than many
have suggested. We really do begin to see 'how acutely the later
Blake understood the social construction of gender'.[83] Moreover
McClenahan picks up on the way Blake shapes 'a radically democratic reader – text exchange' (p. 204) and, like Langland, shows

just how much interpretative liberty this gives to the feminist reader.

Very few feminist writers have the kind of materialist commitments evident in McClenahan's article, although a definite exception to this rule is the Marxist-feminist Jackie Di Salvo whose *War of Titans: Blake's Critique of Milton and the Politics of Religion* (1984) is a neglected classic of radical Blake scholarship. Di Salvo's main aim is to sketch out Blake's proto-Marxist vision of the historical process as evidenced by *The Four Zoas*, and this ambitious project somewhat subsumes her avowed interest in sexual politics. Nevertheless her Blakean re-reading of *Paradise Lost* provides many insights into Blake's understanding of the politics of the family, a subject in which Di Salvo is much interested.[84] Another fascinating perspective is offered in a series of articles by Marsha Keith Schuchard which excavate the murky histories of freemasonry, sexual magic and mesmerism during the eras of Blake's life. Schuchard's work certainly reveals a range of historical debates that should have had a larger place in this study, although we need to wait for her forthcoming books to discover whether her dense archival and biographical writing will be accompanied by fuller treatment of Blake's work in the context of these sexually intriguing subcultures.[85] So far the only writer who has thoroughly demonstrated the fruitfulness of a Marxist-feminist approach to Blake is David Aers. In a series of articles[86] he sets out to historicize and politicize those contradictions in Blake's attitude to women which other writers have noted but not explained. Aers moves beyond the defensive stance of the apologist by paying attention to what he calls 'the dialectic of sex'. His aim is to show that the irreducibly social nature of consciousness, and the power of ideologies in the formation of that consciousness, make it impossible for anyone (even a 'great' writer like Blake) to have an entirely uncompromised sexual 'vision'. Aer's articles would certainly benefit from the inclusion of some specific historical expressions of that dominant sexual ideology which he argues Blake was forced to negotiate, but his work nonetheless represents a most satisfying theorization of the complex subject of Blake's treatment of gender.

There are also a few other distinct clusters of writers who have discussed issues of gender. An archetypal strain of criticism has, for instance, continued in the work of Rachel Billingheimer, who argues in her comparative studies that 'the archetypal female in

Yeats' illuminates 'Blake's eternal female'.[87] Appeals are also continually made to the wisdom of Carl Jung, whose anima and animus remain a sexual partnership perennially fascinating to Blake critics.[88] Indeed comparative studies have continued to flourish in the 1990s. The longest work of this kind is Eugenie R Freed's *"A Portion of His Life": William Blake's Miltonic Vision of Woman* (1994) and it well illustrates both the strengths and weaknesses of this methodology. On the positive side Freed is able to describe in some detail Blake's transcendence of one particularly influential patriarchal tradition and yet, on the negative, his work is examined *only* in terms of that tradition – hence Freed's obsession with the heterosexual couple, with making distinctions between 'good' and 'bad' women and (most perilously) with expounding a philosophy of sexual wholeness and harmony from Blake's troubled epic poems. The greatest weakness of this comparative study is that feminist questions are largely neglected until the very last pages of the book and Blake is, yet again, defended against a horde of critics who 'risk being blinkered by their indignation'.[89] My research shows that this is hardly the case, yet shorter pieces from the comparative school intensify such claims. K.D. Verma's article 'The Woman Figure in Blake and the Idea of Shakti in Indian Thought' (1990) offers remarkably poor reflections on its alleged theme. It rarely addresses the specifics of Blake's work and settles for generalization rather than analysis. It also contains a lengthy footnote upbraiding all feminist critics of Blake with the single exception of Diana Hume George (a popular woman, whose popularity I will address in a moment).[90] Even promising articles like June Sturrock's 'Blake and the Women of the Bible' (1992) contain similar flaws. Sturrock very clearly explains Blake's negative revaluation of Tirzah, Rahab and Mary yet her analysis of *Jerusalem* is at best partial and her assessments universalizing and unsubstantiated: 'like any other human being, he cannot entirely escape the assumptions and limitations of his own historical period or his own psyche'.[91] A strange conclusion as neither subject was addressed in the article. There is also one other group of feminist writers who have taken a comparatist tack and these critics have found it valuable to compare Blake's attitudes to women with those of the other Romantic poets. Diana Long Hoeveler has produced the fullest account in her *Romantic Androgyny: The Woman Within* (1990) and her conclusions are much the same as most of these writers who, like Meena Alexander, feel that 'Blake, of all the English Romantic poets best portrays female desire. Yet not even Blake can finally save himself from the patriarchal postures he condemns.'[92] A fair, if unsurprising, perspective.

Yet with all this work noted it still remains the case that by far the most popular 'feminist' approach has been a psychoanalytical one and I have saved an account of these works until last because I think that they are the most problematic studies of Blake's sexual politics (they are also the longest). These writings fall into two distinct categories: those which hail Blake as a psychological prophet and those which use the theories of various psychologists to analyse, or more correctly diagnose, Blake's poetry. I shall examine these works in accordance with this schema.

The first major work of the prophetic tradition was Diana Hume George's *Blake and Freud* (1980), which was also the first book-length 'feminist' study of Blake to be published. George's central argument is that Blake's theories of feminine psychology represent an advance on Freud's, and that through focusing on Blake's description of normative psychological process in the female and then re-reading Freud in the light of this we will develop a new vision of the later thinker. Blake's insights into sexual psychology are held to be 'significant for social and academic feminism in the 1980s – not because Blake rescues feminism from Freud, but because he brings feminism back to Freud'.[93] And it is this somewhat bizarre practice of using one ambiguously feminist male writer (Blake) to prove the feminist credentials of another (Freud) that makes George's study so unsatisfactory. Her understanding and crystalline explication of Freud's theories are meticulous, as is her painstaking rebuttal of feminist criticism, but the overriding defensiveness of the study ultimately leads to some serious misreadings – misreadings most evident in the book's key chapter '"Is She Also the Divine Image?": Values for the Feminine in Blake'.

This chapter focuses upon what is clearly a key issue for any feminist reader of Blake: how does one distinguish between Blake's depiction of feminine attributes and his attitude towards the individual woman who sometimes embodies them? George's answer is problematic, however, because she has biologist tendencies which are imputed to Blake and which draw her into open conflict with the ground-breaking feminist writers I mentioned earlier. Indeed she writes explicitly about this 'emergent tendency in Blake criticism which I find troublesome' (p. 202). Anti-essentialist writings trouble George because she does not accept the suggestion that manipulative women appear in Blake's poems as a comment upon the patriarchal system which victimizes them to such an extent that the only power they can obtain is of this kind. 'Women are seldom faultless' (p. 204) George darkly comments, as she explains how 'Blake analysed the ways in which women not only submitted to their own denigration but helped it along, and thereby gained power through manipulation in the passive-aggressive mode' (p. 206). There is some truth in this comment but not in its elaboration, for George goes on to contend that 'Blake was as hard on women as on men for the mess that history is' (p. 206), and implicit in this comment is a denial that patriarchy ever existed. Indeed the issue of male power is swept aside and we hear not of systematic exploitation or oppression but rather of female 'self-betrayal' (p. 207). Moreover, George is harsh on those who have suggested otherwise: 'The need to be free of responsibility for Things-as-they-are is, I believe, a disturbing characteristic of the neo-feminist movement, one that implicitly attempts to salvage the exclusive privileges that accrue to the oppressed in an historical scenario in which women are only victims.' (p. 207) One wonders what these privileges could possibly be (or how they accrue to Blakean females such as Hela, Thel or Oothoon).

The main problem with George's study, then, is that it brushes aside the issue of power in its attempt to celebrate the shared wisdom of Blake and Freud, wisdom that appears to pivot around her claim:

> Both men knew that this 'great riddle of sex' was The Problem [sic] that included all other problems. Both men knew that the sexes had done a fine job of making each other and themselves quite miserable, even if they had managed to do little else. And both knew that if there was any telling transformation possible in culture, it must be sexual transformation (p. 227).[94]

A sexually-determinist and effectively de-politicized assessment of Blake's treatment of gender which has earned George the respect of the Blake establishment. Harold Bloom for one believes that she is 'the most responsible and learned of Blake's feminist scholar-critics'.[95]

Very different conclusions are reached by the writers of the diagnostic school, who tend to find Blake a fascinating yet pathological case. The most extended treatment of this kind is Brenda Webster's (paradoxically titled) *Blake's Prophetic Psychology* (1983) which is an extremely traditional piece of Freudian literary criticism in which Webster argues against what she sees as the critical normalizing of Blake, a process that sprung from 'an unwillingness to look at Blake's private self'.[96] The problem is that as we have very little access to 'what was uniquely Blake's as a person' (p. 3) any attempt to examine this private self has to trust rather blindly in the map which is supposedly charting its topography. Webster's own crude Freudian map of Blake's psyche reveals exactly what one would expect it to, and though much could be done with the insight that 'The body of Blake's work is an astonishingly translucent description of the unconscious', Webster's own focus is upon the rather more predictable revelation that 'Gradually, through the medium of his work, he forced himself or was drawn into earlier and earlier life-stages in his efforts to resolve his oedipal dilemma.' (p. 8) Webster's special concern is with the 'fact' that Blake did not manage to resolve his Oedipal complex and in particular she stresses his maintenance of incestuous desire for the mother and the patterns of alternate guilt and rage attendant upon this.

Apart from the reductiveness of this interpretative model the major problem with the study is that Webster domesticates every aspect of Blake's poetry and denying his works all but personal significance is surely inappropriate. Moreover the 'son-centredness' of her Freudian model presents us with a Blake much more monolithically masculinist in his concerns than the corpus of his writings suggest. Indeed Webster's account of 'Blake's real attitude to women' is especially negative and marked by precisely the kind of problems I signalled above: 'In the case of his attitudes toward women, he is largely dramatizing or reenacting early experiences and is too caught up in them to be critical.'[97] Refusal to acknowledge any self-conscious or even self-critical elements in Blake's treatment of gender and sexuality is surely an imperious decision and one which I hope to problematize in the course of this study.

One comment that can be made in Webster's favour is that the scope of her study (the book is a long and well-illustrated 325 pages) ensures that she brings to our attention aspects of

Blake's sexual imagery neglected in the past. The same thing can also be said of the work of Margaret Storch, whose Kleinian writings on Blake and women are nevertheless flawed in much the same way as Webster's. Storch begins her work by pointing to 'an inescapable contradiction between Blake's expressed sympathy for women within his schema of cultural history, and the actual emotional impetus that lies behind his characterizations of women'.[98] Unsurprisingly her conclusion is that this 'powerful antagonism [. . .]' arises from the deeper sources of his being' and though Storch illuminates these 'tensions of his early life'[99] with the help of rather different theories her conclusions are much the same. Melanie Klein's notion that the infant splits the mother into two separate figures to contain its conflicting emotions is held to be a sufficient explanation (however stereotypical such dichotomies may be) and is also taken as grounds for some alarmingly crude biographical contentions.

Such reductionism inevitably has its consequences. Once again, all Blake's meanings are taken to be internal, privatized: 'What he describes as the predicament of contemporary man [. . .] is first of all an urgent portrayal of his own mental condition [. . .] his perceptions about human nature are ultimately perceptions about himself'.[100] Also, the mother-judging dynamic of Kleinian theory leads Storch to exaggerate the presence of threatening women in Blake's poetry: 'Fear and awe of women is the dominant emotion behind Blake's critique of society. Even the cold mechanistic power of Urizen is ultimately subsumed into the female will, and no male figure in the poetry is capable of the range and subtlety of cruelty that often characterizes the women [. . .] Women are benevolent only if under male dominion'[101] – claims which I think my close analyses of Blake's poetry will reveal to be simply false. Moreover, Storch elaborates on Blake's attitudes towards fathers in an equally problematic way – claiming that positive resolution is reached as the father is defeated but embraced and brotherhood becomes an ideal. As in Webster's study, the opportunity of analyzing the anti-patriarchal aspects of Blake's work is radically circumscribed by Storch's exaggerated description of Blake's masculinism, a problem not helped by her fraternal bonding of Blake with that feminist *bête noire* D.H. Lawrence.[102]

Ultimately, any judgment of these works depends upon whether the reader is prepared to accept Storch's claim that, 'When we find insistent and repeated thematic patterns in an artist, it is reasonable to assume that they arise from unconscious sources in the intense psychic struggles of infancy that are never fully resolved in adult life'.[103] I hope that my book will provide some convincing reasons for doubting this diagnostic maxim. Although, in fairness, I will acknowledge that James King's recent biography *William Blake: His Life* (1991) does use a basic Freudian model in a number of highly illuminating ways. Some of his speculations about the poet's hostility to women are dubious but the broad canvas provided by a book-length examination of his life guarantees that King's claims are fully substantiated.[104] At the very least it surpasses Peter Ackroyd's disappointingly shallow examination of Blake's sexual imagination (whatever the reviewers or sales-figures might suggest).

At the end of this review a few synopsizing comments are necesssary for I am convinced that there are a number of quite serious problems with existing feminist studies of Blake's poetry, the most pervasive of which is their schematic nature. Driven by an urge to adjudicate on the issue of whether or not Blake was 'sexist', many critics have become victims of the generalizing 'idiocy' he warned against. Their conclusions are contradictory, with some favouring the early Blake and some the late,[105] but the real problem here is the kind of critical practice this activity requires. Bits of writing (often speeches) are wrenched from their context, individual characters abstracted from the narrative in which they live, concepts discussed as if Blake were the author of algebraic formulas; and as a result the indeterminate, dialogic, revisionary nature of his poetry is often only gestured at. Stereotypical notions and oppositions are repeatedly brought into play, and yet Blake's texts work always to subvert such categorization: he constantly reworked his 'theory' of the female emanation, redefined the nature of Beulah, re-examined the meaning of the female will and offered us not just the 'nurturing Jerusalem' and the 'seductive Vala' but a whole range of female characters who utterly invalidate the virgin – whore paradigm many of these writers seem tacitly to work with.

Moreover because most feminist writers *like* Blake's work they tend to engage in apologist strategies, the most disastrous of which is the positing of monolithically sexist 'times', times whose poisonous influence Blake just could not 'transcend'.[106] In this way a whole generation of female contemporaries are deleted and Blake's negotiation and dialogue with a far from omnipresent contemporary patriarchal ideology is ignored. The sexual and gendered contexts of Blake's work have been grossly misrepresented because the intense sexual debate of the late-eighteenth century, of which I spoke earlier, has been substantially disregarded.[107] The only eighteenth-century feminist that most Blake scholars seem to have heard of is Mary Wollstonecraft and their treatment of her writings is usually limited and often patronizing.[108] In this book I shall move beyond their restricted understandings by examining a whole range of Wollstonecraft's writing in close detail, including her contributions to the *Analytical Review* and her history of the French Revolution. In doing this I hope to show that Blake and Wollstonecraft often addressed the same issues (especially questions of sexual power) and that the profound reflections of each writer are mutually illuminating, both when they concur and when they diverge.

Moreover, this historical insensitivity extends to feminist comments about language, which is seen as the agent of that putatively omnipotent patriarchal culture which allegedly ensnared Blake.[109] I have spoken at length about the historicist and polyphonic theory of language which underpins this study and I need only add here that this deafness to the gendered nuance of much of Blake's language has seriously handicapped feminist treatments of his work.

To conclude, much feminist writing about Blake (with the important exceptions noted above and also some excellent unpublished doctoral dissertations) is simply not worthy of its subject. Most writers lack a sense of history, they lack political commitment and they also lack a combative attitude towards the male intellectual establishment which has so successfully colonized the poet.

## IN CONCLUSION

One of the reasons that early feminist Blakeans produced historically deficient studies was that the general critical environment in which they were working was fairly inhospitable. In recent years, however, various kinds of loosely historicist criticism have challenged the deconstructionist oligarchy that had in the 1980s made a home for itself in Romantic studies. It is in the context of this change in critical emphasis that my own work needs to be seen, especially as the advent of American New Historicism breathed fresh life (albeit in faltering gasps) into the cultural materialist project started so long ago by Raymond Williams.[110] Moreover, in this particular revival of historically sensitive eighteenth-century studies, feminists have at last found a place for themselves, so that the project sketched out by Janet Todd in her *Feminist Literary History* (1987) looks as though it has found some skilled practitioners.[111] It is alongside this kind of work that my book should be read, for as the subsequent summary will make clear this study aspires to be an example of the 'kind of historically specific, archival, ideologically aware but still empirically based' (p. 7) feminist literary practice which Todd so persuasively argued the need for. Feminists in the 1990s have increasingly grasped the potential of wilful interdisciplinary research, for in the words of Madelyn Gutwirth this kind of methodology is vital to our project of 'Changing the Past'.[112] In a small way I hope *William Blake and the Daughters of Albion* will do just that.

As I fully endorse Blake's comment that, 'To Generalize is to be an Idiot To Particularize is the Alone Distinction of Merit' (Anno Ren, E.641) I have limited myself to an attempt to attain 'particular' knowledge of just six of his poems. By looking at a selection of works written/etched in 1789–95[113] I hope both to demonstrate the potential of a feminist-historicist methodology and also to say something about the relationship between the history of these tumultuous years and the texts Blake produced – taking as my guide Bakhtin's comment that the 'inner dialectic quality of the sign comes out fully in the open in times of social crisis or revolutionary change'.[114] During these years British culture, especially political culture, changed immensely and I shall bring out the sexual and gendered subtext of this process of change by illuminating various neglected contexts and reanimating long-silenced voices. As the historical record is so abundant I have had to be selective, nonetheless the range of contexts and voices discussed do, I think, begin to give us a very new sense of what Blake's 'times' were like.

In my second chapter I offer a challenge to orthodox readings of *The Book of Thel* (1789) by examining the poem in the light of the long-running eighteenth-century debate about the education and instruction of young women. By tracing the development of Thel's rational and sceptical consciousness, I demonstrate how

Blake's text exposes the didactic impulse that motivated much conduct literature and how it therefore aligns itself with those feminist writers who were arguing for more expansive and liberating educational opportunities for women. In the course of this exposition I also look at various other contemporary discourses, and in particular I examine writings concerned with the definition of female beauty alongside the discourse of moral motherhood. My alternative view of Thel as a young woman struggling towards a sense of identity in a hostile patriarchal environment comes into focus because I pay close attention to the polyphonic nature of the text and am hence able to apprehend the dialogue which Thel enters into with those 'natural' creatures who try to socialize and/or seduce her into a series of 'appropriate' feminine roles.

In my third chapter on *Visions of the Daughters of Albion* (1793) I try to understand what Oothoon's sexual radicalism meant historically. Various critics have suggested that the text espouses essentially pornographic values and I challenge these largely unsubstantiated claims by examining various erotic discourses current at the time of the poem's publication. The key fact about these sexual discourses is that they were almost exclusively fashioned and employed by male writers, often aristocratic, who were committed to the celebration of starkly phallocentric sexual politics and practice. I touch upon the problems which the existence of this dominant sexual ideology caused Jacobin and women writers when they attempted to write explicitly about physical desire, and point to the way in which their predominant response was to remain silent, or at the very least evasive, on the subject. Blake represents something of an exception here as he openly attempts to appropriate sensuality (perhaps even libertinism) for both the republican and feminist causes, and though I ultimately conclude that the attempt fails I still maintain the view that the poem is a brilliant achievement whose value lies in Blake's acute sensitivity to issues of sexual power. In this chapter I examine both verbal and visual intertexts, and pay special attention to the kinds of female form represented in the commercial engravings that Blake produced and sold.

Although my primary aim is to historicize Blake's treatment of these issues rather than to adjudicate on his political correctness, I do think that by the end of the third chapter something definite can be said about the poet's attitude to women – an

attitude which is exemplified by Oothoon's furious insistence that
when not institutionally 'bound' to man, woman is one who
'knows no fixed lot' (*Visions*, 5:21; E.49). Fundamental to Blake's
political vision is the, albeit faltering, belief that women have
the right to reject all prescribed roles, all instruction and instead
should trust to their own desires and perceptions. Moreover Blake's
female characters are extremely articulate in their defence and/
or pursuit of these freedoms. Both Thel and Oothoon speak fully
for themselves, without the qualification implied by strong authorial intervention.

The problem for the Daughters of Albion in the 1790s was
that they were in a situation of historical deadlock, their progress
– like Oothoon's – was stalled. The reasons for this are complex
but in my fourth chapter I try to throw some light on the matter
by detailing how radical male writers omitted discussions of
women's rights from their numerous pamphlets and manifestos,
and on how this practice is in some ways replicated by Blake in
his own early revolutionary writings: *The Marriage of Heaven and
Hell* (1790) and *America: A Prophecy* (1793). The context focused
in this chapter is broadly that of political discourse, and I look
not only at the significant gender-blindness of such revolutionary classics as Thomas Paine's *Rights of Man* (1791/2) but also at
the problematic nature of works by the few 'republican' feminists who tried to incorporate the rights of women into this kind
of political programme. These texts help us understand why Blake
marginalizes issues of gender when he writes his own explicitly
'political' works and they underline how easy it is for a male
radical to allow his proto-feminist sentiments to dwindle (as
Oothoon gives way to Orc). This also helps us understand the
seeming modesty of most feminist writing of the 1790s: whilst
men thought they sensed the birth of a new world, women were
struggling (largely without recognition) for the most basic of
educational, sexual and property rights.

In my final chapter on *Europe – A Prophecy* (1794) and, much
less centrally, *The Song of Los* (1795) I discuss the way in which
Blake regained and reincorporated a sense of the sexual dynamics
of history and of contemporary political struggle. In this
synopsizing section I look directly at the issue of women and
the French Revolution, and pay especial attention to the mythic
roles assigned to revolutionary women, and to elite figures
like Marie Antoinette, in contemporary political caricature and

propaganda. I also spend a great deal of time contextualizing the misogynist assessment of women's sexuality embodied in the phrase, 'Woman's love is Sin!' (Europe, 5:5; E.62) – for this was one of the main messages broadcast during the revolutionary period, by both conservative and radical writers. My argument is that *Europe* is something of a *tour de force*, as Blake discovers the full potential of the mytho-poetic form he has been developing.

Conclusions must, of course, wait until later, but one framing comment is both legitimate and necessary: Blake is of value to feminism not because he maintained an exemplary and unwavering feminist commitment but rather because he took sexual power seriously and engaged with many of the contemporary discourses and contexts in which it was being exercised or resisted. Moreover, and perhaps more important still, Blake's real 'feminist' gesture is that he constructs a notion of femininity centred upon the concept of dissent. He allows disputatious female voices into his texts in a truly revolutionary way and this polyphonic liberality can be historically located and valued if we look at a pivotal passage from James Fordyce's very popular sermon on *The Conduct and Character of the Female Sex* (1776):

> Ah, my female friends, did you in particular, did you but know, how deeply the male heart is enchanted with those women, whose conversation presents the picture of simplicity and grace, of ease and politeness, in a groupe [sic]; the spirit of whose conversation is a compound of sprightliness, sense, and modesty; who seldom dispute, and never wrangle, who listen with attention to the opinions of others, and deliver their own with diffidence, more desirous of receiving than of giving conviction, more ambitious to please than to conq'er!. Such, believe me, are sure of conquering in the noblest sense.
>
> Paint to yourselves, by way of contrast, a woman who talks loud, contradicts bluntly, looks sullen, contests pertinaciously, and instead of yielding challenges submission. How different a figure!. How forbidding an object!. Feminality is gone: Nature is transformed: whatever makes the male character most rough, and turbulent, is taken up by a creature, that was designed to tranquillize and smooth it. In place of a 'charmer, charming never so wisely', what do we behold? A clamorous, obstinate, contentious being, universally disgustful and odious; fit only to be chased from the haunts of humanity, those peaceful

haunts which it seeks to disturb – Merciful Heaven! Shelter us
from its violence, in the blessed sanctuary of domestic love
and joy, or in the sweet harmonious choir of friendship.[115]

Blake makes this discursively violent creature a central character in all his writing. From the early Hela, who attacks her madly
tyrannical father with the complaint 'thou accursed man of sin
[. . .] I was born thy slave' (*Tiriel*, 6:13–15; E.283) right up to
Enitharmon in *Jerusalem*, Blake's women call the legitimacy of
patriarchy into question by loudly questioning the rightness of
its treatment of them. Blake clearly looked at constructions
of sexual difference like this one and set about redefining femininity in ways which would include precisely those disruptive
qualities which the horrified Fordyce claims de-sex, and indeed
de-humanize, women. Moreover, the family serves no such protective function in Blake's poetry and no great heavenly patriarch is trusted to organize the sexual relationships of humanity.
All is flux and conflict, all is debate and argument, all is open to
challenge and change in Blake's sexual universe; and, as I hope
to demonstrate, this is one of the best reasons for our continued
reading of his poetry.

# 2

# The Sins of the Fathers: Patriarchal Criticism and *The Book of Thel*

I do not want to *make* you any thing: I want to know what Nature has made you, and to perfect you on her plan.

Dr John Gregory

I complain, and no one hears my voice.

(Thel, 3:4; E.4)[1]

Of all the partial readings of Blake's works available to students of his poetry, the most censurable appear in the now bulky corpus of criticism concerned with *The Book of Thel* (1789). Taking Blake's dictum 'Severity of judgment is a great virtue' (Lav, 36; E.585) as my guiding principle I will, by looking at the criticism ensnaring the poem, demonstrate that patriarchal critics have got away with numerous unchastised interpretative transgressions, whilst simultaneously working to reveal the historically specific proto-feminist aspects of the poem suppressed by this patriarchal orthodoxy.

*Thel* may seem a rather diminutive work but it is in fact an immensely important poem,[2] being the first illuminated narrative Blake produced and one he continued to offer for sale throughout his life. Blake's evident commitment to the work, however, was not shared by those men who worked for his canonization; they found it an embarrassing poem and strove, through critical assessments of extravagant condescension, to marginalize it. Northrop Frye blushed even to comment on such a fragile work merely wishing us to note how deft Blake was at avoiding the 'namby-pamby'; David Erdman was similarly uninterested in a work written before the ardour of Orc had arisen and waved the poem aside as 'a sort of mystery play for adolescents', and Damon completed the trinity with his patronizing declaration that this was merely an aberration, Thel being 'far too nice a girl to fit in amongst Blake's furious elementals'.[3]

What is interesting is that though such stances do have a legacy in the constant assertion that *Thel* is the softest, simplest and most accessible of Blake's longer poems (for example, Brian Wilkie recently spoke of 'the pastel Disneyland Thel seems to live in') these three respected patriarchs of Blake studies were, for once, not at all prophetic.[4] Once the metaphysicians had been displaced (Peter Ackroyd's comments about Thel's 'trembling young soul' are woefully outdated) and the poem's protagonist was acknowledged to be an inquisitive and slightly truculent young woman[5] there was a veritable eruption of works impelled by moral imperatives.

The first blast of this particular trumpet was issued by Robert F. Gleckner who, at the end of the 1950s, savaged Thel's behaviour with great ferocity. Not only is she a selfish and vain spiritual failure whose 'real self' is 'ugly, cold, mean' and 'dark' but she is also a despot, bearing 'no distant resemblance' to Urizen who presides over the Vales of Har as its Queen, wearing 'the crown of luxury, pride, material comfort' and 'power'.[6] Moreover, Gleckner maintained this judgemental stance for three decades: in the mid-1980s he continued his critique by designating Thel 'an incipient Vala whose cruelties swarm through all the prophetic books' and completed his assassination of her character by casting aspersions on Thel's sexuality through the contention that she is an 'autoerotic Petrarchan mistress'.[7] Gleckner ended his initial orations with the definitive statement 'in Blake's eyes Thel is obviously a sinner'.[8] If space permitted, it would be fascinating to trace in detail the manifold ways in which critics following him have demanded her repentance. In this chapter I will simply show how in Thel/*Thel* criticism, prescriptiveness and didacticism reign to an extent unprecedented in Blake studies.

Of course there are a few critics who have eschewed this authoritarian stance, but they step in to defend Thel only after denying the significance, or indeed the existence, of her gender. W.J.T Mitchell, for instance, argues that she is a 'surrogate for the reader' and contends that Blake is confronting us 'with a human dilemma that eludes any fixed moral stance'; Steven Cox is equally universalizing in his claim that 'love' troubles Thel and that 'is everyone's problem'; A.G. den Otter offers the ingenious idea that Thel is a 'Barthesian lover' whose drifting desire should not be censured, whilst James King prefers to see Thel as a representative of the poem's author, claiming that 'the maturation crisis of Thel is one Blake himself experienced as he approached thirty-three'.[9] It is only in such incongruously gender-blind readings that Thel finds any support. When critics accept her identity as a young woman didacticism is still the chosen response, with Michael Ferber's recent trenchant attack destined to become a very well-known reworking of the patriarchal orthodoxy. In his Penguin Critical Study (1991) Ferber contends that the poem's moral is that the resisting Thel, with her 'self-regarding [. . .] self-objectifying' tendencies, 'will become a bitter old maid with grey hairs on her head' – the inevitable outcome of remaining a 'wall-flower at the dance of nature'; and just one year later Stephen Behrendt reinforced this evaluation in his longer study of Blake, which presents Thel as a 'wrong-headed' young virgin who has chosen to 'wallow in self-pity and cynicism'.[10]

As the remarks of Gleckner and his heirs intimate, the corpus of criticism forms a kind of dictatorial conduct book of the sort which abounded at the time *Thel* was written and whose motivations, I will argue, the poem exposes. In the past writers have given this kind of intertextual material very short shrift but I intend to show that an awareness of its cultural significance is central to any understanding of *The Book of Thel*. Prior to the 1770s most advice literature was directed towards providing guidance and information for young men, but in the later decades of the eighteenth century the behaviour of young women became a subject of more pressing concern, and brought into print a large band of markedly directive and moralistic writers. As William St Clair remarks, in the context of a review and analysis of this material, 'nothing which went before approached the huge flood of didactic books for ladies that started to build up in the 1780s'.[11] These works took a variety of forms – including fables, letters, lessons, lectures and sermons – but all had the underlying motive of presenting in a palatable form a number of repetitive and repressive maxims. Their authors all hoped to 'lead in sweet captivity the mind/ To virtue' through works which laboured to demonstrate the dictum, 'Improvement and delight go hand in hand'.[12]

The pivot of the ideology governing this conduct literature was an essentialist assessment of the nature and capacities of the sexes, an assessment summarized by Hannah More in her much re-printed collection of *Essays . . . Principally designed for Young Ladies* (1777/5th ed., 1791), 'the mind in each sex has some natural kind of bias, which constitutes a distinction of character, and [. . .] the happiness of both depends, in great measure, on the preser-vation and observance of this distinction'.[13] And it is interesting in the context of *The Book of Thel* that the most essentially female characteristic identified by these writers was a constitutional malleability. Young women were perfectly adapted, and hence morally obliged, to become the servants of other people's needs and desires. For it was asserted that they had, as James Fordyce explained, 'from Nature a peculiar aptitude to please, with a wonderful facility in adapting themselves to the tempers of others', a claim elaborated by Dr John Gregory in his pronouncement on women's essential emotional serviceability: 'The natural softness and sensibility of your dispositions particularly fit you for the practice of those duties where the heart is chiefly concerned. And this, along with the natural warmth of your imagination, renders you peculiarly susceptible of the feelings of devotion'.[14] This concept of emotional duty, often underpinned by a crudely func-tionalist Christianity, was repeatedly invoked to steer women into the path that nature had laid out for them, as endless stric-tures eulogize the virtues of self-denying modesty and altruistic submissiveness: the 'ornament' of the female was 'a meek and quiet spirit'.[15]

The success of this model of femininity was dependent upon the effective challenging and containment of various potentially self-affirming, and hence subversive, female energies. In my next chapter I shall look at how the conduct writers censured and directed women's sexual energy, but in the context of *Thel* it is their treatment of intellectual adventurousness, and their stric-tures against mental rebellion and free thought, which are most pertinent. For a self-conscious trust in one's own judgements and wisdom was something these didactic authors could not counte-nance. Indeed, according to Fordyce this was an inherently un-feminine form of behaviour, for, as he explained 'the Affectation of a Superior understanding' is 'a species of pride irreconcilable with the lovely meekness and modest pliancy which ought al-ways to characterize the sex, and the want of which no talents, no allurements, can ever sufficiently compensate'.[16] This point is maintained so tenaciously because of the purely instrumental attitude these writers have towards female progress and development. As Hannah More made clear 'the end of a good education' was to make women 'good daughters, good wives, good mistresses, good members of society, and good Christians';[17] and if this was to be successful, young women had to become habituated to the renunciation, or at the very least suppression, of their individual ideas and judgements. More is, again, most forceful on this point:

> Girls should be taught to give up opinions betimes, and not pertinaciously carry on a dispute, even if they should know themselves to be in the right. I do not mean that they be robbed of the liberty of private judgement, but that they should by no means be encouraged to contract a contentious or contradictory turn. It is of the greatest importance to their happiness, that they should acquire a submissive temper, and a forebearing spirit; for it is a lesson which the world will not fail to make them frequently practise, when they come abroad into it, and they will not practise it the worse for having learnt it the sooner.[18]

It was on precisely this point that late eighteenth-century feminists took issue with conduct writers, often offering challenges from within the genre of instructional writing. The Marchioness De Lambert, for example, whose *Advice of a Mother to Her Daughter* was published in a 1790 compendium with Gregory's *Father's Legacy*, writes powerfully on the inadequacy of female education and argues for the absolute importance of young women attaining mental autonomy, 'Accustom yourself to exercise your understanding [...] We fill our heads with the notions of other people, and take no care to form any of our own [...] Among our sex the art of thinking is a sort of dormant talent [...] you will find yourself much better supported by your reason than by that of other people'.[19] Prophetically foreshadowing Mary Wollstonecraft the Marchioness concluded, 'Be assured, that the greatest science is to know how to be independent'.[20] Indeed Wollstonecraft herself started her writing career with a number of highly didactic works, including the conduct book *Thoughts on the Education of Daughters* (1787) and she, similarly, subverted the form from within, through a refusal to exercise imperious control over the female intellect: 'It may be observed, that I rec-

ommend the mind's being put into a proper train, and then left
to itself. Fixed rules cannot be given'.[21] And she developed her
ideas on the importance of active education later in the same
work: 'Youth is the season of activity, and should not be lost in
listlessness. Knowledge ought to be acquired, a laudable ambition encouraged; and even the errors of passion may produce
useful experience, expand the faculties; and teach them to know
their own hearts.'[22] Admittedly, Wollstonecraft's moralistic tendencies are still evident here, but this in no way handicapped
her from delineating the oppressive aspects of conduct writing
in her later *Vindication of the Rights of Woman* (1792),[23] a work I
shall draw on later.

Anti-essentialist ideas about women and their education did,
in fact, find expression in a number of works written or published around the time that Blake was working on *The Book of
Thel*. Catherine Macaulay Graham, speaking for a growing number
of liberal educationalists, advanced trenchant arguments in favour of co-education and protested vehemently about the dam-
age done to young women by the inadequacy of the provision
available to them, 'The situation and education of women [. . .]
is precisely that which must necessarily tend to corrupt and
debilitate both the powers of mind and body [. . .] every vigorous exertion is suppressed, the mind and body yield to the tyranny of error, and Nature is charged with all these imperfections
which we alone owe to the blunders of art.'[24] The point these
writers made was that freedom was essential to valuable learning and self-development. Like Mary Hays they all held 'Liberty
to be in the moral world, what the very air we breathe is to
animal and vegetable life'.[25]

Conduct literature and these emergent feminist responses to it
may seem to be matters at some remove from Blake's concerns
in the 1780s, but his engagement with the Bluestocking circle of
Mrs Mathews during these years certainly left its mark on Blake's
writing, as did his engraving work for *The Lady's Magazine* (discussed more fully in Chapter 3). Blake's early *An Island in the
Moon* (1784) evidences a keen awareness of both fashion and
feminine aesthetics. 'Ladies discourses' (*Island*, 8; E.457) were
clearly in his mind at this time, and the works and annotations
roughly contemporaneous with *Thel* also suggest that he was very
much concerned with questions of pedagogy and learning. Blake,
like Wollstonecraft and Macaulay Graham, held that the 'true

method of knowledge is experiment' (*All Religions*; E.1) and his
annotations to Lavater redefine moral worth in ways that have
truly revolutionary implications: in opposition to the notion that
docility is the greatest good Blake insists 'all Act [. . .] is Virtue'
(Lav; E.601). The valuing of, and importance of acting upon, knowledge gained through personal experience and endeavour are the
points of convergence between Blake and these feminist contemporaries, and in this chapter I shall argue that Thel is the first
female character Blake created who develops an intellect capable of this kind of activity. Because of this she stands as a challenge to the writers of conduct literature (both then and now).
In his *Essay on Old Maids* (1785) William Hayley stressed that
'The guardians of female youth cannot caution their pupils too
strongly against the dangerous custom of asking idle and insignificant questions; for a frivolous curiosity, though it amount
not to vice, is, perhaps the most offensive of foibles'.[26] This kind
of irritating questioning and curiosity are Thel's *forte*, though
the knowledge she gains is anything but idle or insignificant. In
this chapter I shall demonstrate that *Thel* is a poem in which the
sceptical enquiries of a determined young woman thoroughly
unmask patriarchal ideology, an ideology which promised women
that heterosexual romantic and maternal roles equalled heavenly
fulfilment, but which Thel discovers amount to nothing less than
death. According to *The Book of Thel* life under patriarchy is a
grave plot. To elaborate this contention I'll briefly run through
the major events of the narrative.

The first contentious question about Thel's biography is what
the realm of the Seraphim is and why Thel chooses to leave it.
One popular belief, emanating from Gleckner, is that this is a
region of deserving higher innocents who, in Michael Ferber's
elaboration, live exalted lives circling around God the sun/Son.[27]
There is but scanty evidence for such rosy claims which anyway
leave their authors with the problem of explaining why Thel would
want to leave such bliss. In opposition I would suggest that we
need to turn, for a more convincing answer, to Mary
Wollstonecraft's insight into the motivation behind patriarchal
associations of the female with the ethereal: 'Why' she said 'are
girls to be told that they resemble angels; but to sink them below women?'.[28] And this is precisely the fate of Thel's older sisters, confined as they are to the dizzyingly futile task of leading
'round their sunny flocks' (*Thel*, 1:1; E.3) – a circuitous occupa-

tion which suggests that these eighteenth-century females, like those sympathized with by Mary Hays, are 'enclosed in a kind of magic circle, out of which they cannot move, but to contempt or destruction'.[29] Yet the youngest sister Thel, having spent slightly less time amongst the sheep, is not so mesmerized, and sensibly decides to leave such an unimpressive life. She has not, however, got much of an idea of what to do once she reaches the illicit 'secret air' (*Thel*, 1:2; E.3), and so laments.

Her lament has received much critical attention, with not a few writers joining David Wagenknecht in his assessment that Thel 'prattles amiably but pointlessly' – a tonal insult reiterated by the many critics who hear only 'whining' and 'foolish prating' in Thel's questions and complaints.[30] Nearly all claim, too, that her main concern is with mortality and the transience of life. Yet however strong this critical consensus may be, it simply is not correct. If Blake had wanted to deal with human finitude (something he didn't believe in anyway)[31] he certainly would not have chosen the form he employs in Thel's lament because what strikes us immediately about her speech is its excessiveness. We could, perhaps, believe mortality was worrying Thel if she had just said 'O life of this our spring! why fades the lotus of the water?/Why fade these children of the spring? born but to smile & fall' (*Thel*, 1:6–7; E.3) but once the torrential flow of similes begins we become aware that something rather more subversive is going on. Blake is, I think, exploding stereotypical notions of youthful femininity by pushing them to their limits and hence revealing their absurdity.[32] These lines can be read as a kind of satire on Burke's highly influential, and roughly contemporaneous, notion of female beauty with its stress on smallness, delicacy and weakness. And if we look closely at part of Burke's Recapitulation, we find a key intertext, whose philosophy Blake exposes:

On the whole, the qualities of beauty, as they are merely sensible qualities, are the following. First, to be comparatively small. Secondly, to be smooth. Thirdly, to have a variety in the direction of the parts: but, fourthly, to have those parts not angular, but melted into each other. Fifthly, to be of a delicate frame without any remarkable appearance of strength. Sixthly, to have its colours clear and bright, but not very strong and glaring.[33]

In the lament Blake focuses especially on the infantilizing implications of Burke's theory, and seems to concur with Mary Hays
that the result of this construction is to reduce women to a state
of 'PERPETUAL BABYISM'.[34] Exquisite beauty connotates trembling fragility, and such weak, almost vaporous, creatures are
likely to submit to the patriarchal moulding I mentioned earlier
without even a whisper. Thel herself is, momentarily, prepared
to accept that gentleness is her defining characteristic (Thel, 1:12–
13; E.3) although for the most part she is not engaged, as Gleckner
claims, in 'masterful self-analysis'[35] but is rather, through parody,
laying bare the flexi-woman construction of femininity canvassed
by such men as Burke and even Blake's own hero, John Caspar
Lavater.[36] A manipulation in which, to use Wollstonecraft's words,
'all women are to be levelled, by meekness and docility, into
one character of yielding softness and gentle compliance'.[37]

So, Thel having opened her new existence by parodying stereotypical notions of female beauty is ready to 'come out' into a
social world where she will defy many other conventional ex-
pectations. This moment of a young Lady's entrance into adult
society was of crucial importance to conduct writers, for it was
the moment of crisis when the efficacy of their strictures received
its first real test. At this point Thel is in a parallel situation to
Hayley's paragon Serena; as he describes her, 'For now she enter'd
those important years/ When the full bosom swells with hopes
& fears'.[38] But, as we will see, Thel cherishes a nobler ambition
than simply 'To love and to be loved'; she has faculties to unfold and independence to attain.[39]

As we move on to look at Thel's conversations, it becomes
essential to value the dialogicality of the text, something which
previous writers have been reluctant to acknowledge.[40] Though
Susan Fox rightly stressed that this is the first poem in which
multiple perspective is the governing principle, most critics have
tended to deny this interactive polyphony and have insisted instead that the Lilly, Cloud and Clod are simply Thel's self-pro-
jections; she being, as Marjorie Levinson puts it, basically a
ventriloquist.[41] In this way Thel's problems are reduced to those
of consciousness only and the insights she gains into the functioning of patriarchy and its justificatory ideologies are dismissed
as examples of Thel's misperceptions.[42] As my case unfolds it
will become clear how far I diverge from the opinions of the
many critics who claim that Thel is ignorant and myopic.[43]

The most important initial point to make about Thel's dialogue with the Lilly is that it does not provide evidence of the poet's enthusiasm for some harmonious natural cycle. Blake did not believe in natural religion, did not feel that you could learn anything from nature and certainly never recommended it as a guide to human action.[44] Rather what he is exploring is the *naturalizing function* of ideology: as the illumination on Plate 2 makes quite clear (*Illuminated*; E.36), the Lilly is a woman much like Thel who has learnt to think of herself as a diminutive weed through patriarchal insinuations, indeed through the insinuations of the ultimate of all patriarchs. She knows that she is a small, weak, watery plant who loves to dwell in lowly vales (*Thel*, 1:16–18; E.3–4) because every morning God the Father spreads his hand over her head and tells her so, daily reminding her that she is a 'humble' 'gentle' 'modest' maid (*Thel*, 1:21–2; E.4), an uninspiring message only slightly sweetened by his promises of life after death in some allegorical abode. And it is the chance of fulfilling this feminine role which is supposed to placate Thel's unease: 'why' asks the Lilly after she has explained her situation 'should Thel complain, / Why should the mistress of the vales of Har, utter a sigh'? (*Thel*, 1–2:25–1; E.4)

Thel continues to object because she has been perceptively observing the situation[45] and has learnt that the Lilly's lot is a great deal more strenuous and perilous than her words have led us to believe. First of all she has self-deprecatingly underestimated her own strength: not only could the gilded butterfly easily perch upon her head but she also nourishes lambs, revives cows and tames horses. But more importantly Thel is distressed by the masochism inherent in giving this kind of nurture. Brenda Webster is right to speak of *Thel* in relation to images of sacrifice and devouring[46] because in minding 'her numerous charge among the verdant grass' (*Thel*, 2:18; E.4) the Lilly actually loses her life. She is cropped by infectious lambs and ultimately dismembered to provide a bed for the infant worm. And it is this self-annihilation that Thel will not accept, she wants an independent life that leaves a mark and her demand 'who shall find my place' (*Thel*, 2:12; E.4) has brought her a great deal of criticism. D.G. Gillham speaks for many when he opines 'Thel has given nothing [. . .] There is no generous impulse here, only a self-centred and self-pitying wail that contrasts with the selflessness of the modest Lilly'.[47] Thel is clearly in trouble for lacking that 'Propensity to devotion, and [. . .] warmth of Affection'[48] which James Fordyce felt to be such essential ingredients in any eighteenth-century woman's character (and twentieth-century too, if we believe the Blakists).

The painfully credulous Lilly, however, simply takes Thel at her word: as she has described herself as 'a faint cloud kindled at the rising sun' (*Thel*, 2:2; E.4) the Lilly assumes that a cloud must obviously be called forth to answer Thel's questions, and having hailed the next interlocutor she shuffles off to perform the hard duties assigned to her in the Vales of Har.

Thel's encounter with the Lilly has allowed her to unfold her reasoning faculties and extend her confidence. Indeed she is decidedly bouyant when the Cloud approaches, addressing him as a little figure and charging him to answer her queries (*Thel*, 3:1; E.4). She will need this self-will, for the Cloud is the only adult male Thel addresses in the Vales of Har, and her feeling that they share a similar problem in lack of recognition for their grievances evaporates immediately she sees his form. Unlike the other creatures Thel encounters, the Cloud is not self-effacing, pale or earth-bound but rather 'shew'd his golden head & his bright form emerg'd, / Hovering and glittering on the air' (*Thel*, 3:5–6; E.4). Thel had thought that he simply shed his water and vanished but this male youth has a much brighter fate, as he tells her 'when I pass away, / It is to tenfold life, to love, to peace, and raptures holy' (*Thel*, 3:10–11; E.4–5). In short, the Cloud seems to enjoy an eternal life of endless happy copulation and though many writers have acknowledged his sexual significance what they have not acknowledged is the deeply suspicious nature of the bliss he enjoys. Annette Levitt roundly condemns Thel for retaining unacted desires in the face of his sexual appeal, insisting that she finds Comus-like danger in a figure who has no negative qualities whatever.[49] But this is an erroneous claim, for the Cloud is merely more honest than Comus about his exploitative masculinist activities: telling us quite openly about his unseen descent upon female flowers and of the marked lack of enthusiasm displayed by his bride the fair-eyed dew, who weeps and 'trembling kneels' as a prelude to their union (*Thel*, 3:12–14; E.5). Hardly the 'companionate marriage' Stephen Cox finds endorsed in the Cloud's speeches.[50] As the title page's illumination makes quite clear, aggressive male sexuality[51] is one of the main problems Thel has to face (*Illuminated*; E.34) and generalized criti-

cism of her virginal fear of the phallus serves only to negate the
legitimacy of her complaints.[52] Why, after all, shouldn't she protest about the prospect of being groped like the woman whose
fate she observes on the title page? Stephen Behrendt's answer
is that such acts of 'aggressive sexual violence [. . .] transpire at
least in part because of a female figures 'unnatural', learned resistance to her natural sexual impulses'[53] but if one does not believe
that what women want and need is a touch of rough trade, this
does not advance the discussion very far. Moreover such criticism tends to obscure the acute perception Thel now has of heterosexual roles and in particular of the divergent parenting
activities of the sexes: having heard the Cloud's account of sexual
union and childrearing Thel declares 'I fear that I am not like
thee' (*Thel*, 3:17; E.5) and one look over the page vividly illuminates why. The headpiece to Plate Four offers an unequivocal
message: Thel stands mimicking the outstretched arms of the
Cloud, but as he gusts energetically on the breeze she looks down
at an infant, lying by her feet (*Illuminated*; E.38). Heterosex means
motherhood, and motherhood in this patriarchal environment
means self-sacrifice. All will indeed say 'without a use this shin-
ing woman liv'd' (*Thel*, 3:22; E.5) if she chooses not to become a
mother and yet, as Thel complains, accepting available maternal
roles is as good as dying and becoming the food of worms. The
speaking of this taboo truth forces the Cloud to reveal his allegiances and he answers her with a piece of exemplary utilitar-
ian sexism (Michael Ferber's claim that his message 'is like
Gabriel's annunciation to Mary' is a startling, though by no means
solitary, misreading).[54] Pompously reclining upon his airy throne
the Cloud shows himself to be a kind of winged Rousseau: 'Then
if thou art the food of worms [. . .] How great thy use, how great
thy blessing' (*Thel*, 3:25–6; E.5).[55] As a woman Thel's greatest
blessing is to be useful[56] and that she rejects such logic becomes
clear when Thel gets a chance to exercise this sacrificial feminine
prerogative.

The Worm is a dual symbol, representing both an infant and
a penis and Thel quite sensibly reacts to each connotation in a
different way. When perceiving the creature as a baby she pities
its naked and helpless form but nonetheless refuses to answer
its cries and nourish it with 'mothers smiles' (*Thel*, 4:6; E.5).[57]
This is a rejection that has done little to endear Thel to her critics, who as we have seen continue to offer up a near universal

cry against her selfishness. And Thel's reaction to its phallic dimensions has done little to ameliorate their displeasure, for her
immediate response – which is certainly not marked by the sexual
pensiveness imputed to her by the Cloud (*Thel*, 3:29; E.5) – is to
express astonishment at its unimpressiveness. Behrendt grandly
describes the Worm as 'a prophet who would lead her (and the
nation of readers for whom she stands) to a promised land of
sensual and sexual freedom'[58] but Blake entertained no such
Lawrencian reverence for the penis. 'The nakedness of woman'
may well be 'the work of God' (*MHH*, 8:25; E.36) but Thel's smirky
'Is this a Worm?', 'Art thou a Worm? image of weakness. Art
thou but a Worm?' (*Thel*, 4:5, 2; E.5) suggests that at least one
aspect of the nakedness of man has no such divine associations.
This has a good deal of political significance because although
Blake was always able to balance negative images of the vagina
(stress on the veil of Vala and so on) with positive ones (the
wonderful bursting flower chorus of *Milton* Book Two) his feelings about the male genitals became more and more wholeheart-
edly negative. By the turn of the century erection is, for example,
treated not as a pleasure but as a veritable affliction (see the
description of the Spectre of Urthona/Los's trials with his 'veiny
pipes' (*FZ*, 50:11; E.333) which draws men into ever more intimate contact with their Spectres (see *Jerusalem*, pl. 6 *Illuminated*;
E.285).[59] With the phallus so radically compromised it is but a
short step to the act of questioning all phallocratic, patriarchal
authority. However suggestive this line of argument is though,
as far as Thel's narrative is concerned, it is the Worm's infant
needs that are most significant, for they bring forth Thel's final,
and most instructive, communicant.

When the Clod of Clay, much critically praised for her 'admirable abjectness' and fantasized about as a 'sexually ripened
mother, sweet for the very fact of being unvirginal',[60] clumps
forward to tend the infant worm we see epitomized the version
of motherhood which Thel has rejected. This decision is made
because she is the very antithesis of the rational or republican
mother whom Wollstonecraft, and many other contemporary
feminists, were stressing the need for.[61] Unlike Wollstonecraft's
reasoning mother who performs her nurturing tasks as a human
duty based on a sense of self-worth and adult capability, the
Clod has accepted without qualification the Cloud's hypocritical
male philosophy: 'we live not for ourselves' (*Thel*, 4:10; echo 3:26–

7; E.5). Hence she has no self-esteem: 'Thou seest me the mean-est thing, and so I am indeed/ My bosom of itself is cold and of itself is dark', has accepted sado-sexual religious rationalizations of her situation: 'But he that loves the lowly, pours his oil upon my head./And kisses me, and binds his nuptial band around my breast'[62] and, most important, is incapable of questioning her condition: 'But how this is [. . .] I know not and I cannot know,/ I ponder and I cannot ponder; yet I live and love' (*Thel*, 4, 5:11–6; E.5–6). Thel, on the other hand, has learnt that she too par-takes with man of the gift of reason and when she sets it up as judge to this most holy mystery[63] soon discovers that the Clod has been seduced into a role of slavery and self-annihilation. Anyone who 'her life exhal'd/ In milky fondness' (*Thel*, 4:8–9; E.5) has been severely gulled if she believes that this amounts to having 'a crown that none can take away' (*Thel*, 5:4; E.5). The Clod, in short, is a living embodiment of Wollstonecraft's claim that, 'The being who patiently endures injustice, [. . .] will soon become [. . .] unable to discern right from wrong'; 'Man, taking her body, the mind is left to rust'.[64] A Clod indeed.

We do, however, need a two-fold vision if we are to appreci-ate the totality of the Clod's role because Blake is not only ex-posing the injustice of her situation; he also – characteristically wanting it 'both ways' – would like us to see the value of her capacity for love however excessively employed. Hence, though Thel maintains her complaint about fading from a significant role in life (*Thel*, 5:12–13; E.6) she is nonetheless deeply moved by the Clod's suffering example, moved enough to engage in some decidedly uncharacteristic, and in fact quite illogical,[65] praise of the Clod's God (*Thel*, 5:8–11; E.6) and, more importantly, moved enough to make the courageous decision to enter Matron Clay's house.

As Plate 6 is where Thel has achieved her general reputation as a cowardly hysterical failure[66] I think it's important just to note initially how brave a figure she actually is. For before Thel reaches her grave plot she passes without flinching through a number of agonized wastelands, 'where never smile was seen' (*Thel*, 6:5; E.6). The fact that the majority of Blake's expositors find it impossible to imagine a young woman who is courageous must not be allowed to blind us to the fact that Blake could, and indeed the disservice done to the poet's feminist sympathies by the existence of a sexist critical orthodoxy is nowhere more evident than in commentary on the voice from Thel's grave. Most critics aim at denying the validity of Thel's vision of her future life. By insisting that the passage 'is entirely subjective' and 'not corroborated by any independent evidence', the majority reiterate the view that the voice is yet another example of her perverted understanding.[67] As Gleckner explained, it is only because Thel is dazzled 'by her own brilliance' that experience looks like 'a chamber of horror'.[68] After all, the voice is speaking of what Thel's life will be like if she grows up in the Clay's house, as part of the community we've seen throughout the poem and any perception of that as destructive must surely be wrong. As Harriet Krammer Linkin authoritatively put it 'No reader questions the vast difference [. . .] between the vales Thel inhabits [. . .] and the startling land unknown'.[69] As my reading has suggested, I do. What Thel is actually hearing is a bitingly honest account of what her life as a woman will be like in an environment where males, through either charm or violence, invade her senses,[70] and as I've tried to show, when stripped of its quasi-religious and pastoral imagery, this is precisely the situation that exists in the Vales of Har. What Thel discovers, in these final lines, is the truth of Lady Pennington's depressing warning to her daughter that she is entering 'into a world full of deceit and falsehood, where few persons or things appear in their true character [. . .] one general mask disguises the whole face of things, and it requires a long experience, and a penetrating judgement to discover the truth'.[71]

*The Book of Thel* manages, however, to move beyond the wariness and/or complicity characteristic of such female conduct writers because Blake allows Thel to engage in subversive sexual speculations. This highly 'unfeminine' practice enables her voice to hint at a solution: by exclaiming against the patriarchal fetishing of the hymen[72] as an oppressive curb to an erotics of mutual delight – 'why a tender curb upon the youthful burning boy!/ *Why a little curtain of flesh on the bed of our desire* (*Thel*, 6:19–20; E.6, my emphasis) – Thel offers a way beyond the deathly future which had seemed to be her, and indeed every woman's, fate. To hear such a vibrant and sexually challenging message emerge from the lips of a young woman who was so unimpressed by earlier displays of the phallus has thrown the critics into disarray, even leading some to wonder whether Thel actually speaks the final two lines.[73] But in fact it is only because of Thel's cumulative scepticism about phallocentric practices that this particular insight is possible.

Opinions differ about the meaning of Thel's final action, although the majority of critics still choose to interpret her flight from the grave as simply the definitive evidence of her personal inadequacy and sexual immaturity. In Jay Parini's words the poem 'ends with an unredemptive thud'.[74] Most alternatives to this judgement hinge upon different understandings of Thel's response to the voice she hears[75] and most complementary to my reading of the poem is the critical path mapped out by a small band of women writers some time ago. In this tradition Thel's final shriek is read, as Anne Mellor hints, as a gesture of violent denunciation[76] and Thel flees back to Har to reanimate her dissenting sighs and moans which the patriarchally saturated Clod had momentarily called down (*Thel*, 5:15; E.6). According to this reading Thel may indeed, as Nancy Bogan tentatively claimed over 20 years ago, become the leader of a protest movement,[77] and the sexual politics displayed on Plate 6 (*Illuminated*, E.40), which ushers her back into the vales, certainly tend to reinforce this claim: a young girl confidently holds the reins of the phallic serpent whilst a young boy directs his attention to  caring for a straggling infant. In the light of this it could be argued that Thel is set to shake things up in the Vales of Har, through her encounters with both the female 'Moles' and the male 'Eagles'.[78] Thel has achieved some of that strength of body and mind which Wollstonecraft thought so essential for women's advancement, and there is no saying what kind of 'revolution' in 'female manners' that might lead to.[79]

The problem with this kind of triumphalist reading is that it is premised upon the belief that Har is a liberating environment, or at the very least a place amenable to sexually and socially radical ideas, and this, as I hope my reading has shown, is a conviction which rests upon the flimsiest of foundations.[80] We can accept Marilyn Bohnsack's blunt and apposite observation that 'Thel wants out' without going on to argue that clear ways out are depicted in the poem, and this, I think, is the point.[81] For the striking fact about *The Book of Thel* is that it offers no alternative to the conventional and stereotypical feminine roles it so astutely caricatures. As Thel progresses she unmasks and rejects heterosexual culture's romantic and maternal myths, but she is not able to construct any kind of workable alternative identity. The only possible escape route hinted at in the poem is the road of libidinal rebellion, but this appears as little more than a tricky retrospective suggestion, and this paucity of solutions points to a situation of historical deadlock which my later chapters explore. For now it is sufficient just to note that Blake has reached some kind of historically specific imaginative limit in his thought about women's rights and roles. He is clearly concerned about the emotional and physical exploitation of young women, and about the oppressive didactic imperative which propelled most contemporary discussions of them, but he is not able to envisage any way for them to end their victimization and become self-determining and autonomous social agents. Sadly, Blake critics usually deny that *The Book of Thel* addresses a specific historical problem. Stephen Cox tells us that 'no one need turn out like Thel [. . .] free choice is always possible and [. . .] energetic choices are always properly rewarded'[82] but, as we shall see, much more than choice and energy are needed to right the wrongs which concerned Blake and his feminist contemporaries.

It need hardly be said that this is not a standard reading of the text. Apart from K.D. Everest's excellent discussion of Thel's specifically female dilemma, and some sensitive unpublished treatments of the same issue, no Blakean writer has pursued any of the feminist implications of this luminously woman-centred poem.[83] In the 1990s this must amount to a critical scandal. Moreover, the perpetuation and amplification of patriarchal understandings of such early works as *Thel* sets a false agenda for the interpretation of Blake's later works. As this book unfolds it will become clear that the sexual questions raised here are central to many of the works which Blake went on to produce, and also that various other critical orthodoxies have, in serious ways, hampered our apprehension of Blake's feminist sympathies. Tilottama Rajan has made the important point that Blake developed 'a counterhermeneutic sensitive to the imperialism of canonical reading' but to date precious few have produced the kind of heretical interpretations she recommends.[84] I hope that *William Blake and the Daughters of Albion* will prove that they ought to, and quickly.

# 3

# 'Slip-Sliding Away': Some Problems with 'Crying Love' in the 1790s

Although the critical character of my first chapters may suggest otherwise, it is the case that venerable Blake scholars do sometimes make the most insightful comments. Such comments, however, are those which seem to be most quickly obscured by the quick-falling dust of time. This is certainly the case with the startlingly neglected[1] contextual remarks S. Foster Damon made as a preliminary to his discussion of *Visions of the Daughters of Albion*. In surprisingly insistent historicist terms he reminds his readers that the 'questionable' nature of eighteenth-century sexual morals and mores must be borne in mind by any critic wanting to understand Blake's treatment of sexuality in that poem, a poem which he insists is 'primarily a protest against the sexual customs of the times'.[2] Adjustments are certainly needed to correct Damon's class prejudices but the path which he pointed out is one that urgently needs following, for neglect of the historical specificities of Oothoon's protest, based largely on the assumption that sex is timeless and stands safely beyond the taints of history,[3] has rendered the greater part of *Visions* criticism repetitive, self-referential or even – as one irritated writer put it – onanistic.[4]

In brief, the orthodox case suggests that *Visions of the Daughters of Albion* is a continuation of *The Book of Thel*,[5] in which the poem's heroine triumphs over the weakness and cowardice that, as we've seen, most critics believe mark Thel's biography. Oothoon in pure 'Blakean' terms becomes that most accomplished of poetic characters: a 'higher innocent'.[6] The criterion used to make this distinction, and assessment, could aptly be called penetrative, as Oothoon's 'success' seems largely to consist in being prepared to undergo the heterosexual assault that Thel feared the future would bring.[7] And the critics who judge Oothoon to be successful usually go on to describe the poem as 'a hymn to free love': the core of Blake's sexual gospel (an interpretative trend started by Blackstone and Bloom, and carried up to the present by Duerkson, Dickstein, Murray, George, Brogan, Crehan, Hagstrum and more problematically Swearingen) – critics in this tradition, like Stephen Cox, still continue to peddle the idea that 'Oothoon's degrading experience of sex asserts the holiness of her love'.[8]

Some more thoughtful understandings of the poem have however begun to emerge, due to the willingness of a number of writers to address the paradox – glossed over by the 'free lovers' – of Oothoon's situation: raped and enslaved yet delivering wildly exuberant sexual rhetoric. Identifying and investigating this paradox is crucial to any convincing reading of the poem and so it is sad that explorations to date have for the most part not been very enlightening. The extant cluster of explanations for this problem are very limited and centre around suggestions that Blake was just ambivalent about sex (Damrosch),[9] or that Oothoon's less than perfect character is responsible (Peterson, Anderson, Haigwood, Ellis, Wilkie)[10] or Blake's equally flawed personality (Ellis, Fox, Mellor, Ostriker, Webster, Haffar).[11] Some writers have even been forced to conclude that the poem's essential contradiction is simply 'mysterious' or 'inexplicable' (Linkin, Stepto, Ferber).[12] And these interpretations are so unsatisfactory largely because attempts to understand the paradox of *Visions* have unfortunately not prompted critics to look in any detail at the historically specific sexual practices and abuses which Damon recommended as a guide, nor – more importantly – at the various discourses that presented and represented them to the eighteenth-century reading and viewing publics. With the single exception of Steven Vine's superb discussion of Oothoon's enslavement (which I shall return to later) commentators have been driven deeper into the corpus of critical literature – with a clutch of very detailed, and undeniably impressive, surveys intent on finding answers, if not truth, by reviewing and revising past criticism (Moss, Haigwood, Goslee, Vogler, Linkin, Hefferman).[13] Thomas Vogler has produced perhaps the most insightful review although he, having been overtaken by post-structuralist suspicions of language's ability to effectively signify, gave up trying to understand any of Blake's messages (which he believes are irredeemably sexist anyway) in favour of examining linguistic and ontological process: 'In my view, the text can be more interestingly read as a text "about" the production of Truth than as a direct assertion of Truth [. . .] If we look at Oothoon's Truth, we can see it riddled with the inevitable paradoxes that mark the systematization of discursive power.'[14] And that's that?

Well, *Visions* criticism, and in particular the appreciation of Oothoon's messages, is certainly in a sorry state but I hope to show that by building on S. Foster Damon's suggestion we can revive the poem's, and the heroine's, fortune. In this chapter I shall argue that Oothoon does indeed continue Thel's story by confronting directly the voice that had given Thel her only glimmer of hope in the death-in-life existence (that 'grave plot') offered by patriarchy: the voice of her constrained, but protesting, sexuality (*Thel*, 6:19–20; E.6). In marked and, as I shall show, problematic contrast to the priorities of his feminist contemporaries Blake places the liberation of women's sexuality at the top of his own 'feminist' agenda, and I shall try to demonstrate that Oothoon's arguments are both an onslaught on the phallocentric sexual ideology that was virulently current in the 1790s (an ideology I shall delineate in some detail) but also that they, at various crucial moments, slide into, and become expressions of, this pornographic culture. My argument is that *Visions of the Daughters of Albion* takes Blake's analysis of sexual exploitation well beyond the at times self-indulgent complaints found in the Notebook poems and *Songs of Experience* (1794), for here Blake attempts to find a place for the unfettered expression of women's desires at a historical moment when the controlling discourses of patriarchy were attempting, with much more effectiveness, to silence the voices of female eroticism. Ultimately I think we must conclude that Blake is unsuccessful in this attempt, but we can best appreciate the significance of his intentions, and begin to comprehend the reasons for, and nature of, Oothoon's ambiguous failure, if we start by looking at what some of these more influential discourses were saying.

What I want to do is to make *Visions* part of a historically specific sexual dialogue, and this intention is greatly aided by various recent developments in scholarship on the history of sexuality. The eighteenth century has traditionally been presented as a frolicsome sexual 'golden age', and this view (echoed incidentally by Ackroyd in his recent biography *Blake*) was only slightly refocused by the more delicate musings of Lawrence Stone upon the allegedly burgeoning practice of 'companionate marriage'.[15] What provoked more serious rethinking was the work of various authors concerned more with representations of sexuality than with postulations about possible practices, and the first influential essay of this kind was Paul Gabriel Bouce's 'Aspects of Sexual Tolerance and Intolerance in XVIIIth-Century England' (1980).[16] Bouce was the first to make the study of the sexual subsoil of 'great' literature his main concern, and to protest against the artificial severing of canonical material from intertexts so rich in information about the state of sexual mentalities. Bouce stressed that this was a vast field, needing a team of interdisciplinary scholars to investigate it, and that it would probably take a quarter of a century to achieve any kind of comprehensive knowledge. Yet these investigations must, he insisted, be carried out because our understanding will remain disastrously partial whilst the secret but life-giving nexus between sub-literature and 'great literature' is ignored. And this valuable project has been continued in a number of essay collections, which have comprehensively destroyed the golden age myth by throwing 'a bridge over the sadly widening gap between literary criticism and social history'.[17]

It is to work generated out of this movement that my chapter is most indebted, and in particular to Peter Wagner's ground-breaking study of eighteenth-century 'erotica': *Eros Revived* (1988). His fleshing out of a pornographic body upon the bones provided by Foucault in his writing about the explosion of sexual discourses apparent during Blake's lifetime is immensely valuable, as is his persuasive, if somewhat phallic, argument for the inexorable 'upward osmosis' of elements of this material into 'great literature'. And after reviewing a host of very different pornographic genres Wagner reaches the conclusion that most of the material is distasteful, exploitative and above all socially and sexually unprogressive.[18] What he did not focus upon, however, are the coercive sexual politics embodied in this intensely conservative body of literature, and whilst I cannot in any way cover as much ground as he does, I intend to re-examine some of the types of material Wagner analysed whilst paying attention to the fact that these were didactic male-authored discourses. Lynn Hunt's fascinating collection *The Invention of Pornography* (1993) clearly shows that the 1790s were definitive in setting modern trends in pornographic writing, but is equally clear that this made little difference to women's involvement in the genre: 'Men wrote about sex for other male readers [. . .] The new fraternity created by these complex intersections of voyeurism and objectification may have been democratic in the sense of social levelling, but in the end it was almost always a levelling for men'.[19] And given this, my overriding concern is to identify the patriarchal values inculcated by these works and Blake's troubled response to them. These values, in fact, are surprisingly similar to those motivating the explicitly instructive conduct literature we looked at earlier[20] – although perhaps this is no great surprise. Like them this pornography centres upon controlling young women, with an intimate oppressiveness quite beyond anything found in conduct writing.

## SEXUAL IDEOLOGY IN THE 1790s

Every day continues to furnish fresh instances of female insatiability, insomuch that one would be inclined to think that most stimulating, indeed maddening, of all disorders to which the human body is liable – the *furor uterinus* – was become epidemic.

The *Bon Ton Magazine* May 1793[21]

Although pornography was not a subversive force in eighteenth-century England,[22] female sexual energy did have numerous unsettling implications. Indeed, when the female objects of pornographic authors' and artists' attentions made even slight autonomous gestures, the potentiality of their libidinousness drastically changed. Active women were often conceptualized, and not always at a sublimated level, as a group of latter-day Eves:[23] necessary but always untrustworthy and possibly evil. Creatures liable, if their desires were allowed to find expression, to bring all the achievements of social order to an end and generate erotic chaos. And, as the *Bon Ton*'s defensively light-hearted quotation suggests, the moment that produced *Visions* was one when it seemed to many that such a disaster might well be imminent. Significant socioeconomic and political shifts doubtless underlie this perceived peak in male anxiety, and indeed many scholars have offered ambitious cross-decade and even cross-century analyses of such fearfulness,[24] but to enter into that kind of speculation is, though tempting, well beyond the scope of this discussion. My aim here is simply to signal the significance of the 1790s as a decade when gender identities and pornographic discourses were in significant transition (something fully discussed by Lynn Hunt and Randolph Trumbach)[25] and to elucidate a few key aspects of the paradoxical yet potent sexual ideology current around the time that Blake was formulating and finally writing *Visions*, that moment just before the moral panic generated by the war with revolutionary France produced its own sexual warnings and stereotypes (discussion of that subject occurs later).

For now it is important to pursue the idea of male fear and hostility and to look at the negative assessments of women's sexuality which generated these feelings, because the most significant aspect of *Visions* is that it seems to find Blake engaged in the difficult task of trying to unmask these fears, and challenge the validity and necessity of the repressive sexual defences which grew out of them. What we find at various moments in the poem is Blake refuting the idea that male control of female desire is a healthy thing, and he refutes this key tenet of the many writers who just couldn't bring themselves to trust women sexually in order to argue that social rejuvenation is directly linked to, if not dependent upon, female sexual freedom. I shall, however, offer an account of the views of some of Blake's more anxious contemporaries before I discuss the poet's ambiguous sensual, if not more correctly sexualized, feminism.[26]

What many male writers seem to have felt is that there was something unspeakably destabilizing in women's erotic potential, and modesty was constantly invoked as a charm against this.[27] A good example appears in John Armstrong's extremely popular *The Economy of Love* (1736/8th ed. 1791), which addresses the subject in these terms:

> Hail MODESTY! fair female honour, hail!
> Beauty's chief ornament, without whose charm
> Beauty disgusts; or gives but vulgar joys.
> Thou giv'st the smile its grace; the heighten'd kiss
> Its balmy essence sweet! *and, but for thee,*
> *The very raptures of the lawful bed*
> *Were outrage and foul riot, rites obscene!*
>                              (my emphasis)[28]

This idea that women's 'obscene' energy could destroy legitimate forms of sexual activity was repeated by various authors, especially those writing marriage guides. For instance the writer of *The Joys of Hymen, or, The Conjugal Directory* (1768) explained to his female readers that a good marriage rested upon the wife refraining from employing her powerful amorous imagination (a capacity which Blake's Oothoon constantly exercises): 'Invent not various ways to taste the bliss,/ But soft and gentle take the melting kiss./ Be modest; *nor to show the woman's force,*/ Disgrace the sex, and spoil the genial course' (my emphasis).[29] Another poem dealing with wifely ideals, which appeared in *The Lady's Miscellany* (1793), made a similar point: 'Let gentle love her bosom warm/ Yes, let her love you truly [. . .] Let modesty her actions guide,/ Or else she'll prove unruly'. It's clear that every man must be vigilant to the movements of this 'force', and 'husband' its dangers in a task parallel to the restraint of female nature that Armstrong explains is a cultivated man's duty:

> ours be the task alone
> To check her rude excrescences; to prune
> Her wanton overgrowth; and where she sports
> In shapes too wild, to lead her gently back,
> With prudent hand, to better form and use (p. 18)

The exact character of this female wantonness is left somewhat vague by these writers. It found, however, explicit expression in the works of John Wilmot, Earl of Rochester whose reputation significantly grew apace (though furtively) throughout the eighteenth century.[30] He energetically descanted in obscene terms on the subject of what men have to fear from women, and the following address to one believed to have been unfaithful is amply illustrative: 'When your lewd cunt came spewing home/ Drenched with the seed of half the town,/ My dram of sperm was supped up after/ For the digestive surfeit water' – the myth of the devouring woman, perfectly elaborated here and in numerous other of the poet's works,[31] gained cumulative currency in the century after Rochester's death. Indeed by the 1780s women's genitals were colloquially known as the 'dumb glutton'[32] and it is worth looking, I think, in a little detail at some of the other discourses in which this misogynist myth found influential expression. In particular it gained currency through its appearance in a number of paramedical works, populist in approach and sensationalist in their quackery,[33] whose special focus was upon masturbation. The solitary vice, thought to be responsible for literally countless mental and physical illnesses, was a key subject in the discursive explosion described by Foucault, but for this discussion an examination of only one work will have to suffice.

*Onania*, and its variants, went through 19 editions in the eighteenth century and sold nearly 38,000 copies.[34] It can, therefore, be assumed to have achieved a fair degree of cultural influence.[35] In its form and tone it resembled numerous pornographic works, especially in the appended supplement which contained a selection of 'reader's letters', each of which, as it unfolded a confessional tale, manoeuvred the reader into the position of a privileged voyeur. Not a few of these letters were allegedly written by concerned young women whose 'shameful' self-manipulations had led to disastrous problems, of which the most frightful was the provocation of the uncontrollable clitoris. The appearance of this organ, in the eyes of many writers, revealed the most dangerous potential of women's sexuality. As the *Onania*'s author commented:

> It is certain, that in some women, especially those who are very salacious, and have much abused themselves by SELF-POLLUTION, the *Clitoris* is so vastly extended, that upon thrusting out of the passage it is mistaken for a *Penis*; such have been called [. . .] Tribades and accounted *Hermaphrodites*, because [. . .] they have been able to perform the Actions of men with other women [. . .] in *Arabia*, they circumcise the women that are so.[36]

Macroclitoris, the condition described above, was a classified disorder which as well as providing a metaphor of the excess of women's sexuality also made it possible to warn women that seeking too much sexual pleasure would, literally, turn them into bisexual or lesbian monsters.[37] Solutions to this problem ranged from casting insults to surgery and straitjackets[38] but what it is essential to note is that these too active women were seen, through their mythical outgrowths, to threaten the most fundamental of hierarchical distinctions: that of the sexes. Well might the primitive sexologist James Graham speculate about the volcanic and even murderous potential embodied in 'the female'. Drawing a self-flattering distinction, he explained, 'From the upper masculine part proceed the light, serenity, life, and strength of our system, so, from the lower or female part (as *alas* from too many *other* female parts) do issue fires and Aetnean or Vesuvian furors, corruptions, diseases, discords, desolation and death'.[39] Yet as so much else evidently issued from these 'female parts' his very opposition is in jeopardy, and the hierarchy legitimated by this crudely phallocratic ideology imperilled.

Fear and defamation of women's sexuality also took other less vividly trangressive forms. Another colloquial name for women's genitals was 'the bite',[40] which also meant to cheat and this as-sociation enabled women's faithless appetite to be conceptual-ized in such extravagant terms that no man was safe, and no woman above suspicion. An illustration of this is provided by the 'man midwives' controversy (still current in 1793),[41] during the course of which male writers developed a standardized ar-gument that women were using the availability of this 'touching gentry' as an opportunity for undetected adulterous stimulation. As in Francis Foster's *Thoughts on the Times* (1779), lurid pic-tures were painted of ladies queueing up to enjoy the services of these pseudo-medical gigolos; and that such arguments were taken seriously suggests the scope of male fears of women's in-satiability. There was simply no moment in a women's life when she was not eager to display and indulge her nymphomaniac nature.[42] And hence male medicine went on to rationalize this appetite as a result of the female body's constant readiness to conceive.[43] It also insisted that women's undiscriminating sus-ceptibilities rendered them sexually inferior to men: 'That lax and pliant Habit, capable of being dilated and contracted on every occasion must necessarily want that Degree of Heat and Firmness which is the characteristic of Man, and which enables him to digest and evacuate his Nutriment in due Time and Proportion'.[44]

Derogatory pronouncements like this, though, were evidently not sufficient to alleviate male anxieties. What seems to have done more to restore self-confidence was the simultaneous, if somewhat illogical, counter-construction of women as essentially malleable passionless objects.[45] For example Armstrong's *Economy of Love* (1736 /8th ed. 1791) has as its centrepiece a wedding night scene in which a passive and incredulously overawed bride is led, blushing and fainting, through a consummation in which she must lie back and melt at the appropriate moment (which she does, without dissent).[46] And John Cleland's outrageously sexualized Fanny Hill is equally lumpen during her nuptials, enduring without protest enormous (everything is enormous in Cleland's world) pains for the sake of 'true love' with her sentimental lover Charles.[47] There were, doubtless, many reasons for the construction of these passive ideals but one of the most important is surely that they helped diffuse the threat of active female sexuality and rendered women subservient to male sexual desires. To avoid becoming the kind of sexual monster described above women were advised to become sheep between the sheets. *The Lover's Instructor* (published throughout the 1790s) makes this quite clear in its section containing <u>Directions in the Choice of a Wife</u>, where prospective lovers are told that, 'there is no single quality of so much importance as sweetness of temper [...] to be so perfectly yours, as to enter into your different passions and affections so deeply, as to feel them with you and for you'. This, of course, is the position Blake's Oothoon eventually slips into, offering not only herself but also other 'girls' to pleasure Theotormon and what is being advertised here is a profoundly unjust erotic economy: women are to give up their desires so that those of their lovers/husbands can be doubled – as the later <u>Rules and Maxims to be Observed by the Ladies for Promoting Matrimonial Happiness</u> instructs, wives must study their husband's 'temper' and 'command' their own; they must 'enjoy his satisfaction with him'.

Other defensive strategies also obtained, one of which was self-compensatory phallic glorification. Cleland was without peer here as his copious metaphors reach epic proportions but most writers dealing with sex in the 1790s propagandized for the power and potency of this 'Tree of Life', that 'master-member of the revels'.[48] It is no accident, I think, that it was towards the end of the eighteenth century that Richard Payne Knight attempted to seriously discuss and perhaps even revive the practice of priapic religion, for many citizens of the century who received his work had been paying homage to the phallus whenever an opportunity arose.[49] What needs to be stressed here is that disjunction which is evident in these sexually explicit discourses – the disjunction between the deification of the male genitals and sexual defamation and distrust of women. Male sexuality could be taken seriously, could even be reverenced, but women were exploited and often humiliated by these writers. Aspects of the female body were, for instance, repeatedly turned into fetishistic objects –

especially 'white snowy breasts', and signified by trivializing nicknames (Apple Dumplin Shop, Diddeys, and so on). Or alternatively women's entire bodies were viewed as simply manipulable material, pliable to the impress of men's temporal appetites. *The Dictionary of Love* (fp. 1753), for example, offered a list of the '30 capital points of beauty' – to which every man is to make 'what alteration his own taste may suggest' as he compiles for himself the ideal woman.[50] At the same time sexual metaphors turned women into assorted objects like the ever present landscape, or animals – naturally less human than men and in need of taming or domestication.[51] This is so often the underside of the sentimental romantic ideals so characteristic of the period.

Furthermore it is important in this prelude to my reading of *Visions* to note that these discourses of sexual humiliation and mockery often involved sadism, as a century-long obsession with punitive penetration found expression in what has been described as 'defloweration mania'.[52] Good sex, in the later eighteenth century, was sex in which female blood was shed. And the increasing popularity of flagellation literature (which reached its eighteenth-century apogee in the 1790's)[53] allowed for both the triumphant depiction of the infliction of pain and the suggestion that women were naturally masochistic. 'Delicious wounds' abound and the *Bon Ton Magazine*'s lurid focus upon the moment when white flesh becomes bloodied and breaks strikingly illuminates the editor's confidence that his cultured readers will enjoy a lingering account of violent penetration; an account polished off in these ringing tones: 'sometimes the wanton, vagrant fibres are directed to the more *secret* sources of painful bliss! sometimes the curious, curling tendrils bask in the *Paphian Grove!* and sometimes [. . .] they penetrate even the *Sacred Cave of Cupid'.*[54]

What emerges from this brief survey, then, is a contradictory but still clearly discernible image of women as genitally ravening if not sexually monstrous, whilst being simultaneously conceptualized as incapable of autonomous erotic desire and therefore in need of brutish if not explicitly violent stimulation. Though women lack the organ which signifies all that is best and 'normal' about sex, they are still seen as essentially and irreducibly sexual creatures.[55] In fact these writings seem to confirm the notion that any ideology, however effective, will be based upon contradiction, and what we find Blake doing in *Visions* is adopting an interrogative stance towards both aspects of this construction. As

I hope to show, the poem enacts a dual exercise in attempting to undo the reductive sexualization of women whilst also trying to redeem their desires from contemporary slurs of devouring bestiality.

## VISUAL REPRESENTATIONS OF THE BODY IN THE LATE EIGHTEENTH CENTURY

One very significant way in which Blake investigated and challenged this relentless sexualization of women was through his experimental and innovatory depictions of female and male bodies. As modes for depicting the female body are of most relevance in the discussion, I will begin by examining the popular models of the female form available to Blake during his formative years as an artist, those years just after his apprenticeship with Basire had ended, and he began to develop his own artistic style and visual vocabulary.[56]

The style predominantly employed by those wishing to foreground women in their art was the French imported rococo, a style which in its 'frothy and frivolous' amorality is usually considered to have had no impact upon, or resonances within, the work of a serious artist like Blake.[57] It is, then, an important and corrective lesson to recall that the first two separate plates Blake was commissioned to produce were a pair of companion 'fancy' pieces after Watteau: *Morning Amusement / Evening Amusement* (1782). These stipple engravings, commissioned by the important print publisher Macklin, were a flattering order for an engraver like Blake who had been trained primarily for the less prestigious work of book illustration.[58] And this introduction to the work of the creator of the *fête galante*[59] was just the start of Blake's liaison with the various genres of rococo art. The most significant, and long-lived connection, came through Blake's role as a member of an engraving team doing work after Thomas Stothard. Stothard was a personal friend of Blake's for many years and one on whom he was heavily dependent for his livelihood and reputation during the first half of the 1780s, with around half of Blake's engraving work between 1780–85 consisting of plates after Stothard's designs.[60] What makes Stothard so central to this discussion is that he was, *par excellence*, a creator of popular female stereotypes, his speciality in this period being images of sexualized innocence, broadcast primarily (though by no means exclusively) through the *Lady's Magazine* (for which he produced no less than 90 plates between 1770–90). Blake spent the first years of his career, then, working for a man whose reputation rested upon his ability to produce consumable women. As the contemporary art commentator Edward Dayes explained, Stothard's 'females display all the loveliness of form that would captivate a stoic, and all the sacred chastity of deportment that would make the libertine blush, and lead him to repentance'.[61]

That such images were not entirely congenial to Blake is quite clear. Not only does his work in this genre add greater linear definition to what are in effect muscleless puppets[62] but the private art which he produced during the 1780s enters into direct, and often contentious, dialogue with Stothard's models (interestingly, Blake gave him a copy of *The Book of Thel*). In these personal productions Blake maintains the centrality of the female form but in contrast he introduces a range of other than sexual significances. Women, from the very outset, play important roles in Blake's rudimentary visual mythology and this demands that their bodies be capable of multiple signification. As, for example, 'An Old Man Appearing on a Cloud to a Young Nude Couple' [92/86], 'A Man and Woman Kneeling and Warming Themselves at a Fire' [95/87], 'An Old Man and a Woman in Contemplative Adoration amid Trees' [99/90], and 'A Crowned Woman amid Clouds with a Demon Starting away' [102/92] (to select just a few examples) make quite clear. Even when some kind of sexual signification is apparent in an image, as for instance in 'A Girl and a Bearded Man Embracing' [91/85], Blake tends not to exploit or eroticize the female form.[63] This particular image is, in its composition and concerns, a forerunner of *Jerusalem* Plate 28 (*Illuminated*, E.307) and offers an image of embrace as an egalitarian 'comingling'.

And it is important to note that ready alternatives to the aforementioned rococo models were not abundant in the 1780s. In the crudest art historical terms, the style which acted as a displacing rival was an insurgent and virtuous neoclassicism, challenging with its oppositional lines of rectitude the serpentine indulgences of rococo art.[64] But though Blake was a friend and admirer of some of Britain's chief proponents of the style (in particular George Cumberland and John Flaxman) he was quick to realize that it could serve equally fleshy purposes as the style it seemed superficially to oppose. Cumberland, for example, used the 'chaste outlines' of neoclassicism for decidedly suggestive ends in his *Thoughts on Outline* (1796) and Blake's contribution to this collection of antique engravings was much the same as his adaptation of rococo models. He attempted to desexualize the forms, through a de-emphasis on Cumberland's flesh bulges and a heightened stress on the flow of outline along an entire torso or limb.[65] Blake also roughened Cumberland's lines, a strategy he was to use (as we will see) repeatedly in his illuminated books when the fetishizing of the female body was being resisted.

Other styles/genres in fashion at this time offered little more to Blake in what can be seen as an attempt to redefine the representation of the female body. The vogue genre of didactic history painting, for instance, was, even at its most earnest, replete with monumental female pathos, a sublime suffering ever teetering on the brink of victimized eroticism. James Barry, whom contemporaries considered 'better entitled to the appellation of Historical Painter, than any other artist in this country', produced many images of this kind – his concern with women's harsh treatment by the forces of commerce and his avowed admiration of Mary Wollstonecraft being always subservient to the production of glistening and recumbent female bodies, ever serene and inviting to the viewer's eye.[66] Although Blake admired Barry's work immensely his own history paintings eschew these conceptualizations of the female body.[67] And less elevated forms were equally barren, presenting grotesque and lascivious models in roughly equal proportions. Blake did in fact produce one work in this genre in the 1780s but on the whole caricature repelled him and introduced into his own art-criticism a singularly moralizing tone. Later stung by the idea that his works were 'ill-proportioned', he told Dr Trusler: 'I perceive that your Eye[s] is perverted by Caricature Prints, which ought not to abound so much as they do. Fun I love but too much Fun is of all things the most loathsom.' (E.702). And when selecting particular individuals for censure he plumped – very sensibly given the artist's insistent celebrations of voyeurism[68] – upon Thomas Rowlandson, declaring that his work was certainly not a fit thing for a Clergyman like Trusler to be enamoured of (E.704).

A very different and important kind of alternative was evident in the art of Henry Fuseli.[69] A number of Blake critics have identified direct intertextual references to Fuseli's work in *Visions* but have regrettably left the issue at the point of mere listing rather than investigating any kind of dialogue or parody.[70] Yet antagonistic referencing I think there is, at this moment of especially close collaboration between the artists[71] – the detailing of which will concern us for a few moments. Blake's life-long maintenance of friendly feelings for Henry Fuseli has baffled Blake critics for some years, with a recent study devoted entirely to their relationship having still to admit it was a 'riddle' if not a 'miracle'.[72] Given this, my aim is not to try to solve the puzzle but rather to suggest that its mysteriousness is even deeper than has to date been realized. What they do share, an inheritance from the writings of Johann Winckelmann, is a commitment to the body (often naked) as the primary vehicle of artistic expression.[73] Although this definite connection in fact points up their most significant difference, for Fuseli's depictions of male and female bodies bear the heavy impress of the sexual fears and defences sketched out earlier (he was, incidentally, a close friend of John Armstrong's). He is, quite simply, a vivid artistic exemplar of that masculinist ideology.

Not only was Fuseli a habitual fetishizer of women (hair being his metonymic fixation),[74] and issuer of artistic sexual stereotypes ('The women of Correggio are seraglio beauties [. . .] of Parmegiano are coquettes [. . .] of Guido are actresses'[75] and so on) but he was also obsessed with what he considered to be women's feral erotic intentions. His art abounds with images of the devouring woman which we saw earlier. Courtesans, witches and mythological harlots bind and gag men in a nightmare world of exaggerated gesture and mannerist horror. And the predictable weapon which Fuseli felt ought to be wielded against such usurpation was the penis. In many scenes of sexual bondage the heroic male offers virile defiance by sporting an 'impressive' erection, and the politics of such images are clear: not only does it take two or even three women to get these men on their backs but there always remains one part of the male anatomy that they will never subdue or exhaust. Phallic power is ever the answer, although Fuseli felt that he was living in an impotent age and in his eyes men suffered accordingly – for as he put it 'The epoch of eunuchs was ever the epoch of viragoes'.[76]

The companion to these images are defensive depictions of sexually defeated women, most obviously his phenomenally successful 'Nightmare', which very effectively worked itself into both the popular and elite imaginations of the age.[77] Fuseli's greatest debt here was to Joshua Reynolds, whose 'Death of Dido' offers an equally consolatory representation of sexually acquiescent orgasmic collapse. Although perhaps the most important intertext of this type in the present discussion is Fuseli's *'Falsa ad Coelum'* which Blake very possibly worked on c. 1790.[78] It shows us the tamed woman hung in a stance of cruciform exhaustion, and is surely an image of the female which Blake is both using and disabusing in his verbal and visual depictions of Oothoon. The other defensive strategy which ran parallel with the presentation of humiliated and victimized women was Fuseli's, by now predictable, argument that in fact they took pleasure in being dominated: 'Female affection', he explained, 'is ever in proportion to the impression of superiority in the object. Woman fondles, despises and forgets what is below her; she values, bears and wrangles with her equal; she adores what is above her'; and Fuseli's ideal woman was one who would adore in just this way, she being a female ever, 'poised between pure helpless virginity and sainted ecstasy'.[79]

Henry Fuseli's art contains, then, numerous stark expressions of the sexual ideology we looked at earlier. And what is equally clear, though rarely developed, is Blake's condemnation of Fuseli for these attitudes.[80] Yet condemn him he did, for Fuseli is the foremost amongst Lavater's 'cotemporaries' [sic] who provoked Blake's ire with their belief that 'Woman's Love is Sin' (Lav, E.601), and we shall see in a moment the ways in which Blake takes issue with both the visual and verbal expressions of this idea. But before going on to this I shall spend a few moments looking at Blake's concurrent renovation of the male figure.

The key to understanding, and appreciating the poet's innovations in this area, lies with Blake's artistic hero Michelangelo, and with the main interpreter and mediator of his significance to the Romantics, Winckelmann (whose ideas were known to Blake through Fuseli's translation). It was Winckelmann's ultimate opinion that though Michelangelo was the greatest artist, he had attained the antique (an ambition, it seems, of virtually every artist in the late-eighteenth century including Blake) only in his male figures: 'only in strong muscular figures, heroic frames; not in those of tender youth, nor in female bodies'.[81] For some admirers, those with masculinist convictions like Fuseli, this was a boon[82] but for Blake it proved to be a serious problem. Indeed

Blake's only area of major dissent was with Michelangelo's insistent patriarchalism.[83] In revising groups of his figures Blake's most significant strategy was to de-emphasize the father[84] – a process that ended in his transformation of the artist's majestic Almighty into a malevolent and often bungling caricature: Urizen.[85]

It was not just the divinity's paternal qualities, though, that Blake rejected. It was also the celebration of male dominance embodied in the figure's bulging musculature.[86] For Blake 'strength is compactness, not extent or bulk' (*DC*, E.545) and the more brawny his figures become the more negative are the connotations – of which the most relevant here is the muscle-bound Bromion (See *Visions*, pl. i; *Illuminated*, E.125). A companion image is that of Nebuchadnezzar on Plate 24 of *Marriage* (*Illuminated*, E.121) – where we see an idealized neoclassical male nude turned inside out, just as Blake exposes the celebration of male strength implied by such models. And he went further than this: throughout the 1780s (and well beyond) Blake set about feminizing the male figures whom he was presenting as heroes. The slender and soft bodies of David, Joseph and his brethren, and most importantly Christ[87] all lack marks of virility and male prowess.

In undertaking this process of feminization, Blake is in some senses following the lead of his successful contemporary Angelica Kauffmann.[88] In her epic scenes male courage is diminished and female suffering heightened, and this de-emphasis of heroic masculine potency did not pass unnoticed, as these lines from John Wolcot/Peter Pindar boorishly illustrate: 'Her Dames so Grecian! give me such a delight!/ But were she married to such gentle males/ As figure in her painted tales – / I fear she'd find a stupid wedding night'.[89] Kauffmann also, significantly, reduced the sexual signification of women in her art by never presenting nudes, indeed the only unclothed figures who feature in her work are children. As Angela Rosenthal pertinently notes, the artist 'closes the aperture upon the waiting male gaze'.[90]

If further evidence is required of Blake's doubts about and dissatisfaction with machismo and phallic glorification, we need only look at the radical alteration he made to Henry Fuseli's shameless celebration of ejaculatory power: 'The Fertilization of Egypt', which appeared in Erasmus Darwin's *Botanic Garden* (1791). Blake removes from the foreground altogether the taut-legged bank-bursting canine god and replaces him with the figure of a fleeing woman. The effect on the patriarch in the background is

telling. He quickly moves from a stance of open-armed homoerotic admiration to one of simultaneous threat and self-clutching fear. This transformed image is the title page of *Visions*
(*Illuminated*, E.127).

After this necessarily brief survey of Blake's early innovations
in the representation of male and female bodies, what we have
seen is the presentation of a more linear female form (beauty, as
Morris Eaves rightly notes, is redefined in unorthodox linear
terms)[91] alongside a more pliant, slight almost de-materialized
male. In contrast to the rapidly solidifying contemporary polarization of male and female bodies – well summed up by French
physician Pierre Roussel 'the essence of sex is not confined to a
single organ but extends, through more or less perceivable nuances, into every part'[92] – Blake is moving towards, if not actually attaining, an androgynous figure style. This is something
which Blake scholars have been reluctant to elaborate the significance of, but feminist art historians have been quick to suggest what it might mean. According to Margaret Walters, Blake
'takes the classical nude and makes male and female approxi-
mate to his own vision of a perfected and bisexual humanity.
Never denying sexual difference, he sees clearly how the exag-
geration of that difference by society imprisons men and women
in mutual and destructive misery'; and Linda Nochlin concurs
on Blake's development of innovatory androgynous figures.[93]

In terms of Blake's development as an engraving-artist,[94] with
a desire to reach the public direct, it is important to realize that
this thematic innovation was intimately related to a technical
one: Blake's development of illuminated printing. Commercially
expedient standardization of engraving techniques, and hence
of forms engraved, had produced a restricted vocabulary for the
depiction of the female form – a visual lexicon which displeased
Blake, as his private art of the 1780s shows. Furthermore special-
ization within the reproductive engraving process, brought on
by the division of labour, had forced him into becoming a specialist in just this kind of material: light erotic 'fancy' pieces.[95]
But with the development of illuminated printing Blake was able
to break away from all this. As Robert Essick, who has written
extensively on Blake's work as a printmaker, has pointed out
the, 'bold and rugged forms of Blake's illuminated books are the
result of conscious choice' and are, 'even to the eye of a casual
observer, completely outside the fashionable tastes of their time'.[96]

Essick is not concerned with the difference in representation of the female form between Blake's reproductive work and his illuminated books, but if we do analyze *Visions* in this way a heated dialogue emerges between the kinds of 'shapely' creatures Blake had spent much of the 1780s engraving and many of the female forms which appear here. The distinction John Berger makes between the naked and the nude[97] helps us to clarify what Blake is doing: 'To be naked is to be oneself. To be nude is to be seen naked by others and yet not recognised for oneself. A naked body has to be seen as an object in order to become a nude [. . .] Nakedness reveals itself. Nudity is placed on display.'[98] Nude images orientated to a male viewer's gaze (for example Plate 3, *Illuminated*; E.131) appear in these illuminations, only to have their validity disputed, and motivations questioned, by the more preponderant representation of naked women (esp. Plates ii, 6 and 8, *Illuminated*; 127; 134; 138). Amongst these the most offensive to the kind of onlooker Berger details must be those who appear on Plate iii (*Illuminated*; E.128). Not only does the larger kneeling woman cover her breasts but the smaller flying figure whom she kisses actually turns her naked back on the viewer.[99] It must be appropriate now to look in some detail at the text which this leaping woman precedes us into: *Visions of the Daughters of Albion*.

## VISIONS OF THE DAUGHTERS OF ALBION

The title page of *Visions* offers clear evidence that Blake was concerned about, and adopted a critical attitude towards, the sexual ideology outlined earlier, for what the plate contains is a succinct visual statement of each element of that mind-set. We have already examined the central pair of self-clutching patriarch and his terrorized female victim. Accompanying them is a serpentine groper who reaches down towards a reclining woman in the top left hand corner, a malevolent conjurer in the top right and an oppositional group of female figures engaged in a decidedly un-Fuselian scarf-dance (*Illuminated*; E.127). As well as being heralds of Oothoon's emergent passions they are perfect examples of the new type of female form which I have argued Blake worked through the 1780s to construct. The muscles on their extravagantly stretched legs and torsos are as emphasized and curvaceous as either their breasts or buttocks. Furthermore they in no way offer themselves to the gaze of an appetitive viewer: one turns her back on us and the other two devote their attentions towards demonstrating to themselves and each other that (female) 'Energy is Eternal Delight' (*MHH*, 4; E.34). It is for these figures, and their potential, that one very strong voice in the poem attempts to 'argue'.

At the poem's abrupt beginning Oothoon occupies the portentous biographical moment favoured by the majority of pornographic/bawdy writers in their depictions of women: she is on the brink of sexual experience. In the vast majority of these fictions young women appear filled with trepidation, weak in desire and will, and in need of brusque, if not brutal, male stimulation. And it takes little effort to demonstrate that through Oothoon Blake strongly refutes such conceptualizations of 'woman's love'.

First, Oothoon rejects the idea that she should be the passive object of male desire and instead claims the right to be the subject of her own libidinous inclination: 'I loved Theotormon/ And I was not ashamed' (*VDA*, iii:1–2; E.45). It is easy to neglect how radical the poem's first two lines are, and we should therefore remember that the late-eighteenth-century's obsession with distinctions between virtuous and non-virtuous females left women, as Patricia Meyer Spacks notes, with 'virtually no freedom of emotional expression'.[100] It was only on the rare occasions when events like popular masquerades legitimated momentary carnivalesque subversions that women were allowed freely to seek sexual partners,[101] and this was – anyway – a liberty bought at the cost of often fetishistic disguise. Blake's Oothoon can have little to do with that kind of deception, she must leap naked (as she does, Pl. iii, *Illuminated*; E.128) if she is to attain a joy equal to that of the title-page's dancers. And it is concern over how this violently immodest gesture will be received that provokes her 'virgin fears'[102] (*VDA*, iii:3; E.45) – for as the following uncharacteristically disgruntled contemporaneous verse makes clear, this is hardly a fit way for a 'virgin' to behave,

> Virgins, you know, by custom 'tis decreed,
> Must ne'er the bounds of modesty exceed;
> Must shut their eyes and ears at nature's call,
> And cold-form'd prudence still must govern all;

> Nor dare indulge the sweetly-pleasing flame,
> For loss of chastity is loss of fame![103]

Second, and perhaps even more offensively, Oothoon offers a direct affront to the idea that a woman's sexuality is only activated by the presence of a man and his, to use one of Cleland's abundantly self-flattering metaphors, 'wonderful machine'.[104] Integral to this phallocentric fantasy was the depiction of female virginity as a visceral hindrance begging to be conquered, and to defuse the bloody climax attendant on this deflowering mania Oothoon literally deflowers herself: 'I pluck thee from thy bed/Sweet flower' (*VDA*, 1:11–12; E.46); thus giving lyrical expression to the blunt statement made by a young woman in a contemporary ballad: 'My thing is my own'.[105]

Oothoon's activities in Leutha's vale have drawn a good deal of critical comment, with some writers arguing that it is a realm of sexual evasiveness and denial in which Oothoon literally 'hides',[106] whilst others, though prepared to admit that she finds her sexuality here, argue that all Oothoon wants to do is give it away, as a gift to give pleasure to a man. Michael Ferber's 'She is about to offer her virgin flower to her lover, of course' is depressingly typical.[107] It is also a serious misreading which distorts the challenging nature of Blake's message, for what she sought were 'flowers to comfort *her*' (*VDA*, 1:4; E.45 – my emphasis) and what she finds in the plucking of this duplicitous symbol is her own potential for multiple and recurrent orgasm. This is the 'soul of sweet delight' that 'Can never pass away' (*VDA*, 1:9–10; E.46), although it can – as she too soon discovers – be 'defil'd' (*MHH*, 9:53; E.37). Nympha was the classical name for the, as we saw, much reviled clitoris, used throughout the eighteenth century by numerous medical writers, and what Blake does by lyrically celebrating Oothoon's handling of this monstrous organ is to deny the late-eighteenth-century's favourite sexual edict: 'A woman's chiefest bliss must flow from man!'.[108] If Blake isn't quite concurring with Kate Millett in her unequivocal statement, 'The root and ultimate source of human understanding about sexual stimulation is autoeroticism',[109] he is certainly in dissent from his age's paranoia over the countless evils of the solitary vice. And it is here that Blake's sexual radicalism lies: in his validation of a woman's right to pleasure herself. Many, and most recently Stephen Cox, have claimed that Blake enlisted 'in the great eighteenth-century crusade against masturbation'[110] but such a bold statement misses the gendered nature of the poem's later complaint, for it is the male youth's absorption in 'The self enjoyings of self denial' (*VDA*, 7:9; E.50) that is objected to, *not* this activity which signals a woman's possession of her sexual selfhood. And it must also be remembered that Oothoon herself is the one who utters this later complaint. She, unlike the majority of Blake scholars, can see that the significance of any action changes depending on who is enacting it, and in a culture which reviled women's physicality this is a vital gesture of self-love, not self-denial. After all, what is the masturbating Oothoon denying herself? The embraces of the rapist Bromion and the sadist Theotormon. But this is to jump ahead.

The 'Golden nymph' (*VDA*, 1:8; E.46), however rich the pleasures she gives, is nonetheless, a duplicitous symbol because she inhabited other discourses too.[111] Most importantly brothel catalogues displayed their youthful wares under this sign, as the following extract describing Miss B-rn from *Harris's List of Covent-Garden Ladies* for 1788 demonstrates, 'This accomplished nymph has just attained her eighteenth year, and fraught with every perfection, enters a volunteer in the field of Venus [. . .] In bed she is all the heart can wish, or the eye admire, every limb is symmetry, every action under cover truly amorous.'[112] And what I think Blake does with this loaded sign is to signify both the assessment Oothoon has of herself and the assessments others have of her: to patriarchal observers any sexually active woman inscribes herself in *Harris's* pages. As Bromion says 'behold this harlot' (*VDA*, 1:18; E.46). There were, in fact, many words capable of describing a woman 'like' Oothoon, of which the most apposite is 'Dell'. According to Francis Grose these were 'Young buxom wenches, ripe and prone to venery, but who have not lost their virginity, which the *upright* man claims by virtue of his prerogative; after which they become free for any of the fraternity. Also a common strumpet'.[113] A definition that gives a clue to how Oothoon's story will proceed – as the flowery bright Marygold of Leutha's vale visually transmutes into the whipheads of Theotormon's cat-o'-nine-tails (Pl. 6, *Illuminated*; E.134).[114]

So, from the moment of Oothoon's immodest flight, her behaviour must be, and is, described by a narrator sensitive to the multiple, and starkly oppositional, significances of her actions. This slippery speaker makes his/her/its first multivocal statement(s) with this conflictual assessment of that flight, 'Over the waves she went in wing'd exulting swift delight/ And over Theotormons reign, took her impetuous course' (*VDA*, 1:14–15; E.46). To Oothoon her journey is one of ecstatic joy, to the men who witness her it is one of impudent sexual usurpation. Not that the rulers of the realm she is entering have any time for a playful plurality of meanings. For what she rapidly discovers is that Thel's suspicions were correct, 'fighting men' do 'in ambush lie' (*Thel*, 6:14; E.6), ready to punish those who fly too violently in the face of patriarchy's 'grave plots'. And if we are to appreciate Blake's insights into the way sexual violence is used for social control when subtler coercions have failed, Bromion's rape has to be viewed as a punishment for Oothoon's usurpation of male sexual prerogatives.[115] For he is not, as some have argued, 'a servant of lust [. . .] devotee of the senses' nor is he one of the 'heroic' rapists who enjoyed a burst of public popularity in the crim-con renaissance of the late- eighteenth century.[116] Rather Bromion is a frightened policeman of a paranoid patriarchy, insisting (in by now predictable terms) that women, like slaves, are naturally masochistic (*VDA*, 1:22–3; E.46) and, more significantly, wanting as quickly as possible to remove from his presence the appalling (*VDA*, 1:17; E.46) thought of a sexually active woman. Bromion might insistently declare the reified and tradable article Oothoon 'mine' (*VDA*, 1:20; E.46) (women's genitals, incidentally, were known as 'the commodity' at this time)[117] but he is also desperate to pass responsibility (gratis it seems)[118] for her containment over to Theotormon. Theotormon however, is in no way able to deal with Oothoon's sexual gesture (let alone the punitive response it provoked). Capable only of evincing a rather flimsy jealousy he prefers to weep into a sea of misery at the enormity of the problem caused by Oothoon's 'innocent' statement of desire – though not before imprisoning her and Bromion in a union of hateful bondage.

The fundamental issue here, however, is not only the nature but also the 'potency' of Theotormon's response. Stephen Behrendt's claim that he is an 'impotent man of words and nothing more'[119] is especially inaccurate, for the most basic fact that the eye sees (even if the heart won't admit it) about *Visions* is that in this poem men, however sadistic, inept or tormented, possess – just because of their sex – real power. The Daughters of Albion's and Oothoon's 'enslavement' is *literal*, not purely mental as so many Blake critics have argued. They cannot simply 'think' themselves free, and this gives us a clue as to how we should solve the first real interpretative problem of the poem: Oothoon's response to the rape.

What it is most important to note is that Blake appears to have taken this form of assault seriously. Unlike his contemporaries, who turned 'ravishment' into entertainment and put the abused woman on trial,[120] Blake suggests here that this kind of violence has profound effects. It certainly does on Oothoon, for no amount of critical apology can erase the fact that she entirely loses her sexual vision as a result of Bromion's rape, and consequently capitulates to the value system of her oppressors.[121] This is where she begins to slip and slide, as her language – in Stephen Vine's words – 'explodes under the pressure of the contradictions that inhabit it'.[122] And Oothoon's assimilation not only perverts her consciousness, and underlines her powerlessness, but it also turns her into the material for voyeuristic sexual fantasies. The very physical agony of her 'purification' transforms Oothoon into a vehicle of sadistic stimulation – as the 'writhing [of] her soft snowy limbs' (*VDA* 2:12 E.46, and see Pl. 3, *Illuminated*; E.131) under the eagles' talons produces the only response to her bodily existence which Theotormon makes (*VDA*, 2:18; E.46). A 'sick mans dream' (*VDA*, 6:19; E.50) indeed, though as we've seen not an uncommon one. The masculine sexual imagination current at this time was ailing, and Blake himself can hardly have been beyond infection – in fact it is worth noting that (male) critics still claim that the ravening birds 'represent Oothoon's ideal of her lover'.[123]

In some senses the poem ought to end here, with the three in a deadlock caused by their utterly incompatible beliefs and by the sex-determined powerlessness of the one visionary character. Yet Blake, evidently, could not leave the issue here – with women's sexuality cast out to/away upon the moralist and the pornographer (revealingly one and the same figure here). He goes on, therefore, to try and enumerate more of its unsettling potential, a process which demonstrates ever more clearly that the putting into discourse of women's libidinousness was, especially for a male writer, a treacherous practice. Vine again captures the contradiction well: 'From the instant of Oothoon's rape onward [. . .] the significance of the body in *Visions* is profoundly divided: it is at once the abject site where patriarchal domination enforces itself most powerfully, and the place from which

Oothoon declares her desire most fiercely'.[124] Her position is, quite simply, impossible and as the poem continues we see Oothoon's rhetoric slip slide away to the point of complete apostasy. Certainly Oithona, the heroine of Blake's Ossianic source poem, who secretly arms herself to do battle with her rapist before dying, exhibits a punitive and outraged aspect which the ever sexy Oothoon wholly lacks.

## 'SLIP-SLIDING AWAY'

As pointing out every ambiguity in Oothoon's incongruous 'rhapsody on liberty'[125] would be rather repetitive I do not intend to offer a comprehensive reading of the remainder of the poem. Rather I shall devote some time to picking out representative examples of Oothoon's discursive self-betrayal. In the interest of brevity I will also forgo any lengthy discussion of Theotormon and Bromion's speeches (the most significant aspect of which, anyway, is that they do not orientate themselves to any part of Oothoon's sexual rhetoric). It would, however, be illogical to pass without comment over the bursts of *uncompromised* lyrical feminist polemic which the poem does contain. For without doubt Blake enables Oothoon to protest in majestic tones which rival the oratorical goadings of Milton, and indeed of any of his later male prophets.

Nancy K. Miller has suggested that we need to be sensitive to the motivations behind any male author's act of becoming an '"I" in drag', and it is very important that we note how strenuously Blake resists the self-flattery that Miller shows is habitually attendant on this practice.[126] He inveighs against the oppression of women and children in the patriarchal family with a fervour equal to that of the angriest Mary Wollstonecraft and this tonal rage has been an instance of honest indignation that most Blake critics have chosen to ignore – destroying as it does their fantasy of 'poor, lovely Oothoon'.[127] Yet it is she who enjoys the honour of being the first to name Urizen, and that this first accusative labelling brands him the 'Creator of *men*' (*VDA*, 5:3; E.48 – my emphasis) ought not to go unnoticed. The primacy of his patriarchal and sexual oppressiveness is a subject worthy of more study than it has to date received. The other inspiring, though of course problematic, aspect of Oothoon is that she continues exuberantly to stress that women must be subjects, not just objects, of desire. Not only does Blake give her an enviable erotic eloquence but he also takes the additional step of saying that women look with desire too. Women, of course, have rarely been encouraged to express their sexuality by look-ing[128] and being the possessor of a libidinous gaze was a very dangerous business in the eighteenth century. Cleland's Fanny Hill, for instance, usurps the right of erotic gazing directly after her violent deflowering, and Charles' defensive gesture against this visual possession of his (as ever) impressive body is swift and direct. As Fanny's account makes clear: 'as if he had proudly meant revenge for the survey I had smuggled of his naked beau-ties, he spurns off the bedclothes, and trussing up my shift as high as it would go, took his turn to feast his eyes with all the gifts nature had bestowed on my person; his busy hands too ranged intemperantly . . .' and so on.[129] Another prostitute in the same text, Harriet, with whom Fanny works at Mrs Cole's acad-emy, also suffered the same kind of experience after spying upon a lithe and frolicsome youth as he bathed naked in the river – which perhaps helps explain why Oothoon's energetic looking for copulatory beauty (*VDA*, 6–7:22–1; E.50) is likely to burn her eyes out.[130]

These elements, though, cannot be our main focus. Rather, we must examine the irony of the Oothoon who offers herself as an expert in vision[131] but who, at crucial moments, is markedly myopic. The overarching reason for Oothoon's apostasy is that Blake will not allow her to relinquish her unexplained, perhaps inexplicable, 'love' for Theotormon (a weakness of much hetero-sexual romance writing) and also that he is the implied addressee of most of her speeches. Moreover she does not/cannot confront Bromion with her feelings about the assault, and indeed moves rapidly towards denying its importance: reducing it to a thing safely contained in a past which is just that and which therefore should be forgotten,

> . . . . the nightingale has done lamenting.
> The lark does rustle in the ripe corn, and the Eagle returns
> From nightly prey, and lifts his golden beak to the pure east;
> Shaking the dust from his immortal pinions . . .
> . . . the night is gone that clos'd me in its deadly black.
>
> (*VDA*, 2:24–7; 29; E.47)

The invocation of the eagle (lately returned from preying on *her*) alerts us to Oothoon's assimilation and its ability to ironize and compromise even her most beautiful oratory. It also introduces one of Oothoon's most suspicious rhetorical strategies: arguing from nature, a practice which punctuates the text. Though Oothoon mocks the idea that human beings ought to learn from animals (*VDA*, 5:8–9; E.48), she nonetheless, and in direct opposition to Thel's wisdom, continually invokes assorted creatures as behavioural guides. Not only do these appeals to a natural cycle ('Does not the worm erect a pillar in the mouldering church yard?/ And a palace of eternity in the jaws of the hungry grave/ Over his porch these words are written. Take thy bliss O Man!' *VDA*, 5–6:41–2; E.49) veer towards the kind of crass sexual politics we see in John Wilke's *Essay on Woman* (c. 1764/1883): 'Let us since life can little more supply/ Than just a few good fucks and then we die',[132] but they also seem to implicate sex in the kind of contemporary pronatalist ideology[133] that Blake, with all his doubts about 'generation', would hardly have endorsed. Even more importantly, given that one of the poem's central problems is the prevalence of sexual violence and violation, they enable the celebration of masochism: 'Sweetest the fruit that the worm feeds on & the soul prey'd on by woe/ The new wash'd lamb ting'd with the village smoke' (*VDA*, 3:17–18; E.47) and as the reasoning slides, taints, defilement and suffering take on positive connotations. Oothoon begins to side with the devourer. That her sexual commitments are hopelessly compromised becomes even more transparent in the section where she attempts most overtly to 'cry love' (*VDA*, 6–7:4–29; E.49–50), for here parodic opposition slides into endorsement with dizzying speed and perplexing intricacy.

Again, I do not want to deny the power of her attacks on modesty, religious repression and the denial of infantile sexuality, rather what I want to do is to demonstrate that they occupy a place within a disintegrating discursive field. Asking a number of questions about this section of the poem helps to focus this instability. Who, for instance, is Oothoon addressing in her tirade against modesty? When was Theotormon ever the sexually incandescent figure Oothoon describes? More significantly, isn't she trapped by the classic patriarchal binary opposition of virgin/whore when she tries to describe her unabashed desires? There are even problems with that orgasmic 'moment of desire!

[. . .] moment of desire!' (*VDA*, 7:3; E.50): the virgin who 'pines' for a man (just as Oothoon pines for Theotormon) will only achieve 'enormous joys/ In the secret shadows of her chamber' (*VDA*, 7:4–5; E.50), which are a shady region far away from the 'sunny beams' that Blake usually lets fall upon scenes of 'Naked [. . .] delight' (for example, see *A Little GIRL Lost*, 9; E.29). Indeed Oothoon becomes cumulatively more desperate as the oration goes on: worrying in distinctly conventional terms about the fading of her beauty and eventually (just as she begins to 'Cry Love', (*VDA*, 7:16–20; E.50) converting herself into the tempting sexual object and emblem of sin that the moralistic Theotormon always worried she was: 'the fruit that hangs before his sight' (*VDA*, 7:20; E.50).[134] So, given that Oothoon's vision has been corrupted, and that her overriding desire has been to liberate Theotormon, the ultimate conclusion of her speech is no surprise,

> But silken nets and traps of adamant will Oothoon spread,
> And catch for thee girls of mild silver, or of furious gold;
> I'll lie beside thee on a bank & view their wanton play. . . . .
>     nor e'er with jealous cloud
> Come in the heaven of generous love; nor selfish blightings
>     bring.
>
> (VDA, 7:23–5; 28–9; E.50)

This harem fantasy[135] marks the moment of Oothoon's most acute apostasy, as she offers to become an energetically ensnaring procuress – an occupation that points to what must be the key historical subtext of this scene: the endemic prostitution of the late-eighteenth century.[136] Now assimilated to the point of being an active accomplice of Urizen[137] in his heterosexual entrapments, Oothoon prepares to subject other women (some of them as 'furious' as she must once have been at such bondage) to sex against their will. In this way she becomes the absolute voyeur of their humiliating suffering, as we have become voyeurs of hers. Moreover, she seems to relish it. Critics have vacillated over the significance of the scene, and it is by no means uncommon to find the suggestion being made that this is a sexual fantasy that Blake himself enjoyed. Thomas Vogler most recently made this accusation, 'If we read it for its "message" how is it any different from the pornosophical message we can find in *Fanny Hill*, or in Sade's transformations of Oothoon into Juliette and Thel into

Justine? Oothoon takes the course of Moll Flanders and Fanny Hill rather than Pamela or Clarissa, but there is a sameness beneath the differences of these works that links them parodically.'[138] The suggestion of sadistic tendencies has lingered around Blake ever since Mario Praz defined his sexual proclivities in these terms in the 1930s,[139] and the longevity of such claims demands that we challenge them, for they seem based on a number of significant errors. Not only do we never see unproblematic relish expressed in Blake's work for sexual humiliation, cannibalism and murder (the staples of Sade's fiction) but the format of much of the Sadean corpus (the programmatic tales of atrocity retold in *120 Days of Sodom* for example and the rigidly ritualistic nature of his orgies)[140] are expressions of desire veritably Urizenic in their regulation. Sade was, as Angela Carter notes, above all a carnographer.[141] The human body interested him at precisely the moment when live flesh became dead meat and though this kind of idea had a currency in Britain in the 1790s[142] it is highly at odds with Blake's contemporaneous commitment to the sensuous body as a road into eternity. The revelation that the body is as soulful and potentially infinite as the spirit is, at this moment at least, quite central to Blake's philosophy.[143]

Oothoon, then, is not primarily organizing a Sadean orgy suited to the tastes of her creator (tastes which, of course, we know very little about). She is, rather, sliding into the final snare, set for any woman who tries to 'cry love' at this particular historical moment. And that her story ends with the most oft-quoted Blakean aphorism 'every thing that lives is holy!' (*VDA*, 8:10; E.50) is a most tragic irony, as the narrator's chilling final words make clear: 'Thus every morning wails Oothoon, but Theotormon sits/ Upon the margin' d ocean conversing with shadows dire./ The Daughters of Albion hear her woes, & eccho back her sighs.' (*VDA*, 8:11–13; E.50). After reading *Visions* we might well ask, is there *no* hope in store? Certainly the illuminations on Plates 6 and 8 (*Illuminated*; E.134; 136) suggest an Oothoon wrenching herself from Theotormon and beginning to awaken the miserably huddled daughters[144] but these really do very little to lighten the generally gloomy conclusion. Given this, a more apt way to end the discussion, than conjuring false signs of optimism, is to look in a little detail at precisely why Oothoon fails and at what that failure means historically.

We have already seen the range of reasons offered by past Blake scholars for Oothoon's 'failure', few of whom even hint that there might be specific historical explanations for the poem's dead-lock. As I noted, there has been a preference for introspective solutions which treat the poem as a closed system, the most sig-nificant intertexts of which are other works in the Blakean cor-pus. In contrast to these readings I would like to offer two precise historical reasons why I think Oothoon remains so depressingly bound. To do this sensitively we must recall that historical de-terminants take many forms, that the limits of an author's possi-ble vision and expression are circumscribed by diffuse social forces and structures. And it is here that the ideas of the Bakhtin school are particularly useful, for Volosinov's stress on the materiality of the sign has helped to clarify the fact that of all the pressures bearing down upon and confining (as well, paradoxically, as lib-erating) the writer the greatest is the state of language. As lan-guage is an amorphous system, ever on the move, it is very difficult to ascertain exactly what possibilities it offers to an author at any specific moment. But with this said, what has become clear during this discussion of *Visions* is that the poem is, as David Punter insightfully notes, 'beached against a discursive limit'.[145] There was simply no way of writing about (or for that matter visually representing) women's sexuality, in the 1790s, which was not implicated in the pornographic linguistic field we looked at earlier. No discourse comes into an author's hands innocent, of course, it always – as a social entity – bears traces of previous usage and because of this some of the signs Blake was com-pelled to employ (for example virgin, whore, nymph) compro-mise the progressive aspects of the text and perhaps even reveal the limited potential of his sexualized feminism. Though Blake may not have aimed to cater for male fantasies the material medium of his art betrayed him: forced to use language per-vaded with lecherous suggestion Oothoon slides into the open arms of an exploitative sign system only too happy to consume 'figures' like her (the heated pornography debates within con-temporary feminism suggest that this is still a huge problem).

The other, and no less important, aspect of this linguistic issue, is that whilst various discourses (of which those of conduct, medicine and pornography have been the most relevant in this discussion) constructed women's sexuality in various reductive and exploitative ways, women were themselves (as we have seen)

simultaneously prohibited from writing or speaking explicitly
about their physical desires. Some feminists today still complain
that eroticism is, virtually, a male preserve but in the 1790s an
even more absolute exclusivity was imperiously guarded.[146] Exaggerated ideas and ideals of female delicacy, and the ever operative double standard, acted as complete prohibitions against
women articulating libidinous intent.[147] Apart from Mary Hays's
depiction of the lacerated Emma Courtney it is virtually impossible to find a woman writer in the late-eighteenth century who
deals explicitly with the subject of sexual desire and pleasure.
Earlier in the century female novelists had offered extremely frank
discussions and treatments of sexuality, but by the 1790s the novel
had become an essentially didactic form,[148] and female desire
was pushed into sublimated gothic subtexts or dissipated by the
sentimentality of 'romance'. In such works sexual pleasure becomes, as it is for Charlotte Smith's heroine Monimia, 'a sensa-
tion of joy that was undescribable'.[149] A few women writers, like
Catherine Macaulay Graham, did have the courage to point out
that, 'the strength which Nature has given to the passion of love
[. . .] has made it the most ungovernable propensity of any which
attends us' but even she refused to centre either the social or
the more narrowly personal implications of this sexual volatility.[150]

At this time, then, respectable women (cf. Poovey's 'Proper
Lady') were not allowed to speak about their desires, let alone
'cry love', for as one female character in a ballad from Ritson's
collection of love songs remarked to her lover (in section IV of
the work, devoted to detailing the dangers of women entertain-
ing the passion of love), 'yours is the province of speaking'.[151]
The shame of verbalizing desire was too great for the prohibition to be trangressed: 'Eyes can speak and tell the lover,/ What
the tongue must not impart/ Blushing shame forbids revealing,/
Thoughts your breast may disapprove.'[152] For a woman to speak
sexually was to become a whore, and indeed the most erotically
verbose females to appear in eighteenth-century literature are
fantastical prostitutes, gifted with total recall, like Cleland's Fanny
Hill. Some of these problems are interestingly focused in Mary
Wollstonecraft's *The Wrongs of Woman* (1797), a novel which, incidentally, seems to imply that a woman will be perceived as on
the brink of madness if she attempts to discuss her passions.
Wollstonecraft took a daring step in this text by insisting on the
importance to women of sexual satisfaction ('we cannot, without

depraving our minds, endeavour to please a lover or husband, but in proportion as he pleases us').[153] Yet even here there is no sustained discussion of physical love – not least because men are viewed with the kind of suspicion that Oothoon's (and Maria's and Jemima's) ordeal suggests is justified (the relevant topic of lesbian desire and its suppression in the 1790s needs a book to itself, but sadly that is yet to be written).

Wollstonecraft gives her heroine a free hand[154] to construct an ideal sexual partner, but the author's sense of the explicitly oppressive in contemporary sexual practice and discourse disfigures this suggestive opportunity. Darnford is a character who looks, variously: absurd (repeating parrot-fashion Maria's feminist polemic and kissing her like a saint); sentimental (he had never known love until he saw her, their love makes the prison into a fairyland); compromised (speaking of his enjoyment of the favours of prostitutes and his amorous dalliance with other women) and who, most importantly, is only sexually attractive because he seduces himself: 'A man of feeling thinks not of seducing, he is himself seduced by the noblest emotions of his soul'.[155] There are, of course, no scenes of sexual encounter in this novel of the passions rather than of manners,[156] and Wollstonecraft's absolute inability to bring physical love into discourse was shared by virtually all the Jacobin novelists. It is striking, and especially relevant in this discussion of the problematic nature of *Visions*, to note that amongst a group of writers who broadly shared Blake's political sympathies there is little if any support for his belief in the liberating potential of sexuality. Indeed amongst the Jacobin novelists it is the aristocracy who are the repository of the sensual and this is an indulgence for which they are heavily criticized.[157] As Marilyn Butler concludes, 'In sexual matters the jacobins thought and as a group behaved (whatever their opponents claimed) like forerunners of the Evangelicals. Their advocacy of reason and restraint often makes them read like their opponents, the conservative moralists', even as they tried to liberate love from parental tyranny and introduce an ideal of candour between the sexes these writers are sexually tepid, if not completely evasive.[158]

Allied to this absence of female, let alone feminist, eroticism was the great difficulty women had in finding a language with which to protest against sexual attack – a difficulty which, perhaps, ultimately determines Oothoon's fate. Anna Clark has discussed this subject at some length, detailing the way in which women who wrote out an account of their ordeal invariably presented the event as an incident from a melodramatic romance.[159] This style, of course, was not an option for a poet like Blake and neither were any of the other available discourses. For example, Oothoon cannot challenge Theotormon and Bromion's sexualized, if tormented, view of her by invoking ideas of reputation or injured modesty because such protests rest upon a religious set of beliefs about decency and morality which the poet had long suspected were based upon hypocrisy and sexist double standards.[160] This is a major problem as women's ability to defend their bodily integrity is central to any feminist sexual politics, and it remains the case that suggestions about how to compel men to respect this integrity are still few and far between. Fundamentally, then, the first historical reason that Oothoon remains bound is that the proliferation of sexual discourses described by Foucault disseminated myriad contradictory yet reductive sexualized constructions of the female, whilst women themselves were prohibited from speaking with any explicitness or freedom about either the problems or the pleasures of their own sexuality.

The second, and intimately related, historical reason for Oothoon's continued bondage has to do with the diffuse and marginal nature of late-eighteenth-century British feminism – a subject which I shall discuss in some detail in the next chapter. For now, it is sufficient to note that although there were many disparate writers concerned with the rights of women in the 1790s, what was lacking at this particular moment was an organized and publicly active women's movement. As Steven Vine so importantly notes, 'Oothoon and the Daughters lack a political constituency that can voice their demands'.[161] *Visions* ultimately, and simply, spins on an axis rather than progressing[162] because the Daughters of Albion were not in any way on the move at the time when Blake wrote it, and his libidinal exhortations seem of only dubious value in such a context. Furthermore there was little reason for political optimism as radical groups and societies which were active at this time – from the LCS to the Lunar Society – were apathetic about women's liberation if not explicitly hostile to it (again, this is something I return to in my next chapter). Blake, then, should probably not be condemned for exploiting women's victimization but should rather be understood to be taking the strength of patriarchy seriously, and realistically evaluating the countless obstacles that stood in the Daughters' way. That Blake realized a gulf existed between the wild and bounding rhetoric of Oothoon and the comprehensive immiseration of the English women whom she needs, though hardly aims, to rouse is made clear on Plate 7 (*Illuminated*; E.135) – where she breaks into her most impassioned oration whilst they huddle distressed by the ocean.[163] The point is that her 'cries' simply do not signify for them – all they can hear are her 'woes' and all they can do is 'eccho back her sighs' (*VDA*, 8:13; E.51). As a result of all this Blake cannot, as Mary Wollstonecraft could not, articulate any effective method of feminist revolution.[164]

These are precisely the kind of particular historical considerations that most Blake critics have disregarded. They argue instead that Oothoon could be free if only she were a little more attentive[165] or – more seriously – suggest that even if she is bound because eighteenth-century feminists could not elaborate a method, Blake himself was able to do so and the poem is therefore a critique of their inability.[166] And, as we have seen, it has been a favourite critical strategy to see Blake transcending the 'contemporary limitations' that handicapped the lesser intellect of Mary Wollstonecraft.[167] In particular Blake is valued for surpassing what is taken to be Wollstonecraft's regrettably conservative attitude towards sexuality and the liberation of desire. This is a line of argument which corresponds with one influential strain in contemporary Wollstonecraft criticism, a strain which is often rather unfair in its assertions, as for example in Cora Kaplan's somewhat ahistorical claim that, 'It is Mary Wollstonecraft who first offered women this fateful choice between the opposed and moralized bastions of reason and feeling', 'Wollstonecraft sets up heartbreaking conditions for women's liberation – a little death, the death of desire, the death of female pleasure'.[168] Arguments of this kind present an unacceptably bloodless Wollstonecraft and lead to the drawing of crude oppositions between her and writers like Blake, in the course of which many important parallels are obscured. For as we've seen, in the earlier discussion of *The Book of Thel* (1789), Blake's unmasking of sentimental constructions of youthful femininity indicates that he had sympathy with Wollstonecraft's doubts about the romantic trivialization of young women, and the way that these social norms rendered them the slaves of heterosexual love (again, see Vine's excellent discussion of this). Also, though more problematically, Blake seems to comprehend Wollstonecraft's complaint that the excessive sexualization of women involves a reductive refusal to see and value them as human creatures. Both were also concerned with how patriarchal society forced women to gain power through the manipulation and exploitation of their sexuality, an issue I shall discuss at length in my final chapter on *Europe – A Prophecy* (1794).

With these important points noted, though, it is of course the case that an essential difference does exist between the two writers, and that is the difference central to this discussion of *Visions*. As we have seen Blake believed that sexual energy and passion would be instrumental in the process of social change, as well as being some of the most important benefits of its achievement. Mary Wollstonecraft had, with good reason, severe doubts about this. Her *A Vindication of the Rights of Woman* (1792) is, as we shall see in the next chapter, a remarkably ambiguous text but it is nonetheless possible to chart a strong distrust of the sensual. Her desire was to make everyone's passion rational, and subordinate it where irrational to the rule of (a probably sexless though clearly gendered) reason. As the place of sexuality, and especially heterosex, in the liberation of women is still a hotly debated issue this is probably not the place to offer an adjudication, but what does need to be said is that Oothoon's fate and the history of the feminist movement in the twentieth century (especially in the 1960s) suggest that giving wholehearted support to Blake's libidinal gospel may not be particularly wise. And this is the note upon which my discussion of *Visions* must conclude. Oothoon remains an inspiring and attractive figure, but one who is also compromised and defeated, and it has been the aim of this chapter to offer a number of historical reasons why she is such a radically ambiguous sexual creation. In the next chapter, I will examine the significant contemporary political debates which provide a key context for this sexual ambiguity.

# 4

# Blake, the Rights of Man and Political Feminism in 1790s

## INTRODUCTION

Be encouraged, all ye friends of freedom, and writers in its defence! The times are auspicious.

Richard Price

From what we now see, nothing in the political world ought to be held improbable. It is the age of probabilities, in which everything is to be looked for.

Thomas Paine

I may excite laughter, by dropping a hint, which I mean to pursue, some future time, for I really think that women ought to have representatives.

Mary Wollstonecraft.[1]

The buoyant and iconoclastic nature of English radicalism in the early 1790s has ensured for it much detailed, and often loving, academic interest.[2] This decade, along with the era of the English Revolution(s) and the years which saw the emergence of the nineteenth-century labour movement, has attained legendary status in traditional histories of the left; and, as E.P. Thompson has so convincingly shown, with very good reason. In his classic study, *The Making of the English Working Class*, Thompson rejected the practice of viewing these years solely in the light of the French Revolution, and argued instead that, 'the agitation of the 1790s [. . .] was an English agitation, of impressive dimensions, for an English democracy'.[3] From this perspective the fundamental characteristic of the period is that it saw the mass political awakening and empowerment, however brief, of sections of the embryonic English working class, who had never before been self-conscious and organized actors upon the stage of national politics.[4] And the formation of this new political constituency was certainly something that Blake and his contemporaries were acutely aware of, especially those middle-class contemporaries who had entered upon a brief, and never very happy, alliance with this new class. As Joel Barlow commented, 'it depends not on me, or Mr Burke, or any other writer [. . .] to determine whether a change of government shall take place [. . .]. It depends on a much more important class of men, the class that cannot write; and in a great measure, on those who cannot read. It is to be decided by men who reason better without books, than we do with all the books in the world.'[5] Radical plebeian societies, of which the LCS is of course the best known, were central in the marshalling of this new force; and with a network of such societies covering the country, political education and agitation flourished.[6] It was when these groups of propagandists began energetically to distribute Part II of Tom Paine's *Rights of Man* (1792) that John Reeves and his friends decided that Associations here needed to protect property and liberty against levelling republicans.

This chapter, however, will not be concerned with historicizing Blake in that particular political context, not least because this task has been substantially completed.[7] Rather, I shall be pursuing an unintended irony embedded in Thompson's claim that the formation of the LCS 'signified the end of exclusiveness, of politics as the preserve of any hereditary elite or property group'.[8] My discussion will be centred upon E.P. Thompson's most significant silence,[9] namely the failure of this 'new radicalism' to include anywhere on its agenda demands for, or even a concern for, the rights of women. More specifically I will be looking at the consequences of this negligence in the work of those few writers – both male and female – who did wish to combine their commitment to mainstream radicalism with incipient feminist interests. Before moving on to any kind of textual examination it is important, however to underline the completeness of this exclusion, for historians have made very few efforts to redeem the gender-blindness, if not outright sexism, of Thompson's plebeian politicians.[10] As a group they continued to foreground issues of parliamentary reform and enfranchisement and showed no more inclination to conceive of women as citizens than had their elite forebears.[11] Politics during these years were as much, if not more, the province of the Freeborn English *Man*, and the 'anti-female locus' of the public house markedly inhibited political participation. Indeed in the light of G.J. Barker-Benfield's comment that at 'the crucial tavern level of this alternative structure [of politics] the culture was powerfully, self-consciously male' it is quite possible that women's opportunities for any engagement in political activity actually decreased during these years.[12] As Jane Rendall notes 'we know nothing of any female involvement in the radical politics in the 1790s': publicly vociferous women do not begin to appear until the post-war period.[13] Future research may necessitate a reappraisal, and it is undeniable that women must have played some significant roles in the LCS as weekend meetings took place in members' homes, but from the evidence we now have, Donna Landry seems correct in her assessment, 'The notion of "revolutionary women" in Britain at the end of the eighteenth century is an impure idealization, a contradiction in terms'.[14] Even the female food riot has been declared a myth.[15]

Given this, it is hardly surprising that Mary Wollstonecraft did not become a public speaker, though she'd certainly have made an excellent one. If women were to influence politics it had to be at one remove, through the men closest to them, and if they did stray into the public arena ridicule or scorn awaited. The experience, for example, of the Duchess of Devonshire during the 1784 election campaign provides ample evidence. She was accused of having gladly exchanged sexual favours for votes, and was eventually driven to give up electoral campaigning altogether.[16] When Charlotte Smith in 1790 protested, 'Women it is said have no business with politics – why not? – Have they no interest in the scenes that are acting around them',[17] the answer had already been decided firmly in the negative. And that decade's emergent plebeian politicians had no intention of changing this assessment. So, however ubiquitous a concept marginality may be at present it does perfectly describe the relationship of women's rights, and women themselves, to the new radical movement and ideologies of the early 1790s. Indeed in some cases there is a striking literalness about this, for example in Thomas Cooper's pamphlet, *Propositions Respecting the Foundation of Civil*

*Government* (1792). For the most part Cooper's text is a meticulous exposition of the standard radical argument that legitimate authority is derived from the consent of the governed. It is only when discussing exceptions that Cooper approaches the issue of women's rights, serious thought upon this issue having convinced him that women have been illegitimately disenfranchised. Yet it is only in the literal margin of a footnote, albeit an expansive one, that Cooper declares this far-reaching decision, 'I have repeatedly considered the subject of the Rights of Women, and I am perfectly unable to suggest any Argument in support of the political Superiority so generally arrogated by the Male Sex, which will not equally apply to any System of Despotism of Man over Man.' And Cooper's failure to make this part of his main argument is even more striking when we consider his amazing feminist booklist and personal contacts: 'I have read the writings of Mrs. M. Graham, of Miss Wolstencroft [sic], of Mrs. Barbauld, of Mrs. Montague, Miss Carter, Miss Seward, Mrs. Dobson, Mrs. Williams, [. . .] in England – I have conversed with Theroigne, with Madame Condorcet, Madame Robut, Madame Lavoisier [. . .] in Paris.' Cooper ends with a flourish which challenges 'the Defenders of male Despotism, [to] answer, if they can "THE RIGHTS OF WOMEN"',[18] but as this discussion unfolds we will see that the more urgent need was for their supporters to give them greater space in their texts. For examples of this kind of marginalization could be duplicated endlessly. In the publishing concerns of the great dissenter Joseph Johnson, for instance, or in the sympathies of radical clubs: only when 40 toasts were being quaffed did the Friends of the Revolution find time to raise their glasses in praise of the 'patriot women of Great Britain'.[19] Complacency and disinterest seem to have been the main culprits. Confident male radicals had caught sight of the new dawn and would let nothing distract their gaze from such lofty libertarian horizons.

However this, as I mentioned earlier, was not quite the whole story. As even the fraternally inclined Thompson notes, there was a small coterie of radicals who did attempt to champion the rights of women[20] and my concern in this chapter will be to look at the works of those few writers who did try to combine a commitment to mainstream radicalism with an interest in feminist issues, who – to borrow Landry's formulation – attempted to broach 'the political discontinuity but ideological comparability of radical republicanism and feminism', a comparability which she reminds us was not necessarily a compatibility.[21] I shall devote quite some time to this exercise because such works are, I think, a vital context for the interpretation of *The Marriage of Heaven and Hell* (1790) and *America: A Prophecy* (1793) – two texts which I shall argue are compromised by Blake's divided loyalties, and by his decidedly intermittent desire to bring about a marriage between these two very different conceptions of the political.

## MALE RADICALS AND THE RIGHTS OF WOMEN

In this introductory section I shall undertake a brief examination of the works of three male writers – William Godwin, Thomas Paine and Thomas Spence – who in varying degrees attempted to incorporate some kind of concern with gender into their general political theories.[22] During this discussion I shall stress the telling fact that for each man retreat to safer, or more personally fulfilling, argument was always available, and often undertaken. None gives a central place to the rights of women in his work and none remains consistent in his argument, but by paying attention to precisely these failures of will, nerve or imagination we can better understand Blake's limitations, as well as appreciate his achievements.

### William Godwin

E.P. Thompson is quite definite about the inclusion of William Godwin within his feminist/libertarian coterie, yet Godwin can have but slender claims to such a location, claims, one suspects, based largely upon his unusual personal practice of conversing seriously with women, and of extending his naturally ponderous but respectful intellect to the understanding of their individual problems.[23] Textually there is little to recommend his classic, *An Enquiry Concerning Political Justice* (1793), and the problems which it presents are of two particular kinds. The first derive from Godwin's clinical and much caricatured necessitarian and perfectionist philosophy and can be simply stated: Godwin has an excessive amount of faith in the minds of 'men' to discriminate truth and act justly. A brief quotation well illustrates this point: 'sound reasoning and truth', Godwin contends, 'when adequately communicated, must always be victorious over error [...] Truth is omnipotent'; a faith endorsed with equal vigour by Tom Paine, 'No man is prejudiced in favour of a thing, knowing it to be wrong [...] such is the irresistible nature of truth, that all it asks, and all it wants, is the liberty of appearing.'[24] Mind figures in his text as an asocial entity, finding its home in a seemingly unsexed body, and when we consider this alongside Catherine Macaulay's, and more especially Mary Wollstonecraft's, catalogue of influences that prevent the female mind from attaining the independence Godwin so cherished, his philosophical eulogies look positively escapist[25] – although it should be noted that the ordeal of writing out this cerebral faith in the context of *Things as They Are* (1794) had, momentarily at least, a rather chilling effect. Much of the anguish of the novel derives from the fact that Caleb Williams and those closest to him are incapable of resisting the influence of society's prejudices and values upon their individual consciousnesses (and, interestingly enough, it is the male mind which is Godwin's concern here and the problems of formulating appropriate masculine and homoerotic identities).

The second set of problems are those raised by the significantly marginal Appendix, 'Of Cooperation, Cohabitation and Marriage'.[26] This is Godwin's most explicit theoretical discussion of gender issues, a discussion which is in fact a subclause to the main section dealing with the 'evils' of co-operation.[27] Certainly some of his comments about marriage have feminist resonances, for example the idea that it is the most odious of monopolies, that it turns women into fetishistic prizes and, more generally, that it is selfish to want to attain complete possession of another person. Yet as Katherine Rogers notes, 'He dealt with women and marriage as an aspect of property, attacking contemporary marriage not because it oppressed women but because it restricted proprietorship in her to one man'.[28] The fundamental difficulty is that Godwin never considered women as a distinct group with hindrances and oppressions specific to their sex, and for this reason tacitly assumed that their liberation would be a natural consequence of the freeing of the human mind, an enlightening event which he looked forward to with great eagerness and in which he placed boundless faith. Looking at Godwin, then, what we see is that the major radical theorist of the early 1790s only hovered around that complex of issues best titled the 'rights of woman' and, moreover, that he felt secure in the belief that his readers would not expect him to do more than this. Godwin's revisions of the text certainly soften its icy anti-emotionalism, but they do nothing to grant women a more central place in his concerns. That the usually verbose Godwin had little to say to Mary Wollstonecraft on their first meeting should come as no surprise, her contentions about what was politically significant differed from his at the most basic level.

**Thomas Paine**

Mark Philp has suggested that our understanding of writers such as Godwin and Paine will be enhanced if we consider the notion of their 'radical careers',[29] and if we follow the vocational political trajectory of Thomas Paine we discover a perturbing picture of cumulative personal success as a writer and politician displacing some initially promising feminist convictions. When Paine first arrived in Philadelphia in December 1774 he originally intended to open a girl's school but this suggestive scheme was soon laid aside, and with Franklin's assistance he instead became the editor of a small paper, *The Pennsylvania Magazine, or American Museum*.[30] Whilst here, and still under the influence of his earlier Quaker sympathies, Paine produced a series of important articles concerned with the rights of women, both politically and within marriage.[31] His 'An Occasional Letter on the Female Sex' (1775) opens with the pertinent comment, 'If we take a survey of ages and countries, we shall find the women, almost – without exception – at all times and in all places, adored and oppressed. Man, who has never neglected an opportunity of exerting his power, in paying homage to her beauty, has always availed himself of their weakness. He has been at once their tyrant and their slave.'[32] Nearly 20 years later Mary Wollstonecraft based her second *Vindication* on just this paradox, and though Paine's discussion of it is weak in places its mere identification is noteworthy. Perhaps more impressive, though, are his 'Reflections on Unhappy Marriages' (1775), which had a fanciful forerunner in the tale 'Cupid and Hymen' (1775) (a diminutive but rather winsome piece which was written with the laudable aim of putting the institution firmly in its place: 'know Hymen', says an indignant Cupid, 'that I am your master. Indulgent Jove gave you to me as a clerk, not as a rival, much less a superior'.[33] And in the more developed 'Reflections', Paine analyses unhappy marriages of three distinct kinds: those made in haste and rapidly repented, marriages made for money which he considers, 'downright prostitution'[34] and, saddest of all, mutually desired unions which over time disintegrate through routine and inattention. Paine demonstrates here a keen emotional sensitivity akin to that found in works by contemporary female novelists, which rarely found expression in the writings of male political theorists and polemicists. Indeed it rarely appears again in his own works, for in the following year Paine produced *Common Sense* (1776) and with this definitive and phenomenally successful entry into active revolutionary politics,[35] any concern with gender is rapidly eclipsed. From reading this pamphlet one would think that in times of conflict it is only 'men's souls' which are tried.

In *Common Sense* Paine accepts the existence of a natural sexual hierarchy which acts as an unfortunate qualification to his otherwise trenchant egalitarianism. Mankind, he explains, 'being originally equals in the order of creation [. . .] equality could only be destroyed by some subsequent circumstance', and yet it is also stated that, 'Male and Female are the distinctions of nature'.[36] Paine sadly continued to stress the significance of this distinction, eventually elaborating it into a theory of an original division of labour, in his poetic remarks upon the time when, 'Adam delv'd in Paradise/ And Eve made beds of roses'.[37] And most importantly belief in this division affected his later writing, for when Paine theorizes about the origins of society he thinks in terms of an original male-only community, postulating that they were brought together by a need to co-operate in labour.[38] This is the basis of a masculinist political philosophy in which fathers, brothers and sons are the only actors. Power is contended for by groups of men,[39] and the independence which grants citizenship, both individual and national, is seen as synonymous with the attainment of manhood – as Paine explained in one of the *Crisis Papers* (1771–83): 'To know whether it be the interest of the continent to be independent, we need only ask this easy, simple question: Is it in the interest of a man to be a boy all his life?'[40] Agency and choice, both political and personal (and the two often elide) is something which rests entirely with men – a fact well focused in this typical passage from *Common Sense* (1776),

'As a man, who is attached to a prostitute, is unfitted to choose or judge of a wife; so any prepossession in favour of a rotten constitution of government will disable us from discerning a good one.'[41]

What is especially distressing about the dwindling of Paine's gendered consciousness is that it is concurrent with the growth of his famous radical optimism. As he pushed women to the edges (and beyond) of his texts, Paine simultaneously expressed more and more expansive political hopes. As he was often to say, though to strictly male audiences, 'we have it in our power to begin the world again'.[42] And this disjunction, and sex-specific orientation, has especially damaging consequences in *Rights of Man* (1791/2) – Paine's key work, written from the heart of international radical politics and rapidly to become one of the foundation texts of the newly formed and burgeoning working class. That any author could deal with issues of illegitimate authority, mysterious prejudice, enforced ignorance and that 'mass of sense lying dormant'[43] and make no mention of women is certainly a great indictment of the radical cultures of the 1790s. Paine, 'intransigent, brash, even cocksure' wrote this text with a firm audience in mind, a firm faith in men to achieve change and with no time for special cases which might hinder the coming of the next political summer: 'to be free, it is sufficient [to] will it'.[44] Mary Wollstonecraft and her female contemporaries must have wondered about the self-evidence of this truth. It is only fair to remark, however, that the final section 'Ways and Means of improving the condition of Europe' does offer something a little more hopeful. Any plan to construct a welfare state tacitly undermines patriarchal authority, as does any criticism of the system of primogeniture. And Paine's plans for payment of benefits on marriage and at the birth of a child certainly have feminist implications, as does his suggestion that 'work-houses' be set up in the metropolis for the use of both sexes. Though it isn't stated explicitly (which, of course, is the problem), Paine evidently envisaged these as an alternative for many women to a life of prostitution, a markedly humanitarian plan in a century of Magdalens and scabrous double-standards. Yet such details do not fully redeem the text because what *Rights of Man* (1791/ 2) represents is a great lost opportunity. It is in fact the high point of an amazing international career which vividly demonstrates the limitations of mainstream radical thought in the early

1790s, limitations about which Thomas Spence, to whom I now turn, had much to say.

## Thomas Spence

> Then let us join heart in hand,
>     Through country, town, and city,
> Of every sex and every age,
>     Young men and maidens pretty.
> To haste this Golden Age's reign,
>     On every hill and valley,
> Then Paradise shall greet our eyes,
>     Through every street and alley.[45]

Spence's main complaint about Paine, and indeed all mainstream radicals, was that they did not envisage a drastic enough redistribution of the land, and this agrarian temporizing provoked some decidedly splenetic, as well as more codified, rebuttals.[46] For Spence the earth was a common treasury and he would countenance no preservation of private property in it. All civil and political rights derive from owning an equal share of the earth, with the key administrative unit in Spence's ideal society being the parish.[47] Thomas Spence was a tireless propagandist of these ideas, living for many of his London years an impoverished and harried life as the often imprisoned 'poor man's advocate'.[48] And as David Worrall has so clearly shown, Spence's culture of artisan radicalism was something Blake was also deeply immersed in. Verbally and visually they share motifs, generic practices and populist convictions.[49] They were also both prompted by an almost boundless egalitarianism to give more than cursory attention to gender issues. And this shared questioning of the natural sexual hierarchy which Paine endorsed is focused in an image which both used of Adam and Eve lying naked together. Spence's comment on the image is the well-known slogan, 'Man over Man he made not Lord'; whilst Blake's couple lie under the arms of a creating genius, and above the line 'All men are alike (tho' infinitely various)'.[50] Linguistically they share Paine's blindness, but through the use of verbal–visual dialectics they begin to move beyond it.

Spence certainly gave the question much more serious thought with his most noteworthy engagement with gender issues coming in letter four of *The Restorer of Society to its Natural Order* (1803), which is concerned in the main with explaining the beneficial effects of divorce. Not only would its availability improve the quality of personal relationships, but Spence also believed that it would help combat the effects of the double-standard and 're-claim' many women in less humiliating ways than the aforemen-tioned Magdalen hospital. His expression is understandably awkward, but the intention should not be undervalued – it was certainly a novel and enlightened cure for one of the eighteenth century's most discussed 'moral evils': 'Another good effect must also flow from such known possibility of separation. Men will no longer be afraid to give a beloved woman a fair trial of dom-estic life, though formerly she may have borne a loose charac-ter, by which many will be reclaimed.'[51] More importantly, Spence also advanced an argument for the conceptualization of the pri-vate sphere as a political domain, indeed as a locus of oppres-sion perhaps more painfully experienced than any other. Indignantly he exclaimed, 'What signifies Reforms of Govern-ment or Redress of Public Grievances, if people cannot have their domestic grievances redressed?'[52] This marks out a very stark difference from Thomas Paine, as does Spence's linking of pol-itical revolution and sexual liberation, though the terms are fa-miliar enough: 'it is to be supposed the Chains of Hymen would be among the first that would be broken, in case of a Revolu-tion, and the family business of life turned over to Cupid, who though he may be a little whimsical, is not so stern a jailor'.[53]

Spence, of course, was no feminist paragon and the lapses which are evident stem largely from his agrarian enthusiasms. Like William Morris after him, Spence has a tendency to dream of rather inane rural idylls, of which a small extract from *A Further Account of Spensonia* (1794) will suffice: 'The merry bells now sounded from every steeple. The glad females, after feasting their manly spouses and paramours, prepared for the dance; and though [sic] the evening revelled in pleasures known to love and inno-cence alone'.[54] Spence also portrays women as closer to nature than men, as having some special kinship with it. This is par-ticularly clear in his allegedly feminist tract, *The Rights of In-fants; or the Imprescriptable Rights of Mothers to Such a Share of the Elements as is Sufficient to Enable them to Suckle and Bring up their Young* (1797).[55] The text's title summarizes its main argument: women enjoy their rights at one remove and in the company of quite a menagerie. She-bears, she-wolves and she-otters, as mothers, also have their right to a portion of the elements. The document certainly contains more ambiguous aspects and 'the woman' speaks with some force of how, 'men are not to be depended on', but for the most part women are such vociferous contenders for rights simply because, 'nature shall [. . .] never be extinguished'[56] in them. When the committee of women, who for the sake of efficiency have taken over the running of the parish, distribute its surplus, calculations of amounts are made on an exemplary egalitarian basis, but the monies are actually handed over, 'to the head of every family [. . .] for every name under his roof'.[57] Spence's achievements and limitations are succinctly codified in the section of *The Constitution of Spensonia* (1803) which deals with 'The State of Citizens', two clauses of which are worth giving in full:

4. Every Man or Woman born, or otherwise having acquired a settlement in a parish of Spensonia and of the age of twenty-one years complete; is admitted to the exercise of the rights of a Spensonian Citizen, as far as their sex will allow.

5. Female Citizens have the same right of suffrage in their respective parishes as the Men: because they have equal property in the country, and are equally subject to the laws, and indeed, they are in every respect, as well on their own account as on account of their children, as deeply interested in every public transaction. But in consideration of the delicacy of their sex, they are exempted from, and are ineligible to, all public employments.'[58]

Spence manages to go exactly half-way towards making women citizens in his utopia but his vision is eventually compromised by the stereotypical notions of femininity lurking in the pastoral interlude cited above.

Thomas Spence, then, achieved a great deal, especially in comparison with his male contemporaries but even he did not devote an entire pamphlet to the specific problems and demands of women. They deserved their share of the land, and along with men the right to terminate unhappy conjugal relationships, but beyond this Spence did not go. His characteristically energetic indignation was not roused by their plight, their concerns never found a place in the pages of his radical part-work *Pig's Meat* (1793–5) and – most importantly for the next part of my discussion – he never extracted the writings of any of his republican feminist contemporaries.[59] In making these editorial decisions

Spence remained securely in the middle of the radical mainstream, and for all his zealousness and temporary bouts of obscurity this is probably where Spence ultimately belongs. The same, however, cannot be said of the women writers whose works I will now examine. The texts and careers of Catherine Macaulay Graham, Mary Hays and, most spectacularly, Mary Wollstonecraft provide evidence of both the starkly masculinist nature of all levels of radical culture in the late-eighteenth century, and also of the immense difficulty involved in trying to combine feminist concerns with republican commitments.

## THE PROBLEM OF POLITICAL FEMINISM IN THE 1790s

Notwithstanding this general diffusion of liberal sentiment, however, I am aware that a disquisition on the rights of woman will expose the author to ridicule; and although he may not draw down the thunders of an attorney-general, Bigotry will frown, and Folly – thrice happy Folly! will jingle her bells, and laugh, at the attempt.

*The Cabinet* (1795)[60]

### Catherine Macaulay Graham

If any eighteenth-century woman author deserves the title 'radical' it must be Catherine Macaulay Graham. Not only does her eight-volume *History of England* (1763–83) stand as the main Whig rebuttal of David Hume's Tory interpretation of the Stuarts and the Interregnum, but she also entered into textual dispute with the theories of Hobbes and Burke, and contributed writings on a number of topical political problems, including the American crisis. She was, in fact, at the centre of the radical cause in Britain from 1760 to 1785, accepted by radicals of the day as their primary theoretical spokesperson and the main point of contact between theorists and activists during the Wilkesite agitation. Her salon, unlike those of her now more famous bluestocking contemporaries, was a wholly political affair in which she was the only female member. And Macaulay's fame was not restricted to this sphere, or even to this country. She was received with pleasure in France and America, and in 1785 undertook a tour of nine of the 13 states of the union, ending with a stay at Mount

Vernon as the guest of George Washington.[61]

What matters most in this discussion, however, is that Catherine Macaulay, for the vast majority of her extraordinary career, studiously avoided any discussion of gender issues. Hers was, as her contemporary Mary Scott noted, 'A name, to ev'ry *son* of freedom dear' and as a contributor on women's rights to a 1788 number of the *Gentleman's Magazine* observed, this was a subject upon which Macaulay was still 'sharpening her pen'.[62] Indeed it wasn't until the very end of her life, when the writer was in fact dying, that she expressed feminist commitments, and the skill and clarity with which Macaulay proceeds in her *Letters on Education* (1790) make this telling belatedness especially regrettable. Upbraiding Rousseau's essentialism, exposing the double-standard, pointing out the necessary corruptions of a trivializing education and insisting even more firmly than Wollstonecraft that the peculiar foibles and vices of women originate 'only in situation' – she, with dexterity, set out what are now seen as the central concerns of late-eighteenth-century feminism. Moreover her analytical skills are brought to bear upon the thorny issue of the power of truth to prevent injustice and facilitate progress, and her account of the trouble it has combating 'fond prejudices' serves as a prophetic rebuke to the vast claims soon to be made for truth's power by Godwin and Paine.[63]

Most important of all Macaulay comments upon the 'total and absolute exclusion of every political right to the sex in general' (p. 210), and if interest in this exclusion had earlier been fostered in a writer of Macaulay's eloquence and erudition the radical culture we've been looking at would, perhaps, have had a very different complexion. But the key point is that nothing in her political milieu encouraged an interest in this subject – she was as Bridget Hill explains 'A Woman in a Man's World'[64] – and hence even in this, Macaulay's one 'feminist' text, the main focus is on other things, namely the titular 'religious and metaphysical subjects'. Indeed it's with some irony that we observe the eighteenth-century's great Whig historian commenting, 'I do not intend to give [. . .] a history of women' (p. 206), and this is a repudiation which has ominous implications. It is a distancing strategy which allows a decidedly superior tone to slip into the discussion: simultaneously rejecting the role of 'apologist for women' Macaulay suggests that we should amuse ourselves, until there is more wisdom in the female world, by making fun of women's follies (pp. 214; 207). Developing in a male intellectual environment had, of necessity, a decisive effect upon Macaulay's style and in particular she shares with Wollstonecraft an inability to evince any sustained expressions of sisterly feeling (a problem, as we have seen, which also beset Blake's Oothoon). At times there seems to be, lurking behind her text, an alter ego who really does think that women are fools. And it is perhaps for this reason that her *Letters on Education* (1790) were so calmly received. The conservative *Critical Review*, for example, focused its attention especially on the educational section of the work, and though disagreeing with Macaulay's contention that there is 'No Characteristic Difference of Sex', it did so in a most light-hearted fashion, ultimately finding itself able to warmly recommend the work for its 'elegant entertainment and instruction'.[65] Ultimately, we probably have to conclude with Mary Wollstonecraft that Macaulay's main value for feminists was not so much what she wrote but what she did: she was a great 'example'.[66] Yet in the early 1790s it seemed just possible that radical women could do more than this and it is to the two women who most assiduously tried to discover what this 'more' might be that I now turn. What most decisively marks the experiences of Mary Hays and Mary Wollstonecraft is a deeply ambiguous relationship with the radical circles which brought them to birth and this is a problem that I shall elaborate upon in some detail.

### Mary Hays

Mary Hays began what was to be a distinctly radical career by taking the leading Baptist progressive Robert Robinson for a spiritual mentor. Through him she was gradually brought into contact with some of the most influential rational dissenters of the time, including the unitarian Theophilus Lindsay and his successor John Disney, for whom Hays wrote sermons. In 1788 she was able to benefit from the opening of New College, Hackney, which gathered a most impressive group of dissenters for its faculty and staged public meetings and lectures. Given such a start, it is hardly surprising that Hays' first publication was a pamphlet written to defend dissenting modes of worship against Gilbert Wakefield's rather ungenerous attack. Her *Cursory Remarks* (1791) were well received and went into a second edition within a year. This success brought Hays into more overtly politicized circles, as she became intimately acquainted with various members of the Johnson coterie, her most lasting relationship being one of lengthy tutelage to William Godwin.[67]

This experience of a succession of male teachers was by no means an uncommon one, as Gina Luria explains, 'for women like Hays, private tutelage with learned men of necessity replaced formal education. Mary Hays, like Wollstonecraft, Amelia Anderson Opie, Helen Maria Williams, Mary Brunton, and Elizabeth Hamilton, circumvented the social proscriptions against female education and filled the vacuum created by the absence of formal training and intellectual vigour for women, by learning through personal instruction with generous men.'[68] Yet however generous these tutors were there were dangers attendant upon developing intellectually in an almost entirely male environment – (I simply cannot accept Gary Kelly's claim that Hays 'adopted an attitude of feminine independence' with her male tutors[69]) – assimilation being something of which Hays was well aware, as she commented in a letter to Godwin: 'I am more used to, and therefore more at ease in the company of men'.[70] A rather unnerving admission from a woman who spent a good deal of her time writing feminist polemic, and one central to the following investigation of some of Hays's works.

Mary Hays first approached the topic of women's rights in her collection of *Letters and Essays, Moral and Miscellaneous* (1793). As with Macaulay's *Letters* feminism is not the work's only concern, although it does occupy a much more prominent place. Generally the text expresses the kind of philosophical radicalism expected from somebody of Hays's background, especially in essays such as 'Thoughts on Civil Liberty' where stress is laid firmly upon the value of the emancipated mind. And when attention is focused on gender this nuance is maintained, with an exemplary instance being the chapter entitled 'On the Influence of Authority and Custom on the Female Mind and Manners', which opens with the truly Godwinian claim: 'Of all bondage mental bondage is surely the most fatal'[71] (again, the fate of Oothoon and all the other Daughters of Albion somewhat nullifies this belief). For the most part the essay is a proficient piece by an avowed admirer of Mary Wollstonecraft, but what interests us here is Hays's strategy of addressing herself to male supporters, something which she does in the following terms: 'Lovers of truth! be not partial in your researches. Men of sense and

science! remember, by degrading our understandings, you inca-
pacitate us for knowing your value [. . .] how impolitic to throw
a veil over our eyes, that we may not distinguish the radiance
that surrounds you' (p. 26). This is the first instance of an important practice which threatens to compromise her work. It posits
men as the agents of change and discourages female self-respect
and self-dependence, problems Hays faced up to in her appro-
priately titled, *Appeal to the Men of Great Britain in Behalf of the
Women* (1798).[72]

This work was originally written in the early 1790s but, for
reasons outlined in its introduction, was not published until the
end of the decade, by which time the anti-Jacobin backlash guaranteed that it had missed its moment. It remains nonetheless an
important document, and one too often viewed only as a pale
reflection of Wollstonecraft's better known *Vindication* (1792). This
is a mistaken practice, for the *Appeal* has much to recommend it.
It is, for example, a less digressive text, moving steadily through
its religious and rationalist arguments for women's rights. Hays
is also a good deal less critical of women. Instead of successive
portraits of frivolous and incompetent females, she lays her stress
on the constrictions which make them so: 'They find themselves
enclosed in a kind of magic circle, out of which they cannot move,
but to contempt or destruction.'[73] Her view of femininity as a
contradictory construction is also something that moves her beyond Wollstonecraft's rather monolithically negative account,
'What a chaos! – What a mixture of strength and weakness, of
greatness and littleness, – of sense and folly, – of exquisite feeling and total insensibility, – have they jumbled together in their
imaginations' (p. 47). Yet even such insights as these are compromised by Hays's authorial position.[74]

Initially Hays seems to have intended to write a straightforward petition, appealing to the men of Great Britain (long known
for their love of liberty) to bring about the gradual emancipation of women. This is certainly the tone of the introductory section
of the work, where she assures her male readers: 'Know, however, that I come not in the garb of an Amazon, to dispute the
field of right or wrong; but rather as a humble petitioner [. . .]
Not as a fury flinging the torch of discord and revenge amongst
the daughters of Eve but as a friend and companion bearing a
little taper to lead them to the paths of truth, of virtue, and of
liberty' (p. v). Hays did not maintain this persona for long. One

reason why she was doubtful about the stance of petitioner was her awareness of how fiercely operative patriarchal ideology was, even upon her dearest mentors. As she comments,

> THAT MEN ARE SUPERIOR BEINGS, WHEN COMPARED WITH WOMEN AND THAT CONSEQUENTLY NATURE AND REASON, INVEST THEM WITH AUTHORITY OVER THE WEAKER SEX [. . .] is [. . .] the grand pivot upon which social and domestic politicks turn [. . .] it must be confessed, that even those who consider the human species, in a more liberal and extensive point of view [. . .] yet suppose the necessity of subordination on one side unavoidable' (pp. 95–6).

This realization creates havoc in a text ostensibly designed to be an appeal to enlightened men. Indeed thought upon it brought Hays to the painful conclusion that such a group probably did not even exist, and forced the bitter, but strikingly perceptive, observation,

> No! No! It is vain to think, that any man, or set of men, or men in short taken in the gross shall by frequent appeals to their best feelings seek out reasons to portion it [that is, authority] away. With a bad grace do men intrusted with power, derive it to each other, and still they keep it within as narrow a circle as possible, but when through necessity, and for the common purposes of life, they admit women to certain puny privileges, and delegate to them a scanty portion of power, with what a niggardly and griping hand do they dispense their favours! With so many useless and mortifying precautions do they trammel their gifts, that they become by passing through such hands, equivalent to prohibitions. (pp. 98–9)

Mary Hays the feminist polemicist was launched, and her most scathing insights are into precisely this male self-interest[75] and the infuriating indolence of those who should have been sympathetic. As she proceeds,

> the truth I believe is, that men in general, think nothing at all about the matter [of women's oppression] except when their pride and resentment are roused, by any little opposition on

the part of women. Or when they do think, they consider the authority which has been assumed by their sex, not only as an inheritance against which no claim can be of any avail; but as a birthright given from above, which it is their duty as much as their inclination to maintain. In short they are fully convinced that they are much fitter to govern women, than women to govern themselves; and therefore waiving all dispute and examination on the subject they doze (pp. 101–2).

The issue, of course, is how to deal with this arrogance and negligent slumber and it is here that the unamenable nature of the historical moment we've been looking at most powerfully impresses itself upon the text. What Hays needs to do, now that she's plumbed the depths of male (radical) disinterest, is to address herself to women. And herein lies the great problem she shares with Mary Wollstonecraft (and, as we have seen, with Blake's Oothoon), because there simply was no female audience for the kind of activist message that Hays's logic requires.[76] Aware of this isolation she retreats to the only available option, appealing to men to be more 'fair', to behave more 'philosophically' – for all this sexism, 'is precisely what we may be permitted to say, is proceeding upon a wrong principle' (p. 102). Back to a reliance on the power of the mind to distinguish 'error' and the omnipotence of 'truth'.

Hays's predicament, then, points to the paradox of her situation. Only the ponderous culture of rational dissent could empower her to enquire so comprehensively into the injustices women endured. And yet this very culture kept these enquiries in a firmly marginal position, whilst simultaneously resisting the militant and ideologically perceptive conclusions to which Hay's thought inexorably led. It was a tricky and unenviable predicament. And it was one in which Mary Hays remained for the rest of her life – relieved only by the temporary spleen-venting of her Godwin-supervised novel *Memoirs of Emma Courtney* (1797). Although in comparison with Mary Wollstonecraft's manifold political discomforts, Hay's tribulations seem relatively pacific.

## Mary Wollstonecraft

By popular assent Mary Wollstonecraft is the late-eighteenth-century's great republican feminist. Her *Vindication of the Rights of*

*Woman* (1792) stands, as one enthusiastic editor put it, as the feminist 'declaration of independence'.[77] Yet her attempt to marry two equally heartfelt political commitments was an extremely painful and problematic enterprise, resulting in a text torn by the most striking ambiguities and contradictions. These were, like those of Mary Hays, the product of Wollstonecraft's personal and historical location and are, in fact, hardly surprising. Wollstonecraft had come to political birth under the kindly eye of Richard Price; the dissenting community at Newington Green had sustained her in times of personal anxiety, and when life looked especially bleak Joseph Johnson had provided emotional and material help in equally generous amounts. She was indebted to them, and the radical mainstream they represented, and she knew it.[78] In her *Vindication of the Rights of Men* (1790), Wollstonecraft began to repay this debt, responding with genuine indignation to Burke's scurrilous attack on Price and offering by way of tribute idyllic visions of enlightened paternalism.[79] Yet even at this early stage in her career Wollstonecraft strains within the confines of the text, digressing into issues that would not have seemed properly 'political' to many.[80] For example, she breaks off to speak about mercenary marriages in which 'love and Hymen' rarely meet, she touches on the need for a different kind motherhood and most importantly she assaults Burke from a distinctly feminist perspective, exposing the pernicious potential of his ideas about diminutive female beaty. As Mitzi Myers explains, Wollstonecraft stands out from the rank and file who opposed Burke by eschewing a narrowly political approach in favour of combining socioeconomic with moral-aesthetic arguments.[81] With this text Wollstonecraft's radical career was well under way, but it took the sting of intimate insult to fully animate her feminist convictions. In 1791 her friend and co-worker Thomas Christie produced a collection of *Letters on the Revolution* (1791) which were published by Joseph Johnson. In these Christie took it upon himself to defend the French constitution and dwelt with admiration on one facet in particular,

> That ancient Salic Law [. . .] was considered by the Assembly as a fundamental and wise regulation [. . .] which merited to be solemnly renewed, and permanently established. Thus this polite people, the most attached and attentive to the sex of any in Europe, have manisfested superior wisdom, in shewing

that they know where to draw the line, and so to honour the sex as not to injure their *real* happiness, or endanger the welfare of society. They have rightly judged, in not raising them out of their natural sphere, in not involving them in the cares and anxieties of state affairs, to which neither their frame nor their minds are adapted.[82]

This was too much. To find a colleague defending the new Republic's single mistake assisted Wollstonecraft back into print and, as Eleanor Nicholes notes, her second *Vindication*'s dedication, 'reads like a direct reply to Christie's defence of the action of Talleyrand and his fellow legislators'.[83] 'Who made man the exclusive judge' (p. 87) in matters of political justice, she wondered, when he comes up with judgements like this, and it is when Wollstonecraft is writing in this reactive vein that she deserves her reputation as one of the greatest of political polemicists. Her chapter five (Animadversions on Some of the Writers Who Have Rendered Women Objects of Pity, Bordering on Contempt) is a set-piece exercise in indignant literary criticism which reads as freshly now as it did 200 years ago. And the anger which protests that, 'the *rights* of humanity have been [. . .] confined to the male line from Adam downwards' drives Wollstonecraft to the most cutting of epigrammatic insights, 'It is justice, not charity, that is wanting in the world!' (pp. 185; 165).

Yet, in this great age of political pamphleteering (Gail Trusdel Pendleton estimates that approximately 'four thousand pamphlets dealing with questions of reform and revolution appeared in England between the fall of the Bastille and the Peace of Amiens')[84] Wollstonecraft stands virtually alone in her effort to use the political disquisition as a vehicle for advancing the rights of women.[85] And fully aware of her isolated position, she finds it extremely difficult to maintain any sureness of voice. Sometimes this simply leads to nervous qualification: 'Let it not be concluded that I wish to invert the order of things' (p. 109) or to pained contradiction, for instance over the issue of whether a woman's first duty is to herself or to her family. But sometimes Wollstonecraft's isolated insecurity has an even more disruptive presence within her text. Unlike Mary Hays who decided that her male contemporaries were too somnolent to take any interest in texts about women's rights, Wollstonecraft seems to have sensed a much more alert and hostile male audience,[86] an audience whom she believed were ever ready to contemptuously 'horse-laugh' (p. 147) at her proposals. And the inhibiting effect that this had upon her programme can be seen most starkly when she approaches the important and touchy subject of parliamentary enfranchisement. One passage is worth quoting at length because it so powerfully illustrates Wollstonecraft's wary sense of audience and the tailoring of her message,

> I may excite laughter, by dropping a hint, which I mean to pursue, some future time, for I really think that women ought to have representatives, instead of being arbitrarily governed without any direct share allowed them in the deliberations of government. But, as the whole system of representation is now, in this country, only a convenient handle for despotism, they need not complain, for they are as well represented as a numerous class of hard-working mechanics, who pay for the support of royalty when they can scarcely stop their children's mouths with bread. How are they represented whose very sweat supports the splendid stud of an heir-apparent, or varnishes the chariot of some female favourite who looks down on shame (pp. 259–60).

The structure of the argument speaks volume, as it moves through a faltering introduction of the subject, to the intrusion of another voice which makes it clear that 'they' (idle women) have a good deal less right to the vote than 'hard-working mechanics' and finally onto the dissolution of the issue of women's enfranchisement, as the passage turns into a piece of standard anti-monarchical rhetoric. Rhetoric, we should note, which finds time very early on to take a swipe at regal mistresses, those puppet punchbags of so much republican propaganda (and women who, as Claire Tomalin has so elegantly shown in her *Mrs Jordan's Profession* (1994),[87] were in as much need at this time of having their rights vindicated as anyone else).

Marilyn Butler and Janet Todd have recently suggested that Wollstonecraft's omissions and evasions may have a tactical basis, and it certainly seems the case that she is deflected from developing implied elements of her argument by an awareness of the unamenability of her radical contemporaries.[88] Wollstonecraft shuffles around certain issues – such as women's citizenship, the government's responsibility to women, the question of whether women should be educated for their own good or that of society[89]– in extraordinarily convoluted and contradictory ways, quite beyond anything explainable simply in terms of rushed authorship. Wollstonecraft, in short, is not quite sure how much it's safe to say and for a very simple reason. She, like Hays, works for the most part with the notion of an implied reader who is male and she also – for want of a female constituency to agitate[90] – undertakes her own 'appeal to the men of Great Britain'. To gain some sense of the immense compromise such supplication necessitates we need only look at the closing paragraphs of the text's most scintillating chapter (Of the Pernicious Effects which Arise from the Unnatural Distinctions Established in Society),

> I then would fain convince reasonable men of the importance of some of my remarks; and prevail on them to weigh dispassionately the whole tenor of my observations. I appeal to their understandings; and, as a fellow-creature, claim, in the name of my sex, some interests in their hearts. I entreat them to assist to emancipate their companion, to make her a *help-meet* for them. Would men but generously snap our chains, and be content with rational fellowship instead of slavish obedience, they would find us more observant daughters, more affectionate sisters, more faithful wives, more reasonable mothers – in a word, better citizens (p. 263).

'It is Justice, not charity, that is wanting in the world'? In humbly pleading her cause Mary Wollstonecraft forgets the basic premise of her argument, viz: women have been denied the rights which she is vindicating by a patriarchal system dependent for its smooth functioning upon female subordination. Morever, to posit the existence of a class of 'reasonable men' open to rational argument, Wollstonecraft has to relinquish her belief in the determining influence of the environment and education, and imagine instead that there are, 'some loop-holes out of which a man may creep, and dare to think and act for himself' (p. 257). Yet as her own experience shows such pockets of socially unencumbered free-thought were extremely few and far between, even in the 'radical' 1790s. And her text closes with a welter of disturbing and contradictory contentions, appealing to 'understanding' men who are at once models to be emulated and 'task-masters' to be reviled; and presenting a picture of women as wilful beasts who may or may not have the potential to be something more, 'Let woman share the rights, and she will emulate the virtues of man; for she must grow more perfect when emancipated, or justify the authority that chains such a weak being to her duty [...] Be just then, O ye men of understanding; and mark not more severely what women do amiss than the vicious tricks of the horse or the ass for whom ye provide provender – and allow her the privileges of ignorance, to whom ye deny the rights of reason, or ye will be worse than Egyptian task-masters, expecting virtue where Nature has not given understanding' (p. 319). Lucy Newlyn speaks of Wollstonecraft's political ideals being 'betrayed from within',[91] but as we've seen, this internal problem was the result of a much greater external betrayal. It was the failure of radical organizations and individuals to make a commitment to, or even take an interest in, the liberation of women that fissured and compromised her text. Thus when her *Vindication* first appeared it was received with 'calm approbation'.[92] Reviewers for the most part ignored its feminist implications, and perhaps most telling of all is the *Analytical Review*'s response: it *defended Wollstonecraft* against the idea that she had jumped on the 'Rights of Man' bandwagon by reassuring its readers that, 'in reality the present work is an elaborate *treatise* on female *education*'.[93] Even those closest to her would not grant Wollstonecraft a place in the political debate she so urgently addressed.

## FEMINISM IN THE 1790s

It is in this paradoxical context of expectant male radicalism and troubled feminist isolation that I believe, *The Marriage of Heaven and Hell* (1790) and, *America: A Prophecy* (1793) should be seen. But before I go on to offer a reading of these works something needs to be said about a very valid objection which could be made to the preceding discussion, namely that my definition of feminism is too narrowly political and monolithically interested in republican partisans. That it ignores other loci of pro-woman thought, and disregards other contexts which enabled female activism and self-empowerment. In some senses these charges cannot be resisted. Though it initially sounds like an oxymoron, feminists have always claimed that 'Feminism is more than politics',[94] and this is certainly true of the late eighteenth century

when women were mobilized most frequently by religious movements. Not only did evangelicalism and associated philanthropic
enterprises offer public roles to middle-class women, but the flowering of millennial movements and Methodist cottage religion
were immensely empowering for their working-class sisters.[95]
Indeed this was sometimes the generator of explicitly feminist
ideas. For example Joanna Southcott, a prophetess with a predominantly female working-class following, developed a theology which undermined patriarchal culture's fondest myth: bluntly
exculpating Eve – 'I cannot see but man is blameable; as well as
the woman; but the author of the whole was the devil' – Southcott
went on to revive the heresy of the female messiah.[96] Also, it
would be absurd to try and purvey the illusion that feminism
began with Mary Wollstonecraft. Long traditions are now well-
established[97] and besides this committed lineage a curiosity about
women marked the entire century, finding expression for example in a spate of women's histories, especially literary ones.[98]
Yet, this is where the problem really begins, for interest in women
was *so* plentiful and diverse that it's very difficult to define where
speculative enquiry about 'the sex' ends and feminist commitment begins. The degree of seriousness with which the question
of women's education was addressed can be a good litmus test,
as can the tone of discussion about sexual politics but beyond
this very few guidelines exist. Indeed the broadness of this feminist
spectrum has provoked much study of political enigmas, especially
such conservative feminists as Hannah More (although from my
perspective the outright hostility to women's rights expressed
by such an exemplary dissenter as Anna Laetitia Barbauld, and
the distinct lethargy of Helen Maria Williams, are perhaps even
more worthy of attention).[99]

I will not, however, be engaging with these paradoxes. Nor
will I be addressing the equally complex question of the relationship between 'feminism and fiction', between the establishment of female pre-eminence in the field of literary endeavour
and the nature of feminist thought in the 1790s. The fact that we
see a 'literary landscape [. . .] dominated by women intellectuals'[100]
will have some bearing on my discusssion of *Marriage* but these
artistic achievements cannot be a major concern. I eschew all the
above issues, whilst noting their importance, because it is still
my contention that feminist writing in the 1790s is markedly and
tellingly deficient. What characterizes it is modesty – often of

tone, always of demand and expectation[101] and this in a decade otherwise marked by the most sanguine revolutionary specula- tion. It is necessary and legitimate, I think, to focus solely on what I have termed political feminism because this could have been the moment when feminism became just that, an organ- ized movement, no longer on the defensive but actually claiming power for women. The 1790s could have been the decade when a century's interested chatter about the woman question burst into a firm-voiced manifesto of radical demands for women's rights. Instead we witness little more than Mary Wollstonecraft's courageous equivocations, themselves savaged by an anti-Jacobin insurgency which attacked them for kinship to a revolutionary movement which never owned them as any part of its programme. In short feminism, for the reasons I've tried to suggest, missed its moment: the Daughters of Albion were denied access to their era's resources of hope. And I have offered such a lengthy pre- amble because this historical failure caused Blake some difficulty. As we have seen in *Thel* and *Visions* (and indeed in many of the *Songs* too) he dealt sympathetically with issues central to every kind of eighteenth-century feminism: the politics of conduct, the practice of mothering, the possibility of genuine liberty for young women and the importance of experiential education. But in the works I will now examine, *The Marriage of Heaven and Hell* (1790) and *America: A Prophecy* (1793) he turns back to the radical main- stream, offering his own revolutionary manifesto and celebratory millennial drama. And in the following discussion I shall stress that these are two very different sets of texts, distinguished by a stark disjunction that can be stated in usefully crude terms: Thel and Oothoon both fail to achieve any kind of lasting liberty, whilst Orc bursts his chains and liberates America and the *Marriage* wins at least one Angel over to the Devil's party. It seems that here too we see 'A Poet's Interpretation of the History of His Own Time',[102] and it is to Blake's own 'radical' disregard of women that I now turn.

## THE MARRIAGE OF HEAVEN AND HELL

As we've seen, the early 1790s were a time when male radicals issued expansive manifestos, if not apocalyptic pronouncements, and Blake was no exception. Having progressed, as Erdman describes it, along a familiar path 'From Wilkite patriotism in the 1770s to humanitarian Christianity in the late 1780s to political radicalism in the 1790s'[103], Blake was ideally situated to respond with joy to this historical moment. The exact nature of his ideological formation may be a little more complex than Erdman suggests, and we certainly need to pay closer attention to the enthusiastic, antinomian and artisanal aspects of his political constitution,[104] but for now it hardly matters exactly where Blake was situated in the heterodox milieu of radical London. 'The times were auspicious' and Blake responded with verve and daring, giving to 'the world . . . whether they will or no' (*MHH*, 24; E.44) the most sophisticated manifesto the decade produced.[105] *The Marriage* has always been seen as a pivotal work in the Blake canon, with Morton D. Paley offering a typical, if rather extreme, assessment when he declares, 'The study of Blake's thought begins with *The Marriage*' in it 'we find a fully developed presentation of Blake's ethic of liberation'.[106] It certainly is a remarkably confident and comprehensive text and for a personal reasons perhaps as noteworthy as the political. During the time Blake was working on the text he was also perfecting his techniques for illuminated printing and, as the 1793 Prospectus: TO THE PUBLIC indicates, he – 'the Man of Genius' – is now 'sure of his reward' (E.692). This presentation of himself as a maker of 'numerous great works' (E.693) feeds into Blake's individual and devilish interpretation of republican priorities. It is an interpretation which is as masculinist as either Godwin's or Paine's, yet Blake's particular artistic nuance generates a gendered subtext which is more subversive than any undercurrent evident in their works. Some of its details are worth pondering.

First, the centrality of desire and the body in Blake's liberational gospel of necessity raises questions of gender. It is not possible to read, on Plate 5, of the restraint of desire without thinking of the fates of Thel and Oothoon, and indeed more generally of just who the restrainer is and who the restrained. The text discussed on this plate, *Paradise Lost*, turns of course upon that key moment when man lost his restraining power over woman, and with its 'woeful' consequences. Yet the point about the treatment of such issues in *Marriage* is that Blake is prepared to leave the gender implications undiscussed: Eve is not mentioned in this now classic, though painfully cryptic, piece of Milton criticism. Another related task Blake sets himself is to formulate a sensual apocalypse, for which the obvious source-bank is the Biblical Book of Revelation. In particular the image of the woman clothed with the sun gained great currency around this time, with many late-eighteenth-century female prophets – amongst them Luckie Buchan, Sarah Flaxmer and Joanna Southcott – explicitly identifying themselves with her.[107] And Blake offers a vivid flamy variant of the image on Plate 3 (*Illuminated*; E.100) but again fails to incorporate anything more of the feminist implications of the symbol, implications which must have been apparent to someone so grounded in radical Protestant culture, where the image had deep political resonances.[108] It's noteworthy too, in the context of the *Marriage*'s diabolic allegiance, that these women prophets saw it as their main task to expose the devil. As Flaxmer pronounced, 'I am the anointed person to reveal Satan'.[109] This may seem simply to be a labour incumbent on all the Lord's anointed, but these women undertook it with an intense personal ferocity, something which is especially true of Joanna Southcott in her amazing pamphlet, *A Dispute between the Woman and the Powers of Darkness* (1802). In this account of Southcott's seven-day trial of spiritual strength with the Devil, she so vigorously defends Eve, herself and all womankind that Satan is goaded to exclaim, 'A woman's tongue no-man can tame. God hath done something to chuse a bitch of a woman, that will down-argue the Devil, and scarce give him room to speak [. . .] It is better to dispute with a thousand men than with one woman'.[110] Blake critics have tended to write Southcott off as, 'more petulant than prophetic',[111] but they evidently shared a heritage and culture and used its symbols and paradigms in importantly gender-specific, and often antithetical, ways.

But perhaps the most important individual concern indulged by Blake, which keeps a gendered undercurrent flowing through the manifesto, is his commitment to championing the power of artistic creativity. And as we'll see later in the discussion, much synonymy is alleged between this power and male potency. However, it is worth noting that we also see some visual representations of rejections of male artists (Plates 1 and 2, *Illuminated*; E.98, 99) and, more importantly, are presented with a number of suggestive creative females. First, there are the female fruit gatherers on Plate 2 (*Illuminated*; E.98). These could well be poetic figures, averting the problem of Eve by working together at the tree of knowledge. And if the next plate has any connection this artistic speculation is confirmed, for at the bottom of Plate 3 (*Illuminated*; E.100) we see a depiction of birth as a paradigm of creative female energy. As if fulfilling Anna Laetitia Barbauld's lines, 'Haste, little captive, burst thy prison doors!/Launch on the living world, and spring to light!'[112] an infant, aping its mother's expansive gesture, flies to birth, following two older children who strain towards the page's edge. These illuminations allude obviously to the 'new heaven' just 'begun' (*MHH*, 3; E.34) and tie this image to the even more explicitly apocalyptic female on Plate 14 (*Illuminated*; E.111) who hovers with arms outstretched over a man who, 'has closed himself up, till he sees all things thro' narrow chinks of his cavern' (*MHH*, 14; E.39). She has a much more renovated view, however. Partaking in the cleansing of his doors of perception with her enveloping flames, she too has creative powers as 'salutary and medicinal' (*MHH*, 14; E.39) as those of the infernal printer Blake. It is not too far fetched to link this to the flowering of female poetic power which Blake witnessed around him during the first decades of his writing career. A formidable generation reached their poetic apogee in the 1790s[113] and though not 'ancient poets' they certainly could not have been ignored by such an acute observer of poetic traditions as Blake.

Yet it is the famous 'Printing House in Hell' plate which most decisively focuses the issue of creativity. And what goes on here seems initially to refute all the above speculations, because what we see is a glowing description of the creative process in terms of a phallanx of penetrative and ejaculatory images. The frame and site of this furious labour must be noted, however, for they are working in one of the text's numerous caves, which if passive is nonetheless the indispensable womb of their art.[114] Moreover, the reader's identification with these representatives of creative energy is rendered markedly problematic[155] by the fact that they are not 'men' but beasts. The human (and male) actors in this sequence enact a decidely uninspiring role: the process ends when the metallic 'living fluids' are 'receiv'd by Men who occupied the sixth chamber, and took the forms of books & were arranged in libraries' (*MHH*, 15; E.40).

There are, then, for the speculative reader some startlingly suggestive undercurrents in the *Marriage* – marginal and interlinear female figures offer wry comment on the masculinist manifesto that is unfolding. But they do no more than this, and indeed their visual presence serves only to underline a verbal absence. The work contains no female pronoun, and no woman is encountered or mentioned in the text's travels: the only meanings granted are figural.[116] In fact, in some ways *The Marriage* is not just a masculinist text, it is a text about the development of a correct model of masculinity[117] – indeed this is one of the dominant meanings of 'The Argument' (*MHH*, 2; E.33). This appropriate masculinity finds its emblem in the archetypal angry (young?) man Rintrah, whose roaring opens and closes this prefatory pointer. The initial problem Rintrah oversees is the just man's meekness; it has led to a perilous keeping of a conformist path that leads only to death. This prohibits fruitfulness, as living things – 'Roses' and singing 'honey bees'– are doomed to exist amongst thorns, and labour to eke out a subsistence on the barren heath. But stanza 2 brings miraculous hope: the male seed arrives and plants the path, generating life even on the bleached bones of death. The just man's troubles are not over, however, for this fruitfulness provokes another unsuitable male to join the drama: the lazy and effeminate 'villain' is tempted from 'the paths of ease' and succeeds in driving the just man away, into the wilderness. For a moment a 'mild' 'sneaking' masculinity seems to have triumphed, but this is to ignore the just man's reaction to his loss and displacement: no longer meek he 'rages in the wilds/ Where lions roam'.

Certainly a cryptic beginning, but not an unfathomable one. If men are to return to paradise they must eschew humility, believe in their own creative power and shake their fires at that which offends. Not a bad description of what Blake does, in this his manifesto. The heavy presence of an implied author who has donned this macho garb is a striking aspect of the text. What we hear is Blake the confident, or more correctly cocky, republican Devil; the disobedient and virile subject[118] seeking out prissy, prosaic (and tacitly female) Angels to outrage and push around[119] a universe which, in its entirety, is quite within his compass. And there can be no doubt that Blake relished the persona. Knocking Swedenborg about *was* great fun, and of course Blake isn't fair in his treatment of the Swedish seer,[120] but why should he be? He's been to Hell and back for his information and no one can outdo that as a source of revelation. The point is to show off, like the young man heroically displaying his naked body on Plate 21 (*Illuminated*; E.118). It is 'great men' (*MHH*, 23; E.43) like the impulsive Christ and the self-confident prophets who matter at this revolutionary moment, not earnest spiritual pedants like Swedenborg.

In some ways Blake's iconoclastic doctrines require such a stance, but so, as we've seen, did the moment. Blake is, like Tom Paine, in high 'career' (*MHH*, 17; E.41) imagining men's 'power to begin the world over again'.[121] Yet Blake was more self-consciously aware of the gender-exclusiveness of his revolutionary programme – only 'the return of Adam into Paradise'[122] (*MHH*, 3; E.34) is guaranteed in *The Marriage* and this, I think, perturbed Blake. The problem was how to allow any voice to that 'special case': woman. Incorporating her concerns into the radical agenda would, of necessity, refashion that agenda – upset it, reshape it, 'domesticate' it. It would hold men back. And, as we've seen, most male radicals had no time for this hindrance. Blake, though, momentarily at least, does attempt to find space for women's voices. In the brilliant polyphonic heart of the text the concerns of these other speakers do find at least some degree of expression. The 'Proverbs of Hell' repudiate any single perspective – even a devilish one – in favour of moments of vocal dissonance.[123]

The refusal of monologic authority evident in this section of the text has long been noted by Blake critics, with Harold Bloom some 30 years ago commenting that the specific 'difficulty' of reading *The Marriage* is to answer the question: 'Where does Blake speak straight?',[124] a question many have attempted to answer, with the most noteworthy, and wrongheaded, response coming from my own *bête noire* Robert Gleckner. Gleckner's essay recently served as the finale to a collection of extracts on the text edited by Harold Bloom.[125] In it Gleckner outlined his unhappiness at past readings and expressed special distress that, 'no guiding principle of interpretation has yet been advanced that will account for the apparent shifts in the authoritativeness of the several speakers'.[126] Gleckner finds this 'problem' most prevalent in the proverbs, and offers a two-fold solution. First, he problematizes Blake's seeming partisanship with the devils and, more importantly, goes on to suggest that 'the authority of rightness resides more often than not in our perception and understanding of the nature of Blake's allusions [to Spenser, Milton and the Bible]'.[127] His response, then, to Blake's liberation of other/ the reader is to seek substitute sources of authority at the heart of patriarchial literary culture. And this must be a deeply misguided practice, because Blake employs radical dialogization for just the incipiently democratic purpose Bakhtin speaks of. Andrew Cooper is perhaps too enthusiastic when he declares, 'Blake's rampant perpectivism annihilates any distinct authorial presence',[128] but this state is approached in the proverbs. It is here that the dominant voice of the young man whose 'career' we've been following is put into real dialogue, a conversational context very different from the loaded set-piece encounters with the Angels.

A cursory reading of the 'Proverbs' may not, however, make this dialogue apparent. What first strikes us is a continuity of tone and message. The plates initially seem to be a writing out of the key epigram 'No bird soars too high, if he soars with his own wings' (*MHH*, 7:15; E.36), as we are incited to follow our desires and be true to our individual genius. In many minds these gnomic exhortations *are* Blake, and the continuing importance, if not dominance, of this perspective can be seen in a unique grouping of four lines which appear on Plate 8. No other collocation of lines has the concentrated presence of those in which Hell tells us what it thinks of the King of Heaven, 'The pride of the peacock is the glory of God./ The lust of the goat is the bounty of God./ The wrath of the lion is the wisdom of God./ The nakedness of woman is the work of God.' (*MHH*, 8:22–5; E.36). Blake lifts irony to the level of the sublime as traditional Godly attributes are given provocatively earthly cognates, which, to complete the affront, have grammatical primacy. Moreover we learn what Hell thinks of woman, and the final line is one of a number which reveal devilish objectification, if not an explicitly sexist mentality (as E.P. Thompson says, the ranting impulse was still very much alive in the 1790s). Take a few affiliate examples: 'Prudence is a rich ugly old maid courted by Incapacity' (*MHH*, 7:4; E.35) – likely to raise a laugh in tavern circles where the dregs of Wilkes' sexualized radicalism lingered, but hardly consistent with the views of *Thel*'s author – a poem which shows both prudence and spinsters in a very different light. Or 'Let man wear the fell of the lion, woman the fleece of the sheep' (*MHH*, 8:30; E.36) – most pleasing to those like Bromion who conceptualize women as sexualized 'chickens' pointlessly shunning the 'ravenous hawk' (*Visions*, 3:2; E.47) but less appealing to those whose fate it is to be devoured (see, too, Proverbs: 27/ 40/44/50). Or again, 'Where man is not nature is barren' (*MHH*, 10:68; E.38), a reductive and self-flattering masculinist aphorism with obviously gendered suggestion in this work bristling with overflowing fountains (*MHH*, 8: 35; E.36) and impregnating joys (*MHH*, 8:26; E.36). And so one could go on. The point is not that this perspective is absent but that a dissenting undercurrent exists. Phallic fantasies are simultaneously indulged and denied: 'Drive your cart and your plow over the bones of the dead [. . .] The cut worm forgives the plow' (*MHH*, 7: 2/7: 6; E.35); and that essentially anti-phallic urge,[129] that willingness to acknowledge the other, finds expression also: 'The most sublime act is to set another before you' (*MHH*, 7:17; E.36) or more suggestively, '[S]He who has suffered you to impose on [her] him knows you' (*MHH*, 9:42, E.37 – my additions).

It would, however, be foolish to overstress the importance of this gendered dialogue. Our confident young man is given equal food for thought by a number of other speakers, for example by what might be called a voice of wonder which looks with humility as well as delight, at the minute particulars as well as the grand concepts (*MHH*, 7:10; 8:33; 8:36; 9:53; 8:56; E.36–7). Or alternatively by voices of experience and cynicism, which often elide as observations such as, 'The fox condemns the trap, not himself [. . .] Expect poison from the standing water' (*MHH*, 8:28; 9:45; E.36–7) slide into, 'Bring out number, weight & measure in a year of dearth [. . .] A dead body, revenges not injuries' (*MHH*, 7:14; 7:16; E.36). The combinations and contrasts of perspective which it is possible to produce from Blake's 70 proverbs are infinite. And it is clear that Blake intended his readers to experiment in this way, as he himself offered one set of possible combinations in 'copy H' of *The Marriage*, where different colours indicate groupings.[130] Here we have Blake at his most writerly, insisting on active engagement and shifting the burden of meaning and value conclusively onto the reader.[131] Yet, however redemptive an account fashionable literary theories enable us to produce (and I willingly confess my desire to redeem this marvellous text), it is impossible to deny that as a radical manifesto *The Marriage of Heaven and Hell* fails to enfranchise, and largely even to represent, women. In this it is a missed opportunity as striking as Tom Paine's failure to extend the rights of men to women. Indeed it's an even greater lost opportunity, for the structuring metaphor for Blake's work is so much more suggestive: there is the potential for the celebration of difference and equality, for the depiction of a conjugal relationship that assaults contemporary

mores by offering a vision of marriage as a union in which neither sex subsumes the other. The title page's central couple (*Illuminated* ; E.98) embody these egalitarian dynamics,[132] the famous
passage on the indispensable contraries is its theoritical justification, the account of the prolific and devouring an instance of
it in action plump with erotic suggestion, the epigram 'Opposition is true Friendship' (*MHH*, 20; E.42) its gnomic representation. And yet the domestic, sexual, gendered meaning of *The
Marriage*'s central metaphor is entirely bypassed,[133] eclipsed by
the same configuration of historical pressures that marred the
work of Blake's radical contemporaries.

It is a depressing but irresistible fact that the more 'political'
Blake's writing becomes the less it is explicitly concerned with
gender issues. *The Marriage*'s appendix 'The Song of Liberty'
demonstrates this clearly. Acting as a bridge between *Marriage*
and *America*,[134] it indicates the kind of subsidiary roles that women
will be allocated in the first major installment of Blake's apocalyptic
myth. Women, or perhaps more correctly females,[135] still have a
central place in the narrative but are cast as entirely passive victims.
Here 'woman' appears as 'The Eternal Female' (*MHH*, 25; E.44)
whose groan is heard across the earth. She can have no active part
in the revolution which is emerging, simply holding its embodiment for a moment in her trembling hands. The real conflict takes
place between two archetypal, as well as temporally significant,
male figures – the as yet unnamed Orc and Urizen.[136] When women
as social rather than symbolic figures do appear at the *Song*'s
end it is merely as objects over whom 'the sons of joy' and 'the
Priests of the Raven of dawn' (*MHH*, 27; E.45) argue – their debate about female virginity being eventually settled, in Orc's favour
in *America: A Prophecy*, the poem to which I now turn.


## AMERICA: A PROPHECY

In the United States of America, the science of liberty is universally understood, felt, and practised, as much by the simple
as the wise, the weak as the strong.

Joel Barlow

Remember all Men would be Tyrants if they could.

Abigail Adams (letter to her husband)[137]

Although *America: A Prophecy* (1793) is in many senses a direct writing out of the theoretical formulations of *The Marriage* (1790), perhaps the most productive initial comparisons can be made with *Visions of the Daughters of Albion* (1793). The same leaping female figure invites us into each text, but what is most striking is the polar experiences of the poems' central characters: Orc and Oothoon. As we saw Oothoon began her poem at liberty, seeking sexual flowers to comfort her and boldly declaring her desires. She ends it in chains, a raped and ultimately apostate figure. In contrast Orc starts his career bound, writhing in torment and howling with lust. Yet his story closes in incandescent freedom: the inspirer of a successful revolutionary war, his phallic heat initiates the final melt-down of mortality.[138] Morever, it is quite clear that the difference in their fates is explainable only in terms of their sex: it is Orc's ability to rape which allows him liberty, it is Oothoon's capacity to be raped that facilitates her bondage. It is hard to avoid the conclusion that in writing *America* Blake shifts his allegiances with dizzying speed – although standard readings of the text have always resisted this interpretation.

There has been much apologism for, if not outright celebration of, Orc's prefatory exploits; with one of his most recent champions making extraordinary claims for his action. Under the influence of Norman Stone's thesis, Stephen Behrendt interprets Orc's behaviour thus, 'In a very real sense Orc enacts, albeit violently, the movement that paralleled the decline of patriarchy and the rise of the egalitarian family [. . .] the 'rape' is a necessary rite of passage that frees both figures into a more enlightened perspective'[139] This, as well as all the earlier talk about Orc as 'promising youngster [. . .] determined to set the world on fire', can only be described as sexist cant for as William Keach notes the 'entire scene is complicit with the worst kind of masculine fantasy'.[140] What Orc actually enacts is an archetypal gesture of predatory sexual violence: 'Orc assay'd his fierce embrace [. . .] Round the terrific loins he seiz'd the panting struggling womb' (*Am*, 1:2; 2: 3; E.51–2). Furthermore this is an act upon which the narrator seems to look with pleasure and approval – informing us that the violation brought joy: 'she put aside her clouds & smiled her first-born smile' (*Am*, 2:4; E.52). And much else in the text strongly suggests authorial satisfaction at the evocation of displays of phallic power. Take for example the passage which announces Orc's first appearance in the prophecy, 'And in the red clouds rose a Wonder o'er the Atlantic sea; / Intense! naked! a Human fire fierce glowing, as the wedge/ Of iron heated in the furnace ... (*Am*, 4:7–9; E.53). Or note the preponderance of muscular, usually naked, youths: on Plate 2 one emerges taut and vigorous from the earth's crevice, on Plate 3 another, Hercules-like, brandishes broken chains, on Plate 5 a number of such youths join together to administer sinewy revolutionary justice and on Plate 6 yet another, proudly phallic, emblematizes the best that resurrected flesh can attain[141] (*Illuminated*; E.140; 141; 143; 144). Textually too the Orc of whom these youths are surely representatives, is given the most powerful libertarian rhetoric. On Plate 6 (*Illuminated*; E.144), for example, text and design are in a unique unison for his delivery of 'Blake's poetic version of the Revolutionary declaration of independence'[142] and on Plate 8 he enjoys the honour of recounting his personal destruction of the much hated decalogue. Finally, and perhaps most important of all, Orc continues to celebrate the sexual violation of women – offering as a model of revolutionized female sexuality a mute creature,[143] 'ravish'd in her cradle night and morn' (*Am*, 8:12; E.54). And whilst she is thus laid out, men are elevated to yet greater heights of revolutionary luminosity, 'Fires inwrap the earthly globe, yet man is not consumd; / Amidst the lustful fires he walks; his feet become like brass, / His knees and thighs like silver, & his breast and head like gold.' (*Am*, 8:15–17; E.54).

It need hardly be added that the poem's historical drama is enacted only by, 'warlike men [...] Brothers & sons of America' (*Am*, 3:3 9; E.52), who congregate as a fraternal phalanx at the ocean's margin. Fairness demands that we note a degree of historical fidelity in this, but we should be cautious about claiming that women had no active combat roles in this, essentially civil, war because they quite evidently did. What Blake is responding to here is the unusually strong contemporary American resistance to acknowledging their contribution and presence. Washington, for example, was acutely embarrassed about, and hostile towards, the 'women of the army'.[144] The American Revolution was even less orientated towards enfranchising women than the French one which followed,[145] and service to it was always envisaged in terms of masculine duty, patriotism and commitment. Tom Paine's cry that the Americans, 'awaken [...] from fatal and unmanly slumbers' was ever the call to arms; and it was yet another war in which metaphorical sons fought their tyrannous fathers, only to become fathers in their stead.[145] Indeed it is interesting to note that the very concept of liberty, of which the revolution's sympathizers were so proud, was itself utterly compromised by this often unconcious sexism. Joel Barlow, when praising America as the place where 'the science of liberty is universally understood' celebrated the patriot's practical political wisdom in these terms, 'They believe that there is nothing more difficult in the management of a nation than the affairs of a family; that it only requires more hands.'[147] And yet his model of this family/state is completely patriarchal, for the men who propounded this 'egalitarian' constitution also felt that universal rights are granted by the limited formulation, 'that all men are equal in their Rights, that *it is impossible to make them otherwise*' (p. 283). And in line with such contemporary writing *America: A Prophecy* seems to be a poem about men and their political disputes, and, equally important, about political disputes as solely male property.

Yet to offer this as a reading of the poem would be illegitimately partial. These masculinist elements – like those evident in *The Marriage* – well deserve scrutiny (especially in a partisan exercise like this book where apologism is always a danger) but once noted we must move beyond them and look at the more subversive aspects of the poem. For much more goes on than simply a celebration of Orc; even in the 'Preludium' the interaction is highly problematic.

Standard readings usually try to do away with difficulties by claiming that all 'human interest' of the events resides in Orc, the Shadowy daughter of Urthona being merely a representative of nature. Harold Bloom states the case most forcefully when he observes, 'A reading of *America* from its very first line can begin by utilizing anyone's best hint for reading William Blake: every female personage finally relates to, or is, a form of nature; every male at last represents humankind, both male and female.'[148] Claims of this sort for her symbolic importance are usually bolstered by further allegations that she is a specific part of nature: the virgin land of America, long a locus, in the European consciousness, of gratifying erotic hopes and nurturing dreams.[149] Blake certainly does draw upon a number of elements of traditional continental iconography; most especially his America owes much to the image of the Indian Princess, 'Crown'd with a helmet & dark hair [. . .] A quiver with its burning stores, a bow like that of night' (*Am*, 1:4–5; E.51), which gained ground as the four continents tradition waned near the end of the eighteenth century.[150] Yet, as we shall see, Blake's use of this figure is extremely ambiguous, for the shadowy daughter is much more than a simple one-dimensional symbol. She becomes an individuated character, whose experience and responses raise awkward questions about gender and sexual politics not usually sparked by iconographic figures, who because operating within a firmly defined context have a fairly limited range of significance.[151]

Let me explain what I mean. One strikingly 'unsymbolic' aspect of the shadowy daughter's behaviour is her response to Orc's attack. The prescribed gesture after such a violation is to fall prostrate and pathetic on the ground: a nation imperilled. But what she does is to offer the first taste of the self-protective and possessive female (il) logic which Enitharmon uses so effectively in *Europe – A Prophecy* (1794),[152] and which Wollstonecraft provides the anatomy of in her second *Vindication* (1792). Trying to wrest some kind of initiative and agency back to herself she entirely falsifies the event: 'I know thee, I have found thee, & will not let thee go' (*Am*, 2:7; E.52). Moreover her sufferings are much more visceral than the 'wounds' which the caricature and pamphlet America usually received: 'O what limb rendering pain I feel, thy fire and my frost/ Mingle in howling pains, in furrows by thy lightnings rent;/ This is eternal death; and this the torment long foretold' (*Am*, 2:14–16; E.52). In this context it is interesting to note that the ostensible 'meaning' of caricature prints of America were themselves occasionally disrupted by just such sexual sufferings. Take for example, 'The Able Doctor; or America Swallowing the Bitter Draught' which appeared in the *London Magazine* in April 1774 as an illustration to parliamentary debates over the Boston Port Bill, and was soon copied for an American audience by Paul Revere.[153] What the image 'means' to show is Lord North, forcing America to accept the Boston Port Bill, assisted in this political aim by Lord Mansfield and Lord Sandwich. They are watched over by Bute and representatives of France and Spain, along with a rather distressed Britain. What is more strikingly seen, however, is a depiction of gang oral rape: the barebreasted figure representing America is pinned to the ground by a group of men, one of whom peers up her skirts whilst pulling her legs apart. Another woman stands in the background, powerless to help and too afflicted to watch.

The results of the vividness of this image are the same as in *America*'s Preludium: sexual politics take on more significance than international ones, the men involved become representatives of male power before they are representatives of British power.

'The Able Doctor' is a noteworthy image for comparison for other reasons too, most importantly because it alerts us to Blake's key inversion of ideas about who and what it was that violated America during the revolutionary period. But before we go on to look in detail at these inversions it is an interesting preliminary to note that Blake introduces violent allusions and associations which were very rarely employed by revolutionary sympathizers in Britain in the 1790s. They, like him, considered the American struggle to be a prophetic prelude and inspirer of the then current French Revolution, but spoke of it in untarnished and glowing terms – as, to quote Mary Wollstonecraft, a 'noble struggle against the tyrannical and inhuman ambition of the British court' which 'seems to form a new epoch in the history of mankind; for amidst the various changes, that have convulsed the globe, it stands forth as the first work of reason'.[154] Moreover, even those who narrated the event by means of a metaphor of male development habitually resisted reference to the potentially violent sexual elements of male adolescence, stressing instead that, 'The americans [sic] indeed were not fired with enthusiastic ardour' and speaking in neutral terms about, 'the infant efforts, the more mature struggles, and the ultimate victories of a race of free men'.[155] These really are noteworthy differences because they form a suggestive backdrop to Blake's uncharacteristic treatment of ravishment in the American Revolution, for as Susan Brownmiller pointed out her study of 'Historical Rape' it was the British and Hessians who were considered to be the violating force.[156] In contemporary accounts the English figure as a dangerously degenerate group, an army posing a sexual threat because they are 'enervated by luxury, debauched by gaming, and corrupted by the pleasures and gaiety of the capital'.[157] It is in accounts of Tory and paid Indian attacks that American chroniclers observed, 'The selfish passions of human nature unrestrained by social ties, [...] Not only the men and warriors, but the women and children, and whole settlements, were involved in the promiscuous desolations'.[158] Indeed David Ramsay felt that such activity had infected the new nation, noting with concern that though, the literary, political, and military talents of the citizens of the US have been improved by the revolution, [. . .] their moral character is inferior to what it formerly was. So great is the change for the worse, that the friends of public order are loudly called upon to exert their utmost abilities, in extirpating the vicious principles and habits, which have taken deep root during the late convulsions.[159]

It was perhaps because he sensed the possibility of such corruption that George Washington called upon the patriots to distuinguish themselves specifically by their respect for women: 'it is expected that humanity to women [. . .] will distinguish brave Americans, contending for liberty'.[160] Generally, though, it is the Colonialists who are conceptualized as violators. Tom Paine, for example, invoked a much more common ravishment of the continent metaphor when arguing against reconcilliation: 'As well can the lover forgive the ravisher of his mistress, as the continent forgive the murders of Britain.'[161] And what Blake does is to starkly reverse these convictions and conventions: presenting the female 'America' raped by the revolutionary figure who is to be the poetic inspiration of the men Washington and Paine call upon to defend her. Hence Orc's behaviour is a good deal more like that of the imperialist conquerors who 'found' the 'new land', than that of the republican patriots who now seek to defend it.[162]

In this way (dear reader, forgive the tangled route I've taken) a historically specific ambiguity is built into the figure of Orc. And this suggestion of identity between reactionary and revolutionary men, based upon shared ideas about female 'material', is not allowed to drop from the poem. The pictorial synonymy of Orc and Urizen on Plates 8 and 10 (*Illuminated*, E.146; 148) has been much commented on,[163] especially Plate 8 where Urizen appears directly above the words, 'I am Orc' (*Am*, 8:1; E.54). This serves to alert us to the problematic nature of Blake's revolutionary 'hero', something manifest in many ways. His energy, for example, is less that of youth or honest desire than of a carnivorous beast, and Blake suggests the dubiousness of this in the same way as he suggested the unsatisfactory nature of Thel's early identity: by allowing the character to issue a long speech of 'self-understanding'. It is not just Urizen but Orc himself who offers these characteristics,[164] Sometimes an eagle screaming in the sky, sometimes a lion,/ Stalking upon the mountains, & sometimes a whale I lash/ The raging fathomless abyss, anon a serpent folding. Around the pillars of Urthona . . .' (*Am*, 1:13–16; E.51). Rintrah might be impressed, but this excessive description in fact signals an overvaluing of personal strength and potency, and a dangerous inclination towards violence. It is clear that Orc is sometimes bloodstained and 'terrible' because he symbolizes Blake's sense of the unavoidable turmoil of revolution, but this is not always the case. Sometimes he is so to indicate the limits of his liberational potential; most specifically no woman could ever be liberated by him and no woman ever is.

David Aers, in two excellent discussions of *America*, focuses very well on the problems of Orcian revolution and poses the key question: 'How does a male-dominated political revolution (which it clearly is in 'America' and the history Blake is mediating) lead to the overthrow of traditional male domination over women in the spheres of work, family, sexuality and relations in general?'[165] Aers's feeling is that Blake on the whole seeks to deny the problem: 'Instead of using the vision of Songs to explore fatal limitations of the Orc mentality, its *un*revolutionary and very traditional devotion to 'masculine' violence, [the] poem claims that at least Orcian revolution achieves sexual liberation and gratification'.[166] Yet Aers's own discussion shows that this is precisely what the poem does not claim, as he is forced to admit, 'In context [. . .] this is far from plausible',[167] and to conclude I shall look at the few plates which crystallize this implausibility.

It is on Plate 15 that the issue of women's liberation is directly addressed and what is most striking is that women remain objects rather than agents of change:

'The doors of marriage are open, and the Priests in rustling
   scales
Rush into reptile coverts, hiding from the fires of Orc,
That play around the golden roofs in wreaths of fierce desire,
Leaving the females naked and glowing with the lusts of
   youth
For the female spirits of the dead pining in the bonds of
   religion;
Run from their fetters reddening, & in long drawn arches
   sitting:

They feel the nerves of youth renew, and desires of ancient
   times,
Over their pale limbs as a vine when the tender grape
   appears.

                                        (*Am*, 15:19–26; E.57).

As is quite clear, this passage on 'female liberation' is nothing
more than a continuation of the 'blasphemous demons' attack
on the church, combined with an account of the power of Orc's
fires which, predictably by now, strip the females naked. Moreover,
the second stanza does not even maintain this nominal concern
with women's liberation: we now hear about the *'female spirits
of the dead'* (my emphasis) whose oppression too has a religious source and whose redemption also comes from being transformed into objects of desire. This time they grow into succulent
grape vines, ripe for plucking (just as the apostate Oothoon turned
herself into a juicy apple for Theotormon's pallid palate).

   These are highly inadequate ways to be included in the general apocalypse – if indeed these lines can really be said to amount
to inclusion.[168] And, as ever, it is the illuminations which make
it quite clear that Blake was aware of this, for they seem to show
what really happens to females who are licked by Orc's flames
(*Illuminated*; E.152). For the most part they are afflicted or cowed,
although one figure does seem to be ascending up the left hand
margin. She, however, is to travel up through a tree stump only
to end exactly where she started, crouched with her head in her
hands, though this time clothed.[169] So, as with *The Marriage* it is
the visual text which maintains a female presence, verbally all
concentrates on the fires of Orc. On Plate 16 (*Illuminated*; E.154),
for example, a group of vegetating women stumble behind the
praying figure of Urizen, enacting a darkly ironic comment[170]
on the adjacent verse which tells of Orc's consuming of the five
gates of limited sensuality. Furthermore the plate also contains
the only visual depiction of a sexual encounter in the poem (excepting the title page where the male partner appears to be dead)
and it acts as a very wry deflation of the pervasive phallic jubi-
lations we've noted. Not only are the figures tiny but their pos-
ture is deliberately awkward, with some reluctance on the male's
side, as the female pulls him towards her. Indeed for all the talk
of Orc's desire we never actually see him or any of his representatives consummating their impulses, except possibly in the

form of the ravening eagle on Plate 13 (*Illuminated*; E.152) which preys upon a grossly fetishized body. The most energetic sexual figures in the poem are female, especially striking is the woman on the title page who straddles her lover's body, desperately trying to embrace and kiss him (*Illuminated*; E.138). He, how-ever, remains supine, gripping a sword and as his body is en-tirely intact the death implied may not be physical.

Speculations, however, about the incipient feminism generated by Blake's provocative verbal–visual dialectic could go on inter-minably, whilst the clear fact remains that *America* is a story of a successful male revolution which achieves the ultimate aim of saving a portion of the infinite (*Am*, 14:17–20; E.56). 'The times' for male radicals had been and were 'auspicious' and Blake re-sponded fully, indeed manfully, to this buoyant moment. He had his own *annus mirabilis* during the heydays of plebeian radical-ism – the early 1790s witness a poetic productivity which was never surpassed.[171] Moreover, Blake was courageous in his com-mitment to this radical cause, for example risking prosecution by publishing a work like *America*, yet still placing his name and location on the title page of this seditious poem. But these details are well-known and well appreciated. What makes Blake worth studying from a feminist perspective is that the trajectory of his radical career is uneasy in its course; it is stalled, deflected, even occasionally halted by an intermittent awareness that other power bases exist, other forms of exploitation operate, that it isn't just 'warlike' men who engage with the political. At the time he wrote the texts I've examined in this chapter Blake had not developed – perhaps even had no interest in developing – an effective method of synthesizing these two sets of political concerns, and hence often let women and their rights slip from his work. Yet this did not remain the case, and in my conclud-ing chapter I shall argue that in his slightly later poem *Europe– A Prophecy* (1794) Blake achieves a remarkable, and to date largely unacknowledged, synthesis of his political concerns. Blake's read-ing and viewing of the gendered and sexualized narratives which told the story of the French Revolution prompted and enabled him to tell his own tale. At least that is the finale I will try to produce.

# 5

# 'Go, Tell the Human Race that Woman's Love is Sin!': Sexual Politics and History in Blake's *Europe – A Prophecy*

## INTRODUCTION

Within the canon of Blake's writings *Europe – A Prophecy* (1794) is generally regarded as the most challenging of his early works. Harold Bloom designates it, 'the subtlest and most difficult of Blake's poems outside of the three epics'[7] and the predominant critical response to *Europe*'s stark complexity and intensification of myth has been to argue that it heralds a move away from historical and political engagement – 1794 being the moment when Blake began a series of less temporal considerations. As W.H. Stevenson commented, 'the trend from *The French Revolution* to *The Book of Urizen* shows a clear movement from "historical" to "pure".[2] According to such critics, then, *Europe* finds Blake flushing away his last few 'impure' historical and political thoughts.

It was, of course, in opposition to this kind of dehistoricizing critical imperative that David Erdman wielded his *Blake: Prophet against Empire* (1969, fp.1954) and it is his historical location of the work that I shall take as my starting point, although sketching out vital areas of dissent and highlighting various omissions will also occupy a good deal of my time. In both *The Illuminated Blake* (1974) and *Prophet*,[3] Erdman argues that *Europe* (as its title suggests) deals with British reactions to developments across the channel between 1792 and 1794. He pays special attention to the vicissitudes and strategies of the English anti-Jacobins and also

133

focuses on the significance of the declaration of war against the French Republic. Vital substantiation for this beguilingly unclut-tered case is found through looking at intertextual connections between *Europe* and a number of mass-produced political car-toons – an interesting exercise which demonstrates conclusively how Blake was well aware that, 'Caricature was [. . .] *the* major art form of the French Revolution.'[4] In contrast to other influen-tial readings of *Europe*, Erdman's account is lucid, accessible and overarchingly unequivocal, and it is sadly ironic that it's this very wish to explicate clearly that leads Erdman into many in-terpretative problems and omissions. Most fundamentally his admirable desire to historicize and demystify Blake means that Erdman undervalues, and perhaps even misunderstands, Blake's use of myth. Speaking dismissively of *Europe*'s 'mythological envelope' is not only a perilous stance for any Blake critic to take (most, after all, would have to agree with Eagleton that he is 'the most astonishing instance we have of a revolutionary myth-maker')[5] but it also expresses an erroneous conception of how Blake and his contemporaries reacted to the 'French Revolution'. Erdman is, at heart, a reflectionist – seeking out exact mirrorings of social facts and historical personages[6] and literature produced in the Romantic period is often unsuited to this approach for, as Marilyn Butler has demonstrated, the main English literary re-sponse to the French Revolution found its form in 'heady metafiction'.[7] It is 'symbolic narratives of the destruction and creation of new worlds' which predominate, and though 'these are not necessarily representations of revolution in the sense that a report or even an allegory is a representation', they power-fully express the experience of this revolutionary epoch, they offer confusing and vividly immediate 're-living(s) of violent and destructive change'.[8]

The mythic aspects of Blake's work, then, should not be viewed as an irritating covering that needs to be pulled off to reveal the real historical message; rather the creation of his myths is itself the *real historical message* and what it tells us is that Blake's revolu-tionary thinking required a form to express it which was flex-ible, which allowed provisionality and enabled ambiguity to thrive.[9] And it is just this potential for equivocation and open-ness that Erdman is hostile to, for it is his aim to offer us an Orc-centred view of the poem which casts Blake as a dogmatic revolutionary sympathizer, throwing his full poetic weight behind the 'French' cause. This is partly understandable given the implicitly reactionary orthodoxy that Erdman was confronting but it is a depiction that radically falsifies *Europe*'s politics, because this isn't Blake's Bastille-year poem, it's not concerned with the exuberance of the early years of the revolution; rather it addresses French events after 1792, to which the major British response was confusion and dismay, even amongst committed radicals.[10] Their main problem was that although expressing fierce hostility to Pitt and his proclamations was natural they could not so easily align themselves with the French republicans – the September massacres of 1792 had already caused alarm and developments in 1793 looked blacker still. With news of the royal executions, the purging of the Girondins from the Convention and the setting up of the Committee of Public Safety (which effectively signalled the start of the 'great terror') appearing in Britain in copious detail Blake was forced into the painful task of re-examining his political convictions. The 'mythological envelope' which Erdman neatly slides away contains evidence of the awkward and urgent questions raised by this activity.

The second, and for the purposes of this discussion much more important, topic on which I dissent from Erdman's reading of *Europe* is in his interpretation of the significance of the poem's female characters. Erdman's historicizing takes us to France but once this context is established he refuses to follow up what the female dominated *Preludium* implies: that this is a mythological mediation of the revolutionary experience of French women.[11] He gives no thought to the idea that Blake employs a complex mythic form because, in part at least, it allows him to meditate upon the roles and representations of women in this revolutionary period. Yet despite Erdman's omission, this is, I believe, the case and the claim that Blake was thinking about women in the French Revolution receives some very useful substantiation if we look at the commercial engraving work that he was doing around the time he wrote *Europe*. The most important piece of evidence is a work simply entitled 'The F. Revolution' which appeared in Vol. 1, 1793 of Bellamy's Picturesque and Literary Museum. This was engraved by Blake from one of C.R. Ryley's designs during the first half of 1793 and 'pictures Louis XVI and Marie Antoinette protected by loyal troops from a revolutionary mob which stormed the palace at Versailles'; its purpose in the magazine being to 'illustrate an unsympathetic "Account of the

Revolution in France, from its commencement to the Death of Louis XVI"'.[12] This engraving, which as Robert Essick notes is Blake's 'most direct and explicit engagement as a pictorial artist with the events unfolding in France', has been entirely overlooked by all previous commentators on the poem;[13] and such disinterest can only have hampered our understanding, for this engraving strongly suggests that the revolutionary experience of at least one group of French women (that is, those of the elite) had been placed on Blake's agenda during the time he was writing *Europe*. Moreover, if we turn to a second series of engravings – the plates Blake produced for John Gabriel Stedman's, *Narrative, of a Five Year's Expedition, Against the Revolted Negroes of Surinam*, published by Joseph Johnson 1792–93[14] – it is clear that less privileged women were also under consideration. Many of Blake's engravings deal with the experiences of female slaves. Works such as 'Flagellation of a female Samboe Slave' and 'A Surinam Planter in his Morning Dress' focus on the specificities of women's powerlessness and this insight about sexual exploitation is extended in an engraving that represents African, American *and* European women: 'Europe Supported by Africa and America'.[15] Here Blake graphically illustrates his awareness of the double exploitation of being female and a slave – an insight which he, of course, developed in *Visions* where the condition of simply being a woman was shown to amount to a form of slavery.

Taken as a group, then, these engravings amount to a series of insights into the paradoxes and complexities of women's power and women's powerlessness at a time of revolution, colonialism and imperial wars – which is one way of summarizing the reading of *Europe* I intend to offer. The poem marks a new stage in Blake's work not just because of its mythic intensification but also because it contains two qualitatively new female figures: the furiously generative shadowy female and, more centrally, the putatively powerful Enitharmon. In this chapter I shall argue that in looking at various representations and accounts of women's experiences in Revolutionary France, Blake was confronted with a stark image of women's brutalized and dismal fate when two hostile patriarchal, and overtly sexist, forces clash. *Europe – A Prophecy* is Blake's response to this situation – where women function simultaneously as significant, though undervalued, agents of revolutionary action whilst also being elevated into figureheads of the challenged old regime, which can be defaced and then replaced without the principle of patriarchy ever being questioned. Something very much like this happened in the French Revolution and was dramatized in the mass of political writings and caricatures about the state of France which appeared in Britain before and during the time Blake was writing *Europe – A Prophecy*. I realize that these are ambitious claims. To establish their pertinence it is necessary to take a long view of British perceptions of the French, and in particular of French women, hence the first sections of this chapter serve a largely contextualizing function. I do not, however, regard this as 'secondary' material. The discourses and debates discussed in these sections provide some of the most valuable material that Blake used to construct his poem. Please read on.

## BRITISH PERCEPTIONS OF WOMEN IN PRE-REVOLUTIONARY FRANCE

[The French Nation] gravely exalts those, whom nature has subjected to them, and whose inferiority and infirmities are absolutely incurable. The Women, though without virtue, are their masters and sovereigns [. . .] in all places and all times, the superiority of the females is readily acknowledged and submitted to by everyone, who has the least pretensions to education and politeness.[16]

David Hume, as the quotation above makes quite clear, had little time for eighteenth-century French society, feeling that at its worst it approached an interminable saturnalia – rife with social and especially sexual inversions.[17] He wasn't alone in this view: for most of the century 'foreign observers identified the women of France as a distinct and probably dangerous species' whose excessive influence over all facets of national life was spoiling and softening the social fabric.[18] Racist stereotypes certainly played a part in popularizing this conception[19] but the French themselves also occupied a good deal of their own time in self-chastisement for allowing women such unnatural power, and in lamenting the degrading outcome of this alleged female rule.[20] The virtual deification of Rousseau for the creation of such utterly non-authoritative women as Sophie is an indication of the degree of male anxiety that this supposed female dominance had created.

The idea that all centres of power were being controlled and infected by women often originated in rumours about the purported sway of such figures as Mme de Pompadour and Mme Du Barry[21] over the machinations of the French court, and though these suspicions ran counter to all fact they became extremely deep-rooted. In reality the professionalization and bureaucratization of an increasingly centralized French government meant that it was, during the eighteenth century, effectively masculinized; the only way that women could obtain even a modicum of power was to prostitute themselves, or be prostituted, to the whims of the French king and his ministers (which many evidently did, or were.)[22] Yet though the only arena in French society where women could exercise any kind of autonomous influence without simply indulging in intrigue were the intellectual Salons of Paris[23] the belief grew, as the century wore on, that all the problems of the increasingly distrusted Old Regime were due to women's meddling, and their virtual usurpation of man's right to rule. And the predominance of such notions was not the result of random accident. They gained their pervasive dissemination because they were the staple subtext of the many 'libelles' peddled by the burgeoning ranks of disenchanted underground writers who spread their ribald political theories to all who had an inclination to look and listen (and the number of the interested grew as the century progressed). These works combined aggressive political pornography[24] with strong patriarchal moralizing and generally climaxed in a message that scapegoated the women closest to the King as the malignest influence in the state. Those who'd passed, as the popular phrase had it, 'from the brothel to the throne' (though as Mary Wollstonecraft pointed out the distinction between the two spheres was a very nice one)[25] had destroyed the monarchy by debasing the King. Of Mme de Pompadour – who was known as 'the whore's bastard' – it was said'That low born slut/ Rules him with insolence, / And she's the one who hands out/ Honours for sale' – whilst sympathy was shown towards the displaced monarch: 'Oh, Louis [. . .] At the feet of Pompadour, I've seen your sceptre fall'.[26]

These 'libelles' were, as Robert Darnton has pointed out,[27] a major influence in desacralizing and ultimately destroying the legitimacy of the Old Regime and though such works may seem only to have relevance in discussions of internal French politics, they are in fact of great importance to this investigation of the formation of Blake's ideas about women and political power because a vast number of them were composed and produced in London. Driven out of legitimate publishing circles by state censorship, monopolizing guilds and police control of the visual publishing industry, many of these 'Rousseaus of the gutter' moved to England, eventually forming a sizeable expatriate community. And they were a group it was hard to miss – attracting as they did a following  posse of bizarre French spies (at least one of whom Blake knew personally) and crying to the press about such infringements of their newly obtained British liberty, by these agents of that tyrannizing absolutist state who had pursued them across the channel.[28] And what is perhaps most important to any reader of Blake is that many of these works (often appearing in English too) contained numerous pornographic engravings: hence by the time Blake had qualified as an engraver and was planning to open a print shop this fraternity of smut purveyors was very well-established and seeking skilled workers and outlets for its material. David Erdman marginally notes that 'Blake of Parker and Blake was not above catering to the tastes of print collectors who wanted pretty, sentimental drawing that was mildly erotic and that mirrored current illusions without disturbing them'.[29] He also speaks of the 'decently erotic and discreetly naked Floras and Venuses designed by Stothard and engraved by Blake, for Parker and Blake',[30] but it doesn't seem inappropriate to suggest that he might will have had the opportunity of stocking prints, or perhaps even engraving plates, that were a good deal more explicit and subversive than that. Late-eighteenth-century popular visual culture, which Blake was situated at the heart of, was saturated with sexual and scatological obscenity[31] and the massive French influence within this (especially in the field of political pornography)[32] makes it, I think, fairly likely that Blake was aware of these 'libelles'. If this is a legitimate speculation, then their relevance to this discussion of the sexual politics of Europe/*Europe* cannot be overstated – for not only did they habitually stress the link between political corruption and women's sexuality; they also implied that any expression of female desire was in itself wickedly voracious. 'Women's love' – as far as these London-based libelists were concerned – was perhaps the gravest of all sins, and came high on the list of aristocratic vices that the Revolution must expunge, or at the very least place under imperious control. The apotheosis of these misogynist theories was reached, predictably, in the years of outright revolution, but before we move on to look at the final wave of political pornography which evidentally helped destroy the putatively powerful female rulers of the old order, it is important to see that the paranoia about female power conjured up by these libelists had, illogically enough, deeply negative implications for the political activities of plebeian French women as well.

## SEXUAL POLITICS AND WOMEN'S PROTEST IN REVOLUTIONARY FRANCE

'if the *citoyennes* were allowed to use this meeting room, thirty thousand women might foment disorder in Paris . . .'.[33]

There is uncommon consent amongst historians about the decisive importance of the roles women of the popular classes played in the French Revolution.[34] All agree that in the years 1789–95 women entered onto the public stage to a degree unprecedented in modern history: women's voices were heard in the pre-revolutionary cahiers, women took part in the storming of the Bastille and were murdered with other patriots in the Champs de Mars. Building on ancient subsistence protests, they marched to Versailles to fetch 'the baker' and his family and whenever famine threatened they demanded bread at fair prices with a ferocity unequalled anywhere in the Revolution. During the terror women were amongst the most violent supporters and enforcers of the law of suspects and they fought, beside men, in the revolutionary army. In many ways women *were* the Revolution: not one of the *journées* would have succeeded without them.

Yet there is a paradox, for historians also seem to agree that these actions were not accompanied by any substantial call for women's rights. With the revolutionary establishment ever fearful that politically active women were threatening to trangress natural boundaries, it seems that no widespread feminist consciousness was able to develop.[35] Despite the central roles women played in revolutionary protests, legislators strangely classified them as 'passive' (that is, decidedly second-class) citizens[36] and although the radical changes made in family and inheritance law must not be undervalued Olympe de Gouges was undoubtedly asking the right question when she indignantly addressed her sisters: 'O women, women, when will you stop being so blind? What advantages have you gained from the Revolution?'[37] because they had gained very little indeed.

1793 was the most definitive, and revealing, year of their struggle – for in the confrontations that it witnessed appropriate republican female roles were unequivocally proscribed and the 'libelliste' prejudices of revolutionary men laid bare. In February 1793 the most important of all the female political clubs was formed: the Society of Revolutionary Republican Women. It ensured political effectiveness for the duration of its brief life by creating a working alliance with well-established revolutionary organizations and sections amenable to its activities, that is, those of the most extreme disposition. As a combined force these unflinching Jacobins purged the 'modérantisme' Girondins from the convention and looked with no little optimism to the new leadership. Events in 1793, however, never went smoothly nor took the course anyone expected: by the end of the year all women's clubs were banned and their members shut, conclusively, out of government. Their defeat can be partly explained as the result of the now institutionalized Montagnards' growing hostility to the politics of the vehement *enragés*, whom the Revolutionary Republican women were aligned with, but this is really only half the answer. The other half must be sought amongst the flood of sexist pronouncements on women's political activity unleashed after Charlotte Corday's eye-catching murder of Jean-Paul Marat.[38]

Corday's execution was one of many prominent women in 1793 (Mme Du Barry, Mme Roland, Olympe de Gouges and, of course, Marie Antoinette also met their death that year)[39] and each guillotining presented revolutionary males with the opportunity of reiterating a few republican principles about women's nature and rights. As Linda Kelly explains, 'in the daemonology of the time, sex, or the want of it, was seen to lie behind all female irruptions into public life'[40] and when chastisements were handed out virtue[41] was the key word: the semi-official *Feuille du Salut Public*, extracting its lesson from de Gouges's death, employed just such a emphasis: 'she wished' it ominously warned 'to be a politician and it seems that the law has punished [her] for forgetting the virtues appropriate to her sex', markedly domestic virtues which it did not hesitate to enumerate: 'Women! Do you want to be Républicaines? [. . .] Be simple in your dress, hard-working in your homes, never go to the popular assemblies wanting to speak there. But let your occasional presence there encourage your children. Then *la Patrie* will bless you, for you will have done for it what it has a right to expect of you.[42] The patriarchal motivations behind this statement become even starker when we note that most members of the Society of Revolutionary Republican Women (and indeed most women in Paris) would have fully condemned de Gouges themselves – but the revolutionary establishment now had political women of whatever stripe in its line of fire,[43] and was simply waiting for a chance to act. This opportunity presented itself quickly when members of the Society became involved in violent public scuffles with female market-traders over their resistance to wearing the revolutionary cockade and *bonnet rouge*. An investigation into this clash was ordered and André Amar's report to the Convention on behalf of the Committee of General Security conclusively outlawed all female political activity. Among the key questions which the report addressed were, '(1) Can women exercise political rights and take an active part in affairs of government? (2) Can they deliberate together in political associations or popular societies?' and its answers left no room for doubt, 'With respect to these two questions, the Committee decided in the negative'.[44] There followed a piece of essentialist reasoning which perfectly elaborates the rapidly solidifying ideology of the two spheres (an ideology wholly antithetical to Blake's own 'revolutionary' belief that woman 'knows no fixed lot' (*VDA*: 5:21, E.49)

> the private functions for which women are destined by their very nature are related to the general order of society; this social order results from the differences between man and woman. Each sex is called to the kind of occupation which is fitting for it; its action is circumscribed within this circle which it cannot break through, because nature, which has imposed these limits on man, commands imperiously and receives no law.[45]

Protest against these arguments seemed, and proved, futile – the next time a deputation of women wearing the *bonnet rouge* entered the paris Commune it was met with 'furious hooting in the galleries'[46] – and Chaumette used the same arguments as Amar to ban women from the Commune's sessions: 'The council must recall that some time ago these denatured women, these *viragos*, wandered through the markets with the red cap to sully that badge of liberty and wanted to force all women to take off the modest headdress that is appropriate to them. The place where the people's magistrates deliberate must be forbidden to every person who insults nature'.[47] And from that time forward it was.

Excluding women from the centres of political power did not, however, mean that the republic had no public use for its *citoyennes*. Once excluded from active politics, and as a means of reinforcing and embellishing this exclusion, women were utilized to represent the abstract principles closest to the republic's heart: a host of 'massively passive' goddesses conveyed a double message of revolutionary values and female compliance.[48] The goddess of Reason is the best known of these deities but she was by no means alone – a whole pantheon existed, and were not always approached in a wholly reverential way.[49] A penchant was developed for full-bosomed divinities and as the new revolutionary (pin-up) calendar suggests there were certain forms of titillation that even the most 'virtuous' republic refused to surrender. The most serious message that this iconography had to convey was the now predictable contention that active politics were a task for men alone; and Lynn Hunt has charted how the changing symbolism of 'the republic' can be seen conveying a shift towards this ideology of the separate spheres.[50] By 1793 Liberty had become a figure of splendid power (not unlike the later model popularized by Delacroix in 'Liberty Leading the People') a woman ready to head the charge against the enemies of her nation, and as such notions of women's role in revolutionary politics were becoming more and more unpalatable, measures were soon taken to displace her: just a few days after women's clubs were outlawed David submitted his proposals for the replacement of Liberty by a gargantuan Hercules (resonances of Blake's Orc and his dealings with the Shadowy Female?). Throughout the terror this violently virile male represented the republic, with Liberty relegated to the role of fragile attainment to be defended by the active force of the revolutionary fraternity.[51] By the mid-decade Hercules' image had been softened slightly – he now appeared in domestic contexts, but his was still the ascendant role, dwarfing his defenceless sisters and underlining David's neoclassical ideology of macho republican virtue (an ideology whose tacitly homoerotic aspects deserve much greater study than they have so far received).[52]

Other symbolic roles were also open to women in the French Revolutionary festivals – although as their essential theatricality suggested active engagement in the drama of history, women, as Mona Ozouf explains, were only grudgingly granted a number of limited roles. Domesticity and maternity were the key values, and pregnant women were 'summoned imperiously' to take their place alongside family tableaux based on the pictures of Greuze.[53] When Robespierre took over, this emphasis was maintained: his supreme being was also a supreme patriarch and although he needed no goddess to bolster his authority, festivals in his honour used hordes of women to emblematize familial cohesion. 'Thousands of women took part, emulating the ancient Greeks of Sparta in their religious processions by marching in separate detachments subdivided into group according to familial functions and singing appropriate songs'.[54] Being packaged in this way grossly misrepresented the contribution women had made to the Revolution's success and powerfully demonstrated what Marie-Claire Vallois describes as, 'the violence of the allegorizing process, that transforms the living into the eternal and abstract'.[55] It also circumscribed acceptable female behaviour within oppressively narrow parameters. However, when compared with the fate of their aristocratic sisters, being converted into a suckling Sophie[56] or the goddess of Reason begins to look a highly attractive option. When faced with women of the people, the new revolutionary patriarchy could achieve its aim of control through enforcing a rigid ideology of motherhood and domesticity. When facing up to the challenge which they believed that elite women posed, however, nothing short of death would suffice. Their corrupting presence had to be erased from the pages of the nation's history, for a new epoch had begun.

As we saw, aristocratic French women were, in the pre-revolutionary period, taken as raw material which the virulent imaginations of the libelists worked up into misogynist parables aimed at undermining the now illegitimate, because allegedly emasculated, Old Regime. These works were exported across the channel and if they managed to avoid the censor[57] found an audience amongst a growing number of discontented French subjects. When the Revolution came, however, these writers immediately returned home and instigated a veritable cultural revolution: men like Brissot and Marat became admired political heroes and found numerous legitimate outlets through which to broadcast their still vituperative messages.[58] And the impact of their works was stark, indeed terrifying. Claude Langlois has remarked that 'Truly, during the revolution ridicule killed' and Peter Wagner takes up the same point: 'it is remarkable that, when the forces of revolution finally struck, sexual atrocities committed especially against the [female] nobility seem to have been inspired by sinister and malicious allegations from political pornography, which had harped in particular on the sexual perversions of the mighty'[59] (my addition). The first example Wagner takes up is especially relevant to this discussion as the Princess Lamballe – who was raped by a gang of soldiers before having her breasts and pudenda cut off and paraded around the city – suffered this fate largely because of her close, reputedly lesbian, relationship with Marie Antoinette[60] (who, horrifically, also had to endure the grisly sight of her friend's severed head, thrust against her prison window). Of all the eighteenth-century French women who were sexually reviled, in both France and England, none attracted the quantity of abuse levelled at the queen and as I shall proceed to argue that Blake makes direct reference to her fate in *Europe*, it is necessary to look at Marie Antoinette's biography (both mythic and literal) in some detail.

## MARIE ANTOINETTE: QUEEN OF THE 'HEAVENS OF EUROPE'

'the greatest of all the joys of the Père Duchesne, (was) having with his own eyes seen the head of the female veto separated from her fucking tart's neck'
>                    Jacques René Hébert reporting the death of
>                    Marie Antoinette.[61]

In the years leading up to the Revolution Marie Antoinette was converted into 'the personification of political misrule' and through this packaging of her as 'First errant wife, then intriguer, and adulteress and finally murderous Austrian wolf' she became the leading character in the eighteenth-century's greatest patriarchal moral fable.[62] This story found its conclusion with, 'the figure of Marie Antoinette [. . .] transfigured into that of the Queen of the Night, the very embodiment of all that the nation . . . [had] become obsessed with destroying',[63] and though this is not the occasion for a pseudo-chivalric defence of Marie Antoinette's character it must be initially noted that the construction of this tale – which I shall sketch out in a moment – demanded a good deal of economy with the truth. The most obvious falsehood (and the one central to Blake's revision of the story) was that this shadowy French female was portrayed as an entirely omnipotent despot when, as Nancy Davenport has noted, the reality of her influence was much less absolutist than that: 'if politics as it has been said, "in a sense has always been a con game", Marie Antoinette [though] often a player, seems never to have controlled her card's (my addition).[64] In fact she was never dealt a very good hand: stripped of her clothing on an island in the Rhine and delivered naked to the French[65] as a hostage to a treaty made between two traditional enemies (the Bourbons and the Habsburgs) in an attempt to check the power of Frederick of Prussia, Marie Antoinette started her adult life with scarcely any power over her own body let alone over the destiny of France. High treason she was certainly guilty of (though having been prostituted to the French under the above treaty her assiduous communications with the republic's enemies should perhaps be seen as a duty well performed) but it says something for her reading of the political situation that she realized that the monarchy was in peril in 1789. If Louis XVI had listened to her early entreaties that they flee the country he would probably have kept his head – though not, of course, his crown. Such speculations are not, however, the subject of this discussion – what most concerns me is to investigate the instrumental role that the notion 'Woman's love is Sin!' (*Europe*, 5:5; E.62) played in Marie Antoinette's downfall.

The circumstance that first called Marie Antoinette's reputation into question was her failure to conceive a child, and though the responsibility for this rested solely with the King and his unfortunate phymosis, much of the pamphleteering nastiness that ran riot centred upon the remedies which the queen was supposedly taking to compensate for her marital disappointments. Given that after three years of marriage Marie Antoinette was only able tentatively to confide to her mother, 'I think our marriage has been consummated'[66] any alleged infidelity would not, perhaps, be wholly censurable but whatever the justification, or even whether any adulterous activity actually took place, made no difference in the mind of her critics. She had been given the

chance to cuckold her husband and it was indicative of dominant beliefs about women's deceptiveness and insatiability that
everyone assumed that given this chance she would naturally
have taken it. The event that really damned the queen in the
nation's mind, however, was the Diamond Necklace Affair[67] and
although it was conclusively proved that she'd been as much a
dupe as the Cardinal de Rohan, the show-trial set up to investigate the scandal provoked the writings which conclusively sealed
Marie Antoinette's fate. In the speculations that followed she was
accused of having sexual liaisons with no less than 34 named
persons[68] and this voracious libido was taken to be indicative of
her attitude towards the nation as a whole: to fulfil her monstrous appetites Marie Antoinette would consume anything she
could lay her hands on, including the nation's coffers. And it
must be re-emphasized that it was not simply elite sexual over-
indulgence that was being objected to and turned into a metaphor for the pillaging of the nation – it was energetic *female* activity,
for the men of the French royal family found their reputations
were generally improved by reports of sexual excesses, however
sordid they may be.[69]

The Diamond Necklace affair started the literary avalanche:
after this there was such avid interest that best-sellers like the
*Essai Historique sur la vie de Marie Antoinette* was published with
yearly revisions to take account of the queens 'new conquests',
and so prolific were libelists on this topic that vendors could
actually specialize in works on the queen.[70] These pamphlets were
not only explicit and malicious (though they were always that),
they also conveyed the kind of political parable I discussed earlier: Louis XVI had been deceived, his wife had usurped his role.
In this heavily visual culture[71] numerous caricatures took up the
story, telling people that whilst the king was at worst a glutton-
ous fool his wife was a principle of active evil (likened to everyone from Judas to Pandora) who had infantilized the king and
seized control of the state.[72] The inscription that accompanies
one particular engraving which depicts Marie Antoinette as an
orgiast illustrates this very well: the king dozes on his throne
whilst the semi-reptilian queen snatches his rod of office: 'A people
is without honour and deserves its chains/ When it stoops beneath the sceptre of queens'.[73] Marie Antoinette's lusts, then, had
disastrously upset governance of the state – the nation was being debased and she must be dealt with.

Elizabeth Colwill has traced the methods employed to deal with this 'favourite revolutionary anti-hero' by one of the most popular sans-culottes newspapers, Hébert's *Le Père Duchesne*, and it's worth looking at her account in a little detail.[74] From the beginning Marie Antoinette acted as a 'scapegoat for France's difficulties', being blamed, as we noted earlier, for feminizing government.[75] She also served as a living call for the reassertion of masculine political authority, and in the early years it was clear that if the king would just behave like a 'man' the constitutional monarchy might yet remain:

> Sire, I speak to you in friendship: believe me, we never let ourselves be led around by our wives. I have one who is sweet as a lamb, because, *foutre*, I always showed her the fist when she wanted to play the mistress. It's even more deadly if a king lets himself be governed by women. Women have caused throughout time the misfortunes of France [. . .] Remember the hideous reign of the Medicis; recall Henri IV always ready to do some stupidity for his mistress [. . .] Tell your wife you took her to breed your children not to mix in the affairs of state and turn your kingdom upside down. Among your people, these people who adore you, you will find security.[76]

As Colwill elaborates, Hébert's strategy was to turn Marie Antoinette into 'Just Another *Citoyenne*', and to imply that she'd never have become such a pestilential influence if the king had been as potent as the men of the people. The key subtext to this was that the queen had got a very wrong idea about her sexuality, and one of the main methods Hébert suggested to displace her from her illegitimately dominant position was to, crudely, screw her back into her rightful place.[77] The scenario presented in a typical work from 1792 demonstrates this admirably: Marie Antoinette is followed through the usual night of lust – indulging herself first with LaFayette, then the Princess Lamballe and finally the King; but the pamphlet tells us, something is missing from each encounter. This something – fear – is eventually supplied by the Chambermaid's plebeian lover, as the queen exclaims: 'I have never been screwed better [. . .] At the sight of his enormous organ I was truly filled with fright'.[78] Louis XVI's impotence (both literal and metaphorical) had allowed the queen to misapprehend the nature of her sexuality: firstly, she'd for-

1. Title-page to *The Book of Thel*

2. Title-page to *Visions of the Daughters of Albion*

3. 'The Able Doctor, or America swallowing the Bitter Draught' (1774)

4.  *Europe – A Prophecy* (Plate 5(6))

The shrill winds wake !
Till all the sons of Urizen look out and envy Los:
Sieze all the spirits of life and bind
Their warbling joys to our loud strings
Bind all the nourishing sweets of earth
To give us bliss, that we may drink the sparkling wine of Los
And let us laugh at war,
Despising toil and care,
Because the days and nights of joy, in lucky hours renew.

Arise O Orc from thy deep den,
First born of Enitharmon rise !
And we will crown thy head with garlands of the ruddy vine ;
For now thou art bound ;
And I may see thee in the hour of bliss, my eldest born.

The horrent Demon rose, surrounded with red stars of fire,
Whirling about in furious circles round the immortal fiend.

Then Enitharmon down descended into his red light
And thus her voice rose to her children, the distant heavens reply.

5.   *Europe – A Prophecy* (Plate 6(7))

6.  *Europe – A Prophecy* (Plate 7(8))

Shot from the heights of Enitharmon;
And in the vineyards of red France appear'd the light of his fury.

The sun glow'd fiery red!
The furious terrors flew around!
On golden chariots raging, with red wheels dropping with blood;
The Lions lash their wrathful tails!
The Tigers couch upon the prey & suck the ruddy tide:
And Enitharmon groans & cries in anguish and dismay.

Then Los arose his head he reard in snaky thunders clad:
And with a cry that shook all nature to the utmost pole,
Call'd all his sons to the strife of blood.

FINIS

7.   *Europe – A Prophecy* (Plate 17(18))

8.  'The Contrast' (1792/3)

gotten the pleasures of fear and second, she'd forgotten that its main function was to produce children for her husband. Marie Antoinette had, in short, become a bad wife and mother and this is, essentially, what she stood trial for.[79]

Though clearly guilty of high treason, answering this charge was not the centre of her trial. The event's real climax came with the distasteful claim that the queen had committed acts of incest with the eight-year-old Dauphin. As Colwill explains the queen stood, 'accused and convicted of embodying all that women should not be. Beneath the final charge of conspiracy lay covert accusations of adultery, home-breaking and infanticide.' Her trial was indeed a, 'watershed in the ideology of womanhood [. . .] In killing the wicked witch, the republic had given birth to the good daughter.'[80] The parable, then, was complete and as we've seen, Pére Duchesne rubbed his hands, although even on her death the queen displeased him, showing not quite enough of that essential quality – fear: 'The bitch was audacious and insolent right to the very end. However, her legs failed her at the moment of being tipped over to shake the hot hand'.[81]

What most shocks me about all these accounts of Marie Antoinette's fate is the intensity of the visceral male hatred directed towards her. Whereas women of all political orientations (and as we'll see nationalities too) were able to acknowledge, and even respect, the queen's courage and final dignity, men seemed bent on sexual humiliation. Events that took place on the day of her execution vividly capture this dichotomy and the account of Rosalie Lamorlière, the servant who tended Marie Antoinette in prison, is especially powerful. Lamorlière came to consider her 'the best and most unfortunate queen' and pleaded that she be allowed to dress herself in private for her journey to the guillotine. Her male guard, however, was unwilling to grant even this small gesture of humanity and hence stood by and watched as Marie Antoinette removed the blood-stained rags which Lamorlière had smuggled in to staunch the flow of the vaginal haemorrhaging which had beset the queen throughout her final days.[82] This truly was, as Jacques Revel describes it, a 'staging of hatred'[83] and we will shortly examine the very different motives that direct Blake's treatment of the queen and the life of her body.

## BRITISH PERCEPTIONS OF WOMEN IN REVOLUTIONARY FRANCE

The preceding pages may seem to have been a continental diversion but they deal with a context well worth sketching because the British imbibed so many French ideas about the effect of women upon public and political life. Throughout the French Revolution any interested British observer – obviously including Blake himself – could obtain a vast amount of information about affairs in France; there was much traffic in both people and ideas between the two countries[84] and rapid reporting of practically every event, often in great detail. Both the *Universal* and *Gentleman's* magazines, for example, made a regular feature of printing extensive extracts from the minutes of the French national convention and publishers' advertisements were full of books on related topics. Most interesting of all was the way in which magazines, most importantly the *Bon Ton*, elected to chronicle events in an overtly sexualized way.[85] And it's to these British interpretations that I now turn.

Disinterested reporting was, of course, an impossibility and it's in the subtexts and vicissitudes of British (especially visual) propaganda that we find the most vital intertexts for Blake's *Europe*. Visual media deserve special attention because, as David Bindman explains, 'Almost all the main events of the French Revolution were given visual form in low quality engravings within weeks of their occurrence', and as Dorothy George's magisterial study shows: 'English impressions of the French Revolution must have been largely coloured by the print-shops. The caricatures – French as well as English – were almost the only rapid pictorial reactions to events in France.'[86] This was, after all, the 'Golden Age' of English Caricature – during the 1790s there were no less than 71 shops or related merchandising operations attempting to do business in London.[87] Blake said he could remember when a printshop was a 'rare bird' but observed to Cumberland that this time was passed (E.706), and it certainly was: caricature was everywhere. Comic strips were produced to decorate wainscoting, illuminated transparencies filled the windows of the shops and Rudolph Ackerman even developed a parachute for aerial distribution of broadsides. Things were also happening on a theoretical level: in 1788 Francis Grose brought out the first systematic instruction book on the subject, *Rules for Drawing Caricature*; by

1791 it was into its second edition, and caricature transparencies formed the basis of popular lectures.

In short you could not help but *see* the revolution and amongst the very first images were vivid depictions of the vociferous French women who marched to Versailles: W. Dent's, 'Female Furies or Extraordinary Revolution' (18 October 1789) and, 'Le Roi Esclave ou les Sujets Rois Female Patriotism' probably by Isaac Cruikshank (31 October 1789) are two fairly typical examples.[88] Neither is particularly sympathetic to the royal family (early prints generally weren't) and the second is of most interest as it not only shows French women insisting that they can fire the cannon as well as their male compatriots but also because it is an English depiction that holds Marie Antoinette responsible for the royal family's vulnerability: 'Oh my wife' exclaims the king 'what have you done?', and whereas he's the 'baker' being returned to Paris the queen is more bluntly referred to as 'the butcheress'. Such suspicion, and indeed outright hostility, were – as Dorothy George notes[89] – characteristic, as British caricaturists showed just how many French stereotypes they had assimilated: as early as 1783 Marie Antoinette was appearing in England amongst women of reputedly loose morals. In 'The Ladies Churchyard', of September 1783 she is shown as a possible future lover of the Prince of Wales – lying in a grave that bears the inscription, 'Death has placed her on her Rump to play her cards Till the Last Trump!' and in the slightly later, 'The Commercial Treaty; or, John Bull Changing Beef and Pudding for Frogs and Soup Maigre!' (November 1786) – a woman who can only be Marie Antoinette is shown dressed in an 'appropriate' recent fashion: with projected bust and 'derrière'.[90]

Evidence that many British observers also saw Marie Antoinette as the holder of illegitimate governmental power can be found in political caricatures too: W. Dent's 'Revolution, or Johnny Bull in France' (25 July 1789)[91] demonstrates this: here the symbol of English freedom (who the author approvingly finds on the rampage in France) is seen tossing Marie Antoinette in the air, causing her clothes to fly up – much to the amusement of the assembled soldiery, whilst Louis XVI is allowed to retain his crown for the small price of kneeling before this representative of the people's power. The anonymous, '*La Chute du Despotisme*/The Downfall of Despotism' (August 1789) and Gillray's 'The Offering to Liberty' (August 1789) make much the same point.[92] Louis XVI is believed to be fairly amiable and amenable to change whilst Marie Antoinette remains a defiant figure of the old regime – associated with torture and the setting sun of political tyranny.

These negative conceptualizations were dominant in both written and visual media until around June 1791 (with the vital exception of Edmund Burke's passionate depiction which will be discussed in some detail later). The foiling of the royal family's attempt to escape to Varennes was something of a watershed and was taken up immediately by numerous popular caricaturists.[93] Of these prints perhaps the most interesting is Thomas Rowlandson's 'The Grand Monarch Discovered in a Pot de Chambre Or The Royal Fugitives Turning Tail' (June 1791).[94] This is especially noteworthy because it suggests that Hébert's obscene discourse had crossed the Channel too: as the soldier who has halted their flight issues a threat, Marie Antoinette screams *'Nous Sommes tous foutus'* (we're all fucked up). Père Duchesne couldn't have put it better himself and the influence of political pornography is unmistakable here – though it's worth noting that British works were rarely as vicious as those produced by the French.

So a new trend had begun, and with the imprisonment of the royal family, the French republic's declaration that it desired to export revolution across the world and a war looking more and more likely, reactionary propaganda began to predominate in England. Moreover, although French women continued to be central in prints and poems, the messages conveyed after 1792 were of a more hysterical kind. Now fears about French sexual laxity and perversion remained a constant, with conservatives quick to endorse William Thomas Fitzgerald's assessment that Paris was 'The doom'd Gomorrah of our modern times!'[95] The republic's legalizing of divorce also seemed to give great substance to these fears, fears cultivated in reactionary propaganda. Hannah More's character Tom explains to his friend who is flirting with French ideas that under their system a man can lose his wife over 'any little tiff'.[96] The sexual politics of this statement are extremely important for it wasn't missed by English observers that it was French women who were taking the greatest advantage of this legislative innovation.

During the 1790s, however, something was added to the usual sexual fears raised by war. Invasion and the violation of women are always present and certainly featured in numerous popular ballads[97] but what's vital is that the danger represented by revolutionary France is predominantly conceptualized not as a threat to women but as a threat *from* them. As John Brewer explains the,

> nightmare world, summoned up by Burke, luridly described in popular pamphlets and graphically portrayed by Gillray, is grotesque. It deviates from the natural order, breaking down categories which distinguish masters from men, men from women, and human from animal forms. In counter-revolutionary propaganda the Jacobins are women, simian creatures or wolves. Paris women are depicted as the most furious and blood-thirsty revolutionaries [. . .] Their conduct means that times are out of joint, that authority has collapsed and family life been destroyed. Medea, the murderer of her brother, Pandora, who loosed chaos on the world; the furies: these are the prototypes of revolutionary women.[98]

It should not surprise us, then, to discover that the design which was probably disseminated most widely in the anti-radical campaign sets up a stark opposition between French and British versions of womanhood. 'The Contrast'[99] opposes British Liberty to the French version by embodying each quality in a female figure: on the British side we see Britannia serenely seated under the stately oak, swathed in symbols of British justice. On the French side is Medusa, rampaging across the corpse of a decapitated man. In her right hand she holds a trident, which extends from the man's groin, upon which she has impaled his head between two hearts. Behind her hangs another male figure, this time dangling limply from a lampstand. The Crown and Anchor Society, who intended this print to be sold by the hundreds, clearly found French women a very specific, and a very great, threat. And they certainly weren't alone in this. David Punter, in his discussion of 'The Sex of Revolution' (1982), also finds evidence of a lurking fear that a precariously maintained British masculinity may be in danger, and in Coleridge's 1791 poem 'Happiness' we see a fine example of this – unbridled desire is a revolutionary force bringing transient bliss but lasting woe, and the diseases that follow 'her' deceptive visitation have 'harpy fangs'.[100] As Punter notes the 'key fear is sexual excess'[101] and it was not just amongst those poets who've been selected for

canonization that this anxiety existed. Betty Bennett, in her collection of popular 'Romantic' war verse, also finds oppositions
set up between French and English women and portrayals of
figures strikingly similar to 'The Contrast's' Medusa. The song
'Church and King' (sung to the tune of *Rule Britannia*) contains
this image: 'while O'er the bleeding corpse of France/ Wild
Anarchy exalting stands,/ And Female fiends around her dance,/
With fatal *Lamp-cords* in their hands'. 'Poor France' according to
this work is 'By too much liberty undone; *Defeat* is better than
excess./ For, having *all*–is having *none*' – and its opposition between freedom as a 'temperate treat' and 'savage mirth and frantic
noise' bringing the 'fever that destroys' has quite obvious sexual
connotations.[102] Indeed the sexual ideology embodied here is much
akin to the kind of restraining advice we saw earlier in our discussion of *Visions*, and has little to do with Blake's commitment
to an eroticized sensual liberty which – as we shall see – finds
its apotheosis in triumphant female orgasm. At the time Blake
was composing and writing *Europe*, then, French women were
seen as a murderous erotic force set to overwhelm British manhood and corrupt the daughters of Albion with their 'sinful'
understandings of 'woman's love'. Fear of the (im)moral Jacobinism
they represented reached its peak at the century's end in the
numerous warnings issued by the *Anti-Jacobin Magazine* (although
any investigation of that fascinating publication is, sadly, a little
outside the parameters of the present discussion).[103]

This didn't mean, however, that the British gave up on French
women entirely – just as the revolutionaries got to work fashion-
ing republican motherhood to redeem its *citoyennes*, the British
conservatives set about the parallel but reverse task of trans-
forming Marie Antoinette from sneered-at court voluptuary into
a symbol of virtuous (this time aristocratic) motherhood.[104] The
most outrageously sentimental paintings and prints of her last
interview with Louis XVI predominated and by the time Marie
Antoinette was hauled onto the guillotine, she had been meta-
morphosed into nothing less than a royalist martyr, delivering
anguished maternal pleas from the scaffold.[105] Charlotte Corday
was also enthusiastically snatched as a figure to be set against
the feared female furies, although the daring and decidedly suggestive nature of her crime made Corday a slightly tricky heroine. Of the many prints that depicted her murder of Marat, a
number omitted to disclose that this young woman had pen-

etrated the flesh of a senior revolutionary patriarch as he lay naked in his bath-tub.[106]

It is clear then that British conceptualizations and interpretations of affairs in France were overtly sexualized or, as a bid to contain this, unconvincingly sanitized. To be 'Frenchified' meant in the 1790s to be 'Infected with the venereal disease'[107] and it's to Blake's negotiations with this idea of corruption and infection that I now turn.

## THE WOMEN IN BLAKE'S EUROPE/*EUROPE*

As my preliminary discussion has demonstrated, Blake produced *Europe – A Prophecy* in an environment alive with fearful and proscriptive ideas about women and the implications of their sexuality. Both English and French men seemed to have suffered anxiety over the maintenance of masculine authority, and both groups saw women's unpredictable and tyrannous erotic energy as a threat to the stability of the state (be it the constitutional monarchy of George III or the Virtuous republic of Maximilien Robespierre). Unrestrained women – whether aristocratic or plebeian – were identified as the root of all social evils and the channel through which they exercised this polluting prerogative was sexual: in the 1790s 'woman's love', however you looked at it, was 'sin'. And given the failure of past writers on Blake to pay any attention to this aspect of his historical context, just sketching it in is – I think – of value. But I hope to do more than that: in the rest of this chapter I will try to argue that Blake's *Europe* is an idiosyncratic but nonetheless indisputable critique of his contemporaries'ideas about women, their sexuality and political power. The tone appropriate to the second half of this discussion is speculative but I feel it is useful to suggest that the contexts I've tried to outline provided most of the materials which Blake's inimitable imagination worked up into *Europe – A Prophecy*.

Blake's first affront to the dominant ideas I have outlined was to render his contemporaries' contentions about women's power and culpability deeply illogical: he reminded them of the existence of patriarchy. Also, and as a reinforcing rider to this, he stresses that sexual perversity is by no means the exclusive province of women, or indeed of the feminine imagination. These issues are addressed in the frontispiece and the 'fairy poem' respectively.

The frontispiece of *Europe* (*Illuminated*, E.156) is probably the best known of all Blake's visual images and it is generally taken to be a frightening yet majestic depiction of 'God the Father' creating the world. If we remove the idea of reverence from this conception, 'common-knowledge' is correct: *Europe*'s frontispiece is an archetypal image of patriarchal power[108] and the primary place it has within this poem clearly indicates that Blake hadn't accepted the popular myth that women reigned in the heavens of *Europe*/Europe. Furthermore his act of 'creation' is one of unequivocal constriction. In contrast to the furiously prolific Shadowy Female and the ambiguous form-giving Enitharmon, this Urizenic God simply sets limits. Beyond satire the image certainly is, beyond culpability for the imprisonment of humanity's sensual existence he is not. The essentially phallocentric nature of European struggle is further underlined by the oppositional title page (*Illuminated*; E.157) where Urizen's coiled adversary is an enormous serpent 'Embodying energy, desire, phallic power'.[109] His dominance over women is made even more clear in one of the prototype versions of the plate (*Illuminated*; E.398) where two females appear dwarfed by his snaky bulk. One lies outstretched against it in seeming prayer and another is crushed, as he bears down upon her loins (Erdman suggests that she is probably 're-ceiving his weight with pleasure'[110] but that, of course, is a matter of personal judgement).

The issue of sexual perversity – perhaps even sadism – is taken up in the bizarre 'fairy' poem which acts as a prefatory pointer in two of the 12 known copies of *Europe*. Carole Kowle has argued convincingly for the importance of the fragment as a key to understanding the later sections of the poem, stressing in particular the linking theme of sensual constriction and the importance of human wilfulness in bringing this about.[111] What most needs highlighting, however, is that the climax of Blake's portrait of the 'cavern'd Man' (*Europe*, iii:1; E.60) focuses upon a specifically male refusal to enter eternity through 'an improvement of sensual enjoyment' (*MHH*, 14; E.39). Line 5 is not simply a picture of *human* perversity but rather is an account of male refusal to joyously ejaculate: 'Thro' one, *himself* pass out what time *he* please, but *he* will not'[112] (*Europe*, iii:5; E.60 – my emphasis); and the male fairy's appropriation of Proverbs ix, 13–18 which warns of the shadowy female who teaches that, 'stolen joys are sweet, & bread eaten in secret pleasant' (*Europe*, iii:6;

E.60) again reinforces this important point. Indeed, the whole tone of this singular framing poem demands comment, for what we seem to see is Blake and his miscreant creation engage in a bout of homosocial flirtation: with this 'small Sir' expressing mock fear at being possessed: 'My master. I am yours. Command me, for I must obey' (*Europe*, iii:10, 12; E.60) and soon after asking laughingly to be fed on 'love-thoughts' (*Europe*, iii:15; E.60). The encounter has a darker side too, because Blake and the fairy are, as Brenda Webster notes, like two naughty schoolboys – practising small-scale meannesses such as knocking down butterflies and more importantly undertaking the sexually sadistic act of plucking the eternal flowers so as to take pleasure from their whimpering (*Europe*, iii:20–21; E.60).[113] Most critics, like Harold Bloom, find the poem 'charming', considering it an evocation of the world of innocence[114] but the activities of Blake and the Fairy could not be further from the ethos of *Songs* . . . – no child there would ever ill-treat even the smallest insect and more importantly such glossing fails to pay attention to where this youthful male cruelty leads. On Plate 7 of Blake's *For Children: The Gates of Paradise* (1793), the knocking down of female spirits with a boy's hat is seen as tantamount to murder – leading Blake to exclaim upon women's christ-like endurance of such commonplace brutality: 'Alas! the Female Martyr – Is She also the Divine Image' (E.263).[115]

The fairy and the poet, then, are prototypical spectres (James Swearingen's recent adoration of the creature really must be questioned)[116] and their plucking of the eternal flowers simply to watch them suffer – unlike Oothoon's roughly contemporaneous gesture of lovingly placing a plucked flower to 'glow between my breasts' (*VDA*, 1:12; E.46) – must alert us to the slant such impish misogyny could have on the poem that follows. *Europe*'s 'Fairy poem' is surely the strangest framing device in Blake's poetry and though I wouldn't want to offer this gendered account as the only reason for its inclusion, I think it is valid to suggest that we must be alert to the sexist bravado and patriarchal nuance that any work dictated by this creature would have. Though, as ever with Blake, at least two voices will be present – for the poet is also still slightly intoxicated by the incense of the female victims (*Europe*, iii:22, E.60).

As we can see, then, the 'Fairy poem' is both a self-contained cameo and a valuable indicator of a number of themes which will be taken up in later sections and it is important to any understanding of the poem to read each of its five segments in this way: as autonomous yet sharing related themes. As this is the case, I will proceed to look at each section in turn – trying both to tease out some kind of narrative whilst simultaneously respecting the integrity of each portion. *Europe*'s 'Preludium' takes up the story of the nameless shadowy female which was started in *America*. In that poem she was raped by the 'hairy youth' Orc (*America*, 1:11; E.51) and is now desperately vulnerable and afflicted with ceaseless generativity: 'My roots are brandish'd in the heavens. My fruits in earth beneath/Surge, foam, and labour into life, first born & first consum'd!/Consumed and consuming! (*Europe*, 1:8–10; E.60). David Erdman seeks to canvass the theory that Orc will eventually be her saviour – rather nonchalantly explaining that she is, 'still somewhat pestiferous because Orc has not yet fulfilled his dragon-slaying, harvest-saving mission'[117] – but this is a serious misreading expressing a faith in male revolutionaries that Blake himself seems not to have possessed. The Shadowy Female's complaint does not, after all, protest about the slowness of this second coming but rather centres upon why Orc ever had to 'come' at all.[118] Having endured one visit from the 'spirit of revolution' she exclaims anxiously, 'O mother Enitharmon wilt thou bring forth other sons?', which is a question generated by her fear that their arrival will blot out her independent existence: 'To cause my name to vanish, that my place may not be found' (*Europe*, 1:4–5; E.60). This Thel-like[119] worry that masculinist revolutionary action will obliterate her female autonomy was, as we saw earlier, confirmed in the fate of active women in the French Revolution and it is interesting that the historically specific illuminations which accompany the Preludium contain only male political actors.[120]

She is, however, like the French women whom she is some way symbolizes, by no means a powerless or defeatist figure. Diana Hume George designates her a 'helpless, blameless urge'[121] but this robs the shadowy female of her vigorous efforts at self-amelioration:

> I wrap my turban of thick clouds around my lab'ring head;
> And fold the sheety waters as a mantle round my limbs [. . .]
> Unwilling I look up to heaven! unwilling count the stars!
> Sitting in fathomless abyss of my immortal shrine.
> I seize their burning power
>
> (*Europe*, 1–2:12–13, 1–3; E.61)

yet the problem is that her labours simply perpetuate an old and, so far, unfruitful dialectic: 'And bring forth howling terrors, all devouring fiery kings' (*Europe*, 2:4; E.61). Orc and Urizen appear again and again – 'terror' and 'king' – locked together in seemingly endless male power struggles.

The figure whom the shadowy female chooses, in some senses, to blame for her situation is Enitharmon – the poem's central character and a female universally despised by Blake critics as either an 'insidiously repressive mother' or a 'domineering spouse'.[122] Such claims have little validity in this section, though, where Enitharmon's actions are prompted by only admirable motives: she wants to curtail her daughter's endless productivity by giving form to the shadowy female's 'vig'rous progeny of fires' (*Europe*, 2:8; E.61). Though Enitharmon stamps the 'myriads of flames' with a Bromion-like 'signet' this at least gives them enough definition to 'roam abroad' (*Europe*, 2:9–10, E.61). It is an act of liberation not possession. It does not however ameliorate the situation and the shadowy female is ultimately left, despite all her efforts, 'void as death' (*Europe*, 2:11; E.61). The overall message of the Preludium seems to be that these two women are caught up in a process in which they have indispensable roles but over which they have no control: their lot is to be 'drown'd in shady woe' without enjoying even a moment of 'visionary joy' (*Europe*, 2:12; E.61). It would be labouring the point to do more than note how suggestively this links with the historical details which I sketched out earlier, and what perhaps is most depressing about the end of this section is that the shadowy female returns to precisely the situation where she started in *America* . 'She ceast & rolld her shady clouds/Into the secret place' (*Europe*, 2:17–18; E.61 and see *America*, 1:7; E.51). If this poem contains any kind of historical allegory, Blake's assessment of women's fate in the European struggles of his day is one with which most twentieth-century feminist historians would concur.

The third section of *Europe*, composed of Plates 3–8, is the most complicated to interpret. We do, however, have one connection with the preceding fragment and this provides a small clue to the segment's meaning: the important birth which the shadowy female had despaired of ever seeing seems to be occurring now (though she's evidently disappeared) and as the chimes with Milton's 'On the Morning of Christ's Nativity' indicate, the

appearance of this secret child is an event with world-historical
significance.[123] Its immediate effects are obvious: the child's birth
seems to have brought unexpected tranquillity, both to the shadowy female's agonizing fecundity and to the sexual and male
power struggles described earlier:

War ceas'd, & all the troops like shadows fled to their abodes.
Then Enitharmon saw her sons & daughters rise around.
Like pearly clouds they meet together in the crystal house.

(*Europe*, 3:3–6; E.61)

Of equal significance is that Los and Enitharmon seem to have
instituted a harmonious conjugal relationship to accompany their
children's unity: 'And Los, possessor of the moon, joy'd in the
peaceful night' (*Europe*, 3:7; E.61). A number of Blake critics have
suggested that this bliss lasts only momentarily because Los's
failure to dominate indicates a 'regressive abdication of [. . .] adult
masculinity'[124] but the more obvious fracturer of their peaceful
joy seems to be Los's need to crow over his achievement of it.
Rather than acknowledging the grave importance of Orc's peace-
bringing birth Los instead spends his time drawing attention to
his own role in it: 'Again' he says (robbing the event of its unique
significance) 'the night is come/ That strong Urthona takes his
rest' (*Europe*, 3:9–10; E.61) and having thus referred to himself
rather pompously by his eternal/unfallen name Los goes on to
note not the arrival of Orc but the meteoric glowing of the newly
released Urizen. Los, in fact, destroys the peace, goading the Sons
of Urizen to 'Stretch forth your hands and strike the elemental
strings!/ Awake the thunders of the deep' (*Europe*, 3:13–14; E.61),
which is a challenge Urizen's male offspring are, of course, only
too ready to take up.

There is much critical debate about who the speakers of the
next 14 lines are[125] and though I have yet to encounter any reading that matches mine I think it is consonant with the tone and
themes of the poem to argue that what we see here are the Sons
of Urizen and Los joining together in a mockery of, and triumph
over, the bound Orc. Plate 4 begins with a narrator setting the
scene: 'The shrill winds wake!/ Till all the sons of Urizen look
out and envy Los' (*Europe*, 4:1–2; E.62). We then receive an account of their reaction to Los and Enitharmon's, however transitory, erotic unity;[126] behaving absolutely in character, Urizen's

sons decide that they can achieve this kind of relationship through acts of brutalizing violence:

> Seize all the spirits of life and bind
> Their warbling joys to our loud strings
> Bind all the nourishing sweets of earth
>
> To give us bliss, that we may drink the sparkling wine of Los
>
> (*Europe*, 4:3–6; E.62)

Their method for achieving peace is simply to deny the reality of conflict: 'And let us laugh at war,/ Despising toil and care,/ Because the days and nights of joy, in lucky hours renew.' (*Europe*, 4:7–9; E.62). The Sons of Urizen also, I think, speak the next four lines – feeling that Orc's presence (in his guise as the 'secret child') is not necessary for their attainment of joy and peace (that is, they don't need a saviour) they go on to mock him. The allusions to the humiliation of Christ are clear, though it is safe to bait Orc not because he is committed to turning the other cheek, but only because he is so firmly chained. Their taunting revolves around this fact:

> Arise O Orc from the deep den,
> First born of Enitharmon rise!
> And we will crown thy head with garlands of the ruddy vine;
> For now thou art bound;
>
> (*Europe*, 4:10–13; E.62)

And Los, who has been silently observing all that his initial goadings prompted, now finishes the section, admitting that he too can accept his son whilst he is bound: 'And I may see thee in the hour of bliss, my eldest born' (*Europe*, 4:14; E.62).

I have spent some time expounding this reading, which effectively refutes the standard idea that Enitharmon taunts Orc, because I think it is vital to do away with the conventional opposition between these two figures – an opposition proferred (though for very different reasons) by both Marxist and archetypal critics and one which rests upon the notion that, 'Enitharmon (is), a malignant queen of heaven [. . .] (who) has bound Orc and kept him secret in order to enslave mankind'.[127] As Kowle's statement demonstrates, readings of this kind create a despotic female figurehead who is blamed for all the abuses of what is in fact a male-run system [Enitharmon is assailed whilst Urizen rules]. Something of this sort, as we saw, happened in eighteenth-century France and it is through the figure of Enitharmon that Blake, I believe, enters most directly into a discussion of women's roles and fate in the French Revolution.

The first place to turn for evidence of this is to the designs on Plates 3–5 (*Illuminated*; E.161–3). These illuminations, quite as much as the Gillray-influenced examples which Erdman discusses,[128] find Blake entering into the discourse of political caricature, and the character being represented is Marie Antoinette; the freshly executed queen of France.

By way of introduction to this exposition of *Europe* I outlined the largely negative depictions of Marie Antoinette that predominated in the 1780s and early 1790s. Picking up on the popular French patriarchal fable that told of the queen's insatiable appetites for both sex and power, British cartoonists cast her as a flirtatious tyrant holding tenaciously onto authority and corrupting the largely progressive Louis XVI, and this is how the few critics who have found some trace of her in *Europe* have described Blake's Marie Antoinette.[129] There is some justification for this as Blake's only direct references to the French Queen certainly seem to draw bluntly on these stereotypes:

> Let the Brothels of Paris be opened
> With many an alluring dance
> To awake the Physicians thro the city
> Said the beautiful Queen of France

> (E.499)

The picky reader might want to quibble about whether it is wholly negative to have those brothels – 'built with [. . .] bricks of Religion' (*MHH*, 8:21; E.36) – exposed to the questioning eye, but generally this seems to replicate the view that Marie Antoinette was little more than Erdman's 'royal whore'[130] – prostituting herself for whatever power she could obtain. What I think *Europe* shows, though, is that the events of the queen's imprisonment and death, and British reactions to these, initiated in Blake's mind a process of revisionist thinking about such views, and that this process culminated in Blake apprehending 'old Nobodaddy aloft'

(E.499) – already lurking behind Marie Antoinette in the Brothel verse – as the most culpable despot in the heavens of Europe/ *Europe*, whilst the queen begins to be seen more as a scapegoat and victim than a tyrant. It is in this poem that we find the embryo of Blake's concept of the female will, that complex of manipulative feminine strategies developed and employed by women to obtain power in an oppressive and restricting patriarchal context.

On Plate 3 (*Illuminated*; E.161), Blake faces up to Marie Antoinette's execution directly: occupying most of *Europe – A Prophecy*'s skyline floats an immense female figure, her hair falling down over her face as she vigorously clutches the back of her neck – preparing herself, evidently, for the inevitable blow. Decapitation was a process that particularly haunted Blake[131] and this is hardly surprising – after 1792 one of the key symbols of France, of course, was the Guillotine and in March 1793 Fores, exhibitors of 'The largest collection of caricatures in the world' (and a London establishment Blake must have known) added to its attractions a correct model of the machine – which stood six feet tall and attracted much horrified attention.[132] Neither is it surprising that Blake's mind should turn towards Marie Antoinette for though most 'Affairs of France' were well-known in England there was, after Louis XVI's death, a great paucity of information about the queen's fate. From March onwards the newspapers[133] circulated rumours and by July whole stories were being made up that gave gruesome accounts of her 'massacre'. In fact she outlived her husband by some nine months, being executed on the 16th of October and by the 23rd the eulogizing proper had begun. The queen's death attracted considerably more attention than the king's, with the first account, on the 23rd, being a full-page statement of her trial and death in *The Oracle*. Once the death was confirmed many other reports followed but *The Oracle*, which had adorned its first account with a heavy black border, kept up an interest the longest publishing, in November and December, a column of anecdotes from the Queen's life and following this up with Mary Robinson's highly popular 'Monody to the Memory of the late Queen of France' (1793).

As I noted earlier, Marie Antoinette's death was the occasion for what appeared to be a remarkable renovation of the queen's image. She was transformed, or so it seemed, from French whore to aristocratic angel (something Blake perhaps alludes to in his character's enormous wings?). Periodicals devoted pages to her fate;[134] sentimental paintings and prints added a layer of the most winsome sensibility and reactionary poetasters produced appalling epitaphs for this, 'BEAUTEOUS MARTYR! AUSTRIA'S pride!/ Epitome of ALL – to worth ally'd!'.[135] But what is most important about all this was that many of these supposedly sympathetic productions continued to raise the spectre of Marie Antoinette's allegedly perverted and/or wanton past by continually alluding to the most outrageous event of her trial: Hébert's claim that she, and the King's sister, had spent their evenings teaching the eight-year-old dauphin how to masturbate. Full-length trial-reports were published,[136] popular ballads (even 'Church and King' ones) were decorated with voluptuous images of a fullbreasted queen and more works were added to the already wellestablished library of political pornography dealing with the life of 'Antonina, Queen of Abo'.[137] This 'Woman's love', then, was still 'sin' and Blake centres this aspect of the representation of Marie Antoinette in Plate 4 – working backwards chronologically as his revisionism is conclusively launched.

Plate 4 (*Illuminated*; E.162) presents us with the distinctive, longhaired female figure who appeared in the previous illumination – only this time she is wingless and naked. In a clear reference to Hébert's accusation, Blake's symbolic queen of France is shown kneeling upon a cloud lifting the bedsheet to reveal a naked male youth. It is at this point that David Erdman's reading partially converges with mine, as he designates her a 'flirting [. . .] Marie Antoinette type'[138] and his unthinking censoriousness reveals, of course, the existence of a weighty historical myth. Erdman, in fact, restates what was the radical orthodoxy of the time – an orthodoxy that sneered at 'the peerless and immaculate Antoinetta of Austria' and later enjoyed joining with Byron in his mockingly ironic assessment that she was 'quite as chaste as most of those in whose honour lances were shivered'.[139] In their minds she was, to quote *The Jockey Club* (1792), guilty of 'incredible and revolting excesses',[140] and thus had no claim upon their sympathy or understanding. Rather, she was an example of impure womanhood and a figure from whose fate many telling moral lessons could be drawn,[141] although it is highly interesting to note that female radicals took a different view. In 1793 Charlotte Smith, for example, expressed a great and forgiving sympathy: 'Ah! much I mourn thy sorrows, hapless Queen!/ And deem thy expiation made to Heaven/ For every fault [. . .] Be they no more remember'd; tho' the rage/ Of Party swell'd them to such crimes [. . .] More than enough/ Thou hast endured'.[142]

That Blake too had moved beyond this position of censure becomes clear if we glance at the small figures who occupy the plate's background, two of which are in the sexually desolated positions shown on *Visions* Plate 1 (*Illuminated*, E.129). Erdman makes this link and concludes that given Enitharmon/Marie Antoinette's 'character', the plate depicts figures who are 'exhausted from some orgy'[143] and who should therefore be understood as morally degenerate. Yet this is an interpretation of the allusion from which I demur, because, as we've seen, the one major sexual discourse connected with 'Marie Antoinette-types' is savage political pornography which manipulated her image for its own ends. Erdman endorses such sexualized accounts of Marie Antoinette's omnipotence but for Blake pornography raised questions of women's powerlessness, hence the reputed female power here depicted appears in the context of a discourse whose essence is the lack of female agency, autonomy and will. So, what I feel is focused on by the dialogue of the back- and foregrounds of this plate is the danger of allowing a sexist mentality to take the victim for the oppressor. The historically specific event alluded to certainly seems to endorse this: Hébert's accusation of incest played a pivotal role in the Queen's condemnation and yet was without substance. Her gravest sexual sin, which was so graphically recounted, was one of which she was wholly innocent.

To see where this revisionism took Blake we need now to look at the writings of Edmund Burke, for his chivalric depiction of Marie Antoinette is the absent centre of this whole discussion and is a notion of the queen which Blake unequivocally – see Plate 5 (*Illuminated* ; E.163) – engaged with.[144]

The initial response to Burke's *Reflections on the Revolution in France* (1789) had, of course, been vast. Dorothy George lists hordes of satirical prints that replied to its extravagant fears, and magazines were full of reviews and discussion of both Burke's style and his political opinions.[145] That only treasury newspapers took Burke (who really did, as Mary Wollstonecraft put it, seem to have a 'moral antipathy to reason') at all seriously in the early days hardly seemed to matter[146] – its distribution was wide and its images soon entered common political discourse. Moreover, by 1793, Burke's hysteria seemed somehow more apposite than the rational tone of his major rebuffer/debunker Paine and, with the death of his heroine, Burke's ideas about French women again came to the fore. *The Post* of 3 August 1793 – for example – speculated about whether Charlotte Corday's daring feat would displace Marie Antoinette as the recipient of Burke's 'amorous panegyric.'[147] Burke, like so many male writers in late-eighteenth-century Britain and France, was obsessed by two radically opposed notions of woman[148] – the sexually savage and politically subversive women of the people who had marched on Versailles and invaded the Assembly; and the apparently exalted Marie Antoinette, 'glittering like the morning star, full of life, and splendour, and joy'.[149] These women, who occupy the central roles in the 12 pages of *Reflections* that make up Burke's story of the Revolution epitomized,[150] superficially act as the two poles of alternatively wicked and pure womanhood. Yet close examination shows the opposition to be a false one for Burke's illogical 'respect' for the queen simply masks a host of sexist prejudices and antagonisms – and by following the thread of Burke's argument about the nature of women a surprisingly strong link is revealed between his beliefs and those of the revolutionaries he so vehemently reviled.[151]

Burke's central case seems to be that, 'All the decent drapery of life' ought not to be 'rudely torn off' because the 'naked shivering nature'[152] of reality is too distasteful to endure. To Burke's mind it is a real blessing that, 'pleasing illusions' can make 'power gentle' and it is even more fortuitous that the whole, 'wardrobe of a moral imagination' is available to render women palatable. Burke's veiled conception is, however, now imperilled because the revolutionary 'new conquering empire of light and reason' threatens to shine on the essence of womanhood and reveal its bestiality. This may seem to be an overly polemical assessment but the word is not too strong – for though Burke worries that egalitarian levelling will reveal the king to be 'but a man', a few more clauses are added to his account of the revelation of Marie Antoinette: 'a queen is but a woman; a woman is but an animal, and an animal not of the highest order'. Burke, in short, shares Hébert's view, that once reduced to the level of woman, the queen is in fact a beast: wolf or harpy, her inhumanity (and indeed every woman's) is incontrovertible.

The similarity between Burke and the revolutionaries does not end here. He may not have been inclined to verbalize his feelings about Marie Antoinette in the expletives Hébert employed but his utterly sexualized view of her is just as intense. Not only do we have the wildly phallic thousand swords threatening to leap from their scabbards in response to the queen's distress but Burke constantly titillates himself (and presumably some of his readers) by referring to her sexual vulnerability: his account of the piercing of her bed as she runs 'almost naked' to seek refuge at the king's feet (p. 164) is little more than a rape-fantasy, and Burke again fantasizes penetration through his imagery of the 'sharp antidote against disgrace' that Marie Antoinette carries close to 'that bosom' (p. 169). As David Punter notes, 'his portrayal of the French Queen expresses less a fear of rape than [. . .] the presentation of a pin-up' and Burke's portrayal of Marie Antoinette as the perfect sexualized victim[153] is precisely what we see replicated in many of the poems written after her death. William Thomas Fitzgerald's lascivious lamentation over Marie Antoinette: 'Her neck exposed – her throbbing bosom bare,/ And sheer'd by ruffian hands her lovely hair'[154] is both typical and sufficient to demonstrate the point.

The prints which answered Burke were also alive to his barely concealed sexual impulses: 'Don Dismallo, After An Absence of Sixteen Years, Embracing His Beautiful Vision' (November 1790),[155] for example, shows Burke intimately clasping Marie Antoinette. Whilst his wife looks on in distress, the queen exclaims, 'Welcome, thrice Welcome to my arms [. . .] thou Adonis of Cavaliers! thou God of Chivalry! do thou vanquish with Sacred Spear, Great Hero, and give me to grasp thy Invisible Shillelee, more powerful than the sword of Rinaldo, or that Terrible Talisman, the Truncheon of Marlborough.' And even more important is Cruikshank's, 'The Doctor Indulged With His Favourite Scene' (? Dec 1790) which shows the queen's ransacked bedroom as the scene of a peep-show.[156] Though Richard Price is the object of the satire it perfectly demonstrates the mentality at work in Burke's, 'enthusiastick ejaculation' (p. 165).

It was images like this that provoked Mary Wollstonecraft to respond to Burke's *Reflections* so vociferously.[157] In her more radical first reply Wollstonecraft took up the case of the 'furies of hell' – a construction she wonderfully deflates with the cool statement: 'Probably you mean women who gained a livelihood by selling vegetables or fish, who never had had any advantages of education.'[158] More important for this essay, however, is her drawing of a parallel between these revolutionary women and the queen – who to her are purely, 'the great and small vulgar' (p. 30). Both, she insists, have been rendered variously inhuman by patriarchal restrictions and Wollstonecraft, possessing 'a plain downright understanding', refuses to 'make a distinction without a difference' (p. 30). Like Blake she is concerned with the ambiguity and provisionality of any woman's power.

This explanatory mode is also present in the more subdued *Historical and Moral View of the Origins and Progress of the French Revolution* (1794). Despite the shadow of the Terror and Wollstonecraft's unfortunate borrowing of material from reactionary historians (not least amongst them Edmund Burke), she still prioritizes the task of defending Marie Antoinette. What most concerns Wollstonecraft is to rewrite Burke's sexual objectification. In this account there is no piercing of the queen's bed, no collapsing in terror at the king's feet, and in pointed contrast to Burke's fleeting glimpse of Marie Antoinette 'almost naked', Wollstonecraft insists she had just enough time to throw 'a wrapping-gown around her'.[159] In short, Wollstonecraft's consideration of the queen as only a woman climaxes not with a picture of Burke's sexual victim but rather with an image of *child-like* vulnerability: the violation of 'the chaste temple of a woman' finds Marie Antoinette at rest, consigning 'her senses to the bosom of sleep, folded in its arms forgetful of the world' (p. 209).

As well as defending the queen against Burke's libertine imagination,[160] Wollstonecraft also continues to explain Marie Antoinette's alleged character – applying her principles of socialization to every aspect of the queen's behaviour. If she behaves like a habitual flirt it says nothing of her nature, for 'In such a voluptuous atmosphere, how could she escape contagion?', and if she is inept in political understanding and a potential disaster for the nation it's because, 'her opening faculties were poisoned in the bud [. . .] A court is the best school in the world for actors; it was very natural then for her to become a complete actress, and an adept in all the arts of coquetry that debauch the mind, whilst they render the person alluring' (pp. 29; 73; 74).[161] In this account Marie Antoinette earns the sympathetic title 'The unfortunate queen of France' because her fate is just one of Wollstonecraft's many 'Observations on the state of Degradation to which Woman is Reduced by Various Causes'.[162]

It is only when the dialogue between these opposed views is taken into account that Plate 5 (in both its pictorial and verbal aspects – see, *Illuminated*, E.163) gains full historical meaning, for here Blake addresses directly Burke's penchant for sexual victimization hidden under the veil of hyperbolic praise and also attends to Wollstonecraft's insight that if woman's love is treated as sin, women will learn to use this notion to defend themselves from assault[163] and gain illict sway. Plate 5's link to this debate is unequivocal: Blake's rethinking of Marie Antoinette's fate has arrived back at the 'Age of Chivalry' as a markedly unenthusiastic and scaly knight gallant stands with his sword ready, in front of two winged women – who supplicate, or serenely wait, for his attention.

The first generation of Blake critics, whose readings are still dominant, have seen this plate as a warning about how women can so easily become the real power behind the throne. David Erdman gives the most complete assertion of this view when he claims that these winged figures are representatives of Marie Antoinette and Queen Charlotte, who in Erdman's reading of history seem to have controlled every event of the revolutionary wars like two master (mistress) puppeteers.[164] Enitharmon's pivotal speech is read, from this perspective, as the pure expression of the female will working through the determined but coy woman who is, according to Frye and his descendants, the most wicked figure in Blake's whole demonology of oppressors – as Stephen Cox fulminates, 'Enitharmon's story is a *plot* in more ways than one [. . .] Enitharmon schemes to dominate the world [. . .] she will use sexuality to ruin sexuality.'[165]

Thankfully some more recent critics have apprehended her function as both victim and agent, but what even they have not done is to historicize Blake's understanding of these particular 'dialectics of sex'[166] and this is an exercise which must be carried out if we are to comprehend how incisive Blake's protofeminism is. I have drawn attention to so many discourses – both French and English – on 'woman's love' because they have such vital resonances in Enitharmon's speech: to understand its full impact Burke, Rousseau,[167] Hébert and the caricaturists must all be borne in mind – for at root what woman's dominion (*Europe*, 5:3; E.62) amounts to is women accepting that they are merely sexual objects (something all these men agree upon) and learning how to exploit that fact to the utmost. And what is most important are the various devices Blake employs to reveal that Enitharmon's speech isn't issued from a position of power but is a response to the position in which patriarchy places women. In this speech, Blake demonstrates an awareness of the pertinence of Mary Wollstonecraft's observation that, 'this exertion of cunning is only an instinct of nature to enable them to obtain indirectly a little of the power of which they are unjustly denied a share; for, if women are not permitted to enjoy legitimate rights, they will render both men and themselves vicious to obtain illicit privileges'.[168]

First, the illuminations that follow Plate 5 present women in positions of subservience to archetypal male rulers (see *Illuminated* ; E.166; 169). Plate 11 (*Illuminated* ; E.169) is particularly relevant here as the *fleurs de lys* waving 'angels' are locked into obeisance to a spectrous pope/king – the phallic serpents issuing from their robes perhaps underlining their assimilation into the patriarchal system.[169] Two other things also indicate that Enitharmon's speech is to be read as an indictment of patriarchal oppression and the manipulativeness it generates. The first is the obvious fact that it offers a recipe for behaviour which is quite as limiting to women as it is for men: in this schema women's dominion amounts to spending your life as a 'little female' spreading 'nets in every secret path' (*Europe*, 5:8–9; E.62). The second, and more important point, is that Enitharmon, however wilful she might seem, is not particularly competent at disseminating these repressive creeds: by line 6 of the speech she has already given the game away by revealing that her allegorical abode is a delusion (it is *she* who describes it as a place 'where existence hath never come' (*Europe*, 5:7; E.62E)). Her lack of power is further revealed in her need for, and choice, of messengers.

In contrast to Urizen in *The Song of Los* (1795) who effectively and efficiently ensures that his 'Laws' are disseminated by simply giving them 'to the Nations/By the hands of the children of Los' (*SL*, 3:8–9; E.67) Enitharmon has continually to call her distributors to 'Arise', in tones that suggest not a little anxiety (five exclaimations of 'O' in 22 lines). This unease is not surprising for the figures she has chosen to ensure female rule are representatives of the two groups of men who throughout Blake's poetry are the archetypal oppressors of women (and they *never* need any prompting). It can hardly augur well for lovely woman's prospects of dominion that the first messenger is the masculinist 'furious king' Rintrah, whose 'eyes rejoice because of strength' (*Europe*, 8:12; E.62) and who presides over a group of male furies who 'each ramping his golden mane shakes' (*Europe*, 8:11; E.62). That Rintrah's bride Elynittria 'Weeps [. . .] in desart shades' (*Europe*, 8:6; E.62) is no surprise and reinforces the dubious value of Rintrah's efforts in Enitharmon's campaign.[170] The second group of messengers is equally inauspicious, for 'Palamabron horned priest, skipping upon the mountains' (*Europe*, 8:3; E.62) is a composite figure of phallic imp (the fairy grown up?) and joy-binding clergyman whose 'Priests of the Raven of dawn' (*MHH*, 25; E.45) brethren instigated the notion of sin that began the whole sense-constricting process in the first place. Sin in Blake is a male concept created to deal with women's sexuality: from Ona's father's sexualized horror at his daughter's 'Naked [. . .] delight' in 'sunny beams' (*LGL*, 9; E.29) to the naming of the erotic songstress Ahania 'Sin' (*Ahania*, 2:34; E.84) by the mortified Urizen, it is men who create and maintain this notion of Holy 'crime' (*LGL*, 4; E.29). There is no better way that Blake could have revealed Enitharmon to be acting within the constraints of patriarchy than to have her try and employ this utterly male concept – as Brenda Webster succinctly puts it, 'Women's triumph [. . .] depends on using the father's code and image'.[171] It is, in short, the most chimerical of all victories.

Given this, section four (Plates 9–13:9; E.63–5) must be approached not as an, 'account of the triumph of woman in Christian culture'[172] but as an ironic unmasking of such an idea: these alleged 'Eighteen hundred years' (*Europe*, 9:5; E.63) of female dominance have no more substance in Blake's conception of western history than a dream that cannot even be remembered on waking (*Europe*, 13:9; E.65).

Section four is a particularly difficult segment of the poem because although references to the reduction of humanity's sensual existence give some sense of continuity, Plates 9–13 move us into entirely new realms and it is here that Erdman's reflectionist historicizing is most convincing.[173] I shall not, however, be following the details of Erdman's account of the developments in British politics in the 1790s because a more general issue concerns me here (as it has done throughout) – which is the way that Blake again reasserts the existence, and poisonous influence, of patriarchal social organization in western history. As the first line of Enitharmon's dream tells us, the last two thousand years have seen, 'Shadows of *men* in fleeting bands upon the winds:/ Divide the heavens of Europe' (*Europe*, 9:6–7; E.63 – my emphasis).

In this section, Blake invalidates misogynist parables which blame women for the pollution of Christian culture, for in his myth the primary figures of evil are male. Plate 11 (*Illuminated* ; E.169) gives the most succinct account of the unfolding of their influence, and again usefully underlines how genuinely powerful tyrants need make no nervous call for messengers to purvey their creeds (view alongside Plate 5, *Illuminated* ; E.163):

> Albions Angel rose upon the Stone of Night.
> He saw Urizen on the Atlantic;
> And his brazen Book,
> That Kings & Priests had copied on Earth
> Expanded from North to South.
>
> (*Europe*, 11:1–5; E.64)

The 'God' who became 'a tyrant crown'd' (*Europe*, 10:23; E.63) as a result of this was not Enitharmon but, as we've seen, the frontispiece's divider ('of the heavens of Europe') and the fact that Blake saw these male power-possessors as his main enemies is made crystalline when Orc moves into action: the target of his wrath is Albion's Angel, not Enitharmon, and indeed every one of the named reactionary figures in this 'historical' section is male. When Enitharmon does finally appear it is only to underline how delusive and ironic any kind of 'woman's triumph' would be in such an environment. For this is a world in which: 'the shadows are filld/ With *spectres*, and the windows wove over with curses of iron:/ Over the doors Thou shalt not; & over the chimneys Fear is written' (*Europe*, 12:26–8; E.64 – my emphasis). In this supposed fantasy-land of female pre-eminence the worst of all negative masculine attributes predominate: houses are dens full of spectrous brutality[174] and religious prohibition. Northrop Frye claims that Enitharmon 'hangs silently over' this scene, 'like a grin without a cat'[175] but what her laughter more probably indicates is a terrible confusion – for whilst 'her' description tells of 'every man bound' (*Europe*, 12:26; E.64), the illumination below suggests that it is women who are ensnared: at the bottom of Plate 12 a contorted female is caught in a spider's web, she folds her hands and prays desperately for deliverance (*Illuminated*; E.170).

The final question, of course, is whether *Europe* offers any kind of remedy to the patriarchal problems it has so vividly outlined, and the shift back into the most intense myth, which occurs after the apocalyptic last trumpet has been blown, suggests that Blake is extremely wary of offering any simple solutions. David Erdman tries to read the text as a largely unbroken and progressive revolutionary narrative[176] but what actually seems to happen is that the final section returns us to the moment just after the 'secret child's birth: 'eighteen hundred years were fled/ *As if they had not been*' (*Europe*, 13:10–11; E.65 – my emphasis), and Enitharmon (in a situation that almost exactly parallels that of *Europe*, 3:5–6; E.61) 'calld her sons & daughters/ To the sports of night/ Within her crystal house' (*Europe*, 13:13–15; E.65). What most needs to be grasped about the speech that Enitharmon commences here is that it is deliberately launched in opposition to the one offered by Los and the Sons of Urizen (do read alongside *Europe*, 3–4:9–14; E.62) in which, as I attempted to argue, Los's egoistical exhibitionism, and their malignant sexism, corrupted sexual harmony almost as soon as it began. And to really appreciate the dialogue Enitharmon enters into, the kind of exposition which I engaged in earlier is again needed – for the complicated myth presented in Enitharmon's song contains some of the most suggestive proto-feminist polyphony anywhere in Blake's poetry.[177]

The first difference between Los and Enitharmon's night-time speeches is that Enitharmon speaks not of herself but to her children, opening the passage with a beautiful piece of protective advice to her daughter: 'Arise Ethinthus! tho' the earth-worm call;/ Let him call in vain;/ Till the night of holy shadows/ And human solitude is past! (*Europe*, 13:16–19; E.65). By paying attention to just a few of the intertextual references here (*Thel's* worm and *Vision's* night most obviously)[178] it becomes apparent that Enitharmon is offering a radical sexual message: religious ideologies have turned sex into a mysterious and alienating experience, and Enitharmon (no doubt thinking about the Sons of Urizen's threats) advises her daughter to shun any contact with men under these circumstances. She then goes on to sing in praise of the mother–daughter relationship:

Ethinthus queen of waters, how thou shinest in the sky:
My daughter how do I rejoice! for thy children flock around
Like the gay fishes on the wave, when the cold moon drinks the dew.

> Ethinthus! thou art sweet as comforts to my fainting soul:
> For now thy waters warble round the feet of Enitharmon
> (*Europe*, 14:1–5; E.65)

Most critics have refused to see any positivity in these lines (with
S. Foster Damon even providing a diagram to explain why this
is the first stage in 'The Repression of Sex under Enitharmon'
and Stephen Cox offering disdainful comment on her 'large and
grotesque family')[179] but in fact this is to deny one of the corner-
stones of Blake's early vision: that maternal love can be a re-
deeming force.[180] Enitharmon, here, is trying to find a way to
stop heterosexual relationships degenerating into the envy and
violence we saw earlier and she continues to suggest that the
encouragement of parental rapture will ensure this: 'Manathu-
Vorcyon! I behold thee flaming in my halls,/ Light of thy mothers soul! I see thy lovely eagles round;/ Thy golden wings are
my delight' (*Europe*, 14:6–8; E.65). This celebratory vision is not,
however, sustained. Corruption enters when Enitharmon attempts
to describe women's sexuality (which is wholly appropriate given
all we've seen in this discussion of eighteenth-century attitudes
to 'Woman's love') and the contradictory nature of her perceptions is focused in Enitharmon's address to Leutha:

> Where is my lureing bird of Eden! Leutha silent love!
> Leutha, the many colord bow delights upon thy wings:
> Soft soul of flowers Leutha!
> Sweet smiling pestilence! I see thy blushing light:
> Thy daughters many changing,
> Revolve like sweet perfumes ascending O Leutha silken queen!
> (*Europe*, 14:9–14; E.65)

The opening line gives the clue to the problem's 'genesis'. Christian
history began by making woman's love sin (that 'lureing bird of
Eden') and Enitharmon simply has not got the power, though
she certainly has the desire, to maintain an alternative vision:
hence the contradictory images of pestilence/perfume that follow. Moreover this situation is not likely to be redeemed, for
her sons (and by implication all men) will not listen to her message. Antamon, the obviously spermy 'prince of the pearly dew',
has left his mother in favour of floating 'Alone' (*Europe*, 14:15,
17; E.65, 66) and with her male listeners implacable Enitharmon

soon slides into propagating the manipulative, but self-protective, sexual politics we heard earlier:[181] 'I hear the soft Oothoon in Enitharmon's tents:/ *Why wilt thou give up womans secrecy* my melancholy child?/ Between two moments bliss is ripe' (*Europe*, 14:21–3; E.66 – my emphasis). The corruption of Enitharmon's alternative vision seems inevitable but the final parallel with Los's speech suggests that this is not necessarily the case, for Enitharmon finishes up in the presence of Orc. In the earlier account of this situation Enitharmon's persecuted position (her daughters were about to be bound by the Sons of Urizen) meant that all this encounter did was to give her the energy to speak;[182] in this version she calls on him to act. In an instructive contrast to Los and the Sons of Urizen's mockery, Enitharmon invites Orc to aid her children:

> Orc! smile upon my children!
> Smile son of my afflictions.
> Arise O Orc and give our mountains joy of thy red light
> (*Europe*, 14:28–30; E.66)

For just a moment Enitharmon's vision and Orc's energy seem to merge and produce a transitory instant of harmony: 'nature felt thro' all her pores the enormous revelry' (*Europe*, 14:34; E.66). Yet the glowing of 'the stars of Urizen' (*Europe*, 14:32; E.66) grows into the dawn of patriarchal day and as morning opens in the east the revelry ends, regimentation returns ('every one fled to his station') and 'Enitharmon', quite understandably, 'wept' (*Europe*, 14:36; E.66). Neither the mother nor the son seem able to permanently alter the father's system.

The events of Plate 14, then, render problematic, to say the least, the standard reading of *Europe* that pits Orc, and eventually Los, as linked revolutionary actors challenging the tyranny of Urizen and Enitharmon.[183] The final plate which attempts in some ways to resolve these European/*European* conflicts is in fact a mass of contradictions. To begin with the opening lines, 'But terrible Orc, when he beheld the morning in the east,/ Shot from the heights of Enitharmon' (*Europe*, 14–15: 36–1; E.66) are open to a number of readings. Peter Butter insists that 'we unequivocally rejoice at the escape of Orc from the seductive Enitharmon'[184] but if we reject the idea that she ever held him captive it is possible to argue that he uses her mountains as a

positive vantage point from which to explode in bloody vengeance
for Urizen's fracturing of his sibling's momentary night-time
harmony. The events that take place in 'the vineyards of red
France' (*Europe*, 15:2; E.66) also lend little weight to the standard 'revolutionary' reading, for whilst Enitharmon certainly 'groans
& cries in anguish and dismay' (*Europe*, 15:8; E.66) Los and Orc
seem hardly to be working in masculine unison: when Los calls
'*all* his sons to the strife of blood' (*Europe*, 15:11; E.66 – my emphasis) one of them is already well immersed in its traumas.
Generational communication is still out of synch. It seems that
Blake's meditations upon women's experience in revolutionary
France, and upon the more general issue of the nature of female
power, have rendered any kind of convincing closure impossible. As David Aers observes: 'while the final plate involves highly
generalized apocalyptic violence, the outcome is wisely not pre-
dicted, the question of sexual emancipation is correspondingly
left suspended, the dialectic is unresolved'.[185] Indeed the final
image we have (*Illuminated*; E.173) suggests something worse:
that we are slipping back into a patriarchal revolutionary consciousness – as the proudly phallic father (Los?) carries a col-
lapsed woman over his shoulder and drags a female child away
from some extravagant wavy flames.[186]

So, despite all that I've tried to contend and convey in this
chapter, *Europe* is still a problematic poem: it is still extremely
hard to interpret, with any degree of certainty, Blake's attitude
to masculinist revolution and its abuse of women. One strategy
which might help would be to examine the final instalment of
his continental prophecy, 'ASIA' from *The Song of Los* (1795). This
poem is certainly relevant, although it hardly clarifies the question. Again we are presented with a wholly male power struggle: the Kings of Asia call forth their priests, counsellors and
admonishers to aid Urizen in his efforts to bind humanity; and
they are answered by an even more violently phallic Orc, who
'raging in European darkness/ Arose like a pillar of fire above
the Alps/ Like a serpent of fiery flame! (*SL*. 7:26–8, E.69). Moreover
the repercussions in human history are equally weighted: concern is expressed for the devastating effect of mortality on 'Adam,
a mouldering skeleton [who presumably alone]/ Lay bleach'd
on the garden of Eden' (*SL*. 7:23–4, E.69). Orc's defeat of death
is similarly orientated: when 'all flesh naked stands', it stands
in the forms of 'Fathers and Friends;/ Mothers & Infants; Kings

and Warriors' (*SL.* 7:33–4, E.69). If this is only a partial description of male humanity, it is infinitely more limited in its description of the female. And yet, given all this and despite all this, what are we to make of the poem's final image? That still shocking, still arresting picture of resurrected human flesh imaged as a wildly orgasmic female grave:[187]

> The Grave shrieks with delight, & shakes
> Her hollow womb, & clasps the solid stem:
> Her bosom swells with wild desire:
> And milk & blood & glandous wine
> In rivers rush & shout & dance,
> On mountain, dale and plain.
>
> (*SL.* 7:34–40. E.70)

What are we to conclude? That the female can only be included in this story of human liberation as a depersonalized and gaping grave, desperate to grasp a thick and life-giving phallus? Or, alternatively, that this is a complete reversal of the masculinist values which preceded it – that 'Urizen Wept' (*SL.* 7:42, E.70) precisely because the waves of female juice now flooding the world are the one force which even he cannot contain?

The method which I have used throughout this book to answer questions like this is a historicizing one, and certainly Blake's version of Asiatic femininity is starkly different from the passive ideals dreamed of by his peers. Contemporaries like William Hodges admitted the sexual appeal of 'eastern' women, who in his account 'bathe in the river [. . .] sporting and playing like Naidds or Syrens' but their submissiveness is central too: 'the simplicity, and perfectly modest character, of the Hindoo women, cannot but wrest the attention of the stranger. With downcast eye, and equal step, they proceed along.'[188] Certainly this is a fascinating context, and one perhaps that I should have elaborated in greater detail, but at this closing point in my study I have chosen not to. And I have reached this decision because I do not believe that any one researcher, however diligent, can attain satisfying knowledge without the benefit of genuine critical dialogue. This central question, and many like it, will remain unanswered, I believe, until more scholars undertake the kind of feminist historicist work I have been recommending. In my brief conclusion I will say a little more about the lacunae that remain in Blake studies and the effects they have had upon my work, but for now I simply ask the reader to ponder Blake's disparate and contradictory images for themselves. What did they mean then? What do they signify now?.

# 6

# 'Conclusion'

'There is neither a first nor a last word' Mikhail Bakhtin[1]

Conclusions are difficult to formulate, especially at the close of an enterprise like this one which has ranged over territory rarely mapped by students of Blake. Although the tone of my arguments has been insistent, fervently so in places, my predominant feeling at the end of this project is not of being engaged in heated debate but rather of speaking into a void, of offering arguments that lack a critical context. For it is still the case that mine are eccentric interests within Blake studies; no community of published scholars[2] exists concerned with the specific questions which I have addressed. Given this I shall devote my brief conclusion to the restatement of why I think this work is necessary and of value, and also to offering some thoughts about how it fits into a larger, and more promising, context of 'Romantic' criticism.

The sense of isolation I have described is in many ways paradoxical, for the early 1990s were years pregnant with possibility for feminists working on writing produced in the late-eighteenth and early-nineteenth centuries. In my introduction I noted the revival of historicist work in this period and the significant contribution feminist scholars have made to the effectiveness of this critical reorientation.[3] It is also important to note that their endeavours have been accompanied, and valuably supplemented, by the first paperback reprinting of the works of a host of 'Romantic' women poets.[4] The implications of the easy availability of this archive are immense. Once students of the period begin to grasp the extent and nature of these productions, the arbitrariness of the traditional, male Romantic canon will come into stark focus. Indeed debates are already raging about 'the limits of Romanticism' and the urgent need for it to be 're-visioned',[5] and as these initial studies begin to crack the edifice we can reasonably assume (or at least unreasonably hope) that the work of future years will see the monolith of Romanticism reduced to a pile of dusty ruins. Shelley's words may well prove prophetic in ways he would never have imagined, 'Nothing beside remains. Round the decay / Of that colossal wreck, boundless and bare / The lone and level sands stretch far away.'[6]

Moreover, the belated incorporation of feminism into the agenda of eighteenth-century studies coincides with the emergence of a widespread awareness amongst feminists of the need to historicize our own endeavours.[7] Feminism, as Joan Wallach Scott insists, 'must be read [...] in its concrete manifestations, and then not only for its programmatic recommendations'[8] and it is convictions of this sort which help clarify the value of a work like mine. Although Blake may eventually be laid to rest in the desert with his Romantic peers (though he was never well suited to their company) his writings demand attention, in the present moment at least, because they engage in powerful and profound ways with so many of the feminist debates specific to his historical context. It has been my overwhelming desire to demonstrate this. *William Blake and the Daughters of Albion* has attempted to show not just that Blake was aware of the ideas of declared feminists of the period (although this certainly needed to be done) but also that he gave serious and sustained attention to the other discourses in which sexual debates were annunciated. In the past, critics of Blake have tended to treat the material which I have focused upon as temporal cultural effluvia. Generic, and always gendered, disdain governed all. Conduct literature was viewed as marginal and lightweight,[9] pornography as peripheral and tasteless, popular caricature only significant for the overtly political messages that it carried. And the kind of intellectualist and elitist imperative behind these judgements needs to be refuted not simply because of its tacit sexism, but also because it denies the social nature of language.

This returns us then to Bakhtin's concept of the 'living utterance'.[10] Any writer who focuses as repeatedly as Blake upon questions of sexual identity, pleasure and difference is engaged with these discourses and debates because 'Each word tastes of the context in which it has lived its socially charged life'.[11] Blake was not formulating and conveying his ideas in a language that belonged to him alone, he shared his medium and wrote in response to many voices. And what we gain by replacing his works within contemporary dialogues is the sense of a historical limit being reached, of feminist thinking of the period arriving at a point of deadlock. The years 1789–95 were pivotal in the history of thinking about the nature, rights and role of women and the texts I have examined engage with the unresolved questions of that moment. What can a young woman like Thel do once she has refused the seductions of conventional and acquiescent feminine roles? What are the options for a female like Oothoon once she has reclaimed her sexuality, if heterosex is the only choice[12] and powerful males classify any erotically awakened woman a whore? Or, how can a committed male radical incorporate the rights of woman into his overtly revolutionary manifestos without casting doubt upon his otherwise sanguine political convictions? Do demands for the rights of men always entail the suppression of the rights of women? These are the issues that Blake addressed in the works he wrote during the early 1790s, and their centrality to his thinking has been too long ignored. Indeed, Blake may actually be of more value to feminist scholars of the period than his 'Romantic contemporaries' because, as we saw in my chapter on *Europe – A Prophecy*, he developed a mythopoetic form which enabled him to investigate the intricate relations of sexual politics and political power.[13]

A rather different kind of comment also needs to be made at this concluding moment, and that is the admission that my arguments may simply be wrong in places. I may be guilty of misplacing emphases, of ignoring important contexts or of missing significant historical nuances; but my point is that until debate about these issues thrives, until my voice becomes part of a sustaining critical dialogue, we quite simply cannot know. And until that point is reached I must console myself with Blake's generous observation that, 'If others had not been foolish we should be so' (*Marriage*, 9:52, E:37). Moreover, although I acknowledge the possible interpretative errors generated by my methodology, I firmly maintain my initial argument that such writing is urgently needed. For it is feminist historicist work which most powerfully demonstrates that feminist readings are not simply 'another perspective' that can be neatly lined up amongst a range of alternative options[14] (especially not within Blake studies as I percieve it). This kind of writing disrupts and refutes critical orthodoxies, and so far this iconoclastic enterprise is only in its most embryonic phase. Historicists have wrested for themselves an indisputable place on the agenda of Blake Studies but feminists have not. It is a depressing admission, but an undeniable one, that the kind of patrician disinterest and sexist erasure outlined in my introduction still beset us. So too does the dishonest strategy of grossly exaggerating Blakist's general concern with questions of sexual politics and practice. Glen E. Brewster's claim, from 1992, that 'Blake's profound interest in re-visioning and re-presenting male–female relationships is acknowledged by virtually every commentator on his work'[15] is typical. It aims to silence by telling feminists that their concerns are critical 'old hat'; in fact nothing could be further from the truth, for the task still facing us is immense.

The readings I have offered of a selection of his texts represent only the smallest of starts, and there is a pressing need for this kind of methodology to be utilized in the interpretation of all Blake's works. The results, I think, would be revolutionary, especially with regard to Blake's great epic poems, for his entire epic project could fruitfully be reconceptualized as an investigation of the personal and political consequences of various expressions of sexual desire and sexual love. After the completion of *Europe* Blake turned or perhaps more correctly returned, in the Urizenic trilogy, to the primal scenes of family conflict, and his agonized reflection upon these scenes became the basis for all the writing which followed. *The Four Zoas* (c. 1797), for example, makes innumerable comments about the anguish and the joy of heterosexual union,[16] *Milton* (c. 1809–10) explores the fallout of obsessive homosocial and homosexual desire and *Jerusalem* (c. 1815–20), on one important level at least, describes the potential and experience of lesbian sensuality. By centring upon a few pivotal passages and contextualizing them as thoroughly as I did in my treatment of *Europe – A Prophecy's* resonant phrase, 'Woman's Love is Sin', these extensive works would be radically illuminated.[17] And what I feel would be revealed is the thought with which I want to close this study. This kind of investigation would not produce for us a feminist Blake, it would not bring into focus or excavate a body of exemplary feminist statement (if this existed it would surely have been found by now). Rather what I think we'd discover is a writer who devoted himself to the task of giving a form to sexual error, who was by turns a searching critic of patriarchy but also a hectoring misogynist. Who, most fundamentally, questioned and endlessly reconstructed the sexual mythologies through which he and his contemporaries made sense of their experience and the experience of others. For Blake 'the loins' are 'the place of the Last Judgment' (*Jerusalem*, 44:38; E:194), sexual identity is the most defining yet problematic aspect of selfhood and in this study I hope to have shown that the poet's historically specific reflections upon this subject are pertinent and suggestive to both his contemporary moment and to ours. Other feminist writers have gestured at conclusions of this kind, but without the weight of archival evidence that I have provided, their claims and insights lacked substance, and were easily overlooked or brushed aside. It is my hope that the arguments offered in *William Blake and the Daughters of Albion* are less ethereal, less speculative and better able to stand as serious reflections upon the sexual issues that occupied Blake's imagination throughout his creative career. It is also my hope that the academically influential critics who have been so woeful in their understanding of these issues will soon lay down their pens and acknowledge that their 'wish' has been (and Blake must have the last word) 'to lead others when they should be led' (*The Voice of the Ancient Bard* (L.11; E.32).

# Notes and References

## 1  Blake Studies: A Critical Survey

1. Bakhtin, 'Toward a Methodology for the Human Sciences', in *Speech Genres and Other Late Essays*, ed. by Caryl Emerson and Michael Holquist (Austin, Texas: University of Texas Press, 1986), p. 170.
2. 'Blake' (1920), rep. in *T.S. Eliot: Selected Prose*, ed. by John Haywood (Harmondsworth: Penguin, 1965), pp. 159–62 (p. 162). For a rather different treatment of this issue see Nelson Hilton, 'Blake and the Apocalypse of the Canon', *Modern Language Studies*, 16, 1 (Winter 1988), 134–49.
3. Some of these deficiencies are being remedied by writers whose work I shall discuss later, the following are especially valuable: Jon Mee, *Dangerous Enthusiasm: William Blake and the Culture of Radicalism in the 1790s* (Oxford: Clarendon Press, 1992); David Worrall, *Radical Culture: Discourse, Resistance and Surveillance, 1790–1820* (Hemel Hempstead: Harvester Wheatsheaf, 1992) and E.P. Thompson, *Witness Against the Beast: William Blake and the Moral Law* (Cambridge: Cambridge University Press, 1993).
4. 'Toward a Methodology', p. 170.
5. A good sense of the scope of this debate can be found in the 44 works (89 vols) reprinted in the series, 'The Feminist Controversy in England, 1788–1810', ed. by Gina Luria (New York and London: Garland Publishing Inc, 1974). See too, *Women, the Family and Freedom: The Debate in Documents*, Vol. I 1750–1880, ed. by Susan Groag Bell and Karen M. Offen (Stanford: Stanford University Press, 1983).
6. Valentin Nikolayevich Vološinov, *Marxism and the Philosophy of Language* (Cambridge, Mass: Harvard University Press, 1986), p. 21 [Note: one issue as yet unresolved by Bakhtin scholars is that of the authorship of a number of disputed texts, in these instances I use the name 'Bakhtin' to refer to all the authors of the so-called 'Bakhtin school': Mikhail Bakhtin, Valentin Nikolayevich Vološinov and P.N. Medvedev].
   Bakhtin's now fashionable theories have been appropriated by a variety of critics And it is beyond the scope of this study to detail their different interpretations. However, the kinds of understanding of his work which inform my study are provided by such writers as, Terry Eagleton, 'Wittgenstein's Friends', in *Against the Grain* (London: Verso, 1988), pp. 99–130; Tony Bennett, *Formalism and Marxism* (London and New York: Methuen 1979), pp. 75–96; Ken Hirschkopp, 'Bakhtin, Discourse and Democracy', *NLR*, 160 (1986), 92–113; *Bakhtin and Cultural Theory*, ed. by Ken Hirschkopp

and David Shepherd (Manchester: Manchester University Press, 1989) and Graham Pechey, 'Bakhtin, Marxism and Post-Structuralism', in *Literature, Politics and Theory*, ed. by Francis Barker *et al.* (London and New York: Methuen, 1986), pp. 104–25.

7. Peter Ackroyd, *Blake* (London: Sinclair-Stevenson, 1995), p. 162.
8. *Philosophy of Language* pp. 14; 19.
9. Various types of 'double-voiced discourse' are summarized in *Problems of Dostoevsky's Poetics*, trans and ed. by Caryl Emerson (Manchester: Manchester University Press, 1984), p. 199.
10. *Philosophy of Language*, p. 41; *Discourse in the Novel*, in *The Dialogic Imagination*, ed. by Michael Holquist (Austin, Texas: University of Texas Press, 1981), 259–422, (p. 276); *Philosophy of Language*, p. 23.
11. As Clive Thomson notes, 'there is general agreement that the addition of the category of gender to the theory of the dialogic is possible. But the addition of this discursive category entails adjustments in the utopian tendency of Bakhtin's dialogic', 'Mikhail Bakhtin and Contemporary Anglo-American Feminist Theory', *Critical Studies*, 1, 2 (Summer, 1989), 141–61, (p. 158). From the same volume see too, Myriam Diaz-Diocaretz, 'Bakhtin, Discourse and Feminist Theories', 121–39, and Nancy Glazener, 'Dialogic Subversion: Bakhtin, the Novel and Gertrude Stein', in *Bakhtin and Cultural Theory*, pp. 109–29. Also of interest are Dale Baur, *Feminist Dialogics: A Theory of Failed Community* (New York: University of New York Press, 1988) and Jacqueline Howard, *Reading Gothic Fiction: a Bakhtinian Approach* (Oxford: Clarendon Press, 1994).
12. *Philosophy of Language*, p. 86.
13. *Discourse in the Novel*, p. 293.
14. For Bakhtin's views on poetry see, *Discourse in the Novel*, esp pp. 296–300 and David H. Richter's excellent article, 'Dialogism and Poetry', *Studies in the Literary Imagination*, 23, 2 (Spring 1990), 9–27.
15. See especially the early chapters of, *Problems of Dostoevsky's Poetics*.
16. Epic and Novel, in *The Dialogic Imagination*, pp. 3–40, (p. 7).
17. *Discourse in the Novel*, pp. 286; 297.
18. Ibid, p. 298.
19. *Dostoevsky*, p. 252.
20. *Literal Imagination: Blake's Vision of Words* (Berkeley, Los Angeles and London: University of California Press, 1983), p. 2.
21. Although my comments about Hilton are largely negative, his work in chapters six and seven on, 'Spinning and Weaving [The Text, 1]', pp. 102–26 and, 'Veil, Vale, and Vala [The Text, 2], pp. 127–46, touches on many issues central to a feminist historicist reading of Blake.
22. Hilton's review of Leopold Damrosch, *Symbol and Truth in Blake's Myth*, in *BQ*, 15, 4 (Spring 1982), 192–96, (p. 196).
23. Hilton elaborated his ideas in, 'Literal Tiriel Material', in *Critical Paths: Blake and the Argument of Method*, ed. by Dan Miller, Mark Bracher and Donald Ault (Durham and London: Duke University Press, 1987), pp. 99–110, (pp. 99–100). And note that Morton Paley,

for instance, speaks of Hilton as one of the, 'best writers on Blake' who has been able to 'assimilate post-structuralist theory to [his] own critical sensibilities', *SiR*, 21, 3 (Fall 1982), 426.

24. Gleckner, 'Most Holy Forms of Thought', in *Essential Articles for the Study of William Blake, 1970–1984*, ed. by Nelson Hilton (Hamden, Conn.: Archon Books, 1986), pp. 91–118, (p. 100).

25. Ibid., preface.

26. *The Index of Unnam'd Forms: Blake and Textuality*, ed. by Nelson Hilton and Thomas Vogler (Berkeley, Los Angeles and London: University of California Press, 1986) is replete with references to Derrida, Lacan, Foucault, Barthes, Freud, Nietzsche and even Julia Kristeva, but no member of the Bakhtin school is invoked. Given this the collection is seriously deficient, although the essays of David Simpson and Robert Essick traverse a little of the ground which I have pointed to. Essick's more detailed study, *William Blake and the Language of Adam* (Oxford: Clarendon Press, 1989), is also noteworthy in this context. He focuses upon linguistic issues but, strangely, given his otherwise exemplary historicist writings, finds no place for comment upon the Bakhtin school's ideas.

27. *Philosophy of Language*, p. 82.

28. Creating States ... (Toronto: University of Toronto Press, 1994), p. xiv.

29. *Rethinking Blake's Textuality* (Columbia and London: University of Missouri Press, 1993), pp. 1; 2.

30. 'Representations of Revolution: From *The French Revolution to The Four Zoas*', in *Critical Paths*, pp. 244–70, (pp. 244; 246).

31. Other 'radical' critics who have invoked in some way the ideas of Bakhtin are: Stewart Crehan, *Blake in Context* (Dublin: Gill and Macmillan Humanities Press, 1984), pp. 185; 188; Edward Larrissy, *William Blake* (Oxford: Basil Blackwell, 1985), *passim*, and David Punter in a number of articles reworked in *The Romantic Unconscious: A Study in Narcissism and Patriarchy* (Hemel Hempstead: Harvester Wheatsheaf, 1989). The only Blake critic who has used Bakhtin in an extensive way is Graham Pechey, in '*The Marriage of Heaven and Hell*: A Text and Its Conjunctions', *Oxford Literary Review*, 3, iii (1979), 52–76.

32. Norma A. Greco, 'Mother Figures in Blake's *Songs of Innocence* and The Female Will', *Romanticism Past and Present*, 10, 1 (Winter 1986), 1–15, (p. 6).

33. To gain some sense of the quantitative mass of Blake studies one need only look at a number of bibliographies; in particular, G.E. Bentley Jr, *Blake Books* (Oxford: at the Clarendon Press, 1977), pp. 707–1001; Joseph P. Natoli, *Twentieth Century Blake Criticism* (New York and London: Garland Publishing Inc, 1982); Mary Lynn Johnson, 'William Blake', in *The English Romantic Poets: A Review of Research and Criticism* 4th edition, ed. by Frank Jordan (New York: The Modern Languages Association of America, 1985), pp. 113–253 and at the annual, 'Blake Circle' bibliography that appears in *Blake: An Illustrated Quarterly*.

34. The classic misogynist account of Blake's attitude to women appears in Bernard Blackstone's chapter, 'Desire, Love and Marriage', in his *English Blake* (Cambridge: Cambridge University Press, 1949), pp. 288–99.

35. Eaves, 'Introduction', to 'Inside the Blake Industry: Past, Present and Future', *SiR*, 21, 3 (Fall 1982), 389–443, (pp. 389–90). Its contributors were the honoured David Erdman along with Robert Essick, Hazard Adams, Joseph Viscomi, W.J.T. Mitchell, Nelson Hilton, Morton D. Paley, Karl Kroeber, Robert Gleckner and John E. Grant. It is extraordinary that Mary Lynn Johnson (herself a noteworthy omission from the list) should acknowledge of the Blake Industry that, 'No art historian, British or commonwealth subject, neoclassicist or feminist scholar of any gender or discipline – sits on the board of directors', whilst also claiming, 'the clan is representative enough to air the main agenda of Blakists within the whole of academia', in *The English Romantic Poets*, p. 250. See too her defence of the 'Blake Industry', pp. 148–9.

36. Comments of this nature appear in the contributions of David Erdman, p. 394 and Karl Kroeber, p. 428. Only W.J.T. Mitchell's, 'Dangerous Blake' deals at length with questions of sexuality, pp. 410–16 – especially in his section on 'Obscenity', pp. 413–14.

37. 'Post-Essick Prophecy', 400–3, (p. 400).

38. 'What Is To Be Done', 425–7, (p. 426). Mary Lynn Johnson also notes, 'In the middle eighties, formalist and archetypal critics continue bracing themselves for a long-predicted tidal wave of phenomenological, structuralist, semiotic, and deconstructionist interpretations of Blake that will reshape the critical landscape', *The English Romantic Poets*, p. 251 and in a later collection, *Critical Essays on William Blake* (Boston, Mass: G.K. Hall, 1991), the editor Hazard Adams somewhat grudgingly represents, 'the so-called postmodernist emphasis on difference, deconstruction, Hegelian negation, and language', (p. 6) with extracts from Steven Shaviro's, '"Striving with Systems": Blake and the Politics of Difference', and Robert Essick's, *William Blake and the Language of Adam*.

39. 'Dangerous Blake', p. 416. The kind of works he is referring to are Steven Shaviro, '"Striving with Systems": Blake and the Politics of Difference', *Boundary* 2, 10, 3 (1982), 229–50. See also the collection *Critical Paths*, especially Dan Miller's, 'Blake and the Deconstructive Interlude', pp. 139–67, and of course Hilton and Vogler's, *Unnam'd Forms: Blake and Textuality*.

40. *William Blake: Modern Critical Views*, ed. by Harold Bloom (New York: Chelsea House Publishers, 1985), editor's note. Bloom includes Susan Fox's, '*Milton: Beulah*', pp. 133–44, but not her groundbreaking feminist essay, 'The Female as Metaphor in the Poetry of William Blake'.

41. As I noted, Fox's article had to wait until the next year to be reprinted in the collection, *Essential Articles*, pp. 75–90. It appeared alongside Alicia Ostriker's, 'Desire Gratified and Ungratified: William Blake and Sexuality', pp. 211–36. Peter Otto's review of these two

collections usefully pinpoints the important differences between them, and the different Blakes which emerge, *BQ*, 21, 1 (Summer 1987), 29–31.

42. See Hilton and Vogler's editorial comments on their inclusion policy in *Unnam'd Forms*, 'Acknowledgements Note' and also the revealing exchange between Hilton and Margaret Storch: *BQ*, 25, 4 (Spring 1992), 171–3/ *BQ*, 26, 4 (Spring 1993), 161.

43. Adams frames the one feminist essay, from Alicia Ostriker, in his collection with the somewhat misleading comment that it 'discusses [. . .] the sexuality of the Blakean body', *Critical Essays*, p. 5.

44. Leopold Damrosch's discussion of 'The Problem of Dualism' is divided into sections on: Vegetated and Spiritual Bodies / Contraries / Emanations / Sex / Beulah / Eden, in his *Symbol and Truth in Blake's Myth* (Princeton, NJ: Princeton University Press, 1980), pp. 165–243. Steven Cox, *Love and Logic: The Evolution of Blake's Thought* (Ann Arbor: University of Michigan Press, 1992).

45. David Fuller, *Blake's Heroic Argument* (London: Croom Helm, 1988), pp. 224–80.

46. Note especially Otto's acknowledgement that, 'such a course must inevitably be selective [. . .] a number of issues which arise from and complicate my readings – most glaringly, the extent to which Blake's 'sexism' qualifies or even undermines his constructive vision and visionary deconstruction – are not dealth with', *Constructive Vision and Visionary Deconstruction: Los, Eternity and the Productions of Time in the Later Poetry of William Blake* (Oxford: Clarendon Press, 1991), pp. 32–3.

47. Rodney M. Baine and Mary R. Baine, *The Scattered Portions: William Blake's Biological Symbolism* (Athens: The University of Georgia Press, 1986); Martin Bidney, *Blake and Goethe: Psychology, Ontology, Imagination* (Columbia: University of Missouri Press, 1988); Lorraine Clark, *Blake, Kierkegaard and the Spectre of Dialectic* (Cambridge: Cambridge University Press, 1991); Robert F. Gleckner, *Blake and Spenser* (Baltimore: Johns Hopkins University Press, 1985); Harvey Birenbaum, *Between Blake and Nietzsche: The Reality of Culture* (Lewisburg: Bucknell University Press, 1992) and on and on. My point is not that these studies, and the many other works on Blake which appear every year, totally disregard issues of gender, but that other subjects are considered to be of more pressing importance. Such a judgement has significant political implications which this study will tease out.

48. Essick, 'Female Will . . . ', *Studies in English Literature 1800–1900*, 31 (1991), 615–30 (p. 615).

49. Eaves, *The Counter-Arts Conspiracy . . .* (Ithaca and London: Cornell University Press, 1992), p. 255.

50. 'Checklist', *BQ*, 28, 1 (1994), p. 6.

51. 'Checklist', *BQ*, 28, 4 (1995), p. 144.

52. See, for example, *The Observer Review*, 3/9/95, p. 14; *The Times*, 11/9/95, p. 17 and 14/9/95, p. 38. Whatever the reviewers might say, however, Ackroyd was decidedly remiss in neglecting to com-

ment on Joseph Viscomi's account of William and Catherine's complex working relationship, *Blake and the Idea of the Book* (Princeton, NJ: Princeton University Press, 1993), passim but esp. pp. 129–42.

53. 'The Genitals are Beauty' was a mixed media exhibition which took place 6–17 February 1995 at The House of William Blake in South Molton Street, London. See Jim Dewhurst, 'Is the Tyger All About IT?', *The Journal of the Blake Society at St James*, 1 (Spring 1995), 33–6 (p. 35).

54. Mark Schorer, *The Politics of Vision* (New York: Henry Holt and Co., 1946); Jacob Bronowski, *A Man Without A Mask* (London: Secker and Warburg, 1944); David Erdman, *Blake Prophet Against Empire* (Princeton, NJ: Princeton University Press, 1969, fp 1954) and E.P. Thompson, *The Making of the English Working Class* (Harmondsworth: Penguin Books, 1986, fp 1963), passim.

55. Eagleton, 'The Ballad of English Literature', in *Against the Grain*, p. 185.

56. *Blake*, p. 160.

57. Schorer, *The Politics of Vision*, p. xi.

58. 'Blake: The Historical Method', in *William Blake: Modern Critical Views*, pp. 19–34, (p. 20).

59. *Prophet Against Empire*, p. 254. Note too that in 1991 Hazard Adams was still contending that, 'Erdman's work was immediately recognized and still is recognized as the most important study to appear on the political implications of Blake's writings', *Critical Essays*, p. 4.

60. On familial and sexual mores see, pp. 109–17 and for the sexual politics of artistic style see the chapter, 'Republican Art', pp. 192–238 in *Blake In Context*.

61. For Crehan's comment on context see, 'Blake, Context and Ideology', *BQ*, 20, 3 (Winter 1986–87), 104. Robert Essick also remarks on the inhibiting nature of Erdman's throughness in 'William Blake, Thomas Paine and Biblical Revolution', *SiR*, 30 (Summer 1991), 189–212, (p. 189).

62. Larrissy makes a number of suggestive asides about Blake's treatment of gender and sexual oppression, but his other concerns prevent any sustained elaboration. See for example, *William Blake*, pp. 2–4; 122–6.

63. Punter has been a prolific writer on Blake and the articles most relevant to this discussion are, 'Blake, Trauma and the Female', *NLH*, 15, 3 (1984), 475–90 and 'The Sign of Blake', *Criticism* 26 (1985), 313–34, both of which are reworked in the work I have quoted, 'Romanticism and the Self: An Engagement with Blake', in *The Romantic Unconscious*, pp. 68–117, (p. 101). The problems of Punter's mode of address are discussed by W. Ruddick in his review of the latter work, which is described as, 'A brilliant book [...] but one whose insights seem fated to be denied to a great many of its readers by the extreme unpredictability of its assertive mode of procedure and the mandarin nature of its style', *Literature and History*, 2nd ser. 2, 1 (Spring 1991), 109–11, (p. 111). A

notable exception to this discursive problem is Punter's wonderfully lucid introduction to the collection of Blake's poems which
he recently edited, *William Blake: Selected Poetry and Prose* (London
and New York: Routledge, 1988), pp. 1–19.

64. Michael Ferber, 'Nature and the Female', in *The Social Vision of
William Blake* (Princeton, NJ: Princeton University Press, 1985), pp.
89–115, (p. 112).

65. It should also be noted that he has continued to express similar
views on Mary Wollstonecraft's inadequacies, commenting that,
'Oothoon is [. . .] a much more radical and liberated soul than
Wollstonecraft, who disparaged love, despised sensations and con-
sidered this life to be a preparation for the next', *The Poetry of
William Blake* (London: Penguin, 1991), p. 70.

66. Behrendt, *Reading William Blake* (Basingstoke: Macmillan, 1992),
p. 84.

67. Eagleton's preface to Larrissy's, *William Blake*, pp. ix–xi, (p. xi).

68. In neither of the revised editions of *Blake: Prophet Against Empire*,
(1969/1977) does Erdman show any awareness of how feminist
historians have changed our sense of Blake's context, and, as we
have seen, he gave the issue very short shrift in the *SiR* (1982)
special which discussed the future of Blake Studies.

69. See chapter two, '"Every Honest Man is a Prophet": Popular Enthusiasm and Radical Millenarianism', *Dangerous Enthusiasm*, pp.
20–74. The female prophets Sarah Green (p. 33), Eliza Williams
(p. 47) and Maria de Fleury (p. 60) are no more than glanced at.

70. *Witness Against the Beast*, p. xiii.

71. *Blake, Ethics and Forgiveness* (Tuscaloosa and London: University
of Alabama Press, 1994), passim.

72. *Historicizing Blake*, ed. by David Worrall and Steve Clark
(Basingstoke: Macmillan, 1994). See especially John Beer, 'Blake's
Changing View of History: The Impact of the Book of Enoch', pp.
159–78 and his talk about the 'heroic penis' (p. 165).

73. Clark, 'Blake and Female Reason', in his *Sordid Images: The Poetry
of Masculine Desire* (London and New York: Routledge, 1994), pp.
138–87.

74. 'The Presence of Cupid and Psyche', in *Blake's Visionary Forms Dramatic*, ed. by David V. Erdman and John E. Grant (Princeton, NJ:
Princeton University Press, 1970), pp. 214–43. Some examples of
thoughtful but gender-blind studies of Blake's treatment of sex
and sexuality are: John Sutherland, 'Blake: A Crisis of Love and
Jealousy', *PMLA*, 87 (1972), 424–31; Dennis M. Welch, 'In the Throes
of Eros: Blake's Early Career', *Mosaic*, 11 (1977–78), 101–13 and
Thomas Frosch, 'The Sexes', in *The Awakening of Albion: The Renovation of the Body in the Poetry of William Blake* (Ithaca and London:
Cornell University Press, 1974), pp. 159–77.

75. 'The Woman Scaly', *Midwestern Modern Languages Association Bulletin*, 6 (1973), 74–87.

76. Susan Fox first talked about Blake's treatment of gender in various sections of her book on *Milton*, 'Contraries and Progression',
pp. 194–222 and the two appendixes, 'Illustrations and Structure',

pp. 223–32 and 'Revisions and Structure', pp. 233–8, in *Poetic Form in Blake's Milton* (Princeton, NJ: Princeton University Press, 1976). These ideas were, however, substantially revised in the article I am dealing with, 'The Female as Metaphor in the Poetry of William Blake', *Critical Inquiry*, 3 (Spring 1977), 507–19, (p. 507).

77. 'Desire Gratified and Ungratified: William Blake and Sexuality', *BQ*, 16, 3 (Winter, 1982–83), 156–65, (p. 164).

78. Anne K. Mellor, 'Blake's Portrayal of Women', *BQ*, 16, 3 (Winter, 1982–83), 148–55, (p. 148); '"All the Lovely Sex": Blake and the Woman Question', in *Sparks of Fire: Blake in a New Age*, ed. by James Bogan and Fred Goss (Richmond, Cal.: North Atlantic Books, 1982), pp. 272–5. The most reductive production of this kind is Howard O. Brogan's, 'Blake On Woman: Oothoon to Jerusalem', *CEA Critic*, 48, 4/49, 1 (1986), 125–36.

79. Michael Ackland, 'The Embattled Sexes: Blake's Debt to Wollstonecraft in *the Four Zoas*', *BQ*, 16, 3 (Winter, 1982/1983), 172–83 and Judith Lee, 'Ways of Their Own: The Emanations of Blake's *Vala*, or *the Four Zoas*', *ELH*, 50 (1983), 131–53.

80. Catherine Haigney, 'Vala's Garden in Night the Ninth: Paradise Regained or Woman Bound?', *BQ*, 20, 4 (Spring, 1987), 116–24.

81. 'Blake's Feminist Revision of Literary Tradition in "The Sick Rose"' in *Critical Paths*, pp. 225–43, (p. 228).

82. Jon Mee makes some interesting comments on how, 'The reader is enfranchised' within Blake's texts, *Dangerous Enthusiasm*, pp. 15–18, (p. 18) and Stephen Behrendt focuses extensively upon the experience of reading his works in *Reading William Blake*, passim.

83. 'No Face Like the Human Divine?: Women and Gender in Blake's *Pickering Manuscript*', in *Spirits of Fire: English Romantic Writers and Contemporary Historical Methods*, ed. by G.A. Rosso and Daniel P. Watkins (London and Toronto: Associated University Presses, 1990), pp. 189–207, (p. 189). More generally see discussion, pp. 193–9.

84. *War of Titans: Blake's Critique of Milton and the Politics of Religion* (Pittsburgh: University of Pittsburgh Press, 1984), esp. 'Part III Paradise Lost: A Blakean Reading', ch. 9, 'The Politics of the Family', pp. 311–46. See too the antecedent of this, 'Blake Encountering Milton: Politics and the Family in *Paradise Lost* and *The Four Zoas*', in *Milton and the Line of Vision*, ed. by Joseph Wittreich (Wisconsin and London: Wisconsin University Press, 1975), pp. 143–84. The Blake establishment has not received DiSalvo's work very warmly, see for example Robert Gleckner's review of her book, *BQ*, 19, 4 (Spring 1986), 146–50.

85. See, 'Blake's Healing Trio', *BQ*, 23, 1 (Summer 1989), 20–32; 'The Secret Masonic History of Blake's Swedenborg Society', *BQ* 26, 2 (Fall 1992), 40–51 and 'Blake's "Mr Femality": Freemasonary, Espionage and the Double-sexed', *Studies in Eighteenth Century Culture*, 22, 1 (1992), 51–71. Of future interest is, *The Men of Desire: Swedenborg, Blake and Illuminist Freemasonry* (forthcoming).

86. 'William Blake and the Dialectic of Sex', *ELH*, 44 (1977), 500–14; 'Blake: Sex, Society and Ideology', in *Romanticism and Ideology*, ed. by Aers *et al.* (London: Routledge and Kegan Paul, 1981), pp.

27–43. This concern with gender is maintained in his, 'Representations of Revolution . . . ', in *Critical Paths*, pp. 244–70.

87. 'The Female in Blake and Yeats', *CEA Critic*, 48, 4/49, 1 (1986), 137–44, (p. 137). Billigheimer reiterates her sentiments at greater length in her book, *Wheels of Eternity: A Comparative Study of William Blake and William Butler Yeats* (Dublin: Gill and Macmillan Ltd, 1990).

88. Jungian Studies of Blake include June K. Singer, *The Unholy Bible: A Psychological Interpretation of William Blake* (New York: Putnam's Sons for C.G. Jung Foundation of Analytical Psychology, 1970); Christine Gallant, *Blake and the Assimilation of Chaos* (Princeton, NJ: Princeton University Press, 1978) and Jerry Caris Godard, *Mental Forms Creating: William Blake Anticipates Freud, Jung and Rank* (Lanham, New York and London: University Press of America, 1985). For a convincing critique of these approaches see Margaret Shaefer's review of Singer's *Unholy Bible*, *BQ*, 24 (Spring 1973), 100–4.

89. '*A Portion of His Life* . . .' (London and Toronto: Associated University Presses, 1994), p. 125.

90. 'The Woman Figure . . .', *Comparative Literary Studies*, 27, 3 (1990), 193–210. See footnote, pp. 207–8.

91. 'Blake and the Women of the Bible', *Journal of Literature and Theology*, 6, 1 (March 1992), 23–32, (p. 32). Another example of the comparative approach, though of a rather different sort, is Peter J. Sorensen's 'The Pistis Sophia: The Fall and Redemption of Blake's Female Characters', in his *William Blake's Recreation of Gnostic Myth* (New York and Salzburg: Edwin Mellen Press, 1995), pp. 37–58.

92. Alexander, *Women in Romanticism* (Basingstoke: Macmillan, 1989), pp. 20–21; Hoeveller, *Romantic Androgyny* (Pennsylvania and London: The Pennsylvania State University Press, 1990). Similar conclusions are reached by: Sarah McKin Webster, 'Circumscription and the Female in the Early Romantics', *PQ*, 61, 17 (Winter 1982), 51–68; Deborah A. Gutschera, '"A Shape of Brightness": The Role of Women in Romantic Epic', *PQ*, 66, 1 (Winter 1987), 87–108 and Melanie Bandy, *Mind Forg'd Manacles: Evil in the Poetry of Blake and Shelley* (Alabama: The University of Alabama Press, 1981), esp. chs. 5 and 6. Different ones in *Romanticism and Feminism* ed. by Anne K. Mellor (Bloomington and Indianapolis: Indiana University Press, 1988).

93. *Blake and Freud* (Ithaca: Cornell University Press, 1980), p. 25. Other works of the prophetic school are Jerry Caris Godard's, *Mental Forms Creating*, and Morris Dickstein's, 'The Price of Experience: Blake's Reading of Freud', in *The Literary Freud*, ed. by Joseph H. Smith (New Haven: Yale University Press, 1980), pp. 67–111.

94. The work, of course, has many more admirable features. Her defence of Freud in, 'Freud and Feminine Psychology', pp. 209–28 is both painstaking and lucid, and George also offers an invaluable survey of past writing on the subject of Blake and women, 244–7.

95. Bloom praises George in his collection, *William Blake*, p. vii. A more even-handed appreciation of the work is offered by Thomas Vogler in his review, *BQ*, 16, 2 (Fall 1982), 121–4.

96. *Blake's Prophetic Psychology* (London and Basingstoke: Macmillan, 1983), p. 2.

97. 'Blake, Women and Sexuality', in *Critical Paths*, pp. 204–24, (pp. 223; 224) presents a succinct account of Webster's belief in Blake's misogyny.

98. Storch's ideas are contained in three pieces of writing: 'Blake and Women: "Nature's Cruel Holiness"', *American Imago*, 38 (1981), 221–46; 'The 'Spectrous Fiend' Cast Out: Blake's Crisis at Felpham', *MLQ*, 44 (1983), 115–35 and *Sons and Adversaries: Women in William Blake and D.H. Lawrence* (Knoxville: The University Of Tennessee Press, 1990). The quotation is from 'Nature's Cruel Holiness', p. 221.

99. 'Nature's Cruel Holiness', pp. 223; 224.

100. *Sons and Adversaries*, p. xii.

101. 'Nature's Cruel Holiness', pp. 237; 246. It should be noted that some of the crudeness of Storch's claims is softened in the more lengthy elaboration and justification of her method which introduces, *Sons and Adversaries*.

102. A number of other writers have considered the relationship between Blake and Lawrence, among the more noteworthy are Myra Glazer Schotz's articles, 'For the Sexes: Blake's Hermaphrodite in Lady Chatterley's Lover', *Bucknell Review*, 24, 1 (1978), 17–26; 'Why the Sons of God Want the Daughters of Men: On William Blake and D.H. Lawrence' in, *William Blake and the Moderns*, ed. by J. Bertholf and Annette S. Levitt (Albany: State University of New York Press, 1982), pp. 164–85 and John Colmer, 'Lawrence and Blake', in *D.H. Lawrence and Tradition*, ed. by Jeffrey Meyers (Amherst, MA: University of Massachusetts Press, 1985), pp. 9–20.

103. Storch, *Sons and Adversaries*, p. 26. There have been a few more recent psychoanalytical treatments of Blake which are a good deal less diagnostic, see for example Mark Lussier's thesis, 'Mirror and Vortex: Blake and Lacan' (Texas A&M University, 1989) and Mark Bracher's, 'Rousing the Faculties: Lacanian Psychoanalysis and the Marriage of Heaven and Hell in the Reader', in *Critical Paths*, pp. 168–203. Julia Kristeva's notion of the symbolic and semiotic realms has also been invoked on a couple of occasions: by Robert Essick, 'How Blake's Body Means', in *Unnam'd Forms*, pp. 197–217, (p. 211, n. 27) and in the same volume by Thomas Vogler, 'Re: Naming MILTON', pp. 141–76, (pp. 144–7) – who also uses the concepts of écriture féminine and phallocentrism.

104. See especially, 'The Female Will 1798–1800', in *William Blake: His Life* (London: Weidenfeld and Nicolson, 1991), pp. 119–30.

105. Susan Fox, for example, favours the late Blake, 'The Female as Metaphor', whilst Brenda Webster charts a cumulative masculinism, *Blake's Prophetic Psychology*, and 'Blake, Women and Sexuality'. Margaret Storch accepts half Webster's case, although she finds

evidence of sexual reconciliation in some of Blake's late wood-
cuts, 'Conclusion: Pastoral Reconciliation in Blake's Illustrations
to *Virgil* and *Job*, and in Lawrence's *Lady Chatterley's Lover*', in *Sons
and Adversaries*, pp. 179–90. Alternatively, Harold Brogan, evidently
wanting it both ways, concludes that Blake goes, 'full circle in his
view of woman', 'Blake on Woman', p. 134. Schematic accounts of
Blake's attitudes are generally confusing.

106. Just about every feminist Blakean has gestured at social and cultural contexts which are held to be uniformly hostile to his proto-
feminist sentiments. Karleen Middleton Murphy speaks of his
'masocentric culture', 'All the Lovely Sex', p. 275, Diana Hume
George apologetically tells us that, 'Blake was the product of his
acculturation', *Blake and Freud*, p. 197 and, most worrying of all,
Anne K. Mellor trenchantly argues, 'Blake had not escaped the
restrictive patriarchal thinking of his day [. . .] Blake continued to
think in terms of the binary systems he inherited from the eighteenth century enlightenment', 'Blake's *Songs of Innocence and of
Experience*: A Feminist Perspective', *Nineteenth Century Studies*, II
(1988), 1–17, (pp. 14–15). Susan Fox, however, comes a little closer
to a useful assessment when she comments that Blake 'more than
any other male writer of his time recognised the destructive effect
of received attitudes towards women, but who was nevertheless
to some extent a victim of those attitudes', ibid., p. 519 – a remark
which intimates, even though it does not detail, the kind of sexual
debate and conflict Blake was engaged in.

107. Apart from various references to Mary Wollstonecraft (dealt with
in the next note) feminist Blake critics have been largely uninterested in the sexual debate of the late-eighteenth century, and in
the texts which enacted it. A partial exception is Norma A. Greco's,
'Mother Figures in Blake's *Songs of Innocence*', pp. 11–12, which
does find time to glance at the mythologizing of women as religious beings which occurs in such works as William Duff's *Letters
on the Intellectual and Moral Character of Women*.

108. Mary Wollstonecraft has been referred to by Blake critics throughout
this century, and I have already commented on a number of uses
of her work (Ferber, Ackland, Lee and McClenahan). She is usually invoked in discussions of *Visions*, as I shall detail later, and a
number of writers have also paid some attention to the engravings Blake produced to illuminate her books. See for example Robert
Essick, 'The Figure in the Carpet: Blake's Engravings in Salzmann's
Elements of Morality', *BQ*, 12 (1978), 10–14; Dennis Welch, 'Blake's
Response to Wollstonecraft's "Original Stories"', *BQ*, 13 (1978),
4–15 and Mitchell Orm, 'Blake's Subversive Illustrations to
Wollstonecraft's 'Stories', *Mosaic*, 17, 4 (1983), 17–34. Speculation
about the poem *Mary* is also popular, as in G.E. Bentley's, 'A Different Face: William Blake and Mary Wollstonecraft', *WC*, 10 (1979),
349–50.

My objection to the majority of the works which deal with
Wollstonecraft and Blake is that they usually try to prove Blake's

superiority as both thinker and feminist. Michael Ackland's claim that Blake, 'in his [. . .] reworkings of Wollstonecraft [. . .] shows himself capable of transcending the received assumptions that are also embodied in her work', 'The Embattled Sexes', p. 180, is a privileging that also motivates Nelson Hilton's more subtle and intertextually exemplary, 'An Original Story' in *Unnam'd Forms*, pp. 64–104. Indeed this type of assessment has become a kind of critical orthodoxy, with Kelvin Everest's introductory guide to Romantic poetry telling its readers that Blake, 'developed her views on the subjection of women in his own brilliant and strangely original illuminated poems [. . . whose] range takes him beyond Wollstonecraft's perspectives', although she is at least acknowleged to be, 'a crucial part of the intellectual matrix which made Blake's art possible', *English Romantic Poetry* (Milton Keynes and Philadelphia: Open University Press, 1990), p. 21.

109. The notion that the language available to Blake was inherently sexist is advanced by a number of writers, including Karleen Middleton Murphy, 'All the Lovely Sex', pp. 274–5; Anne K. Mellor, who speaks of the 'linguistic prisons of gender-identified metaphors inherent in the literary and religious culture in which he lived', 'Blake's Portrayal of Women', p. 184 and Diana Hume George, who explains that, 'Blake's problems with portrayals of sexuality and of women [. . .] are problems of symbol formation that express themselves in the limitations of language', *Blake and Freud*, p. 199.

110. The important issues raised by New Historicism are all discussed in the volume, *The New Historicism*, ed. by H. Aram Veeser (New York and London: Methuen, 1989) and 'the New Historicist diaspora' further explained in *The New Historicist Reader* also ed. by Veeser (New York and London: Routledge, 1994), p. v. Especially relevant here is John Klancher's, 'English Romanticism and Cultural Production', *The New Historicism*, pp. 77–88.

The kind of works which have questioned the role of deconstruction in Romantic studies, and enacted a move towards more historicist/materialist investigations, are collections like: *Revolution and English Romanticism: Politics and Rhetoric*, ed. by Keith Hanley and Raman Seldon (Hemel Hampstead/New York: Harvester Wheatsheaf/St Martin's Press, 1990); *Romantic Revolutions: Criticism and Theory*; ed. by Kenneth R. Johnson *et al.* (Bloomington and Indianapolis: Indiana University Press, 1990) and more particularly, *Spirits of Fire: English Romantic Writers and Contemporary Historical Method*, ed. by G.A. Rosso and Daniel P. Watkins (London and Toronto: Associated University Presses, 1990); *Revolution in Writing: British Literary Responses to the French Revolution*, ed. by Kelvin Everest (Milton Keynes and Philadelphia: Open University Press, 1991); *Beyond Romanticism New Approaches to Texts and Contexts 1780–1832*, ed. by Stephen Copley and John Whale (London and New York: Routledge, 1992) and *Reflections on Revolution: Images of Romanticism*, ed. by Alison Yarrington and Kelvin Everest

(London: Routledge, 1993). Marilyn Butler's 'Repossessing the Past: the Case for an Open Literary History', in *Rethinking Historicism* (Oxford; Basil Blackwell, 1989), pp. 64–84 is a classic justification of this kind of method, a method exemplified in Butler's own work, and especially in her *Romantics, Rebels and Reactionaries: English Literature and its Background 1760–1830* (New York and London: Oxford University Press, 1982).

111. The collection edited by Felicity Nussbaum and Laura Brown which presented *The New Eighteenth Century* (London and New York: Methuen, 1987) gave feminist scholars a great deal of space; as do most of the collections listed above – especially Whale and Copley's *Beyond Romanticism*. Excellent expositions of this kind of method are provided by Gillian Beer, 'Representing Women: Re-presenting the Past', in *The feminist reader*, ed. by Catherine Belsey and Jane Moore (Basingstoke: Macmillan, 1989), pp. 63–80 and, of course, by Janet Todd, *Feminist Literary History: A Defence* (Cambridge/ Oxford: Polity Press in association with Basil Blackwell, 1988).

112. Gutwirth, 'Changing the Past: A Feminist Challenge', *ECS*, 28, 1 (Fall 1994), 29–36, (p. 34).

113. A number of other writers focus especially on the Lambeth books, see in particular Leslie Tannenbaum, *Biblical Tradition in Blake's Early Prophecies: The Great Code of Art* (Princeton, NJ: Princeton University Press, 1982); John Howard, *Infernal Poetics: Poetic Structures in Blake's Lambeth Prophecies* (London and Toronto: Associated University Presses, 1984) and the works of Jon Mee and E.P. Thompson discussed above.

114. Philosophy of Language, p. 23.

115. *The Character and Conduct of the Female Sex, and The Advantages To Be Derived by Young Men from the Society of Virtuous Women* (London, the Strand: T. Cadell, 1776), pp. 82–4.

## 2 The Sins of the Fathers: Patriarchal Criticism and *The Book of Thel*

1. Dr John Gregory, *A Father's Legacy to His Daughters*, in *The Young Lady's Pocket Library, or Parental Monitor* (Dublin: Printed by Graisberry and Campbell, for John Archer, 1790), p. 22. Interestingly, as Nelson Hilton notes, '*Thel* accounts for half of Blake's poetic uses of "complain" and its cognates', *Literal Imagination: Blake's Vision of Words* (Berkeley and Los Angeles: University of California Press, 1983), p. 30.

2. On the importance of the poem see, *The Book of Thel, A Facsimile and Critical Text*, ed. by Nancy Bogan (Providence: Brown University Press, 1971), pp. xiii–xiv and W.J.T. Mitchell, *Blake's Composite Art* (Princeton, NJ: Princeton University Press, 1978), p. 78.

3. Northrop Frye, *Fearful Symmetry: A Study of William Blake* (Princeton, NJ: Princeton University Press, 1974. fp. 1947), p. 233; David Erdman, *Blake: Prophet Against Empire* (Princeton, NJ: Princeton University Press, 1969. fp. 1954), pp. 130, 132; S. Foster Damon, *A Blake Dic-*

*tionary* (New England: Brown University Press, revised ed. 1988, fp. 1965), p. 401. Special attention is given to these three critics because of the authority they continue to exercise over Blake studies. For example in his foreword to the 1988 edition of Damon's *Dictionary*, Morris Eaves declared, 'if Blake is where you're going, Frye, Erdman, and Damon should be your guides. As an introductory offer they remain unbeatable', p. ix.

4. Brian Wilkie, *Blake's Thel and Oothoon* (Victoria, Canada: University of Victoria, 1990), ELS Monograph Series, No. 48, p. 64. Martin K. Nurmi calls *Thel* 'completely accessible to anyone', *William Blake* (London: Hutchinson, 1975), p. 69; Raymond Lister speaks of it as 'the simplest' of Blake's prophetic works, *William Blake* (London: G. Bell and Sons, 1968), p. 35 and as recently as 1988 (when the sheer volume of past readings must have cast doubt upon its transparency and lightness) David Fuller was still suggesting that, 'perhaps ultimately the most valuable qualities of *Thel* are not thematic but tonal – its delicacy and gentleness', *Blake's heroic argument* (London: Croom Helm, 1988), p. 33. The poem is, in the words of Eugenie R. Freed, simply 'charming', '"Sun-Clad Chastity" and Blake's "Maiden Queens": Comus, Thel and "The Angel"', *BQ*, 25, 3 (Winter 1991/1992), 104–16, (p. 106).

5. Peter Ackroyd, *Blake* (London: Sinclair-Stevenson, 1995), p. 116. He would have done well to digest E.B. Murray's explanation of why, 'the only apposite meaning Blake could have supposed his prospective contemporary audience to associate with the word "Thel" was the word female"', 'Thel, *Thelyphthora*, and the Daughters of Albion', *SiR*, 20 (1981), 275–97, (p. 276).

6. See Gleckner, *The Piper and the Bard* (Detroit: Wayne University Press, 1959), pp. 157–74 (pp. 168; 171) and 'Blake's Thel and the Bible', *BNYPL*, 64 (1960), 574–80, (p. 579).

7. Gleckner's views were reiterated in the later, *Blake's Prelude: Poetical Sketches* (Baltimore and London: Johns Hopkins University Press, 1982) and especially in *Blake and Spenser* (Baltimore and London: Johns Hopkins University Press, 1985), pp. 28–47; 287–302, (pp. 39; 47).

8. Gleckner, 'Bible', p. 578. The importance of Gleckner's censorious work has been noted by Mary Lynn Johnson, 'Together [. . .] Gleckner and Tolley shifted critical attention from the metaphysical to the moral sphere, where it now rests', *The English Romantic Poets, A Review of Research and Criticism Fourth Edition*, ed. by Frank Jordan (New York: Modern Language Association of America, 1985), p. 215.

9. W.J.T. Mitchell, 'The Form of Innocence: Poetic and Pictorial Design in *The Book of Thel*', in his *Blake's Composite Art*, pp. 78–106, (pp. 80; 81). Other humanists include, Steven Cox, *Love and Logic* (Ann Arbor: The University of Michigan Press, 1992), pp. 61–7, (p. 65) and Elaine Kauver, 'The Sorrows of Thel: A Freudian Interpretation of *The Book of Thel*', *Journal of Evolutionary Psychology*, 5, 3–4 (1984), 210–22/6, 3–4 (1985), 174–88, (p. 185). See too, A.G. Den Otter, 'Thel: The Lover', *English Studies in Canada*, 16, 4

(Dec. 1990), 385–402, (p. 385) and James King, *William Blake: His Life* (London: Weidenfeld and Nicolson, 1991), pp. 66–7, (p. 67).

10. Michael Ferber, 'The Book of Thel', in his *The Poetry of William Blake* (London: Penguin Books, 1991), pp. 52–63, (pp. 52; 58; 62) and Stephen C. Behrendt, *Reading William Blake* (Basingstoke: Macmillan, 1992), p. 78. Sadly this didactic urge has found its way into the usually more enlightened realm of unpublished doctoral writing on Blake, where Alexander Gourlay asserts, 'Throughout most of the poem [. . .] she is an ignorant theologian, a bad rather than a good shepherdess, an uninspired poet, and an immature bride; her virginity signifies her ignorance', 'Blake's Sisters: A Critical Edition, with commentary, of *The Book of Thel* and *Visions of the Daughters of Albion*' (University of Iowa, 1985), p. 31.

11. William St Clair, 'Women: the evidence of the advice books', in his *The Godwins and the Shelleys* (London and Boston: Faber and Faber, 1991), pp. 504–11, (p. 505). Useful discussions of conduct literature are provided by Joyce Hemlow, 'Fanny Burney and The Courtesy Books', *PMLA*, 65 (1950), 732–61; Mary Poovey, *The Proper Lady and the Woman Writer* (Chicago and London: Chicago University Press, 1984), pp. ix–xix; 3–47; Jane Spencer, *The Rise of the Woman Novelist* (Oxford: Basil Blackwell, 1986), pp. 15–18; Nancy Armstrong and Leonard Tennenhouse, *The Ideology of Conduct* (New York and London: Methuen, 1987) and 'Conduct' in, *Women in the Eighteenth Century*, ed. by Vivian Jones (London: Routledge, 1990), pp. 14–56. The collection of microfilms entitled 'Women Advising Women' (Marlborough: Adam Matthew Publications, 1992) is also invaluable.

12. These lines from Thomson serve as an epigram to, *The Young Lady's Pocket Library*. Note also Hannah More's desire 'To Make Amusement and Instruction Friends' in The Prologue to her didactic verse-tale, *The Search After Happiness: A Pastoral Drama*, 8th ed. (London: T. Cadell, 1785. fp. 1773).

13. Hannah More, *Essays On Various Subjects, Principally Designed for Young Ladies*, 5th ed. (London: T. Cadell, 1791. fp. 1777), p. 13. Another example of such ideas can be found in Edward Moore's fable, 'The Lawyer, and Justice', which outlines at length the God-given particularities of each sex: 'To weaker woman he assign'd/ That soft'ning gentleness of mind [. . .] Man, active, resolute, and bold,/ He fashioned in a diff'rent mould', from his *Fables for the Female Sex*, which were reprinted in *The Young Lady's Pocket Library*, pp. 219–24, (pp. 219; 220).

14. James Fordyce, *The Character and Conduct of the Female Sex* (London: T. Cadell, 1776), p. 19; Dr John Gregory, *A Father's Legacy to His Daughters*, reprinted in *The Young Lady's Pocket Library*, pp. 4–5. Female conduct writers also accepted the cruel necessity of young women developing a constitutional pliancy, as the Countess Dowager of Carlisle advised, 'Habituate yourself to that way of life most agreeable to the person to whom you are united [. . .] Let an early examination of his temper, prepare you to bear with inequalities to which all are more or less subject', *Thoughts in the Form of Max-*

*ims Addressed to Young Ladies, on Their First Establishment in the World* (London: T Cornell, 1789), pp. 1; 4.

15. Fordyce, ibid., p. 50.
16. Fordyce, ibid., p. 78.
17. Hannah More, *Essays . . . for Young Ladies*, p. 133. The subtext of much conduct writing is an intense concern with the moral degeneracy of society and the role of women in its renovation. John Moir, for example, expresses a common sentiment when he contends, 'Could we make good women of our daughters, an effectual reformation would soon take place in every department of society', *Female Tuition; or, An Address to Mothers, on the Education of Daughters*, 2nd ed. (London: J. Murray, 1786), p. vi.
18. More, ibid., p. 145.
19. Marchioness De Lambert, *Advice of a Mother to Her Daughter*, reprinted in *The Young Lady's Pocket Library*, pp. 133; 158–9.
20. De Lambert, ibid., p. 161.
21. Mary Wollstonecraft, *Thoughts on the Education of Daughters*, in *The Works of Mary Wollstonecraft*, ed. by Janet Todd and Marilyn Butler (London: William Pickering, 1989. fp. 1787), 4, p. 21. Her attraction to the didactic mode is most evident in *Original Stories from Real Life* (1788).
22. Wollstonecraft, *Education of Daughters*, 4, p. 45.
23. Her critique of conduct literature can be found in a series of articles published in the *Analytical Review* and especially in *Vindication of the Rights of Woman* (London: Penguin, 1986. fp. 1792), chapter 5, 'Animadversions on Some of the Writers Who Have Rendered Women Objects of Pity, Bordering on Contempt'. The conviction that drives Wollstonecraft's critique is the belief, 'that all the writers who have written on the subject of female education and manners, from Rousseau to Dr Gregory, have contributed to render women more artificial, weak characters, than they would otherwise have been; and consequently, more useless members of society', p. 103.
24. Catherine Macaulay Graham, *Letters on Education* (London: C. Dilly, 1790), pp. 207; 47 and see, too, 'Amusement and Instruction of Boys and Girls to be the Same', pp. 45–50. Of importance here is the tradition of liberal educationalists which begins with Vicesimus Knox, James Burgh and Thomas Day, and continues in the later writings of Erasmus Darwin and the Edgeworths. A useful summary of some of their ideas is provided by Barbara Branden Schnorrenberg, 'Education for Women in the Eighteenth Century: An Annotated Bibliography', *Women and Literature*, 4, 1 (1976), 49–55. The other locus of productive ideas about women's intellect and education was the Bluestocking circle, a group discussed by Sylvia Harcstark Myers, *The Bluestocking Circle* (Oxford: Clarendon Press, 1990), esp Part IV; Marilyn L. Williamson, 'Who's Afraid of Mrs Barbauld? The Bluestockings and Feminism', *International Journal of Women's Studies*, 3, 1 (1980), 89–102 and Evelyn Gordon Bodek, 'Salonières and Bluestockings: Educated Obsolescence and Germinating Feminism', *Feminist Studies*, 3 (1976), 185–99.

25. Mary Hays, *Appeal to the Men of Great Britain In Behalf of Women* (New York and London: Garland Publishing, 1974. fp. 1798), p. 106. It should be noted that although this work was published late in the 1790s, Hays actually began work on it at the start of the decade.

26. William Hayley, *A Philosophical, Historical, and Moral Essay on Old Maids* (London: T. Cadell, 1785), p. 20 and more generally Chapter II, 'On the Curiosity of Old Maids', pp. 19–33. W.J.T. Mitchell is one of the few critics to note Thel's, 'pondering [...] rational, skeptical attitude' in his *Blake's Composite Art*, p. 88 and A.G. Den Otter explores her questioning mind in, 'The Question and *The Book of Thel'*, *SiR*, 3, 4 (Winter 1991), 633–55.

27. Gleckner, *The Piper*, pp. 162–3; Michael Ferber, 'Blake's *Thel* and The Bride of Christ', *BS*, 9 (1980), 45–56, (p. 49). The idea that a male sun-god is situated at the heart of the poem is also advanced by Eugenie R. Freed, '"Sun-Clad Chastity"', p. 109. Alternatively the positivity of the realm of the Seraphim is questioned by a few writers including W.J.T. Mitchell, ibid., p. 83 and Margaret Hood and Marilyn Bohnsack, who both sense some kind of female rebellion in Thel's refusal to tend her flocks. See 'Thel – Daughter of Beauty', in Hood's 'The Pleasant Charge: William Blake's Multiple Roles for Women' (University of Adelaide, 1987), pp. 39–44, (p. 41) and 'Ambiguity in *The Book of Thel*, in Bohnsack's, 'William Blake and the Social Construct of Female Metaphors' (University of Miami, 1988), pp. 51–103, (p. 65).

28. Mary Wollstonecraft, *Rights of Woman*, p. 194.

29. Mary Hays, *Appeal*, p. 111.

30. David Wagenknecht, *Blake's Night: William Blake and the Idea of Pastoral* (Cambridge, Mass: Belknap Press of Harvard University Press, 1973), p. 155 and Robert Gleckner speaks of 'Thel's persistant whining', *Blake and Spenser*, p. 230. See, too, John Howard, *Infernal Poetics: Poetic Structures in Blake's Lambeth Prophecies* (Toronto and London: Associated University Presses, 1984), p. 52; Nelson Hilton, *Literal Imagination*, p. 31 and Alexander Gourlay who complains about Thel's 'foolish prating', 'Blake's Sisters', p. 59. An interpretation closer to my own is offered by Marilyn Bohnsack who notes how the poem 'mimics the most limiting and trivial kind of female experience dictated by the social world of eighteenth century privileged classes', 'Ambiguity in *The Book of Thel*', p. 95.

31. This critical commonplace was recently reiterated by Michael Ferber: 'of course the issue of *Thel* is precisely time, how to face time's passing and one's own death', *The Social Vision of William Blake* (Princeton, NJ: Princeton University Press, 1985), p. 152. In this context it is worth noting that in 1788 Blake had written, 'The desire of Man being Infinite the possession is Infinite & himself Infinite' (*NNR* b. VII; E.3).

32. On exploding feminine stereotypes see Mary Ellmann, *Thinking About Women* (London: Virago, 1979), pp. 55–147. Jon Mee usefully points to the 'overload of sensibility' evident in this passage in *Danger-*

*ous Enthusiasm: William Blake and the Culture of Radicalism in the 1790s* (Oxford: Clarendon Press, 1992), p. 153.

33. Burke, *A Philosophical Enquiry into the Origin of Our Ideas of the Sublime and Beautiful*, 6th ed. (London: J. Dodsley, 1770, fp. 1757), p. 222. Useful discussions of the gendering of Burke's aesthetic ideas are provided by Ronald Paulson, 'Burke, Paine and Wollstonecraft: The Sublime and the Beautiful', in, *Representations of Revolution* (New Haven and London: Yale University Press, 1983), pp. 57–87; W.J.T. Mitchell, 'Eye and Ear: Edmund Burke and the Politics of Sensibility' in his *Iconology: Image, Text, Ideology* (Chicago and London: The University of Chicago Press, 1986), pp. 116–59, (pp. 129–31) and especially Vincent De Luca who comments on Blake's 'post-Burkean understanding of beauty', *Words of Eternity: Blake and the Poetics of the Sublime* (Princeton, NJ: Princeton University Press, 1991), pp. 45–7, (p. 46).

   Burke's feminist contemporaries were unimpressed by his *Enquiry* and offered a number of overt critiques. See Mary Wollstonecraft's, *A Vindication of the Rights of Men* (1790), in *The Works* , 5, pp. 45–7; Catherine Macaulay Graham, *Letters on Education*, pp. 43–4; 47–8 and Mary Hay's delightfully incisive unmasking: 'What a chaos! What a mixture of strength and weakness, – of greatness and littleness, – of sense and folly, – of exquisite feeling and total insensibility, – have they jumbled together in their imaginations, – and then given to their pretty darling the name of woman!', *Appeal*, p. 97.

34. Hays, ibid., p. 97.

35. *The Piper*, p. 163.

36. Lavater claimed, 'The primary matter of which women are constituted appears to be more flexible, irritable, and elastic, than that of man. They are formed to maternal mildness and affection; all their organs are tender, yielding, easily wounded, sensible, and receptible [. . .] This tenderness, this sensibility, this light texture of their fibres and their organs, this volatility of feeling, render them so easy to conduct and to tempt; so ready of submission to the enterprise and power of man', quoted in *Britannic Magazine*, 4 (1796), p. 109.

37. Wollstonecraft, *Rights of Woman*, p. 195.

38. William Hayley, *The Triumphs of Temper*, 12th ed. (London: T. Cadell and W. Davies, 1803. fp. 1781), p. 2. Lynne Vallone focuses on this dangerous quasi-autonomous moment in her discussion of 'The Crisis of Education: Eighteenth Century Adolescent Fiction for Girls', *Children's Literature Association Quarterly*, 14, 2 (1989), 63–7. All the advice books so far referenced are addressed to young ladies who are about to make their, 'first entrance [. . .] into the great and critical world', *Thoughts in the Form of Maxims*, p. viii (an event which Mary Wollstonecraft acerbically described as the bringing 'to market [of] a marriagable miss', ibid., p. 289).

39. Hayley, ibid., p. 6 (chimes with Wollstonecraft, *Rights of Woman*, p. 85).

40. The most recent essay to discuss dialogue in *Thel* does in fact acknowledge that, 'as soon as Thel discovers other voices, she replaces her monologue with dialogic responses that are amiable and communicative', Otter, 'The Lover', p. 394 but for the most part critics generally identify dialogic 'dysfunction' in the Vales of Har. A recent example of this is, Harriet Kramer Linkin, 'The Function of Dialogue in *The Book of Thel*', *CLQ*, 23 (1987), 66–76. For a general discussion of Blake and dialogicality see Dana Gulling Mead, 'From "Topoi" to Dialectic: The Progression of Invention Techniques in the Poetry of William Blake' (Texas Christian University, 1985). See in particular her chapter IV, pp. 76–104, which compares dialogues in *Thel* and *Visions* to Plato's Georgics, and reveals examples of Bakhtin's dialogic language and Kristeva's non-disjunctive characters.

41. Susan Fox, *Poetic Form in Blake's Milton* (Princeton, NJ: Princeton University Press, 1976), pp. 7–8. Marjorie Levinson, 'The Book of *Thel* by William Blake: A Critical Reading', *ELH*, 47 (1980), 287–303, (p. 289, and passim). Levinson goes on to contend, 'it is her own words, her own identity, herself as craving or Desire that furnishes the content of the creatures' speeches', p. 290 and Wagenknecht agrees that Thel is engaged in 'self-communication', *Blake's Night*, p. 152, as does Christopher Heppner: 'the whole process of the poem is really self-interpretation [. . .] it is herself that she questions in her encounters with the "Representatives" of her feelings as they are called into existence by her own words', '"A Desire of Being": Identity and *The Book of Thel*', *CLQ*, 13 (1977), 79–98, (p. 86).

42. This idealist fallacy is expressed most succintly by Heppner who claims, 'If Thel could change her perspective and see her external world as part of herself [. . .] she would find herself in a different state', ibid., p. 85.

43. So many critics have insulted Thel's intellectual and perceptual capacities that Dennis M. Read's exclamation against 'her consummate ignorance', 'Blake's "Tender Stranger": Thel and Hervey's *Meditations*', *CLQ*, 18 (1982), 160–67, (p. 167), and Gleckner's insistence on, 'Thel's essential myopia', 'Bible', p. 573 amount to little more than random examples. Michael Ferber continues this form of assessment with his claim that Thel, 'has looked askance and asquint', *The Book of Thel*, p. 61.

44. For examples of critics who have tried to turn Blake into a worshipper of nature, and a refutation of their arguments, see Donald R. Pearce, 'Natural Religion and the Plight of Thel', *BS*, 8 (1978), 23–35. Andrew J. Welburn has also offered a gnostic Blake who has very little time for the wisdom of nature: 'Blake, Initiation and *The Book of Thel*', in his *The Truth of the Imagination* (Basingstoke: Macmillan, 1989), pp. 99–122. The best clue, however, is given by Tilottama Rajan, 'the book of nature is a reversible trope [. . .] the natural may be something written', *The Supplement of Reading* (Ithaca and London: Cornell University Press, 1990), pp. 197–274, (p. 244).

45. The intensity of Thel's gaze is quite marked as she encounters the Lilly (Pl. 2, *Illuminated*, E.36) and this habit of close and intent observation is also noticeable on the title page and on Plates 4 and 5 (*Illuminated*, E. 34; 38; 39). Those critics who suggest that Thel is a victim of her own slip-shod perceptions would do well to ponder these examples.

46. See, '*Tiriel and Thel*: Forms of Devouring and Self-sacrifice', in her *Blake's Prophetic Psychology* (London and Basingstoke: Macmillan, 1983), pp. 31–60 and Joanne Carrie Lisberger, 'Violence and the Lost Maternal: Problems of Sacrifice, Biblical Authority, and Feminine Desire in Narrative' (Boston University, 1991).

47. Gillham, *William Blake* (Cambridge: Cambridge University Press, 1973), p. 182. Practically every critic has judged Thel too concerned with herself: from Damon's, 'She is [. . .] self-centred', *Dictionary*, p. 52, through Mary Lynn Johnson's string of complaints about her self-enclosure, self-absorption, sick self-involvement, in, 'Beulah, "Mne Seraphim", and Blake's Thel', *Journal of English and Germanic Philology*, 69 (1970), 258–77, to Diana Hume George's association of Thel with that ultimate of all self-absorbed figures, Narcissus: 'Thel [. . .] functions as Freud's narcissistic woman, who wants to be loved but cannot love in return', *Blake and Freud* (London and Ithaca: Cornell University Press, 1980), p. 98.

48. Fordyce, *Character and Conduct*, p. 45.

49. Levitt, 'Comus, Cloud and Thel's "Unacted Desires"', *CLQ*, 14 (1978), 72–83. The comparison between the cloud as, 'the non-moral principle of the fertilizing male' and the exploitative enchanter Comus was first made by Damon, *Dictionary*, p. 52. Levitt builds upon this idea, insisting that, 'where Comus speaks against Milton's views, the cloud, speaks for Blake', p. 78. Thel, therefore, is at error for resisting his message of Blakean sexual liberation in favour of an 'inaccurate fairy tale view of the world', p. 82. This idea is supported, with no little energy, by Vernon E. Lattin, 'Thel, in spite of the Cloud's clear example of the way to freedom and love, can only worry about being the food of worms, and remains alone and afraid to give her body', 'Blake's Thel and Oothoon: Sexual Awakening in the Eighteenth Century', *The Literary Criterion*, 16, 1 (1981), 11–24, (p. 19).

50. Cox, *Love and Logic*, p. 62.

51. Though David Erdman made the important point that Erasmus Darwin's emphasis on aggressive masculinity is particularly relevant to *Thel*, *The Illuminated Blake* (New York: Anchor/Doubleday, 1974), p. 33, most writers have chosen to ignore this in favour of enthusing over the positivity of the sexual encounter depicted on the title page. For example, W.J.T. Mitchell claims, 'The title page depicts the courting dance of the Cloud and Dew as a whirling vortex of pleasure', *Composite Art*, p. 105. It is strange that a writer so conversant with the corpus of Blake's visual art should fail to note the distress of the female figure in this encounter, especially since her stance of upreaching arms is a gesture Blake repeatedly

used to indicate female sexual distress. See, for example, the cancelled Plate c of *America: A Prophecy* (*Illuminated*; E.394) and Janet Warner, *Blake and the Language Art* (Kingston and Montreal/Gloucester: McGill-Queen's University Press/Alan Sutton, 1986), p. 105.

52. When Linkin speaks censoriously of Thel's deep 'fear of the phallus', 'Function of Dialogue', p. 69, without any hint that Thel may have good reason for this, she is expressing a completely orthodox view.

53. Behrendt, *Reading William Blake*, pp. 81–2.

54. Ferber, 'The Book of Thel', p. 56 and John Howard offers an equally oblivious assessment when he comments that the Cloud, 'states the message of selfless innocence', *Infernal Poetics*, p. 50.

55. An extract from Rousseau quoted, with no little displeasure, by Mary Wollstonecraft makes this connection quite clear: the 'education of women should be always relative to men. To please, to be useful to us, to make us love and esteem them, to advise, to console us, to render our lives easy and agreeable – these are the duties of women at all times, and what they should be taught in their infancy', *Rights of Woman*, p. 175.

56. Wagenknecht did pick up on the Cloud's hypocrisy and on the specifically female fear Thel has of being assessed only in terms of her use-value, *Blake's Night*, p. 158. Otter also offers a critical account of the Cloud, 'The Lover', pp. 395–6.

57. This suggests that Harold Bloom is seriously misguided in his contention that the worm, 'appeals powerfully to [Thel's] repressed maternalism', *Blake's Apocalypse* (London: Victor Gollancz, 1963), p. 57. Brian Wilkie makes the same mistake: 'the part of Thel that is struggling to mature is attracted to what nudity represents: sexual fulfilment and maternity', *Thel and Oothoon*, p. 75.

58. Behrendt, *Reading William Blake*, p. 81.

59. On the problematic penis see David G. Reide, 'The Symbolism of the loins in Blake's *Jerusalem*', *SEL*, 21 (1981), 547–61.

60. John E. Grant, 'Two Flowers in the Garden of Experience', in *William Blake, Essays for S. Foster Damon*, ed. by Alvin H. Rosenfeld (Providence: Brown University Press, 1969), pp. 333–67, (p. 342); Brian Wilkie, *Thel and Oothoon*, p. 76. Thel's behaviour is often set in antithesis to that of the Clod and always with negative implications. See for example Mary Lynn Johnson, 'Beulah, "Mne Seraphim"', p. 269 and Nelson Hilton who claims that 'the Clod of Clay points up Thel's inability and erroneous vision', *Literal Imagination*, p. 30. The same kind of censure of Thel's meanness in refusing to become a mother, though transmitted at a more subliminal level, is contained in Alexander Gourlay and John E. Grant's, 'The Melancholy Shepherdess in Prospect of Love and Death in Reynolds and Blake', *BRH*, 85 (1981), p. 169–89.

61. One of the best discussions of the rise of the moral mother is provided by Jane Rendall, 'Feminism and Republicanism: "Republican Motherhood"' in her *The Origins of Modern Feminism* (Basingstoke

and London: Macmillan, 1985), pp. 33–72. It was Wollstonecraft's belief that, 'To be a good mother, a woman must have sense', *Rights of Woman*, p. 266.

62. This nuptial band is reminiscent of the restraining riband bound round the breast of Hayley's heroine Serena, its function to quell the rising of anger in the service of good temper: 'When Spleen's dark powers would touch that breast to swell/ This guardian circture shall those powers repel', *Triumphs of Temper*, p. 22.

63. The chimes are with Wollstonecraft, 'Who made man the exclusive judge, if woman partake with him of the gift of reason?', *Rights of Woman*, p. 87 and Blake, 'A Little BOY Lost', (L. 15–16: E.29).

64. Wollstonecraft, ibid., p. 180; 171. Blakeans have not agreed with Wollstonecraft's censure of Cloddish ponderlessness. While she stressed that, 'when forbearance confounds right and wrong, it ceases to be a virtue', p. 118 Thel's critics sing in praise of the Clod's limitless self-sacrifice. As Gleckner explains, 'the clay gives to all; she is the great earth mother [. . .] By merely living and loving, acting and being, she has attained the higher innocence, and this is all you know and all you need to know', 'Bible', p. 578; *The Piper*, p. 169.

65. Thel's response is clearly designed to please the sensibilities of the pietistic Clod but it is wholly uncharacteristic and makes no sense, for there is no causal connection between her comment on God's cherishing of the Worm (*Thel*, 4:8–11; E.6) and her repeated complaint about fading away (*Thel*, 4:11–13: E.6). W.J.T. Mitchell picks up on this, *Composite Art*, p. 92 and even Gleckner comments upon these incongruities, *Blake and Spenser*, p. 300.

66. Donald Pearce, 'Natural Religion', offers a survey of the work of those male critics who, from 1890 onwards, have judged Thel to be a failure. Harold Bloom's view that the poem, 'ends in voluntary negation', *The Visionary Company* (Ithaca and London: Cornell University Press, 1971), p. 53 is such a critical commonplace that even a reader as alert as Elizabeth Langland is seduced: 'the girl's refusal to enter her graveplot, to encounter the sexuality and death implicit in the naked worm, defines her failure', 'Blake's Feminist Revision of Literary Tradition in "The Sick Rose"', in *Critical Paths: Blake and the Argument of Method*, ed. by Dan Miller, Mark Bracher and Donald Ault (Durham and London: Duke University Press, 1987), pp. 225–43, (p. 233). Note, too, that Nelson Hilton suggests that the intense lamentation of Plate 6 is perhaps '"hysteric", given Thel's psychological state', *Literal Imagination*, p. 31.

67. Pamela Dunbar, *William Blake's Illustrations to the Poetry of Milton* (Oxford: Clarendon Press, 1980), p. 11 and Zachary Leader declares, 'the world [Thel's voice] speaks of is a projection of her own fears and limitations rather than any objective or independent reality', *Reading Blake's Songs* (Boston: Routledge and Kegan Paul, 1981), p. 94. See, too, Lattin's comments on Plate 6 and Thel's, 'perverted understanding of sexual existence', 'Sexual Awakening',

p. 21. Other views have been offered: Elaine Kauver contends that the voice Thel hears is her superego, 'The Sorrows of Thel', pp. 182–3, whilst John Howard claims that, 'This vision is the true perspective of her earlier moans, revealing to Thel her former delusion', *Infernal Poetics*, p. 52.

68. Gleckner, *The Piper*, p. 169.

69. Linkin, 'Function of Dialogue', p. 71 and Leader concurs: the 'voice [from the grave] brutally denies the teachings of Lilly, Cloud, Clod and Worm', *Blake's Songs*, p. 94. Thankfully a small band of writers do agree with my contention that the voice speaks of a realm much like the Vales of Har and hence continues an already established complaint. See Welburn, 'Blake, Initiation', p. 113; Bohnsack, 'Ambiguity', p. 84 and Philip Cox, who rightly comments that 'the substance of the lament is the same as that of Thel herself from the very start of the poem', '"Unnatural Refuge" Aspects of Pastoral in William Blake's Epic Poetry' (University of York, 1989), p. 6.

70. Heppner very nearly concurs with my argument about Thel's senses, 'Desire of Being', p. 94 and Marilyn Bohnsack makes the point rather more forcefully in her comment, 'Compelled to step into the grave, Thel sees what existence for the fallen Eve is like – Experience with a vendetta for women', ibid., p. 84. A number of more orthodox writers also note the masculine nature of the grave's threat, see Mitchell, *Composite Art*, p. 93 and Gleckner, *Blake and Spenser*, pp. 333–4, n. 17.

71. Lady Pennington, *An Unfortunate Mother's Advice to Her Absent Daughters*, reprinted in, *The Young Lady's Pocket Library*, p. 64.

72. When Thel's voice exclaims against that, 'little curtain of flesh on the bed of our desire' she is not protesting at the physical existence of the hymen (in itself a diminutive membrane of 'little' importance) but rather, as Hilton says, against 'the significance invested in it', *Literal Imagination*, pp. 130–32, (p. 130). (Michael Ferber, therefore, is deeply misguided in his claim that, 'Thel has made a fetish of genital sex', 'The Book of Thel', p. 61). For an account of some eighteenth-century significances see Paul Gabriel Bouce, 'Some Sexual Beliefs and Myths in Eighteenth Century Britain', in, *Sexuality in Eighteenth Century Britain*, ed. by Bouce (Manchester: Manchester University Press, 1982), pp. 28–46, (pp. 33–5) and, Roy Porter, '"The Secrets of Generation Display'd": Aristotle's Masterpiece in Eighteenth Century England', in, *'Tis Nature's Fault: Unauthorized Sexuality during the Enlightenment*, ed. by Robert Purks MacCubbin (Cambridge: CUP, 1987), pp. 1–21, (p. 12).

73. Wagenknecht suggests that these lines are, 'perhaps dramatically inappropriate to [Thel's] consciousness', *Blake's Night*, p. 162 and most critics simply refuse to acknowledge that Thel could have any sexually radical ideas or desires. For example Levitt claims that Thel flees because she cannot bear to hear her future self rejecting restraints on sex, 'Cloud, Comus', p. 81. See also George, *Blake and Freud*, p. 94; 97; Janet Warner, *Blake and the Language of Art*, p. 34; Margaret Storch, *Sons and Adversaries* (Knoxville: The

University of Tennessee Press, 1990), p. 86 and S. Foster Damon, who rather than accepting the dynamism of female sexuality speaks misogynistically of, 'the girl's natural revulsion from the impulses of her maturing flesh', *Dictionary*, p. 400.

74. Jay Parini, 'Blake and Roethke: When Everything Comes to One', in, *William Blake and the Moderns*, ed. by Robert J. Bertholf and Annette S. Levitt (Albany, New York: University of New York Press, 1982), pp. 73–91, (p. 77).

75. A few dissenting perspectives do exist. W.J.T. Mitchell suggests that, 'Thel's shriek and flight' may 'be seen not as a failure to face life, but as the sign of a revelation', *Composite Art*, p. 91. A.G. Den Otter expounds at length the idea that 'Thel rushes back to the undefined possibilities awaiting her in the Vales of Har', 'The Lover', p. 399 and also in his 'The Question', p. 655; whilst Alexander Gourlay feels that the poem isn't a failure because Thel will eventually learn from her errors, she will 'in all likelihood, [be] transformed and redeemed', 'Blake's Sisters', p. 72.

76. The two key writers in this important tradition are, Anne K. Mellor, 'Blake's Designs for *The Book of Thel:* An Affirmation of Innocence', *PQ*, 50 (1971), 193–207, (p. 205) and Nancy Bogan, 'A New Interpretation' in *Thel, A Facsimile*, pp. 21–31, (p. 31).

77. Bogan, ibid., p. 30. These interpretations have not been well received by the Blake establishment, with Donald Pearce commenting that Bogan's assessment of Thel as a protester, 'may well be the most bizarre suggestion yet in the entire range of Thel criticism', 'Natural Religion', p. 28. Students of Blake have, however, occasionally followed the lead given by these women with Marilyn Bohnsack offering perhaps the best elaboration: 'Following the footsteps of her other Biblical prototype, Lilith, she rebels and flees. Her action, which seems disobedient and unrepentant, brings about the complete identification of women with "otherness"', 'Ambiguity', p. 84.

78. Discussion of the motto is provided by Otter, 'The Question', pp. 633–7, although he is not much interested in its obvious gendered significance.

79. Wollstonecraft, *Rights of Woman*, p. 81; 132.

80. As we've seen even astute critics tend to take a rosy view of Har, and of the opportunities available to Thel. Even Margaret Hood contends that Thel is faced with a 'multiplicity of potential roles', 'Daughter of Beauty', p. 264.

81. Bohnsack, 'Ambiguity', p. 79. It is crucial to understand that each realm which Thel enters presents her with precisely the same feminine roles, though the degree of idealization with which they are portrayed diminishes as the poem progresses and Thel becomes more sceptical. Bohnsack picks up on this: 'Thel may be an early attempt by Blake to act out the drama of a woman's life both as it appears to be and as it is', p. 96. She rightly finds, 'Blake ironically balancing the real female world of childbearing, pain, and possible death with the "arbitrary fantasy" of silly social decorum', p. 95.

82. Cox, *Love and Logic*, p. 65.
83. Everest, 'Thel's Dilemma', *Essays in Criticism*, 37, 3 (1987), 193–
    208. The studies of *Thel* which have emerged since Everest's arti-
    cle show very little interest in the pressing historical and political
    issues he raises. See, for example, Scott Simpkins, 'The Book of Thel
    and the Romantic Lament', *South Central Review*, 5, 1 (1988), 25–
    39; James E. Swearingen, 'Will and Desire in Blake's *Thel*', *ECS*,
    23, 2 (1989–90), 123–39; A.G. Den Otter, 'Thel: The Lover' and 'The
    Question'; Eugenie R. Freed, '"Sun-Clad Chastity"'; Brian Wilkie,
    *Thel and Oothoon*, and Michael Ferber, 'The Book of Thel'. Even
    when awareness is expressed it seems to have little impact upon
    critical interpretations, see especially the incongruous remarks which
    conclude Stephen Behrendt's censorious offering, *Reading William
    Blake*, pp. 74–84. Sadder still is Gerda S. Norvig's, 'Female Subjec-
    tivity and the Desire of Reading In (to) Blake's *Book of Thel*', *SiR*,
    34 (Summer 1995), 255–71, which contains the vital but far too
    short section, 'Identification and Empathy: Thel's Feminism
    and Blake's Cultural Critique' (pp. 270–71) – as she admits, 'I do
    not have space here to do more than hint at this line of argument'
    (p. 271).

    As ever, the only works which have treated issues of gender
    and sexual politics seriously and at length are unpublished theses
    and dissertations. As my discussion has made clear the most out-
    standing readings of *Thel* are provided by Margaret Hood, 'Thel –
    Daughter of Beauty' and, especially, Marilyn Bohnsack, 'Ambigu-
    ity in *The Book of Thel*'. Jackie Labbe is also working on an article
    which promises to compliment these valuable works.
84. Rajan, *The Supplement of Reading*, p. 9. See, too, the shorter version
    of her article, 'En-Gendering the System: *The Book of Thel and Visions
    of the Daughters of Albion*', in *The Mind in Creation*, ed. by J. Doug-
    las Keane (Quebec: Mc Gill's–Queen's University Press, 1992), pp.
    74–90.

## 3 'Slip-Sliding Away': Some Problems with 'Crying Love' in the 1790s

1. I have consulted approximately 50 pieces of criticism on *Visions*
   and no writer makes reference to this aspect of Damon's text.
2. S. Foster Damon, *A Blake Dictionary* (Hanover and London: Brown
   University Press, 1988. fp. 1965), p. 437; and see, 'The Fifth Window', in his *William Blake: His Philosophy and Symbols* (London:
   Dawsons of Pall Mall, 1929), pp. 98–104.
3. Charles Cherry has commented that in *Visions* Blake, 'is not confronted with dealing with history', 'The Apotheosis of Desire: Dialectic and Image', *Xavier University Studies*, VIII (Summer 1969),
   18–31, (p. 29) and Stewart Crehan speaks of 'the sexual act' as
   one of the few spheres of human activity that remains outside
   and resists external pressures, see his *Blake in Context* (Dublin: Gill
   and Macmillan, 1984), p. 50.

4. John G. Moss, 'Structural Form in Blake's *Visions . . .*', *Humanities Association Bulletin*, 22, 2 (1970), 9–18, (p. 9).
5. Innumerable critics have drawn parallels between Thel and Oothoon, including all the founding fathers of Blake studies: Damon, Frye, Erdman and Bloom. Characteristic recent readings include: Vernon E. Lattin, 'Blake's Thel and Oothoon: Sexual Awakening in the C18th', *The Literary Criterion*, 16: 1 (1981), 11–24; E.B. Murray, 'Thel, Thelyphthora and The Daughters of Albion', *SiR*, 20 (Fall 1981), 275–97 and Michael Ferber, 'Towards Revolution', in his *The Poetry of William Blake* (London: Penguin Critical Studies, 1991), pp. 64–88, (pp. 67–74).
6. The most succinct account of Oothoon as a 'higher innocent' is provided by Morton Paley in his study, *Energy and Imagination* (Oxford: Clarendon Press, 1970), pp. 35–6.
7. As Robert P. Waxler has commented, 'Thel's image of rape becomes a fact in Oothoon's reality', 'The Virgin Mantle Displaced: Blake's Early Attempt', *Modern Language Studies*, 12: 1 (Winter 1982), 45–53, (p. 48).
8. Harold Bloom, 'Commentary', in David Erdman's *The Complete Poetry and Prose of William Blake* (New York: Anchor Press/Doubleday, 1982), p. 900. Bernard Blackstone, *English Blake* (Cambridge: Cambridge University Press, 1949), pp. 291–3; Harold Bloom, *Blake's Apocalypse* (London: Victor Gollancz, 1963), pp. 101–16; Ronald Duerkson, 'The Life of Love: Blake's Oothoon', *CLQ*, 13 (1977), 186–94; Morris Dickstein, 'The Price of Experience: Blake's Reading of Freud', in *The Literary Freud*, ed. by Joseph H. Smith (New Haven: Yale University Press, 1980), pp. 67–111; E.B. Murray, 'Thel, *Thelyphthora*'; Diana Hume George, *Blake and Freud* (London and Ithaca: Cornell University Press, 1980), pp. 127–44; Howard O. Brogan, 'Blake On Woman: Oothoon to Jerusalem', *CEA Critic*, 48/49: 4/1 (1986), 125–36; Crehan, *Blake in Context*, pp. 116–17; Jean Hagstrum, *The Romantic Body* (Knoxville: University of Tennessee Press, 1985), pp. 114–15 and James E. Swearingen, 'The Enigma of Identity in Blake's *Visions . . .*', *Journal of English and German Philology*, 91 (1992), 203–15. Final quotation from Stephen Cox, *Love and Logic* (Ann Arbor: University of Michigan Press, 1992), p. 113.
9. Leopold Damrosch, *Symbol and Truth in Blake's Myth* (Princeton, NJ: Princeton University Press, 1980), pp. 195–205.
10. Jane Peterson, 'The Visions of the Daughters of Albion: A Problem of Perception', *PQ*, 52 (1973), 252–64; Mark Anderson, 'Oothoon, Failed Prophet', *Romanticism Past and Present*, 8, 2 (1983), 1–21; Laura Ellen Haigwood, 'Blake's *Visions of the Daughters' of Albion*: Revising An Interpretative Tradition', *San Jose Studies*, 11, 2 (1984), 77–94; Helen Ellis, 'Blake's "Bible of Hell": Visions of the Daughters of Albion and the Song of Solomon', *English Studies of Canada*, 12 (1986), 23–36 and Brian Wilkie, *Blake's Thel and Oothoon* (Victoria, Canada: University of Victoria, 1990), ELS Monograph Series, No. 48.
11. Ellis, ibid.; Susan Fox, 'The Female as Metaphor in William Blake's Poetry', *Critical Inquiry*, 50, (Spring 1977), 507–19, (pp. 512–13); Anne

K. Mellor, 'Blake's Portrayal of Women', *BQ*, 16, 3 (Winter 1982–83), 148–55; 'Blake's Songs of Innocence and of Experience: A Feminist Perspective', *Nineteenth-Century Studies*, 2 (1988), 1–17, (p. 16); Alicia Ostriker, 'Desire Gratified and Ungratified: William Blake and Sexuality', *BQ*, 16, 3 (Winter 1982–83), 156–65; Brenda Webster, *Blake's Prophetic Psychology* (Basingstoke: Macmillan, 1983), pp. 91–109 and Dana K. Haffar, 'The "Women" in Blake's Early Writings and the "Females" of the Prophecies' (Oxford, October 1984), p. 32.

12. Harriet Krammer Linkin, 'Revisioning Blake's Oothoon', *BQ*, 23, 4 (Spring 1990), 184–94, (p. 192); Michele Leiss Stepto, 'Blake, Urizen and the Feminine: The Development of a Poetic Logic' (University of Massachusetts, 1978), p. 99; Michael Ferber, *The Social Vision of William Blake* (Princeton, NJ: Princeton University Press, 1985), pp. 111–12.

13. Steven Vine, '"That Mild Beam": Enlightenment and Enslavement in William Blake's *Visions . . .*, in *The Discourse of Slavery*, ed. by Carl Plasa and Betty J. Ring (London: Routledge, 1994), pp. 40–63; John Moss, 'Structural Form'; Haigwood, 'Revising an Interpretative Tradition'; Nancy Moore Goslee, 'Slavery and Sexual Character: Questioning the Master Trope in Blake's *Visions of the Daughters of Albion*', *ELH*, 57, 1 (Spring 1990), 101–28; Thomas Vogler, '"In Vain the Eloquent Tongue": An Un-Reading of *Visions of the Daughters of Albion*', in *Critical Paths: Blake and the Argument of Method*, ed. by Dan Miller, Mark Bracher and Donald Ault (Durham: Duke University Press, 1987), pp. 271–309; Linkin, ibid. and James A.W. Hefferman, 'Blake's Oothoon: The Dilemmas of Marginality', *SiR*, 30 (Spring 1991), 3–18, (pp. 3–5).

    The essays of Moss, Haigwood, Goslee, Vogler, Linkin and Hefferman all do, of course, more than simply review and revise what has gone before them, but it remains the case that a distinct tendency exists in *Visions* criticism for imagining that answers to the poem's paradox will become apparent if past criticism is interrogated thoroughly enough. Note, too, that another group of writers, led by Kathleen Raine, have chosen to ignore the sexual problems raised by the poem altogether. See her, 'Oothoon in Leutha's Vale', in *Blake and Tradition* (Princeton, NJ: Bollingen Series XXXVII, Princeton University Press, 1986), I, pp. 166–79; Jane Peterson, 'A Problem of Perception'; Howard Hinkel, 'From Energy and Desire to Eternity: Blake's *Visions*', *Papers on Language and Literature*, 15 (1979), 278–89 and Mark Bracher, 'The Metaphysical Grounds of Oppression in Blake's *Visions*', *CLQ*, 20 (1983), 164–76.

14. Vogler, ibid., pp. 275; 300, and for his belief in Blake's sexist messages see, p. 300. It should, however, be noted that Hefferman uses post-structuralist theory for rather less nihilistic purposes in his account of Oothoon as an exemplary marginal figure, who unsettles patriarchal categorization through her search for, 'a genuine alternative to the language of male authority and assertion' and, 'her resistance to classification, her refusal to be polarized', ibid., pp. 5; 6.

15. Some examples of this golden age approach are, Bernhardt J.

Hurwood, *The Golden Age of Erotica* (London: Tandem, 1968); 'Introduction' to, *Venus Unmasked*, ed. by Peter Fryer and Leonard de Vries (London: Arthur Barker, 1967), pp. 7–14; Peter Webb, 'Eighteenth and Nineteenth Centuries', in his *The Erotic Arts* (London: Secker and Warburg, 1983), pp. 136–74 and Patrick J. Kearney, *A History of Erotic Literature* (London and Basingstoke: Macmillan, 1982), especially the 'Introduction', pp. 7–18 and, 'The 18th Century: The Flowering of Libertinism', pp. 53–100.

See, also, Lawrence Stone, *The Family, Sex and Marriage in England 1500–1800* (Harmondsworth: Penguin, 1977), especially the section, 'The Companionate Marriage', pp. 217–53; and the work of Jean Hagstrum, who recently acknowledged his debt to Stone in his collection of essays, *Eros and Vision: The Restoration to Romanticism* (Evanston: North Western University Press, 1989), p. xv. Hagstrum's literary and art-historical writings have played a significant role in popularizing more refined ideas about eighteenth-century sexual ideals and mores. See his *Sex and Sensibility* (Chicago: Chicago University Press, 1980) and *The Romantic Body*. Peter Wagner offers a useful critique of Hagstrum's, *Sex and Sensibility*, especially his failure to take cognizance of popular 'erotica', in his 'Researching the Taboo: Sexuality and Eighteenth Century English Erotica', *Eighteenth Century Life*, 8, 3 (May 1983), 108–15.

16. In this account I draw upon Bouce's two essays 'Aspects of Sexual Tolerance and Intolerance in XVIIIth Century England', *British Journal for Eighteenth Century Studies*, III (Autumn 1980), 173–91 and, 'The Secret Nexus: Sex and Literature in Eighteenth Century Britain', in *The Sexual Dimension in Literature*, ed. by Alan Bond (London: Vision, 1982), pp. 70–89.

17. Amongst the works which have pronounced the Golden Age myth dead are, *Sexuality in Eighteenth Century Britain*, ed. by Paul Gabriel Bouce (Manchester University Press: Manchester, 1982), pp. xi–xii and *Sexual Underworlds of the Enlightenment*, ed. by G.S. Rousseau and Roy Porter (Chapel Hill: University of North Carolina Press, 1988).

18. Peter Wagner, *Eros Revived: Erotica of the Enlightenment in England and America* (London: Secker and Warburg, 1988), concluding remarks. Note, too, his comment that 'We are still very much unaware of the links between the canon of so-called "high literature" and the rich subsoil of erotica', p. 303. There is, however, a problem with Wagner's definition of the term erotic as 'writing about sex within the context of love and affection', p. 5, namely that most of the 'erotica' presented in his text fails to meet these criteria. See, too, Wagner's introduction to the collection of essays he edited, *Erotica and the Enlightenment* (Frankfurt am Main: Peter Lang, 1991), pp. 9–40. Especially important is his observation, 'In the field of erotica, the eighteenth century did not make clear cut demarcations between genres or kinds of discourse', (p. 26).

19. Hunt, 'Introduction: Obscenity and the Origins of Modernity, 1500–1800', in the collection she edited, *The Invention of Pornography* (New York: Zone Books, 1993), pp. 9–45, (p. 44).

20. Vivien Jones makes a similar point. Constructions of women's sexuality and sexual rights in conduct books and pornography are, she says, 'ideologically inseparable'. See her anthology, *Women in the Eighteenth Century* (London and New York: Routledge, 1990), p. 57.

21. *The Bon Ton Magazine*, XXVI (May 1793), 100–1.

22. In its lack of political subversiveness British pornography differed markedly from that which appeared in France throughout the eighteenth century. These continental materials are dealt with in my discussion of Blake's *Europe – A Prophecy*. It should, however, be noted that radicalism and pornography did have a more suggestive nexus at a slightly later date. See, Iain McCalman, 'Unrespectable Radicalism: Infidels and Pornography in Early Nineteenth-Century London', *Past and Present*, 104 (1984), 74–110 and *Radical Underworld: Prophets, Revolutionaries and Pornographers in London, 1795–1840* (Cambridge: Cambridge University Press, 1988), and in particular, 'Grub Street Jacks: obscene populism and pornography', pp. 204–31.

23. *The Festival of Love, or, a Collection of Cytherean Poems*, Procured and Selected by G-E P-E, A New Edition (London: M. Smith, 1789), provides a number of examples of eighteenth-century women being branded as Eves, including the epigram, 'So num'rous are these modern Eves,/ A Forest Scarce could find them leaves', p. 48.

24. Some examples of writers offering sexual grand theories, and by no means concentrating exclusively on male anxiety, are those in Hunt's collection, *The Invention of Pornography* along with Randolph Trumbach, 'Modern Prostitution and Gender in Fanny Hill: Libertine and Domesticated Fantasy', in *Sexual Underworlds*, pp. 69–85; Trumbach, 'London's Sapphists: From Three Sexes to Four Gender in the Making of Modern Culture', in *Body Guards: The Cultural Politics of Gender Ambiguity*, ed. by Julia Epstein and Kristina Straub (London: Routledge, 1991), pp. 112–41; David Punter, 'Blake, Trauma and the Female', *New Literary History*, 153 (1984), 475–90 and especially relevant here Nancy Cott, 'Passionlessness: An Interpretation of Victorian Sexual Ideology, 1790–1850', in *A Heritage of Their Own: Towards a New Social History of American Women*, ed. by Nancy Cott and Elizabeth H. Pleck (New York: Simon and Schuster, 1979), pp. 162–81.

25. See works of Hunt and Trumbach listed above, as well as Trumbach's, 'Erotic Fantasy and Male Libertinism in Enlightenment England', in *The Invention of Pornography*, pp. 253–82.

26. Brian Wilkie has commented that Blake's feminism in *Visions and America* can 'seem limited, by a too-exclusive identification of feminism with erotic sexuality', but he goes on to redeem this emphasis, *Thel and Oothoon*, pp. 83–4, (p. 84).

27. Modesty, of course, was the watchword of the conduct literature that we examined in the previous chapter. As the anonymous author of, *Female Virtues: A Poem* (London: T. Cadell, 1787) put it, modesty was considered to be 'innate purity, the highest gem/ Of fe-

male virtues', p. 13. See especially, James Fordyce's disquisition, 'On Modesty of Apparel', in *Sermons to Young Women, In Two Volumes* (London: A. Miller and T. Cadell, J. Dodsley and J. Payne, 1766), I, pp. 43–81 and J. Burton's, *Lectures on Female Education and Manners*, 1st American Edition (New York: Samuel Campbell, 1794), whose Lecture XIII deals with 'Modesty, a Female Virtue'. As we shall see both Blake and Mary Wollstonecraft reacted violently to strictures of this kind.

28. *The Economy of Love* (London and York: N. Frobisher, 1791), p. 34. Although the work was first published in 1736 it was constantly reprinted throughout the century. The eighth edition I worked with was published in 1791 and the entire work was also included in *The Festival of Love* (1789), pp. 120–40. As Roy Porter importantly notes, 'the sexual knowledge people were acquiring through print was old-fashioned', 'Forbidden Pleasures: Enlightenment Literature of Sexual Advice', in *Solitary Pleasures*, ed. by Paula Bennett and Vernon A. Rosario III (New York and London: Routledge, 1995), pp. 75–98, (p. 89).

29. *The Joys of Hymen, or, The Conjugal Directory: A Poem in Three Books (1768)*, reproduced in *Venus Unmasked*, pp. 130–5, (p. 133). For a discussion of this work see, Roy Porter, 'Love, Sex and Medicine: Nicolas Venette and his *Tableaux d'amour conjugal*', in *Erotica and the Enlightenment*, ed. by Peter Wagner (Frankfurt am Main: Peter Lang, 1991), esp. pp. 96–7, 113–16.

30. Fifty editions of Rochester's work appeared between his death and the end of the eighteenth century – see, *The Complete Poems of John Wilmot Earl of Rochester*, ed. by David Vieth (London and New Haven: Yale University Press, 1968), p. xxxiii. Rochester's reputation was also kept alive and diffused in jest books such as, *Rochester's Jests; or The Quintessence of Wit* 4th ed. (London, 1770. fp. 1766) and, *The Whimsical Jester, or, Rochester in High Glee* (London 1784, 1788); and in chapbooks such as, *Joaks upon Joaks; or, No Joak like a true Joak* (Printed in London, 17—), which reprinted a condensed version of the poet's 'Whim Against Women', p. 13. At a more elite level the *Bon Ton Magazine* (1791–95) also made knowing reference to, 'the witty and facetious Earl of Rochester', IX (Nov. 1791), p. 323.

31. *A Ramble in St. James Park*, pp. 40–46, (p. 44) and see for example, *Song 'Fair Chloris in a Pigsty Lay'*, pp. 27–8; *Signior Dildo*, pp. 54–9 and 'The Mock Song', pp. 136–7, in *The Complete Poems*.

32. On the myth of the devouring woman see Paul Gabriel Bouce, 'Some Sexual Beliefs and Myths in Eighteenth Century Britain', in *Sexuality in Eighteenth Century Britain*, pp. 28–46, (pp. 41–3); Francis Grose, *A Classical Dictionary of The Vulgar Tongue* 2nd Edition, Corrected and Enlarged (London: S. Hooper, 1788).

33. See Peter Wagner, 'Medical and Para-Medical Literature', in *Eros Revived*, pp. 8–46 and Roy Porter and Lesley Hall, 'Masturbation in the Enlightenment: Knowledge and Anxiety', in their, *The Facts of Life: The Creation of Sexual Knowledge in Britain, 1650–1950* (New

Haven and London: Yale University Press, 1995), pp. 91–105.

34. My account of *Onania* and its variants draws upon Peter Wagner's discussion of the texts, especially his essay: 'The Veil of Science and Morality: Some Pornographic Aspects of the *Onania* ', *British Journal for Eighteenth Century Studies*, 6 (1983), 179–84. A useful discussion is also provided by Ludmilla Jordanova, who argues that the work celebrates in language the practices it condemns and must be 'seen in the larger context of conduct books in general', 'The Popularization of Medicine: Tissot on Onanism', *Textual Practice*, 1 (1987), 68–79, (p. 64).

35. Though it is worth remembering that the impact of these works is hard to gauge because scholarship on the subject is still in its infancy, see *Solitary Pleasures*, passim .

36. 'A Supplement', in *Onania: or, the Heinous Sin of Self-Pollution* (16th ed. London, 1737), p. 134.

37. I am indebted here to Lynne Friedli's comments about the clitoris in her fascinating essay, '"Passing Women" – A Study of Gender Boundaries in the Eighteenth Century', in *Sexual Underworlds*, pp. 234–60, (p. 247) and to Jordanova, 'Tissot on Onanism', p. 76.

38. John Wilkes, in the notes to his *Essay on Woman* (Chelsea, 1888. fp. c. 1764), called the clitoris 'a bastard plant' and said of it 'at Lesbos it was the formidable rival of Pego. The Lesbian ladies knew perfectly the virtues of it, and preferred it to the other plant – most absurdly, in my opinion', (n, p. 9). For an account of the complicated, but politically interesting, publishing history of the Essay, see: Henry Ashbee (Pisamus Fraxi), *Bibliography of Prohibited Books*, Reprint Intro G. Legman (London and New York, 1962), I, pp. 198–236. Paul Gabriel Bouce details the various 'cures' outlined for masturbating women, 'Aspects of Intolerance', pp. 179–80.

39. James Graham quoted by Roy Porter, 'Sex and the Singular Man: the Seminal Ideas of James Graham', *Studies on Voltaire and the Eighteenth Century*, 228 (1984), 3–24, (p. 20).

40. Francis Grose, *Dictionary*.

41. My account of the 'Man Mid-wives' controversy is drawn from Roy Porter, 'A Touch of Danger: The Man-Midwife as Sexual Predator', in *Sexual Underworlds*, pp. 206–32. An example of a brief contemporary treatment of the theme is, 'The Accoucheur: A Tale', in the *Bon Ton Magazine*, VII (Sept. 1791), 262.

42. According to G.S. Rousseau and Roy Porter it was in this century that, 'the dread figure of the nymphomaniac began to loom large in the proto-psychiatric imagination', *Sexual Underworlds*, p. 3. See also G.S. Rousseau, 'Nymphomania, Bienville and the rise of erotic sensibility', in *Sexuality in Eighteenth Century Britain*, pp. 95–119.

43. Noted by Vivien Jones, *Women in the Eighteenth Century*, p. 58.

44. *The Ladies Dispensatory; or, Every Woman Her Own Physician* (1740) in, Jones, ibid., pp. 83–5, (p. 83). Note that this was reprinted later in the century.

45. Nancy Cott's, 'Passionlessness' thesis is apposite here, as are the

comments I made about feminine malleability in my earlier discussion of conduct literature.

46. *The Economy of Love*, pp. 13–14. Other instances of overawed brides can be found in *The Festival of Love*, see for example, 'From L-Y W-Y, To A Female Friend, Single, Descriptive Of The Nuptial Joys', pp. 82–91.

47. For the 'wedding night' encounter, see *Fanny Hill or Memoirs of a Woman of Pleasure* (London: Penguin, 1985. fp. 1750), pp. 78–80. This text became infamous as soon as it was published in the middle of the eighteenth century; and when the *Gentleman's Magazine* came to write an obituary for Cleland in February 1789 it lamented that the works' 'poisonous contents are still in circulation', Lix (Feb, 1789), p. 180. For an account of editions of the text and the variants it spawned, see *Bibliography of Prohibited Books*, III, pp. 60–72.

For a discussion of Cleland's penchant for the sizable penis see, Carol Houlihan Flynn, 'What Fanny Felt: The Pains of Compliance in *Memoirs of A Woman of Pleasure*', *Studies in the Novel*, 19, 3 (Fall 1987), 284–95.

48. For penis as Tree of Life see, 'The Geranium' in *The Festival of Love*, pp. 24–7 and Cleland, *Fanny Hill*, p. 153. For a discussion of Cleland's phallic metaphors and their epic proportions, see Nancy K. Miller, '"I'S" In Drag: The Sex of Recollection', *The Eighteenth Century*, 22 (1981), 47–57, (p. 54); Frederick Burwick, 'John Cleland: Language and Eroticism', in *Eroticism and the Enlightenment*, pp. 41–69, (p. 55) and Julia Epstein, 'Fanny's Fanny: Epistolarity, Eroticism and the Transsexual Text', in *Writing the Female Voice*, ed. by Elizabeth C. Goldsmith (Boston: Northeastern University Press, 1989), pp. 135–53. As Epstein observes, 'the phallus is everywhere and is everywhere worshipped', (p. 136).

49. See Knight's essay, *A Discourse on the Worship of Priapus, And its Connexion with the Mystic Theology of the Ancients* (London: T. Spilsbury, 1786). This work, including its contemporary reception, is usefully discussed by G.S. Rousseau, 'The Sorrows of Priapus', in his *Perilous Enlightenment: Pre and Post Modern Discourses* (Manchester: Manchester University Press, 1991), 3, pp. 65–108; Peter Funnell, 'The Symbolical Language of Antiquity', in *The Arrogant Connoisseur: Richard Payne Knight 1751–1824*, ed. by Michael Clarke and Nicolas Penny (Manchester: Manchester University Press, 1982), pp. 50–64 and Randolph Trumbach, 'Erotic Fantasy and Male Libertinism in Enlightenment England', in *The Invention of Pornography*, pp. 253–82, (pp. 271–82).

50. *The Dictionary of Love* (1753) in *Venus Unmasked*, pp. 71–2. This was, incidentally, translated from the French of Jean-François Dreux du Radier by John Cleland, and reprinted in 1776. See Roger Lonsdale, 'New Attributions to John Cleland', *Review of English Studies*, XXX, No. 119 (August 1979), 268–90, (pp. 285–7).

51. For the female body as a country, set to be discovered, see Paul Gabriel Bouce, 'Chthonic and Pelagic Metaphorization in Eighteenth Century English Erotica', in *'Tis Nature's Fault': Unauthorized Sexuality*

*during the Enlightenment*, ed. by Robert Purks Maccubbin (Cambridge: Cambridge University Press, 1987), pp. 202–16. And for a discussion and examples of women as race horses see Peter Wagnen, *Eros Revived*, pp. 142–3 and also the, 'List of Sporting Ladies' and 'Eclipse Races' by Philo-Pegasus, both in *Venus Unmasked* pp. 31–3; 120.

52. Peter Wagner, ibid., p. 240. Fanny Hill's experiences with Mr Norbert are a parody of this mania, pp. 170–75. The desire to see female blood is so pervasive in eighteenth-century sexual literature that the reader is directed to any text so far discussed, although Fanny's 'first' defloweration is perhaps the most vivid example, pp. 77–9. It is noteworthy, too, that this kind of obsession necessitates the repeated use of military metaphors, talk about 'attacks [...] on the virgin fort' abounds – see, for example, *The Whole Pleasures of Matrimony* (Aldermary Churchyard, London, 17—), pp. 12–14, (p. 14).

53. For a discussion of flagellation and much else see Peter Wagner, 'Freaks and Kinky Sex', in *Eros Revived*, pp. 21–41 and also Richard J. Wolfe, 'The hang-up of Franz Kotzwara and its relationship to sexual quackery in late 18th-century London', *Studies on Voltaire and the Eighteenth Century*, 228 (1984), pp. 47–66. Also of interest is the paraphrase and commentary of the Abbé Boileau's flagellation tract, *The History of the Flagellants, or The Advantages of Disciple* (London: Fielding and Walker, 1777), which appeared in a second edition entitled, *Memorials of Human Supersition* (1784). These not only recount tales of women being whipped by defensive monks for attempting to corrupt them, but the first edition contained a number of suggestive engravings of women about to be scourged, or poised in pensive mood amidst flagellatory equipment (see engravings opposite pages 161; 222; 340).

54. From the account of the Female Flagellists Club in *The Bon Ton Magazine*, xxii (December 1792), 378–80. For 'delicious wounds' and a 'welcome rape' see, *The Festival of Love*, pp. 27–8; 153.

55. Vivien Jones sums up this illogical construction in much the same way, *Women in the Eighteenth Century*, p. 58 and Felicity Nussbaum concludes her very interesting discussion of gender and character with the comment, 'Positioned in contradiction (between excessive sexuality and lack of desire, between virtue and vice), eighteenth-century "woman" is defined as all of a kind, yet characterless', 'HETEROCLITES: The Gender of Character in the Scandalous Memoirs', in *The New Eighteenth Century*, ed. by Nussbaum and Laura Brown (London and New York: Methuen, 1987), pp. 144–67, (p. 167).

56. This account of Blake's early development as an artist is indebted, in a general sense, to: Anthony Blunt, *The Art of William Blake* (New York: Columbia University Press, 1959); Anne K. Mellor, *Blake's Human Form Divine* (Berkeley: University of California, 1974); David Bindman, *Blake As an Artist* (Oxford: Phaidon, 1977); Bindman, *William Blake: His Art and Times* (London: Thames and Hudson, 1982); Robert Essick, *William Blake: Printmaker* (Princeton, NJ:

Princeton Univerity Press, 1980) and Albert Boime, *Art in An Age of Revolution* (Chicago and London: Chicago University Press, 1987).

57. My comments on rococo art are especially indebted to Albert Boime, ibid., and to Margaret Walter's chapter, 'Revolutionary Eros', in her study, *The Nude Male: A New Perspective* (London: Paddington Press Ltd, 1978), pp. 204–27. An interesting aspect of this subject is also discussed by Mary D. Sheriff, who raises questions about the tacit sexism of certain derogatory assessments of rococo art – as a weak feminine style, squeezed between the masculine virility of the Baroque and the Neoclassical, in her *Fragonard: Art and Eroticism* (Chicago and London: Chicago University Press: 1990), passim.

58. For more information on 'Morning Amusement'/'Evening Amusement' see Robert Essick, *The Separate Plates of William Blake* (Princeton, NJ: Princeton University Press, 1983), pp. xxii; 125–31 and figs 58; 59.

59. For Watteau, see: Donald Posner, *Watteau; A Lady At Her Toilet* (London: Allen Lane Penguin Press, 1973); *Antoine Watteau* (London: Weidenfeld and Nicolson, 1984) and, Marianne Roland Michel, *Watteau* (New York: Alpine Fine Arts, 1984).

60. Robert Essick's chapter on 'Blake's Book Illustration' in *Printmaker*, pp. 45–54 is especially useful on the relationship with Stothard. For an idea of the kind of images Blake was working on, see all the examples of work after Stothard described and reproduced in Robert N. Essick, *William Blake's Commercial Book Illustrations* (Oxford: Clarendon Press, 1991). In particular, see the plates for Joseph Ritson's, *Select Collection of English Songs*, pp. 34–5, plates 38–46.

61. Dayes, quoted by Shelley Bennett, 'Changing Images of Women in Late Eighteenth Century England: The "Lady's Magazine", 1770–1810', *Arts Magazine*, SSIX (1981), 138–41, (p. 139). My comments on Thomas Stothard and female stereotypes in *The Lady's Magazine* are indebted to Bennett's article, and to the more general discussion offered in her *Thomas Stothard: The Mechanisms of Art Patronage in England Circa 1800* (Columbia: University of Missouri Press, 1988). See, too, E.B. Bentley, 'Blake's Elusive Ladies', *BQ 26*, 1 (Summer 1992), 30–33. Edward Dayes, in fact, wrote at some length about Stothard's speciality, explaining that, 'His drawings are highly esteemed, as they are decorated with all the charms of beauty: his female figures are angelic, light, tripping, and full of grace [ . . . ] his women fascinate'. Although even an admirer like Dayes felt that this female subject matter made Stothard rather a light artist, closing his account with the defensive comment that, 'if his works are slight, an ample compensation is made in the general good arrangement of the whole', *The Works of the Late Edward Dayes Containing . . . Professional Sketches of Modern Artists*, ed. by E. W. Brayley (London, 1805), pp. 351–2.

62. Mellor notes this of Blake's adaptation of Stothard's figures, *Human Form*, p. 105. See, too, Stephen C. Behrendt, 'The Function of Illustration – Intentional and Unintentional', in *Imagination on a*

*Long Rein*, ed. by Joachim Moller (Marburg: Jomas Verley, 1988), pp. 29–44, (pp. 31–2).

63. These numbers refer to reproductions and discussions of the listed works in the 'Plates' and then the 'Text' volumes of Martin Butlin's, *The Paintings and Drawings of William Blake* (New Haven, Connecticut: Yale University Press, 1981). For other relevant images see his discussion in the 'Text' volume of Blake's, 'Illustrations to English History, c. 1779 and c. 1793', pp. 16–25 and 'Miscellaneous Early Works, Mainly in Pen and Wash c. 1775–1790', pp. 26–69.

64. See Walter's, *Nude Male*, pp. 204–19 and Boime, *Art in an Age of Revolution, passim*, on the distorting simplicity of such a model – a model whose basic sexual ideology was succinctly expressed by Henry Fuseli, 'The forms of virtue are erect, the forms of pleasure undulate', Aphorism 194, in *The Mind of Henry Fuseli: Selections from His Writings*, ed. by Eudo C. Mason (London: Routledge and Kegan Paul, 1951), p. 146. See too Stewart Crehan's lengthy discussion of the politics of these styles, 'Unique Style or Visual Ideology?', 'Republican Art' and 'Blake's Visual Art', in his *Blake in Context*, pp. 183–279.

65. Mellor notes this of Blake's adaptation of Cumberland's figures, *Human Form*, p. 116.

66. *The Works of the Late Edward Dayes*, p. 316. Even in Barry's early work (of which Blake owned a copy), *An Account of a Series of Pictures [ . . .] at the Adelphi* (London: William Adlard, 1783), the artist was expressing feminist sympathies (pp. 45–6; 61; 73; 81–2). Moreover he became an avid supporter of Mary Wollstonecraft and her ideas, and continued to protest against the abuses of eighteenth-century society through such comparative claims as the following, 'the ancient nations of the world entertained a very different opinion of female capabilities, from those modern Mahometan, tyrannical, and absurd degrading notions of female nature', *A Letter to the Dilettanti Society* (1793), in *The Works of James Barry ESQ Historical Painter* 2 vols (London: T. Cadell and W. Davies, 1809), pp. 594–9, (p. 594). Yet Barry also felt that the essence of woman was the desire to please, *A Letter*, p. 597 and it is this idea which seems to have informed his paintings of the female. See, for example, the variants of, 'King Lear Weeping over the Body of Cordelia' (pp. 42; 102–3; 56–7; 121–2), 'The Birth of Pandora' (pp. 43; 134; 141–2), 'Venus Rising from the Sea' (pp. 53–5), 'The Birth of Venus' (pp. 123–4) and 'Iachino Emerging from the Chest In Imagen's Chamber' (pp. 103–4) in William L. Pressly, *James Barry: The Artist as Hero* (London: Tate Galley Publications Dept, 1983). As Pressly comments, 'Barry's studies of female nudes are often extremely sensual', 'Nude Figure Studies', pp. 136–9, (p. 137).

For more general discussion of this interesting artist see William L. Pressly, *The Life and Art of James Barry* (New Haven and London: Yale University Press, 1981); Sarah Symmons, 'James Barry's *Phoenix*: An Irishman's American Dream', *SiR*, 15 (Fall 1976), 531–48 and, William Vaughan, '"David's Brickdust" and the Rise of the British

School', in *Reflections of Revolution*, ed. by Alison Yarrington and Kelvin Everest (London and New York: Routledge, 1993), pp. 134–58. For Blake and Barry see Symmons, pp. 531–4 and Vaughan, pp. 141–4.

67. I'm thinking especially of such images as, 'Tiriel Supporting the Dying Myratana and Cursing His Sons', c. 1789, Butlin, *The Paintings and Drawings*, 223/198, which is interesting in its use of the Lear theme. Also the series of works dealing with scenes from English history, 'Edward and Elenor', 58/63; 'The Penance of Jane Shore in St. Pauls's Church', 61/69 and 'The Ordeal of Queen Emma', 177/59.

68. Relevant are the kind of images reproduced and discussed by Peter Wagner in *Eros Revived*, pp. 266; 270; 284–8, and of works like, 'Actresses' Dressing Room at Drury Lane' (246), 'Sleeping Woman Watched by a Man' (211) and 'Female Dancer with a Tambourin' (244) in *The Drawings of Thomas Rowlandson in the Paul Mellon Collection*, compiled by John Baskett and Dudley Sudgrove (London: Barrie and Jenkins, 1977) or 'Old Rene and Sleeping Girl' (58) and 'The Life Class' (71) in *The Art of Thomas Rowlandson* (Virginia: J.H. and Art Series International, 1990). More sympathetic discussions of his art are provided by Ronald Paulson, *Rowlandson: A New Interpretation* (London: Studio Vision, 1972) and John Hayes, *Rowlandson: Watercolours and Drawings* (London: Phaidon Press Ltd, 1972).

69. This brief account of Henry Fuseli's art draws upon, Jeffrey Daniels, 'Sado-Mannerism', *Arts and Artists*, 9, 11 (Feb 1975), 22–9; 'Fuseli on Women', in *The Mind of Henry Fuseli*, pp. 142–8; Peter Tomory, *The Life and Art of Henry Fuseli* (London: Thames and Hudson, 1972), *The Poetical Circle: Fuseli and the British* (Australian Gallery Director Council, 1979); Nancy L Pressly, *The Fuseli Circle in Rome* (New Haven, Connecticut: Yale Centre for British Art, 1979); Nicolas Powell, *Fuseli The Nightmare* (London: Allen Lane Penguin Press, 1973); Carol Louise Hall, *Blake and Fuseli: A Study in the Transmission of Ideas* (New York: Garland Publications in Comparative Literature, 1985); *Henry Fuseli, 1751–1825*, exh. Cat ed. by Gert Schiff (London: Tate Gallery, 1975); D.H. Weinglass, *Prints and Engraved Illustrations by and after Henry Fuseli: A Catalogue Raisonné* (Aldershot: Scolar Press, 1994) and Kathleen Russo, 'Henry Fuseli and Erotic Art of the Eighteenth Century', in *Eros in the Mind's Eye*, ed. by Donald Palumbo (New York: Green Wood Press, 1986), pp. 39–57. Peter Wagner, *Eros Revived*, pp. 105; 106; 282; 289–91 and Albert Boime, *Art in an Age of Revolution*, pp. 260–304 also offer some interesting comments, as does Stewart Crehan, *Blake in Context*, pp. 228–9.

70. The most startling example of mere listing is provided by Nelson Hilton, who after stating that, 'The graphic designs of *Visions* ask us to think of Fuseli from the beginning' and reproducing the parallel images offers no discussion of them whatever, 'An Original Story' in *Unnam'd Forms: Blake and Textuality*, ed. by Nelson Hilton and Thomas Vogler (Berkeley: University of California Press, 1986), pp. 69–104, (p. 84).

71. Especially relevant here is the work they did together for Erasmus Darwin's, *The Botanic Garden* (1791). For comment upon their close collaboration, see Ruthven Todd, 'Two Blake Prints and Two Fuseli Drawings, with some possibly pertinent speculations', *BN*, 5 (1972), 173–81 and Robert Essick, *William Blake's Commercial Book Illustrations*, p. 6.

72. Hall uses these terms to describe their friendship, *Blake and Fuseli*, p. 6.

73. Hall discusses the Winckelmann connection, ibid., pp. 67–100, and see especially, 'Naked Beauty Displayed', pp. 81–8. Pressly also comments on the unique style Fuseli, and his circle, developed in Rome, one in which the 'heroic nude [is] the main vehicle of expression', *Fuseli Circle*, p. vii.

74. Schiff is especially insightful on Fuseli's hair fetish in his chapter, 'Fuseli, Lucifer and Medusa', in *Henry Fuseli*, pp. 15–20.

75. See Fuseli's, 'Aphorisms, Chiefly Relative to the Fine Arts', in *The Life and Writings of Henry Fuseli, ESQ M. A. R. A [ . . .] The Former written, and the latter edited, by John Knowles*, 3 vols (London: Henry Colburn and Richard Bentley, 1831), III, pp. 63–150, (pp. 141–4).

76. Fuseli, ibid., pp. 141–4. Other useful discussions of Fuseli's sexual politics are provided by D.H. Weinglass, '"The Elysium of Fancy": Aspects of Henry Fuseli's Erotic Art', in *Erotica and the Englightenment*, pp. 294–353 and Kathleen Russo, 'A Comparison of Rousseau's "Julie" with the Heroines of Greuze and Fuseli', *Women's Art Journal*, 8 (1989), 3–7. The kind of images I'm thinking of are works like, 'Symplegma of a Bound and Naked Man with Two Women' (1770–8), which is reproduced in *Eros Revived*, p. 291 and the variation with 'Three Women', which is in *Henry Fuseli*, p. 19, fig. 7.

77. For the Nightmare's popularity, see 'Impact and Repurcussions', pp. 77–96, and, 'Appendix II: Checklist of Caricatures and Satirical Prints', in Powell's *Nightmare*.

78. For accounts of 'Falsa ad Coelum', and speculation on who produced it, see Essick, *Separate Plates*, pp. 175–6 and David Bindman, *The Complete Graphic Works of William Blake* (London: Thames and Hudson, 1978), pp. 469–70.

79. Fuseli, *Aphorisms*, pp. 144; 143.

80. One writer who has noticed that Blake is chastising Fuseli in this annotation is Nelson Hilton, 'Original Story', p. 75.

81. Johann Joachim Wincklemann, *Reflections on the Sculpture of the Greeks* (1765), trans. Henry Fuseli (Menston, UK: Scolar Press, 1972), p. 23.

82. Powell notes that for Fuseli, 'Winckelmann's reservations were almost recommendations: he was always to prefer muscular figures to tender youths', *Nightmare*, p. 27.

83. For Michelangelo's patriarchalism see Walter's, 'Michelangelo' in her *Nude Male*, pp. 128–151.

84. For this de-emphasis of the father see, Jenijoy La Belle, 'Blake's Visions and Re-visions of Michelangelo', in *Blake in his Time*, ed. by Robert Essick and Donald Pearce (Bloomington and London: Indiana University Press, 1978), pp. 13–22.

85. As David Bindman notes, 'The most striking contribution of satirical method in Blake's art lies in the depiction of Urizen himself, whose true nature is revealed behind the benevolent Renaissance image of God the Father created by Michelangelo and Raphael', *William Blake: His Art and Times*, p. 26.

86. During the eighteenth century, organs common to both sexes came to carry deeply gendered metaphorical loads. Part of this was the feminization of the nervous system and the masculinization of the musculature. See Ludmilla Jordanova, *Sexual Visions: Images of Gender in Science and Medicine between the Eighteenth and Twentieth Centuries* (Hemel Hempstead: Harvester Wheatsheaf, 1989), pp. 58–9.

87. Anne K. Mellor refutes this alleged feminization of Christ, in the course of offering the argument that Blake was, 'constantly sexist [in his] portrayal of women', 'Blake's Portrayal of Women', *BQ*, 16, 3 (1982–83), 148–55, (p. 148).

88. This account of Angelica Kauffmann is heavily dependent upon Albert Boime's discussion of the artist, *Art in an Age of Revolution*, pp. 108–16; Angela Rosenthal, 'Angelica Kauffmann's Ma(s)king Claims', *Art History*, 15, 1 (1992), 38–59 and in lesser ways too, Wendy Wassyng Roworth, 'Biography, Criticism, Art History: Angelica Kauffmann in Context', in *Eighteenth Century Women and the Arts*, ed. by Frederick M. Keener and Susan E. Lorsch (New York, Westport, London: Greenwood Press, 1988), pp. 209–23.

89. J. Wolcot, *The Works of Peter Pindar, Esquire*, 5 vols (London: John Walker, 1794), I, p. 45. Discussed by Boime, ibid., pp. 113–14.

90. Rosenthal, 'Angelica Kauffmann's Ma(s)king Claims', p. 44.

91. Morris Eaves, *William Blake's Theory of Art* (Princeton, NJ: Princeton University Press, 1982), pp. 18–19; 36.

92. Pierre Roussel, quoted and discussed in Londa Schiebinger, 'Skeletons in the Closet: The First Illustrations of the Female Skeleton in Eighteenth Century Anatomy', *Representations*, 14 (Spring 1986), 42–82, (p. 51).

93. Walters, *Nude Male*, p. 241 and Linda Nochlin alludes to Blake's 'reversal of natural scale, androgynous figure style, and intensified drawing', in her essay, 'Florine Stettheimer: Rococo Subversive', in *Women, Art and Power and Other Essays* (New York: Harper and Row, 1988), pp. 109–35, (pp. 112–14).

94. See Robert Essick, *Printmaker*, Parts One and Two, pp. 3–81, for a fascinating discussion of the significance of Blake's technical innovations in the period focused upon. I have only been able to offer the crudest précis.

95. It is, therefore, no accident that the only surviving plates by the Parker and Blake partnership are two light erotic 'Fancy' pieces after Stothard: 'Zephyrus and Flora' and 'Callisto'. For discussion see Essick, *Separate Plates*, pp. 139–44, figs 62, 63.

96. Essick, *Printmaker*, pp. 60; 66. See, too, D.W. Dorrbecker, 'Innovative Reproduction: Painters and Engravers at the Royal Academy of Arts', in *Historicizing Blake*, ed. by David Worrall and Steve Clark (Basingstoke: Macmillan, 1994), pp. 105–24, (p. 137).

97. Blake critics are divided on the significance of Blake's use of unclothed figures, with the poles being set by S. Foster Damon, who
contends, 'Blake's own nudes are probably the first in English art
which are completely devoid of any suggestion of sensuality. They
exist in a world where clothing was never dreamed of', *Dictionary*,
p. 303 and Anne K. Mellor who declares, 'Blake's nudes are calculated to both arouse and express erotic desire', *Human Form*, p. 146.
98. John Berger, *Ways of Seeing* (Harmondsworth: BBC and Penguin
Books, 1986. fp. 1973), pp. 54–6, (p. 54). Also relevant are the more
recent studies: Gill Saunders, *The Nude – a New Perspective* (London: The Herbert Press, 1989) and Lynda Nead, *The Female Nude:
Art, Obscenity and Sexuality* (London: Routledge, 1992).
99. The sex of this leaping figure has never been settled. See Janet
Warner for a discussion of its place in Blake's artistic vocabulary,
and for a little evidence to support my claim that it is female, is
indeed Oothoon as she starts her trip over the waves in winged
exulting swift delight, *Blake and the Language of Art* (Canada: McGill-
Queen's University Press, 1984), pp. 124–7.
Berger comments, 'Almost all post-Renaissance sexual imagery
is frontal either literally or metaphorically – because the sexual
protagonist is the spectator-owner looking at it', ibid., p. 56.
100. Specks, '"Ev'ry Woman is at Heart a Rake', *Eighteenth Century Studies*,
8 (1974–75), 27–46, (p. 46).
101. See Terry Castle, 'The Culture of Travesty: sexuality and masquerade
in eighteenth century England', in *Sexual Underworlds*, pp. 156–80.
102. Her fears are not, as Harold Bloom has suggested, 'due to sexual
inexperience', 'Commentary', in *The Complete Poetry*, p. 901. This
is a fallacious claim repeated by John Howard, who speaks of 'the
fears of virginity', *Infernal Poetics*, p. 102.
103. From 'To a Female Friend', in *Festival of Love*, pp. 82–91, (p. 83).
104. Cleland, *Fanny Hill*, p. 62.
105. From the ballad of that title in the 1789 collection, *Festival of Love*,
pp. 374–6.
106. Bloom claims Oothoon is evading sexual reality in Leutha's vale,
'Commentary', in *The Complete Poetry*, p. 901, and few writers have
acknowledged that this is the place where Oothoon learns to pleasure
herself. For example, Alexander Gourlay speaks of the 'virgin stu-
pidity' she displays here, 'Blake's Sisters', p. 126; John Howard
suggests that it is the 'vale of hidden sexuality' and that Oothoon
turns 'to Theotormon for fulfilment', *Infernal Poetics*, p. 102 and
Brian Wilkie decides that this symbolic sexual plucking occurs,
'essentially, in Oothoon's mind', *Thel and Oothoon*, p. 71. James
Heffernan makes a more interesting comment on the section when
he notes, 'there is virtually no dialogue in the poem: no communication between Oothoon and the men. The only external dialogue we get is the loving exchange between Oothoon and the
nymph at the beginning of the poem', 'Blake's Oothoon', p. 7.
107. Ferber, 'Towards Revolution', p. 68. It is a critical commonplace
that Oothoon is preparing to 'give' herself, with David Erdman

offering the most succinct conventional view when he calls Oothoon, 'a virgin bride [ . . .] willing [ . . .] to give him the flower of her virginity', 'Blake's Vision of Slavery', *Journal of the Warburg and Courtauld Institutes*, XV, 3–4 (1952), 242–52, (p. 247).

108. 'To a Female Friend', in *Festival of Love*, pp. 82–91, (p. 91). Nelson Hilton notes this about *Nympha* in a footnote to his main discussion, 'Original Story', p. 81.

109. Kate Millett, 'Beyond Politics? Children and Sexuality', in *Pleasure and Danger: Exploring Female Sexuality*, ed. by Carol Vance (London: Routledge and Kegan Paul, 1984), pp. 217–24, (p. 219) and see too, of course, *Solitary Pleasures: The Historical, Literary and Artistic Discourses of Autoeroticism*.

110. Cox, *Love and Logic*, p. 118.

111. Nymph of course appeared in other, less stark, contexts but the suggestion of sexual playfulness was constant. See, for example, the many times Charlotte Smith uses the term in her romance, *The Old Manor House* (London: Pandora Press, 1987. fp. 1794), pp. 146; 230; 257; 316; 358; 495. Conduct writers also made use of the wayward suggestiveness of the word, as, for example, in Edward Moore's epigram to his *Fables for the Female Sex*, 'Truth under fiction I impart, / To weed out folly from the heart, / And show the paths, that lead astray, / The wandering nymph from wisdom's way'. All his tales were reproduced in, *The Young Lady's Pocket Library, or Parental Monitor* (Dublin: John Archer, 1790). These lines also appear in the first fable, 'The Eagle, and the Assembly of Birds', pp. 187–91, (p. 187).

112. 'Harris's List of Covent-Garden Ladies: or, the Man of Pleasure's Kalender, for the year, 1788', in *Venus Unmasked*, pp. 185–9, (p. 186). For a discussion of the *Lists*, see Bouce, 'The Secret Nexus', pp. 85–6.

113. Francis Grose, *Dictionary*.

114. As Erdman notes, 'The knots on the whip look uncannily like the heads of the Marygold flowers', *The Illuminated Blake* (New York: Anchor/Doubleday, 1974), p. 134.

115. Northrop Frye is the most overt in his denial that the encounter between Oothoon and Bromion is rape, calling it instead an 'extramarital amour', *Fearful Symmetry* (Princeton, NJ: Princeton University Press, 1974. fp. 1947), p. 239. But he is hardly alone in this emphasis. Very few critics have taken the assault seriously, to the point that even feminist writers, like Haigwood, can be found making statements such as, 'Oothoon is not a rape victim, but an active and aggressive participant in her experience', 'Revising an Interpretative Tradition', pp. 81–2. She goes on to accuse her of committing a 'verbal rape' of Theotormon, p. 88. The issue of rape functioning as a form of social control is taken up, with great pertinence, by Susan Brownmiller, *Against Our Will* (Harmondsworth: Pelican, 1986 fp. 1975) and Anna Clark, *Women's Silence, Men's Violence: Sexual Assault in England 1770–1845* (London: Pandora Press, 1987).

116. See Brownmiller, 'The Myth of the Heroic Rapist' ibid., pp. 283–308 and for its currency in late-eighteenth-century England see Anna Clark's account of John Motherill in her Chapter, 'Women's Pain, Men's Pleasure: Rape in the Late Eighteenth Century', ibid., pp. 21–45. Also, Peter Wagner, 'The Pornographer in the Courtroom: trial reports about cases of sexual crimes and delinquencies as a genre of Eighteenth century erotica', in *Sexuality in Eighteenth Century Britain*, pp. 120–40, and, 'Trial Reports and "Criminal Conversation"', in his *Eros Revived*, pp. 113–32. Quotation is from, Mark Bracher, 'The Metaphysical Grounds of Oppression', p. 165.

117. Francis Grose, *Dictionary*, 'A woman's commodity; the private parts of a modest woman, and the public parts of a prostitute'.

118. The fact that the slave-trader Bromion is prepared to give his possession Oothoon away free rather spoils Erdman's argument that he raped her to increase her market value, *Blake: Prophet Against Empire* (Princeton, NJ: Princeton University Press, 1969), pp. 226–48. For an interesting account of the extra money given for the 'breeding female' slaves whom Erdman alludes to, see Brownmiller, 'Slavery', pp. 153–69.

119. Behrendt, *Reading William Blake* (Basingstoke: Macmillan, 1992), p. 92.

120. For rape as entertainment, see the writings of Peter Wagner and also some of the extracts from rape trials reproduced for the amusement of readers in *The Bon Ton Magazine*. For example, XXVI/XXVII (April/ May 1793), which carry accounts of the trials for rape of John Curtis, pp. 70–71, and James Lavander, pp. 97–8. These amply demonstrate that the female complainant is, in fact, the one whose behaviour is under examination. For more on these issues see Anna Clark, *Women's Silence, passim*.

121. Harold Bloom argues that Oothoon's gesture in allowing the eagles to prey upon her is ironic: she never really believed herself defiled and soon rallies 'into the full rhetorical power of her new freedom', 'Commentary', in *The Complete Poetry*, p. 901. James Hefferman recently agreed with Bloom's identification of irony here and went on to offer an account of the rending as a positive sexual experience, 'if Bromion can turn sexual intercourse into an act of violent aggression, she can turn brutal punishment into a kind of sexual intercourse', 'Blake's Oothoon, p. 12. Michael Ferber concurs, 'it certainly brings about Oothoon's inward purification, the restoration of her virginity through her love for Theotormon', '*Visions*', p. 70. It is , in Alexander Gourlay's words, 'an act of self-sacrificial martyrdom that directly recalls the fate of the masculine revolutionary Prometheus', 'Blake's Sisters', p. 125. In essence these writers all agree with Harriet Linkin's assessment that Oothoon is undergoing, 'a developmental process that results in her acquiring prophetic stature by the conclusion of the poem', 'Revisioning Blake's Oothoon', p. 188.

Amongst the contributions of modern critics Mark Anderson's account of Oothoon's failure, and especially his comments on the nadir reached in the eagle's scene, is outstanding, 'Oothoon Failed

Prophet', *passim*. Much criticism written after around 1985 is also sensitive to a number of the issues I touch upon, with even Michael Ferber allowing that this is a turning point in the poem, p. 71.

122. Vine, '"That Mild Beam"', p. 41.
123. Michael Ferber, 'Blake's *America* and the Birth of Revolution', in *History and Myth*, ed. by Stephen Behrendt (Detroit: Wayne State University Press, 1990), pp. 73–99 (p. 85).
124. Vine, '"That Mild Beam"', pp. 42–50 (p. 42).
125. Alicia Ostriker, *Blake: The Complete Poems* (Harmondsworth: Penguin, 1987), p. 904.
126. Nancy Miller, 'I's In Drag: The Sex of Recollection', *passim*, see, too, Julia Epstein who comments that the text, 'erases the subjectivity of its heroine-narrator because Fanny Hill's subjectivity is appropriated by male self-celebration [ . . . ] The woman's voice emerges transsexually from Cleland's pen as a mask for the work's fundamentally homoerotic economy', 'Fanny's Fanny', pp. 148; 149 and Phillip E. Simmons who observes that in *Fanny Hill*, 'sex speaks the language of male pleasure and mastery from behind the mask of a female narrator', 'John Cleland's *Memoirs of a Woman of Pleasure*: Literary Voyeurism and the Techniques of Novelistic Transgression', *Eighteenth Century Fiction*, 3, 1 (Oct 1990), 43–63, (p. 44).
127. Hazard Adams, *William Blake: A Reading of the Shorter Poems* (Seattle: Washington University Press, 1963), p. 141.
128. Margaret Walters offers an interesting discussion in her introduction to *The Nude Male*, pp. 7–18.
129. Cleland, *Fanny Hill*, p. 83.
130. Of some relevance too might be this information from Francis Grose's *Dictionary*: Eight Eyes. I will knock out two of your eight eyes; a common Billingsgate threat from one fish nymph to another: every woman, according to the naturalists of that society, having eight eyes; viz – two seeing eyes, two lubeyes, a bell-eye, two pope's-eyes, and a ××× eye. We might well ask which of Oothoon's eyes are in 'happy copulation'.
131. Thomas Vogler notes and then discusses the fact that, 'Oothoon presents herself as a specialist of perception' in his section, 'Eyes and Hearts', 'in Vain', pp. 280–88, (p. 283). Vine, too, writes well on the problems of Oothoon's vision, '" That Mild Beam"', *passim*.
132. Wilkes, *Essay on Woman*, p. 8.
133. On pronatalism see Roy Porter, '"The Secrets of Generation Display'd": *Aristotle's Master-Piece* in Eighteenth-Century England', in *'Tis Nature's Fault*, pp. 1–21.
134. For another fruity woman who eventually gets raped, see Blake's Notebook verse, 'I asked a thief to steal me a peach' (E. 468–9).
135. The subject of late-eighteenth-century harem fantasies can be pursued in a number of texts. See, for example, 'Oriental Dreams', in Alev Lytle Croutier's, *Harem: The World Behind the Veil* (Soho: Bloomsbury Publishers, 1989), pp. 173–91; *Exoticism and the Enlightenment*, ed. by G.S. Rousseau and Roy Porter (Manchester and New York: Manchester University Press, 1990) and Nigel Leask,

*British Romantic Writers and the East: Anxieties of Empire* (Cambridge: CUP, 1992).

136. It is no wonder that 'Most through Midnight Streets', Blake heard the cries of prostitutes, as approximately one in every six of the female population of London in 1793 was involved in this kind of employment, Crehan, *Blake In Context*, p. 59. For some idea of their experiences, see Trumbach, 'Modern Prostitution and Gender', in *Sexual Underworlds*, pp. 69–85 and Vern L. Bullough, 'Prostitution and Reform in Eighteenth-Century England', in *'Tis Nature's Fault'*, pp. 61–74.

137. Anderson is insightful on this point, 'Oothoon Failed Prophet', pp. 14–15.

138. Thomas Vogler, 'in Vain', p. 307.

139. Mario Praz, *The Romantic Agony* (London: OUP, 1970. fp. 1933), p. 290. This argument has been expounded most recently by Camille Paglia who claims that he 'is the British Sade', 'Sex Bound and Unbound', in her *Sexual Personae* (London and New Haven: Yale University Press, 1990), pp. 270–99, (p. 270). More generally see Julian Baird, 'Swinburne, Sade, and Blake: The Pleasure – Pain Paradox', *Victorian Poetry*, 9 (1970), 49–75.

140. See Lucienne Frappier-Mazur, 'The Social Body: Disorder and Ritual in Sade's *Story of Juliette*', in *Eroticism and the Body Politic*, ed. by Lynne Hunt (Baltimore: Johns Hopkins University Press, 1991), pp. 131–142.

141. Carter notes, 'Sade explores the inhuman sexual possibilities of meat [ . . .] Carnal knowledge is the infernal knowledge of the flesh as meat', *The Sadeian Woman and the Ideology of Pornography* (New York: Harper Colophon Books, 1978), pp. 138; 141. See, too, her chapter, 'Speculative Finale: The Function of Flesh', pp. 137–50. For a less temporizing critique of Sade see Andrea Dworkin, 'The Marquis de Sade (1740–1814)', in her, *Pornography: Men Possessing Women* (London: The Women's Press, 1981), pp. 70–100.

142. Francis Grose *Dictionary* includes a couple of relevant entries: Beef – To be in a man's beef; to wound him with a sword. To be in a woman's beef; to have carnal knowledge of her. Cold Meat – A dead wife is the best cold meat in a man's house.

143. David Coward draws a very useful distinction between Blake and Sade, 'Pornocrat or Libertine?', *TLS*, No. 4585, 15/2/91, p. 5.

144. For conflicting views of this final illumination, see Linkin who considers it a positive image, undercutting the negative assessment of the narrator, 'Revisioning Blake's Oothoon', p. 185 and Janet Warner who comments that it is 'a sad and ironic echo of the hovering bearded form menacing her on the title-page [ . . .] What seems to be suggested is that Oothoon's failure to become one with Theotormon has made her an image of the very forces she was trying to overcome', *Language of Art*, pp. 94–5.

145. David Punter, *The Romantic Unconscious* (New York: Harvester Wheatsheaf, 1989), p. 82. See too Tilottama Rajan, 'En-gendering the System: *The Book of Thel* and *Visions*', in *The Mind in Creation*

ed. by J. Douglas Keane (Quebec: McGill-Queens University Press, 1992), pp. 74–90 (p. 87) and Steve Vine, '"That Mild Beam"', *passim*.

146. Gary Kelly speaks of 'female erotic desire' as a 'banned topic' at this time, 'Revolutionary and Romantic Feminism: Women, Writing and Cultural Revolution', in *Revolution and English Romanticism*, ed. by Keith Hanley and Raman Seldon (Hertfordshire: Harvester Wheatsheaf, 1990), pp. 107–30, (p. 115) and Lynn Hunt's collection, *The Invention of Pornography*, provides plenty of evidence.

147. An example of this exaggerated concern for female delicacy appears in the preface to Joseph Ritson's, *A Select Collection of English Songs* (London: J. Johnson, 1783), where the 'fair readers' are reassured, 'Throughout the whole of the first volume, the utmost care, the most scrupulous anxiety has been shewn to exclude every composition, however excellent, of which the slightest expression, or the most distant illusion could have tinged the cheek of Delicacy, or offended the purity of the chastest ear' (p.v). The preface writer of *The Festival of Love* also makes a cynical allusion, p. iv. For a contemporary 'explanation' of the double standard, see *The Bon Ton Magazine*, XXII (December 1792), 375–6.

> The colourings of vice, however odious in the male part of the human species, are yet infinitely more abhorrent when displayed in the opposite sex. Man, from the robust texture of his organization, as well as from the superiority of his strength, assumes, and is indeed capable, of debaucheries which women are in general ashamed of, and unequal to. Say what modern refined philosophers may, the fairest of creation never looked so fair nor so desirable as when, by soft and gentle qualities, they are contrasted to the rougher manners of mankind.

And on the third point it is interesting to note that James Graham, the primitive sexologist, mused over what the revelations might be, '*Were we to be made acquainted* with the real sentiments of the sex'. Quoted by Porter, 'Sex and the singular man', p. 14 (my emphasis).

148. Janet Todd charts this move from the sexually explicit, through the sentimental, to the moralizing in women's fiction in her excellent study, *The Sign of Angelica* (London: Virago, 1989). Developments in women's poetry of the period are, sadly, neglected in the present study. I hope, however, to rectify this in my article, '"My Thing is My Own": Inarticulate Eroticism in Women's Verse of the Late Eighteenth Century' (forthcoming).

149. Charlotte Smith, *The Old Manor House*, p. 29

150. Catherine Macaulay Graham, *Letters on Education* (London: C. Dilly, 1790), pp. 220–21.

151. *A Select Collection of English Songs*, I, Class IV, Song IV, By Lady Wortley Montague, pp. 159–60, (p. 160).

152. Ibid., I, Songs Omitted in Class IV, p. 261 and see all the songs in Class IV for a number of other striking illustrations of this theme.

Blake produced by far the majority of plates for the long 'Love Songs' section of Ritson's collection. See reproductions of these in Robert Essick, *The Commercial Engravings*, pp. 34–5, figs 38–46.

153. Mary Wollstonecraft, *The Wrongs of Woman* (Oxford: OUP, World's Classics, 1984. fp. 1797), p. 153. As Donna Landry notes, we see in this novel the 'reinscription of sexuality [ . . .] What had been excluded from the discourse of the *Vindication* returns, the voice of female labor and the emancipatory possibilities of a less constrained sexuality than British law and social custom of the 1790s would admit', 'A Shifting Limit: *The Wrongs of Woman: Or, Maria. A Fragment'*, in her, *The Muses of Resistance* (Cambridge: Cambridge University Press, 1990), pp. 268–72, (p. 271). Kelly concurs, 'Maria reclaims female sexuality from instrument of the trivialization and oppression of women in contemporary society to manifestation of women's equality of "mind"', *Revolutionary Feminism: The Mind and Career of Mary Wollstonecraft* (Basingstoke and London: Macmillan, 1992), pp. 206–23, (p. 215).

154. Wollstonecraft, ibid., 'He was [ . . .] plastic in her impassioned hand – and reflected all the sentiments which animated and warmed her', p. 189.

155. Wollstonecraft, ibid., p. 155. Kelly speaks of Maria and Darnford's 'revolutionary egalitarian love', *Revolutionary Feminism*, p. 218 but I feel Donna Landry is closer to the truth in her assessment that, 'the relation with Darnford offers no real alternative to Maria's disastrous marriage', 'A Shifting Limit', p. 271.

156. Wollstonecraft, Author's Preface tells us 'In writing this novel, I have rather endeavoured to pourtray [sic] passions than manners', ibid., p. 73.

157. The Jacobin novelists' harsh critique of the moral licence and sensuality of the aristocracy is discussed by Mark Philp, *Godwin's Political Justice* (London: Duckworth, 1986), pp. 178–9 and Marilyn Butler, *Jane Austen and the War of Ideas* (Oxford: Clarendon Press, 1976), pp. 44–5. In this context it is interesting to compare the comments of Thomas Holcroft's rakish sensualist Coke Clifton with some of Blake's ideas, for example his claims that: 'Roses grow for me to gather: rivers roll for me to lave in. Let the slave dig the mine, but for me let the diamond sparkle. Let the lamb, the dove, and the life-loving eel writhe and die; it shall not disturb me, while I enjoy the viands. The five senses are my deities; to them I pay worship and adoration, and never yet have I been slack in the performance of my duty', *Anna St Ives* (London: OUP, 1970. fp. 1792), p. 63.

158. Butler, ibid., p. 45. As she notes there is a distinctly 'puritanical streak in the English jacobin novel'. Mark Philp also remarks that, 'The attitude expressed in these novels toward sexuality [ . . .] was, if anything, more conservative than that found in the novels of sensibility', ibid., p. 179. I have also drawn upon the remarks of Jean Hagstrum, *The Romantic Body*, p. 20.

159. Anna Clark, *Women's Silence: Men's Violence*, centres this issue

throughout her text. For melodramatic retellings, see p. 81.

160. 'pale religious letchery' (*MHH*, 25; E. 45) is a target of Blake's indigation throughout the early 1790s. Note especially the woman in the 'den nam'd Religion' who murdered the minister because he wanted her to become his 'whore' (FR, 3: 35–7; E. 287).

161. Vine, '"That Mild Beam"', p. 40.

162. David Erdman speaks of the poem spinning, rather than progressing, *Prophet*, p. 228.

163. John Sutherland focuses on the dissonance between image and text on plate 7, 'Blake: A Crisis of Love and Jealousy', *PMLA*, 87 (1972), 424–31, (p. 425).

164. In *Vindication*, for instance, Wollstonecraft gets no further than imagining that co-educational schools and (perhaps) women MPs might be the answer to the question of how? As Sarah McKim Webster notes, 'We do not feel at the end of "visions" that we have more than glimpsed a new possibility [...] even the most outspokenly feminist of the early Romantic period leaves a significant gap between critique and proposal, between an understanding of the state of affairs and an imaginative (concrete) projection of change', 'Circumscription and the Female in the Early Romantics', *PQ*, 61, 1 (1982), 51–68, (p. 67).

165. Mark Anderson's otherwise very impressive reading of the poem is seriously damaged by his somewhat circular and ahistorical conclusion that, 'The fact that she cannot end her oppression does not mean that Blake has failed to envision the means by which she might have been able to do so [...] The point is not that Oothoon fails to free herself, but that she could have done so – if she had read her own prophecy well enough [...] She ultimately fails as a prophet because she fails to perceive her own reflected state, and therefore cannot change herself in response to her prophecy', 'Oothoon: Failed Prophet', pp. 17–18.

166. A number of female scholars have suggested that Blake is offering a critique of late-eighteenth-century feminism in *Visions*, with the most unequivocal statement coming from Laura Haigwood, 'I am strongly persuaded by Nelson Hilton's work that Blake was familiar enough with contemporary feminist theory and the personal life of one of its proponents, Mary Wollstonecraft, *to conceive and execute a subtle critique of feminism's internal contradictions and inconsistencies*', 'Revisioning an Interpretative Tradition', p. 90 – my emphasis. A depressing image of Blake as a typical male feminist.

167. Michael Ackland, 'The Embattled Sexes: Blake's Debt to Wollstonecraft in *The Four Zoas*', *BQ*, 16, 3 (Winter 1983), 172–83. The titular debt proves in fact to have been largely the other way round, for, as we have seen, according to Ackland Blake, 'succeeded in freeing her perceptions from many of their contemporary limitations', p. 180. The most patronizing assessments of Wollstonecraft, and accounts of Blake's ability to see beyond her, are offered by, Michael Ferber, *The Social Vision of William Blake*, pp. 112–13 and Nelson Hilton whose 'An Original Story' turns Mary Wollstonecraft's

painful relationship with Henry Fuseli into the key subtext of *Visions* and pays no attention to any of her arguments in *Vindication*, which is predominantly viewed as the text in which she wrote out her unhappiness and anger at Fuseli. An example of a polarization of their views on sex which favours Wollstonecraft is offered by Brenda Webster, *Blake's Prophetic Psychology* (Basingstoke and London: Macmillan, 1983), pp. 107–8.

Thankfully some more thoughtful studies are beginning to emerge. See especially Steve Clark, 'Blake and Female Reason', in his *Sordid Images: The Poetry of Masculine Desire* (London: Routledge, 1994), pp. 138–87 and Steve Vine's ever informative, '"That Mild Beam"', pp. 42–50.

168. Cora Kaplan, 'Pandora's Box: Subjectivity, Class and Sexuality in Social Feminist Criticism', in *Making a Difference: Feminist Literary Criticism*, ed. by Gayle Greene and Coppelia Kahn (London and New York: Methuen, 1985), pp. 146–76, (p. 155) and 'Wild Nights: Pleasure/Sexuality/Feminism', in *The Ideology of Conduct*, ed. by Nancy Armstrong and Leonard Tennenhouse (New York and London: Methuen, 1987), pp. 160–84, (p. 167). For a critique of Kaplan's argument, see Janet Todd, 'Readings of Mary Wollstonecraft', in her *Feminist Literary History: A Defence* (Oxford: Basil Blackwell, 1988), pp. 103–17, (pp. 103–10) and Gary Kelly, who like Todd, also comments on the readings of Jacobus and Poovey, *Revolutionary Feminism*, p. 226. Also interesting in this context is Tom Furniss, 'Nasty Tricks and Tropes: Sexuality and Language in Mary Wollstonecraft's *Rights of Woman*', *SiR*, 32, 2 (1993), 177–209.

## 4 Blake, the Rights of Man and Political Feminism in the 1790s

1. Richard Price, *A Discourse on the Love of Our Country* 2nd ed. (London: T. Cadell, 1789), p. 50. Thomas Paine, *Rights of Man* (London: Penguin Classics, 1985. fp. 1791), p. 146. Mary Wollstonecraft, *Vindication of the Rights of Woman* (London: Penguin Classics, 1986. fp. 1792), pp. 159–60.

2. For a detailed account see Albert Goodwin, *The Friends of Liberty* (London: Hutchinson and Co, 1979), and for added emotional involvement E.P. Thompson, *The Making of the English Working Class* (London: Penguin Books, 1986. fp. 1963), especially, 'Part One: The Liberty Tree', pp. 17–203.

3. Thompson, ibid., p. 111.

4. Others concur on the emergence and importance of this new political constituency, see E. Royle and James Walvin, *English Radicals and Reformers, 1760–1848* (Brighton: The Harvester Press, 1982), especially 'The Rise of Popular Radicalism', pp. 48–63; H.T. Dickinson, *Liberty and Property: Political Ideology in Eighteenth Century Britain* (New York: Holmes and Meier, 1977), especially, 'The New Radicalism Aims and Assumptions', pp. 240–58; Gwyn A. Williams, *Artisans and Sans-Culottes, Popular Movements in France and Britain during the French Revolution* 2nd ed. (London: Libris,

1989); and John Brewer traces the impact upon caricature prints of the emergence of 'the people' into politics, *The Common People and Politics, 1750–1790* (Cambridge: Chadwyck-Healey, 1986).

5. Joel Barlow, *Advice to the Privileged Orders* 3rd ed. (London: Joseph Johnson, 1793. fp. 1791), Part I, pp. 21–2. This was also reproduced in Thomas Spence's *Pig's Meat* (London: 1795), III, p. 56 under the title, 'On the Importance of Men Who Cannot Read in Revolutionary Transactions'.

6. On the LCS see, *Selections from the Papers of the LCS 1792–1799*, ed. Mary Thrale (Cambridge: Cambridge University Press, 1983) and Royle and Walvin, *English Radicals*, pp. 50–4.

7. David V. Erdman, *Blake: Prophet Against Empire* (Princeton, NJ: Princeton University Press, 1969. fp. 1954) is still the best book on Blake's political context, although the works of Jon Mee, *Dangerous Enthusiasm: William Blake and the Culture of Radicalism in the 1790s* (Oxford: The Clarendon Press, 1992); David Worrall, *Radical Culture: Discourse, Resistance and Surveillance, 1790–1820* (Hemel Hempstead: Harvester Wheatsheaf, 1992) and E.P. Thompson, *Witness Against the Beast* (Cambridge; Cambridge University Press, 1993) are invaluable supplements. None of these writers is primarily concerned with issues of gender or women's history, but I am nevertheless indebted to their comments and suggestions.

8. Thompson, *The Making*, p. 24.

9. For a sophisticated feminist critique of Thompson's text see Joan Wallach Scott, 'Women in *The Making of the English Working Class*', in her *Gender and the Politics of History* (New York: Columbia University Press, 1988), pp. 68–90. See, too, Harvey J. Kaye and Keith McClelland, *E.P. Thompson: Critical Perspectives* (Cambridge and Oxford: Polity Press in association with Basil Blackwell, 1990).

10. On this issue of disregard and/or sexism, see Royle and Walvin, *English Radicals*, pp. 185–8; H.T. Dickinson, *Liberty and Property*, pp. 251–4; Sheila Rowbotham, 'The new radicalism of the eighteenth century', in her *Hidden from History* (London: Pluto Press, 1974), pp. 19–22; Barbara Schnorrenberg (and Joan E Hunter), 'The Eighteenth Century Englishwoman' in *The Women of England*, ed. Barbara Kammer (London: Mansell, 1980), pp. 183–228, (pp. 202–205) and Catherine M. Rogers, 'Radicalism and Feminism', in her, *Feminism in Eighteenth Century England* (Brighton: The Harvester Press, 1982), pp. 181–208. An alternative perspective is offered by Barbara Taylor who speaks of, 'The Rights of Woman: A Radical Inheritance', in her *Eve and the New Jerusalem* (London: Virago, 1983), pp. 1–18.

11. On the exclusion of women from citizenship, including the franchise, see *Women and Politics in the Age of the Democratic Revolution*, ed. by Harriet B. Applewhite and Darline G. Levy (Ann Arbor: University of Michigan Press, 1990). Useful, too, is Claire Tomalin, Appendix I 'Eighteenth-century References to Votes for Women' in her *The Life and Death of Mary Wollstonecraft* (London: Penguin Books, 1985. fp. 1974), pp. 336–8.

12. G.J. Barker-Benfield, 'Mary Wollstonecraft: Eighteenth-Century Commonwealthwoman', *Journal of the History of Ideas*, 50, 1 (Jan–Mar 1989), 95–115, (p. 113). On Public House meetings and the LCS, see *Selections from the Papers*, pp. xviii; xxvi and Royle and Walvin, *English Radicals*, p. 51.

13. 'Introduction' to *Equal or Different: Women's Politics 1800–1914* (Oxford: Basil Blackwell, 1987), p. 7. For women's protest and politics after the war, see Iain McCalman, 'Females, Feminism and Free Love in an Early Nineteenth Century Radical Movement', *Labour History* (Aust), 38(1980), 1–25; Dorothy Thompson, 'Women and Nineteenth Century Radical Politics: A Lost Dimension', in *The Rights and Wrongs of Women*, ed. by Ann Oakley and Juliet Mitchell (London: Penguin, 1976), pp. 112–38; Gail Malmgreen, *Neither Bread Nor Roses: Utopian Feminists and the English Working Class, 1800–1850* (Brighton: John L. Noyce, 1978); Barbara Taylor, *Eve and the New Jerusalem* and David Worrall, *Radical Culture*, esp. pp. 162–3.

14. Donna Landry is quoted from, 'The 1790s and after: revolutions that as yet have no model', in her *The Muses of Resistance* (Cambridge: Cambridge University Press, 1990), pp. 254–80, (p. 254). See Williams on the possibility of a major re-evaluation, *Artisans and Sans-Culottes*, pp. xxxiv–xxxv and Thrale on loci of LCS meetings, *Selections from the Papers*, p. xxvi.

15. See John Bohstedt's, 'Gender, Household and Community Politics: Women in English Riots 1790–1810', *Past and Present*, 120 (August 1988), 88–122 and the revised version, 'The Myth of the Feminine Food Riot: Women as Proto-citizens in English Community Politics, 1790–1810', in *Women and Politics*, pp. 21–60. Bohstedt's articles deflate this myth most effectively through his demonstration that, 'plebeian women left formal institutional politics to men [ . . . ] Women did not appear in political movements until after 1815', 'Gender, Household', pp. 118–19.

16. Karl Von Donsteinen provides an interesting account of the Duchess's experiences, 'The Discovery of Women in Eighteenth Century Political Life', in *The Women of England*, pp. 229–58, (pp. 235–8) and John Brewer comments on the political cartoonists' ribald treatment of Fox, Sam House and the Duchess of Devonshire, *The Common People*, pp. 36–7.

17. Charlotte Smith, *Desmond, A Novel* (London: G.G.J. & J. Robinson, 1792), I, Preface, p. iii.

18. Cooper's *Propositions*, formed part of his *A Reply to Mr Burke's Invective* (Manchester: M. Falkner + Co., 1792), pp. 93–109. Quotations are from a large footnote, pp. 98–9.

19. On toasts see Tomalin, *The Life and Death*, p. 154, and on Johnson and women's rights, see Gerald P. Tyson, *Joseph Johnson: A Liberal Publisher* (Iowa City: University of Iowa Press, 1979), pp. 49–51. Tyson, however, tries to make rather more of Johnson's concern than the evidence will allow. See, too, Robert Essick, 'William Blake, Tom Paine and Biblical Revolution', *SiR*, 30 (Summer, 1991), 189–212, (pp. 191–3). In his discussion of Johnson's publishing con-

cerns in the early 1790s Essick has nothing to say about any 'feminist' productions. Another striking example of this radical disinterest can be found in the works of Charles Pigott, which were published anonymously. Despite the fact that his *The Female Jockey Club* (London: D.I. Eaton, 1794) addressed itself at some length to the dangers of female abuses of political power, his earlier, *The Jockey Club: or a Sketch of the Manners of the Age* (London: H.D. Symonds, 1792), had no space to discuss the political rights of less elite women.

20. Thompson, *The Making*, pp. 178–9.
21. Landry, *The Muses*, p. 257. A formulation which she discusses brilliantly, pp. 257–8.
22. The question of male radicals' engagement with the rights of women is a subject which could, of course, be extended well beyond the limits of this study. One particularly interesting area of future work would be the texts of the Jacobin novelists, especially Thomas Holcroft and Robert Bage.
23. I am grateful to Gary Kelly for explaining to me some of the reasons for Godwin's personal appeal to women; and for his suggestion that Godwin has been a victim of historical misunderstanding, if not ridicule. The greatest counter to such ideas is William St Clair's brilliant biography, *The Godwins and The Shelleys* (London and Boston: Faber and Faber, 1991. fp. 1989).
24. Tom Paine, *Rights of Man*, pp. 157; 159. William Godwin *Enquiry Concerning Political Justice* (London: Penguin, 1985. fp 1793), p. 140.
25. See Catherine M. Rogers on Godwin, *Feminism in Eighteenth-century England*, pp. 181–2. As she comments, 'Considering the depth and exhaustiveness of his criticism of society [ . . .] it is remarkable that Godwin never thought to question the irrational assumptions that restricted women', p. 182.
26. Mark Philp has written the definitive study of Godwin's *Enquiry* and his circle, and my comments here are indebted in a modest way to his *Godwin's Political Justice* (Ithaca: Cornell University Press, 1986).
27. 'From these principles it appears that everything that is usually understood by the term co-operation is, in some degree, an evil', p. 758.
28. Rogers, *Feminism in Eighteenth Century England*, p. 182. For another account, doubtful of Godwin's interest in feminism, see Claire Tomalin, *The Life and Death*, pp. 243; 244; 245; 259–260; 294–5. See, too, William St Clair, *The Godwins, passim* and especially, Ch. 12 'Women', pp. 141–56.
29. 'The Radical Careers of Thomas Paine and William Godwin in the 1790s', a talk given by Dr Philp at the conference, 'Britain and the French Revolution' (Rewley House, Oxford: Jan. 1991).
30. Details of Paine's early biography from Gregory Claeys' '"Apostle of Liberty": a life of Thomas Paine', in his *Thomas Paine Social and Political Thought* (Boston: Unwin Hyman, 1989), pp. 20–38.
31. William Kashatus III discusses the Quaker base of Paine's feminism, 'Thomas Paine: A Quaker Revolutionary', *Quaker History*,

73, 2 (1984), 38–61. I am also grateful to Dr Bruce Woodcock for supplying me with a copy of his paper, 'Reason and Prophecy: Paine, Blake and the Dialectic of Revolution', and for his comments about Blake, Paine and feminism. Both have had a considerable impact upon the following discussion. More general comparisons of Blake and Paine are provided by James A. Stevenson, 'Reflections on William Blake and Thomas Paine', *San Jose Studies*, 15, 3 (Fall 1989), 62–70 and Essick, 'William Blake', *passim*.

32. 'An Occasional Letter on the Female Sex', *Pennsylvania Magazine*, (August 1775), reproduced in *The Complete Writings of Thomas Paine*, ed. by Eric Foner (New York: The Citadel Press, 1945), I, pp. 34–8, (p. 34).

33. 'Cupid and Hymen', *Pennsylvania Magazine*, (March 1775), in *The Complete Writings*, I, pp. 1115–18, (p. 1116).

34. 'Reflections on Unhappy Marriages', *Pennsylvania Magazine*, (June 1775), in *The Complete Writings*, I, pp. 1118–20, (p. 1119).

35. Blake's contemporaries had great faith in the influence of literature upon the course of the American Revolution. As David Ramsay commented, 'In establishing American independence, the pen and the press had equal merit to that of the sword', *The History of the American Revolution* (London, 1790), II, p. 319. When Mary Wollstonecraft reviewed this work, she chose to reproduce Ramsay's praise of Tom Paine for his authorship of *Common Sense*, *An Rev*, 10 (1791), 149–55.

36. *Common Sense* (London: Penguin Classics, 1986. fp. 1776), pp. 71–2. The distinction is again noted in *Rights of Man*, p. 67.

37. Poetic lines from, 'On the British Constitution', in *Miscellaneous Poems By Thomas Paine* (London: R. Carlile, 1819), pp. 16–17.

38. For speculations about the origins of society see especially, *Common Sense*, pp. 66–7 and *Rights of Man*, pp. 163–4.

39. Winthrop D. Jordan usefully addresses some of these issues, 'Familial Politics: Thomas Paine and the Killing of the King, 1776', *The Journal of American History*, 60 (1973), 294–308.

40. 'Crisis Paper III', *The Complete Writings*, II, p. 79.

41. *Common Sense*, p. 71.

42. Ibid., p. 120.

43. *Rights of Man*, p. 176.

44. *Rights of Man*, p. 210. E.P. Thompson, *The Making*, p. 104. Anna Wilson makes an excellent comparison between Paine's secure sense of audience and Wollstonecraft's isolation, 'Mary Wollstonecraft and the Search for the Radical Woman', *Genders*, 6 (Nov 1989), 88–101.

45. *The Rights of Infants* (1797), reprinted in, *Pig's Meat: Selected Writings of Thomas Spence*, ed. by G.I. Gallop (Nottingham: Spokesman, 1982), pp. 111–26, (p. 121).

46. Examples of vitriolic dispute include, *The End of Oppression* (1795), reprinted in *Pig's Meat*, pp. 91–6 and its slightly later ironic 're-cantation'. Codified disagreement can be found in the appendix to *The Rights of Infants* (1797) which is composed of 'A Contrast between Paine's *Agrarian Justice* and Spence's *End of Oppression*',

in *Pig's Meat*, pp. 123–6. See, too, Malcolm Chase, 'Paine, Spence and the 'Real Rights of Man', *Bulletin of the Society for the Study of Labour History*, 52, 3 (1987), 32–40.

47. Two useful accounts of the organization of Spence's utopia are G.I. Gallop, 'The Structure and Functioning of Spensonia', *Pig's Meat*, pp. 28–40 and H. Gustav Klaus, 'Early Utopias in England 1792–1848', in *The Literature of Labour* (Brighton: Harvester Press, 1985), pp. 22–45, (pp. 23–7).

48. On Spence's London years see P.M. Ashraf, *The Life and Times of Thomas Spence* (Newcastle: Frank Graham, 1983), pp. 41–99; Malcolm Chase, *The People's Farm* (Oxford: Clarendon Press, 1988), pp. 45–77; Iain McCalman, *Radical Underworld* (Cambridge: Cambridge University Press, 1988); Marcus Wood, 'Eaton, Spence and Modes of Radical Subversion in the Revolutionary Era', in his *Radical Satire and Print Culture, 1790–1822* (Oxford: Clarendon Press, 1994), pp. 57–95 and David Worrall, *Radical Culture*.

49. My thoughts about Spence and Blake were greatly stimulated by David Worrall's talk on 'Blake in the Context of Artisan Radicalism' which took place at the Blake Society, July 1991 and by his recent book, *Radical Culture*. Jon Mee also makes interesting reference to Blake and Spence throughout his *Dangerous Enthusiasm*.

50. A selection of Spence's coins, including the one I discuss, can be seen in David Bindman, *The Shadow of the Guillotine* (London: British Museum Publications, 1989), pp. 198–203 (pp. 200; 203). Bindman's interpretation of the image, however, is the reverse of mine. Blake's version appears in *All Religions Are One*, on Plate 10, principle seven (*Illuminated*; E.26). A similar image, but with a rather different extract of text, can be seen on Plate five, principle 2 (*Illuminated*; E.25).

51. 'Letter Four' of *The Restorer of Society to Its Natural State* (1803) in *Pig's Meat*, pp. 138–9, (p. 139).

52. Ibid., p. 139.

53. Ibid., p. 139.

54. *A Further Account of Spensonia* (1794) in *Pig's Meat*, pp. 80–90, (p. 86). This was also reprinted in Spence's *Pig's Meat*, 2nd ed. (London: 1794), II, 205–18.

55. Malcolm Chase makes rather large feminist claims for the text, *People's Farm*, pp. 37–9; 65. Gustav H. Klaus is more reasonable in his assessments and interesting generally on some gender-related changes in later work, 'Early Utopias', *passim* and footnote, p. 183. See, too, David Worrall's account of Spence, whom he concludes, 'was, at best, an opportunist feminist', *Radical Culture*, pp. 31–3, (p. 32).

56. *The Rights of Infants*, reprinted in *Pig's Meat*, pp. 115; 118.

57. Ibid., p. 119.

58. *The Constitution of Spensonia* (1803) reprinted in *Pig's Meat*, pp. 166–86, (pp. 170–71).

59. Other radical part works, like Daniel Eaton's, *Hog's Wash, or a Salamagundy for Swine* (1793–95) showed a similar uninterest,

although *The Cabinet* produced *By A Society of Gentlemen* in Norwich did contain a comprehensive two-part discussion, 'On the Rights of Woman' I (1795), 178–85/II (1795), 36–49.

60. *The Cabinet*, ibid., I, p. 178.

61. Account drawn from Barbara Brandon Schnorrenberg, 'The Brood Hen of Faction: Mrs Macaulay and Radical Politics, 1765–1775' *Albion*, 11, 1 (1979), 33–45; Gina Luria, 'Introduction', *Letters on Education* (New York: Garland Publishing, 1974. fp. 1790), pp. 5–9; Florence and William Boos, 'Catherine Macaulay: Historian and Political Reformer', *International Journal of Women's Studies*, 3, 1 (1980), 49–65; Lucy Martin Donnelly, 'The Celebrated Mrs Macaulay', *William and Mary Quarterly*, 6 (1949), 173–207; Bridget Hill, *The Republican Virago* (Oxford: Clarendon Press, 1992) and also her, 'The Links between Mary Wollstonecraft and Catherine Macaulay: New Evidence', *Women's History Review*, 4, 2 (1995), 177–92. Useful, too, are the comments of G.J. Barker-Benfield, 'Mary Wollstonecraft', p. 115; Karl Von Donsteinen, 'The Discovery of Women', pp. 238–9 and Mary Hays, *Female Biography; or Memoirs of Illustrious and Celebrated Women, of All Ages and Countries* (London: Richard Phillips, 1803), V, pp. 287–307.

62. *Gentleman's Magazine*, 58, 1 (Feb 1788), 98–101, (p. 99). Mary Scott, *The Female Advocate* (Los Angeles: University of California, Augustan Reprint No. 224, 1984. fp. 1774), p. 27.

63. *Letters on Education* (Dublin: C. Dilly, 1790), pp. 203–4.

64. *The Republican Virago*, pp. 130–48.

65. *Critical Review*, n.s. 2 (1790), 611–18, (p. 618).

66. Mary Wollstonecraft, *Rights of Woman*, pp. 206–7, (p. 206) and Schnorrenberg continues to value Macaulay in this way, 'The Brood Hen', p. 45. For a summary of the ground Macaulay and Wollstonecraft share, see Moira Ferguson and Janet Todd, 'Feminist Backgrounds and Argument in A Vindication of the Rights of Woman', in *Vindication of the Rights of Woman*, ed. by Carol H. Poston, 2nd ed. (New York and London: W.W. Norton and Company, 1988), pp. 317–28, (pp. 319–20). On Macaulay's feminism, see Florence Boos, 'Catherine Macaulay's *Letters of Education* (1790): An Early Feminist Polemic', *University of Michigan Papers on Women's Studies*, 2 (1976), 64–78.

67. Account drawn from Gina Luria, 'Introduction' to, *Letters and Essays, Moral and Miscellaneous* (New York: Garland Publishing, 1974. fp. 1793), pp. 5–15. See, too, Luria's, 'Mary Hays's Letters and Manuscripts', *Signs*, 3, 2 (1977), 524–30; Frida Knight, 'Literary Friendships. 1 William Godwin and Mary Hays', in her *University Rebel: The Life of William Frend* (London: Victor Gollancz, 1971), pp. 198–213 and William St Clair, 'The Godwins', *passim*.

68. 'Letters and Manuscripts', p. 526.

69. Kelly, *Women, Writing and Revolution* (Oxford: OUP, 1993), p. 91. Whilst this work gives much needed treatment to Hays's corpus, I am violently at odds with Kelly's belief in the existence (however defined) of 'revolutionary feminism' in the 1790s.

70. To Godwin 8 March 1796, in *The Love-Letters of Mary Hays*, ed. by Annie F. Wedd (London: Methuen, 1935), p. 233.
71. *Letters and Essays*, p. 19.
72. Katherine M. Rogers makes some useful comments about Hays' *Appeal* in her 'The Contribution of Mary Hays', *Prose Studies*, 10, 2 (1987), 131–42. Most recent criticism, however, seems more concerned with Hays' fictional work.
73. Mary Hays, *Appeal to the Men of Great Britain In Behalf of the Women*, ed. by Gina Luria (New York: Garland Publishers, 1974. fp. 1798), p. 111.
74. Vivian Jones stresses the importance of where women write from, and of looking at, 'What debates have enabled their critiques of sexual power relations', in the collection of extracts she edited, *Women in the Eighteenth Century* (London and New York: Routledge, 1990), pp. 192–3.
75. An example of Hays dealing with the issue of male self-interest can be found on pp. 115–16, where she examines the myth of women's beauty giving them power: 'the heavenly softness of the sex, that with a glance can disarm authority and dispell rage'.
76. On this lack of a female audience, see Anna Wilson, 'The Search for the Radical Woman', *passim*.
77. Miriam Brody, ed. and Intro., *Rights of Woman*, p. 7. This is a view of Wollstonecraft fervently propounded by Gary Kelly throughout his *Revolutionary Feminism: The Mind and Career of Mary Wollstonecraft* (Basingstoke and London: Macmillan, 1992).

Wollstonecraft scholarship is a vast body of literature, into which I have only dipped. In addition to the general political studies of Dickinson, Rowbotham and Rogers already noted, I am especially indebted to Jane Rendall, *The Origins of Modern Feminism* (Basingstoke: Macmillan, 1985), pp. 60–64; Janet Todd, 'Radicals and Reactionaries: Women writers of the late eighteenth century', in her *The Sign of Angellica* (London: Virago, 1989), pp. 218–35; Elissa S. Guralnick, 'Radical Politics in Mary Wollstonecraft's *A Vindication*', in Poston, *Vindication*, pp. 308–17; Irene Coltman Brown, 'Mary Wollstonecraft and the French Revolution or Feminism and the Rights of Man', in *Women, State and Revolution*, ed. by Sian Reynolds (Brighton: Wheatsheaf Books, 1986), pp. 1–25; Virginia Sapiro, *A Vindication of Political Virtue – The Political Theory of Mary Wollstonecraft* (Chicago and London: Chicago University Press, 1992) and Marilyn Butler and Janet Todd editors' 'Introduction' to *The Works of Mary Wollstonecraft* (London: William Pickering, 1989), pp. 7–30. All these writers address in some way the 'political' aspects of Wollstonecraft's feminism, which I shall be discussing; as do Wilson, Landry and Barker-Benfield, whose insights I have already drawn upon.

It is important also to note that much debate about, and rethinking of, Wollstonecraft's politics is at present taking place – as events such as the recent conference, 'Mary Wollstonecraft: 200 Years of Feminism', (University of Sussex, 5–6 December 1992), so amply

238 *Notes and References*

testify. Of especial interest to this study is the work of Barbara Taylor, whose talk, 'The Fantasy of Mary Wollstonecraft' and article, 'Mary Wollstonecraft and the Wild Wish of Early Feminism', *History Workshop Journal*, 33 (1992), 197–219, suggest that her forthcoming book will be an invaluable resource for those concerned with the writer's radical context.

78. Various writers have written about these aspects of Wollstonecraft's relationship with the 'radical mainstream'. Eleanor Nicholes offers a useful discussion of the 'germinal effect' of Wollstonecraft's years at Newington Green; she also speaks about the Johnson coterie, 'Mary Wollstonecraft', in *Romantic Rebels: Essays on Shelley and His Circle*, ed. by Kenneth Neill Cameron (Cambridge, Mass: Harvard University Press, 1973), pp. 34–58, (p. 50). G.J. Baker-Benfield is perhaps definitive on these early years, putting forward an excellent case for the formative influence of the gender-sensitive, but by no means feminist, thinkers of the last commonwealth generation: Price, Priestley and James Burgh, 'Mary Wollstonecraft', *passim*. Myzi Myers is insightful on Wollstonecraft's relationship with Price, 'Politics from the Outside: Mary Wollstonecraft's First *Vindication*', *Studies in Eighteenth Century Culture*, 6 (1977), 113–32, (pp. 118–19), as is Timothy J. Reiss, 'Revolution in Bounds: Wollstonecraft, Women and Reason', in *Gender and Theory*, ed. by Linda Kauffman (Oxford: Basil Blackwell, 1989), pp. 11–51, (pp. 21–5). On Wollstonecraft and Joseph Johnson, see Tomalin, *The Life and Death*, pp. 89–109.

79. Mary Poovey discusses these aspects of Wollstonecraft's first *Vindication* and concludes, 'what Wollstonecraft really wants is to achieve a new position of dependence within a paternal order of her own choosing', in her *The Proper Lady and the Woman Writer* (Chicago and London: The University of Chicago Press, 1984), pp. 56–68, (p. 66).

80. On this issue, see Myers, 'Politics from the Outside', *passim*. Also, Gary Kelly argues that Wollstonecraft attacked Burke by trying to 'capitalize on her character as a woman', 'Mary Wollstonecraft as *Vir Bonus*', *English Studies in Canada*, v, 3 (Autumn 1979), 275–91, 275) and goes on to discuss her first *Vindication* in *Revolutionary Feminism*, pp. 84–106. Another useful account of the work is offered by Virginia Sapiro, *A Vindication of Political Virtue*, pp. 186–223, (esp pp. 202–4).

81. Myers, ibid., pp. 119–21 and for the aesthetic arguments contained in the text see Barker-Benfield's discussion of Wollstonecraft and the Burkean sublime and beautiful, 'Mary Wollstonecraft', pp. 104–5.

82. Thomas Christie, *Letters on the Revolution of France, and on the New Constitution* (London: Joseph Johnson, 1791), p. 218.

83. Eleanor Nicholes, 'Mary Wollstonecraft', p. 53. Nicholes is extremely insightful about dynamics within the Johnson circle, as is Sapiro in her section, 'Gendering Theories of the Body Politic' where she notes that, 'Wollstonecraft's gender politics extends the possibilities of liberal strains of democratic theory [...] By explicitly

gendering the argument, Wollstonecraft offered a special challenge to her friends', *A Vindication of Political Virtue*, pp. 289–96, (pp. 296; 295).

84. Pendleton, 'Towards a Bibliography of the Reflections and Rights of Man Controversy', *Bulletin of Research in the Humanities*, 85 (1982), 65–103, (p. 65).

85. Mary Poovey discusses the ways in which the political disquisition was a male domain, *Proper Lady*, pp. 56–7 and Laurie A. Finke discusses how alien philosophic discourse was for women, '"A Philosophic Wanton": Language and Authority in Wollstonecraft's *Vindication of the Rights of Woman*', 155–76. Of related interest is Elizabeth Fox-Genovese's discussion of the problematic nature of the ideology of individualism for eighteenth-century feminists, 'Individualism and Women's History', in her *Feminism without Illusions: A Critique of Individualism* (Chapel Hill and London: The University of North Carolina Press, 1991), pp. 113–38.

86. As with all issues of audience, Wilson is the most important critic and she comments explicitly on the 'accusing voices of the masculine tradition' which haunt Wollstonecraft in *Rights of Woman*, 'Mary Wollstonecraft', p. 100. Laurie A. Finke also notes her 'belief that she is writing for an unsympathetic audience – she conceives of and addresses her readers primarily as men, not as other women', '"A Philosophic Wanton"', p. 159. Of general interest here is Amy Elizabeth Smith's, 'Roles for Readers in Mary Wollstonecraft's *A Vindication of the Rights of Woman*', *Studies in English Literature*, 32, 3 (Summer 1992), 555–70.

87. *Mrs Jordan's Profession: The story of a great actress and a future king* (London: Penguin, 1995).

88. Todd and Butler, 'Introduction' to *The Works*, p. 16. It's worth noting that enfranchisement was the one issue over which sympathetic readers did demur. The *Analytical Review* anticipated this, see Appendix, 13 (1792), 481–9, (p. 488) and see, too, the *Monthly Review*, ns8 (June 1792), 198–209 which bluntly admitted, 'We do not see, that the condition or the character of women would be improved, by assuming an active part in civil government', p. 208. Landry makes some very useful comments about how Wollstonecraft was, 'Pushing at the limits of ideological possibility within her historical moment', *The Muses*, p. 258. It is worth commenting too, in this context, on E.P. Thompson's suggestive, but undeveloped, suggestion that Wollstonecraft be seen as 'a casualty [...] of transition', 'Disenchantment or Default? A Lay Sermon', in *Power and Consciousness*, ed. by Conor Cruise O'Brien and William Dean Vanech (London: University of London Press Ltd, 1969), pp. 149–81, (p. 180).

89. Wollstonecraft does at one moment claim, 'speaking of women at large, their first duty is to themselves as rational creatures', *Rights of Woman*, p. 257 but on the whole women are to be educated so that they will be better mothers: 'Republican Mothers'. On the general issue of women as political citizens see Virginia Sapiro, *A Vindication of Political Virtue*, passim.

90. As Poovey comments, 'Wollstonecraft is generally *not* challenging women to *act*', *The Proper Lady*, p. 79 and Wilson elaborates, 'If men are everywhere, women are nowhere: the audience of women that Wollstonecraft deserves – requires – is absent', 'Mary Wollstonecraft', p. 97.

91. 'The Works of Mary Wollstonecraft', *The Review of English Studies*, XLII, 165 (Feb 1991), 67–77, (p. 77).

92. R.M. Janes, 'On the Reception of Mary Wollstonecraft's *A Vindication of the Rights of Woman*', in *Vindication of the Rights of Woman*, pp. 293–307 (p. 297).

93. *An Rev*, 12 (March 1792), 241–9, (p. 248). R.M. Janes also comments, 'The ability to ignore the work's political implications crossed party lines', ibid., p. 299. Although it is worth noting that later in the decade conservatives were much more alert to the work's radical allegiances, as the *Anti-Jacobin Review* observed, 'Her doctrines are almost all obvious corollaries from the theorems of Paine. If we admit his principle, that all men have an equal right to be governors and statesmen [. . .] there can be no reason for excluding women or even children', 1 (July 1798), 95.

94. Barbara S. Schnorrenberg (and Joan E. Hunter), 'The Eighteenth Century Englishwoman', p. 205. The concept of 'politics' has also, of course, been discussed and redefined by feminists, with Sheila Rowbotham's recent study showing how many different practical meanings the term can have for women. See her *Women in Movement: Feminism and Social Action* (London: Routledge, 1992).

95. As Gail Malmgreen comments, 'Feminist historians should not forget that women took to the public platform on behalf of religion long before they were stirred by politics', *Religion in the Lives of English Women, 1760–1930* (London and Sydney: Croom Helm, 1986), p. 5. See, too, Dale A. Johnson, *Women in English Religion, 1700–1925* (Lewiston, NY: Edwin Bellen Press, 1985); Jane Rendall, 'Evangelicalism and the Power of Women', in *The Origins*, pp. 73–107; Deborah M. Valenze, *Prophetic Sons and Daughters: Female Preaching and Popular Religion in Industrial England* (Princeton, NJ: Princeton University Press, 1985) and more generally, Gerda Lerner, *The Creation of Feminist Consciousness* (Oxford: OUP, 1993).

96. See especially, *A Dispute between the Woman and the Powers of Darkness* (London: E. Spragg, 1802). On Southcott generally, see James K. Hopkins, *A Woman to Deliver Her People* (Austin: University of Texas Press, 1982). Hopkins estimates that 63 per cent of Southcott's followers were women, p. 77.

97. Margaret Kirkham argues strongly for the importance of a feminist tradition in *Jane Austen, Feminism and Fiction* (New York: Methuen, 1986, fp. 1983), especially in 'Part One: Feminism and Fiction: 1694–1798', pp. 3–50. And *First Feminists, British Women Writers, 1578–1799*, ed. by Moira Ferguson (Bloomington: Indiana University Press, 1985) offers an invaluable collection of extracts. See, too, Joan Kelly, 'Early Feminist Theory and *La Querelle des Femmes*', in her *History and Theory: The Essays of Joan Kelly* (Chi-

cago: Chicago University Press, 1984), pp. 65–109; *Feminist Theorists: Three Centuries of Women's Intellectual Traditions*, ed. by Dale Spender (London: The Women's Press, 1983); Virginia Sapiro, 'Wollstonecraft and Feminist Traditions', in her *Vindication of Political Virtue*, pp. 175–85 and Carolyn Woodward, 'Naming Names in Mid-Eighteenth Century Feminist Theory', *Women's Writing* 1, 3 (1994), 291–316.

98. Alice Brown in *The Eighteenth Century Feminist Mind* (Brighton: Harvester press, 1987), constantly notes in passing the instrumental and 'curious' elements in eighteenth-century feminist thought. Some examples of women's histories include Antoine Leonard Thomas, *An Essay on the Character, Manners and Genius of Women in Different Ages – Transl. from the French of Mons Thomas by Mrs Kindersley* (London: J. Dodsley, 1781); William Alexander, *The History of Women* (London: W. Strahan & T. Cadell, 1779), 2 vols and *Biographium Faemineum. The Female Worthies: or; Memoirs of the Most Illustrious Ladies of All Ages and Nations* (London: S. Crowder & J. Payne; J. Wilkie & W. Nicoll; J. Wren, 1776) 2 vols.

99. See for example Barbauld's poem, 'The Rights of Woman' (c. 1795; pub. 1825) which ends with the message, 'separate rights are lost in mutual love', in *Eighteenth-Century Women Poets*, ed. by Roger Lonsdale (Oxford and New York: OUP, 1989), pp. 305–6, (p. 306). Marilyn Williamson writes about Barbauld's conservative attitudes in her article, 'Who's Afraid of Mrs Barbauld? The Bluestockings and Feminism', *International Journal of Women's Studies*, 3, 1 (1980), 89–102, (pp. 90–92). Mitzi Myers analyzes the writings of More and Wollstonecraft, 'Reform or Ruin: "A Revolution in Female Manners"' in *Studies in Eighteenth-Century Culture*, ed. by Harry C. Payne (Madison: University of Wisconsin Press, 1982), II, pp. 199–216; as does Donna Landry, 'Mary Wollstonecraft and Hannah More Reconsidered', *The Muses*, pp. 257–60. Landry also incorporates a convincing critique of Myers, arguing for political difference as well as feminist similarity. Two other alternate views of More are presented by Kathryn Sutherland, 'Hannah More's Counterrevolutionary Feminism', in *Revolution in Writing: British Literary Responses to the French Revolution*, ed. by Kelvin Everest (Buckingham: Open University Press, 1991), pp. 27–63 and Elizabeth Kowalski-Wallace, *Their Fathers' Daughters: Hannah More, Maria Edgeworth and Patriarchal Complicity* (New York and Oxford: OUP, 1991).

100. Stuart Curran, 'The I Altered', in *Romanticism and Feminism*, ed. by Anne K. Mellor (Bloomington and Indianapolis: Indiana University Press, 1988), pp. 185–207, (p. 187). Kirkham, *Jane Austen, Feminism and Fiction*; Todd, *The Sign of Angelica* and Dale Spender, *Mothers of the Novel* (London: Pandora Press, 1986) all address this issue but the most outstanding work on the complex relationship between feminism and fiction is Jane Spencer's, *The Rise of the Woman Novelist* (Oxford: Basil Blackwell, 1986). An excellent survey and supplement is provided by Cheryl Turner's, *Living by the Pen: Women Writers in the Eighteenth Century* (London and New York: Routledge,

1992), especially, 'Earlier Interpretations of the development of Eighteenth Century Women's Fiction', pp. 5–17. Of general interest are Catherine Gallagher, *Nobody's Story: The Vanishing Acts of Women Writers in the Marketplace, 1670–1820* (Oxford: Clarendon Press, 1994) and Edward Copeland, *Women Writing about Money: Women's Fiction in England, 1790–1820* (New York: Cambridge UP, 1995).

101. R.M. Janes sums up this modesty very well, 'If we take feminism to mean demands for specific changes in women's civil disabilities, including the right to vote, Wollstonecraft herself hardly qualifies, and her followers, Hays and Robinson, do not even make the attempt', 'On the Reception', p. 302. Alice Brown also comments on the limitations of feminism in the 1790s, *The Eighteenth Century Feminist Mind*, pp. 138–9.

102. This, of course, is the subtitle to Erdman's *Blake: Prophet Against Empire*.

103. Erdman, ibid., p. 37.

104. I have already mentioned the works of Worrall, Mee, McCalman and Thompson which have sophisticated our perceptions of Blake's radicalism. Marilyn Butler is especially good on its contemporary nuance, *Romantics, Rebels and Reactionaries* (New York and Oxford: OUP, 1982), pp. 41–53, and Edward Larrissy, *William Blake* (Oxford: Basil Blackwell, 1985) and Michael Ferber, *The Social Vision of William Blake* (Princeton, NJ: Princeton University Press, 1985) deal with Blake's complex Protestant heritage and his problematic relationship with mainstream dissent.

105. David Worrall has argued that the structure of *Marriage* operates like that of radical part-works such as *Pig's Meat*, 'Blake in the Context of Artisan Radicalism', and Jon Mee shows how the diverse nature of the work reflects, 'the suspicion of standardized forms within the vulgar culture of enthusiasm', 'The Radical Enthusiasm of Blake's *The Marriage of Heaven and Hell*', *British Journal for Eighteenth Century Studies*, 14, 1 (Spring, 1991), 51–60, (p. 54). See, too, the expanded version of this article, '"Every Honest Man is a Prophet": Popular Enthusiasm and Radical Millenarianism', in his *Dangerous Enthusiasm*, pp. 20-74.

106. *Energy and Imagination* (Oxford: Clarendon Press, 1970), p. 1. A very useful summary of the grand claims that have been made for the poem as a manifesto, and a critique, is offered by Dan Miller, 'Contrary Revelation: *The Marriage of Heaven and Hell*', *SiR*, 24 (Winter 1985), 491–509.

107. As J.F.C. Harrison comments, 'The later eighteenth century produced its full share of prophetesses', *The Second Coming, Popular Millenarianism, 1780–1850* (London and Henley: Routledge and Kegan Paul, 1979), p. 31. He discusses a number of them, including Buchan and Flaxmer, pp. 30–38, as well as giving an extensive account of Joanna Southcott's life and followers. See especially, 'The Woman Clothed with the Sun', pp. 86–134. Jane Rendall also writes usefully on these issues, *The Origins*, pp. 101–6 as, in marginal ways, does Thompson, *Witness*.

108. On Blake's seventeenth-century radical Protestant heritage see Larrissy, *William Blake*; Ferber, *The Social Vision*; Mee, *Dangerous Enthusiasm*; Thompson, *Witness* and A.L. Morton, *The Everlasting Gospel* (London: Lawrence and Wishart, 1958). The issue of which feminist ideas may have filtered through has been rather neglected by scholars working on this heritage, though I am grateful to Edward Larrissy for the pointers he has given me and to Jon Mee, who alerted my attention to reprints of the works of the prophetess Anna Trapnel. An account of her prophetic career was offered in, *Wonderful Prophecies* 4th ed. (London: M. Ritchie, 1795), p. 33.
109. Flaxmer, *The Dragon Overcome. Explanation of Part of the Twelfth Chapter of the Revelations Concerning the Woman Clothed with the Sun* (London: 1795), p. 19.
110. Southcott, *A Dispute*, p. 32.
111. Morton D. Paley, 'William Blake, the Prince of the Hebrews and the Woman Clothed with the Sun', in *William Blake: Essays in Honour of Sir Geoffrey Keynes*, ed. by Morton D. Paley and Michael Phillips (Oxford: Clarendon Press, 1973), pp. 260–93, (p. 281). The feminist aspects of Southcott's life and work are outlined extremely well by Barbara Taylor, 'The Woman Power Religious Heresy and Feminism in Early English Socialism', in *Tearing the Veil*, ed. by Susan Lipshitz (London: Routledge and Kegan Paul, 1978), pp. 119–44 and Jane Rogers, 'The Weaker Sects', *The Guardian* (9/5/91), 33.
112. 'To a Little Invisible Being Who Is Expected Soon to Become Visible' (c. 1795, pub. 1825), in *Women Poets*, pp. 307–8, (p. 308).
113. On this generation of poets see Stuart Curran, 'The I Altered', Marlon B. Ross, *The Contours of Masculine Desire: Romanticism and the Rise of Women's Poetry* (New York and London: OUP, 1989); Rebecca Gould Gibson, '"My Want of Skill": Apologias of British Women Poets, 1660–1800', in *Eighteenth Century Women and the Arts*, ed. by Frederick M. Keener and Susan E. Lorsch (New York, Westport, Conn, London: Greenwood Press, 1988), pp. 79–86 and J.R. de J. Jackson, *Romantic Poetry by Women: A Bibliography, 1770–1835* (Oxford: Clarendon Press, 1993).
114. As Morris Eaves comments '*The Marriage* takes place in a rocky landscape of steeps, abysses, caves, chambers and dungeons', 'A Reading of Blake's *Marriage of Heaven and Hell*, Plates 17–20: On and under the Estate of the West', *BS*, 4 (1972), 81–116, (p. 86). Brenda Webster discusses the cave, including comment on the 'birth' of books in the printing-house sequence, *Blake's Prophetic Psychology* (Basingstoke: Macmillan, 1983), pp. 76–9, (p. 79).
115. Mark Bracher notes these problems of identification in his discussion of the cave sequence, 'Rousing the Faculties: Lacanian Psychoanalysis and the *Marriage of Heaven and Hell*', in *Critical Paths: Blake and the Argument of Method*, ed. by Dan Miller, Mark Bracher and Donald Ault (Durham: Duke University Press, 1987), pp. 168–203, (pp. 200–1).
116. I am grateful to Steve Clark for directing my attention to this absence of female pronouns, though the inference we draw from it

is rather different. Michelle Leiss Stepto comments on the reduction of the female to only figural meaning, 'Blake, Urizen and the
Feminine: The development of a poetic logic' (University of Massachusetts, 1978), p. 79.

117. The theorization of historical and cultural constructions of masculinity is a growing academic activity, although few scholars have
commented upon the eighteenth-century's versions. John Tosh's
two review articles explain the situation well: 'Books About Masculinity', *History Workshop* 35 (Spring 1993), 259–63 and 'What Should
Historians Do with Masculinity', same journal, 38 (Autumn 1994),
179–202. The most relevant recent studies are, *Manliness and Morality: Middleclass Masculinity in Britain and America, 1800–1940*, ed.
by J.A. Mangan and James Walvin (Manchester: Manchester University Press, 1987) and *Manful Assertions: Masculinities in Britain
since 1800*, ed. by Michael Roper and John Tosh (London: Routledge,
1991).

118. Graham Pechey comments on Blake's stance as 'the disobedient
subject' and also on the contemporary republican currency of the
'diabolic', '*The Marriage of Heaven and Hell*: A Text and Its Conjunctions', *Oxford Literary Review*, 3, iii (1979), 52–76, (pp. 54–5;
74). Something illustrated visually by John Brewer, 'Popular Politics and Satanic Radicals, the 1790s', in *The Common People*, pp.
39–40.

   We should, however, note that the infernal regions were not
entirely redeemed in the early 1790s, for example in *Pig's Meat*
3rd ed. (London: 1793), I, a number of extracts were reproduced
from a pamphlet, 'The Rights of Devils', pp. 111–13; 128–32; 138–
40, which present Hell not as a region of anarchic democracy but
as the original absolute monarchy. An idea also drawn upon in
the pamphlet, *Pain [sic] Sin and The Devil Intercepted Correspondence from Satan to Citizen Paine Wherein is Discovered a Secret Friendship
between Honest Thomas and a Crowned Head, in spite of his Avowed
Principles of Opposition to all Monarchy* (London: J. Aitken, 1793).
These are perhaps noteworthy ambiguities, although the sexually
subversive aspects of the region remained constant. See, for example, one of Beelzebub's, 'Letters on Education', in the *Gentleman's Magazine*, lix, pt. 1 (1789), 507–9. In this particular epistle he
ironically explains how he relies upon pleasure to bring him many
recruits and warns readers that, 'I have always said that TOO MUCH
LIBERTY AND LUXURY would make Britain my own', p. 507.
The context of diabolic allusion in the 1790s is a fascinating one,
which I shall explore more fully at a later date. The most comprehensive study of this context is provided by Peter A. Schock, although his article is unconcerned with questions of sexuality and
gender, '*The Marriage of Heaven and Hell*: Blake's Myth of Satan
and Its Cultural Matrix', *ELH*, 60, 2 (1993), 441–70.

119. Daniel Stempel notes this coercive element in Blake's treatment of
the Angel, 'Angels of Reason: Science and Myth in the Enlightenment', *Journal of the History of Ideas*, 36 (1975), 63–78, (pp. 73–4); as

does Morris Eaves, 'A Reading', pp. 110–16, (p. 111). The will to power seemingly evident here is usefully illuminated by David Clark, '"The Innocence of Becoming Restored": Blake, Nietzsche and the Disclosure of Difference', *SiR*, 29, 1 (Spring 1991), 91–113, (pp. 91–6).

120. Blake's feelings about Swedenborg have received much attention. Hopefully, *Blake and Swedenborg: Opposition is True Friendship*, ed. by Harvey F. Bellin and Darrell Ruhl (New York: Swedenborg Foundation, 1985), closes the discussion. Some useful contextual studies of Swedenborgianism have, however, been produced: see John Howard, 'An Audience for *The Marriage*', *BS*, 3 (Fall, 1970), 19–52 and Michael Scrivener, 'A Swedenborgian Visionary in *The Marriage*', *BQ*, 21, 3 (Winter 1987–88), 102–4. Jon Mee's recent article, 'The Radical Enthusiasm', judiciously weighs each writer's claims. Also of interest is Robert Essick's discussion of the Johnson circle's reaction to Swedenborg, 'William Blake', pp. 192–4; Marsha Keith Schuchard, 'The Secret Masonic History of Blake's Swedenborg Society', *BQ*, 26, 2 (Fall 1992), 40–51 and of course Thompson's *Witness*.

121. *Common Sense*, p. 120. Eaves' comments on the vocational aspects of the Angel's use of the word 'career', 'A Reading', p. 83.

122. Sarah Flaxmer's remark may be relevant here, 'the Lord is not going to call the men into Paradice [sic], and shut the women out', *The Dragon Overcome*, p. 23.

123. On the proverbs see Michael F. Holstein, 'Crooked Paths without Improvement: Blake's Proverbs of Hell', *Genre*, 8 (1975), 26–41; Hatsuko Niimi, 'The Proverbial Language of Blake's *Marriage of Heaven and Hell*', *Studies in English Literature*, 1982; 58 (Eng No.), 3–20; June Singer, *The Unholy Bible: A Psychological Interpretation of William Blake* (New York: Harper and Row, Colophon Books, 1970); John Villabobos, 'William Blake's "Proverbs of Hell" and the Tradition of Wisdom Literature', *Studies in Philology*, 87, 2 (1990), 246–59; Gavin Edwards, 'Repeating the Same Dull Round', in *Unnam'd Forms: Blake and Textuality*, ed. by Nelson Hilton and Thomas Vogler (Berkeley, Los Angeles and London: University of California Press, 1986), pp. 26–48 and especially, Marvin D.L. Lansverk, 'The Wisdom of Many, The Vision of One: The Proverbs of William Blake' (University of Washington, 1988). The two latter writers both focus upon the subversive aspects of Blake's proverbs.

The Bakhtinian connection has bubbled around ever since Northrop Frye spoke about the work, with its symposium setting, containing elements of Menippean satire, and Graham Pechey, 'A Text and Its Conjunctions', expounds and employs Bakhtin's theories in an exemplary fashion. See, too, Craig Howes, 'Rhetorics of Attack: Bakhtin and the Aesthetics of Satire', *Genre*, 19 (1986), 215–43.

124. 'Dialectic in *The Marriage of Heaven and Hell*', *PMLA*, 73 (1958), 501–4, (p. 501). Dana Gulling Mead summarizes the views of a number of the most influential theorists of Blake's dialectic in her 'From Topoi to Dialectic: The Progression of Invention Techniques

in the Poetry of William Blake' (University of Tennessee, 1989), pp. 70–74.

125. Bloom's collection of essays is prime evidence for my contention that a patriarchal 'Blake Industry' exists. Nine of his ten contributors are men and the one woman admitted is the safely Freudian Diana Hume George. Moreover, every one of the male contributors was a Professor at the time of publication, Diana Hume George was not.

126. Gleckner, 'Roads of Excess', p. 103.

127. Ibid., pp. 108–9.

128. 'Irony as Self-Concealment in *The Marriage of Heaven and Hell*', *Auto/ Biography Studies*, 2, 4 (winter 1986–87), 34–44, (p. 34).

129. Mark Bracher devotes a great deal of his article to the task of identifying 'our [sic?] phallic fantasies', 'Rousing the Faculties', p. 192. Most of his remarks are of dubious value, but the detailed treatment he gives to the Proverbs yield a few rewards, from which I have drawn my comments, pp. 192; 197.

130. Others have addressed themselves to groups of proverbs: Bloom 'Introduction', pp. 13–14; Bracher, ibid., pp. 183; 190–98 and Webster, *Prophetic Psychology*, pp. 68–73.

131. Even Harold Bloom acknowledges the importance of individuality of response to the Proverbs, ibid., p. 15, and Michael Holstein elaborates on how Blake urges us 'to submit to no one's authority [. . .] all invite a reader to bring new combinations of proverbs to bear on each individual proverb. Here is the point of closest contact between poet and reader', 'Crooked Paths', p. 39.

132. W.J.T. Mitchell makes some pertinent comments about the dynamics of the title page, *Blake's Composite Art* (Princeton, NJ: Princeton University Press, 1978), pp. 10–11, as does Michael Tolley, 'Marriages of Heaven and Hell: Blake's Enigmatic Titlepage', in *Symposium on Romanticism*, ed. by Deirdre Coleman and Peter Otto (Centre for British Studies, University of Adelaide, 1990), pp. 8–23.

133. M.H. Abrams claims, 'all contraries, in Blake, operate as opposing yet complementary male–female powers', *Natural Supernaturalism* (New York: W.W. Norton, 1973. fp. 1971), p. 260. Yet *The Marriage* provides no explicit evidence of this, for as Stepto comments, 'Blake succeeds in divesting *The Marriage* of sexual difference at its most conspicuous level of generalization', 'Blake, Urizen', p. 79. John Howard offers a strangely but strongly gendered account of the poem, which is also interesting in this context. See his *Infernal Poetics: Poetic Structures in Blake's Lambeth Prophecies* (London and Toronto: Associated University Presses, 1984), pp. 61–96.

134. Martin Nurmi makes it clear that the *Song of Liberty*, 'furnishes a bridge between *The Marriage* and *America: A Prophecy*, making an apocalyptic application of the general doctrine of *The Marriage* in the political context of *America*', 'Polar Being', in *The Marriage*, pp. 59–71, (p. 71).

135. Dana K. Haffar addresses this distinction, 'The "Women" in Blake's Early Writings and the "Females" of the Prophecies' (Oxford: October 1984).

136. See, too, Randel Helms, 'Blake's Uses of the Bible in 'A Song of Liberty', *ELN*, 16 (1979), 287–91.
137. *Adams Family Correspondence*, ed. by Lyman Butterfield (Cambridge, Mass: The Belknap Press of Harvard University Press, 1963), I, pp. 369–71, (p. 370). Joel Barlow, 'The Advantages Accruing to Mankind from a Habitual Consciousness of Their Being Equal', an extract of his *Advice to the Privileged Orders*, reproduced in *Pig's Meat*, 3rd ed. (London, 1793), I, 283–4, (p. 283).
138. Jean Hagstrum comments with masterful euphemism on the relationship between the works, 'The two most vigorous Lambeth prophecies, the *Visions* [. . .] and *America*, which open respectively the gates of courtship [. . .] and the doors of marriage [. . .] both begin with consummated sexual acts', *The Romantic Body* (Knoxville, Tennessee: University of Tennessee Press, 1985), pp. 114–15. David Aers is more perceptive on Orc's gesture, 'He enters with an act of masculine violence that looks much like the rape opening the *Visions*', 'Representations of Revolution: From The French Revolution to The Four Zoas', in *Critical Paths*, pp. 244–70, (p. 250). And Stepto makes some interesting remarks about the substitution of Orc for Oothoon, 'Blake, Urizen', p. 100.
139. 'This Accursed Family: Blake's *America* and the American Revolution', *The Eighteenth Century*, 27 (Winter 1986), 26–51, (p. 41). It should be noted that Behrendt has recently offered a dramatic revision of this interpretation, 'An Example: Five Plates from *America*', in his *Reading William Blake* (London and Basingstoke: Macmillan, 1992), pp. 25–35, (p. 29) although his 'History when Time Stops: Blake's *America* . . . ', *Papers on Language and Literature*, 28, 4 (Fall 1992), 379–97 returns to the original emphasis.
140. Northrop Frye, *Fearful Symmetry* (Princeton, NJ: Princeton University Press, 1974. fp. 1947), pp. 205–9, (p. 206) and Keach, 'Blake, Violence and Visionary Politics', in *Representing the French Revolution*, ed. by James Hefferman (Boston: University Press of New England, 1992), pp. 24–40, (p. 33). Orc has been the subject of much comment. Some examples of writers who view him in a positive light include: David Erdman, *Prophet*; Randell Helms, 'Orc: The Id in Blake and Tolkien', *Literature and Psychology*, 20 (1970), 31–5; George Quasha, 'Orc as a Fiery Paradigm of Poetic Torsion', in *Blake's Visionary Forms Dramatic*, ed. by David V. Erdman and John E. Grant (Princeton, NJ: Princeton University Press, 1970), pp. 263–84; Minna Doskow, 'William Blake's *America*: The Story of a Revolution Betrayed', *BS*, 8 (1979), 167–86; Michael Ferber, *The Poetry of William Blake* (London: Penguin, 1991), pp. 65; 75–88 and John Howard who claims that, 'As a personification of desire, Orc manifests a completely positive impulse to freedom', *Infernal Poetics*, p. 110.

Amongst those who've raised problems, are David Aers, 'Representations of Revolution'; James McCord, 'West of Atlantis: William Blake's Unromantic View of the America War', *The Centennial Review*, 30, 3 (Summer, 1986), 383–99; Aileen Ward, 'The Forging of

Orc: Blake and the Idea of Revolution', *Tri-Quarterly*, 23/24 (1972), 204–27 and Julia Wright, '"Empire Is No More": Odin and Orc in America', *BQ*, 26, 1 (Summer 1992), 26–9. Innumerable possible definitions of the character are offered by Edward J. Rose, 'Good-Bye to Orc and All That', *BS*, 4 (1972), 135–62.

141. For comment on Plate six, see Irene Chayes, 'Blake's Ways with Art Sources: Michelangelo's The Last Judgement', *CLQ*, 20, 2 (1984), 60–89, (p. 67) and Stewart Crehan, *Blake in Context* (Dublin: Gill and Macmillan Humanities Press, 1984), pp. 246–7.

142. Erdman, *Prophet*, p. 144.

143. Aers comments on the voicelessness of Blake's revolutionary/revolutionized women, 'Representations', p. 251. Again, the contrast with Oothoon and her eloquence is noteworthy.

144. On women in the America Army and Washington's feelings about them, see Joan Hoff Wilson, 'The Illusion of Change: Women and the American Revolution', in *The American Revolution*, ed. by Alfred F. Young (Dekalb, Illinois: Northern Illinois University Press, 1976), pp. 383–447, (pp. 391; 422–3); Linda Kerber, *Women of the Republic* (Chapel Hill: University of North Carolina Press, 1980), pp. 56–8 and Charles E. Claghorn, *Women Patriots of the American Revolution: a Biographical Dictionary* (Metuchen, NJ and London: The Scarecrow Press, 1991).

145. For women's experiences during and after the Revolution, see Hoff Wilson, ibid.; Kerber, ibid.; Mary Beth Norton, *Liberty's Daughters: The Revolutionary Experience of American Women, 1750–1800* (Boston: Little, Brown and Company, 1980) and *Women in the Age of the American Revolution*, ed. by Ronald Hoffman and Peter J. Albert (Charlottesville: University Press of Virginia, 1989). Jane Rendall concludes her review of such materials with the comment, 'politically, the independence of the new American republic brought with it no immediate prospects for change and, in the course of the 1780s and 1790s, conservative voices surfaced against even the most modest proposals to improve the situation of women', *The Origins*, p. 67.

146. *Common Sense*, p. 89, as Winthrop D. Jordan comments, 'As for Paine, it can be claimed that he performed a vital service to America – but a momentary one – the sons of the revolution soon lapsed into acclaiming their staunchest leader as the father of his country', 'Familial Politics', p. 308. I have already given many examples of the American conflict being perceived in terms of a father – son antagonism, but it is important just to note that Britain was also sometimes conceptualized as an unnatural mother, often a diseased prostitute. See Hoff Wilson, 'The Illusion', pp. 390; 405–6; 433.

147. Joel Barlow, 'The Advantages', p. 283.

148. *Blake's Apocalypse* (London: Victor Gollancz, 1963), p. 119. Erdman makes a similar point, though with a little more reluctance, 'since these females are not so much people as states of nature, the males must continue to stand for both mankind and womankind – a difficulty of many man-made allegories', *Prophet*, pp. 253–4. His

own, 'Fatness of the Earth', pp. 243–63, argument, however, is entirely dependent upon the reader's forgetting any allegorical problems.

149. See Annette A. Kolodny on these fantasies: 'The Land as Woman: Literary Convention and Latent Psychological Content', *Women's Studies*, 1 (1973), 167–82 and, 'Laying Waste the Fields of Plenty: The Eighteenth Century', in her *The Lay of the Land: Metaphor as Experience and History in America* (Chapel Hill: The University of North Carolina Press, 1975), pp. 26–70. See, too, S. Foster Damon on this point, and also on the meaning of the American Revolution to late-eighteenth-century radicals, *William Blake: His Philosophy and Symbols* (London: Dawsons of Pall Mall, 1929), pp. 109–12, (p. 109).

150. See E. McCluny Flemming's two magisterial articles, 'The American Image as Indian Princess, 1765–1783', *Winterthur Portfolio*, II (1965), 65–81 and 'From Indian Princess to Greek Goddess: The American Image, 1783–1815', *Winterthur Portfolio*, III (1966), 37–66. Clare Le Corbeiller also demonstrates the Eurocentrism of these conventions in her, 'Miss America and Her Sisters: Personifications of the Four Parts of the World', *Bulletin of the Metropolitan Museum of Art*, 19 (1961), 209–23.

151. As Aileen Ward rightly comments, Blake 'never specifies' the Shadowy Daughter's significance, 'she serves as a reminder that his mythic narrative makes sense at many levels of meaning, cosmological and psychological as well as political', 'The Forging', p. 211. And James McCord notes how Blake 'personifies the continent in strikingly unconventional ways', 'Blake's Unromantic View', pp. 386–7, (p. 386).

152. David Aers addresses the issue of the genesis of the 'female will' and concludes that pondering a number of questions raised by *America* was a decisive factor, 'Blake: Sex, Society and Ideology', in *Romanticism and Ideology*, ed. by Aers *et al* (London: Routledge and Kegan Paul, 1981), pp. 27–43, (p. 32). I take his argument a little further and find traces of it already apparent in the work.

153. For a reproduction and discussion of 'The Able Doctor', see Wendy Shadwell, 'Britannia in Distress', *America Book Collector*, 7, 1 (Jan 1986), 1–12, (pp. 6–7). Note, too, Ronald Paulson, 'John Trumbull and the Representation of the American Revolution', *SiR*, 21, 3 (Fall 1982), 314–56, which deals with many of the issues of sexual politics that I raise – including comment on 'The Able Doctor', pp. 343–4. And on caricatures more generally: R.T. Halsay Haines, '"Impolitical Prints": The American Revolution as Pictured by Contemporary English Caricaturists. An Exhibition', *BNYPL*, 43, 11 (1939), 795–829; *The American Revolution in Drawings and Prints*, ed. by Donald H. Cresswell (Washington: Library of Congress, 1975), esp. pp. 239–405; Michael Wynn Jones, *The Cartoon History of the American Revolution* (New York: G.P. Putnam's Sons, 1975), esp. 'The Colonies Alight 1773–1776', pp. 41–84; Peter D.G. Thomas, *The American Revolution* (Cambridge: Chadwyck-Healey, 1986) and

M. Dorothy George's, 'America in English Satirical Prints', *William and Mary Quarterly*, 10 (1953), 511–37 and George, 'From the American Revolution to the Coalition', in her brilliant *English Political Caricature: A Study of Opinion and Propaganda* 2 vols (Oxford: Clarendon Press, 1959), I, pp. 150–71. As she comments, 'With the news of the Boston Tea Party, which reached London in January 1774, America absorbs the caricaturists. The Prints not only reflect opinion but were weapons of war', p. 150.

154. Mary Wollstonecraft, *An Historical and Moral View of The French Revolution* (1794), in *The Works*, 6, p. 20.

155. Wollstonecraft's review of David Ramsay, *The History of the American Revolution* (1790), in *An Rev*, 10 (1791), 149–55, (p. 149). The male development metaphor was used in a review of C. Stedman's, *The History of the Origin, Progress and Termination of the American War* (1794), in the *An Rev*, 21 (March 1795), 235–44, (p. 235) – Stedman himself comments on their lack of passion in a section quoted on p. 242. Ronald Paulson's comments about British sympathizers' fondness for fiery Orc figures is a slight qualification to my argument, see his 'John Trumbull', *passim*, and his review article in *BQ*, 11 (1978), 291–7.

156. Susan Brownmiller, 'The American Revolution', in *Against Our Will* (London: Pelican Books, 1986. fp. 1975), pp. 115–21, (p. 119).

157. The debauched English appear in the review of Stedman's, *The History*, noted above, p. 240.

158. The quotations from David Ramsay's *History*, are from Vol. II, pp. 144–5; 150. It should be noted that Ramsay also acknowledged that the Americans undertook acts of retaliation which were equally brutal and directed towards civilian targets, again see Vol. II, pp. 144–5. On the issue of British rapists and the American psyche, see Paulson, 'John Trumbull', pp. 345–6.

159. Ramsay, ibid., II, pp. 324–5.

160. Washington quoted by Susan Brownmiller, *Against Our Will*, p. 119.

161. *Common Sense*, p. 99.

162. Deborah Dorfman qualifies parallels between the bride-stealing King Ariston and Orc, but still has to conclude that the rape is a '*conquest* with a questionably liberative effect', '"King of Beauty" and "Golden World" in Blake's *America*: the Reader and the Archetype', *ELH*, 46(1979), 122–35, (p. 126 – my emphasis). Julia Wright offers an impressive historicist account of the ways in which the American patriot's contradictory relationship with indigenous peoples and women is mediated in the figure of Orc. Her brief article, '"Empire Is No More"', is the best piece of recent criticism on the poem.

163. Aers comments that, '*America* figures an ominous collusion between Orc and Urizen, the values of the masculine, violent revolutionary and the masculine, violent conservative. Orc's "cloudy terrors", his "fierce flames" giving "heat but not light" converges with Urizen depicted in fires, "But no light from the fires"', 'Representations',

p. 251. And Ronald Paulson, having decided that, 'for Blake paradox seems to be the characteristic feature of revolution itself', of course addresses this visual one, 'Blake's Lamb-Tiger', in his *Representations of Revolution* (New Haven and London: Yale University Press, 1983), pp. 88–110, (p. 110). More generally, see Barton R. Friedman, 'Through Forests of Eternal Death: Blake and Universal History', in his *Fabricating History: English Writers on the French Revolution* (Princeton, NJ: Princeton University Press, 1988), pp. 38–66, especially the section, 'Frost and Fire', pp. 46–9.

164. Another of Aers points, 'Contrary to some scholars' impressions, it is not merely Urizen who sees Orc as a dehumanized terror', ibid., p. 250.

165. Aers, 'Sex, Society and Ideology', p. 32.

166. 'Representations', p. 251. David Punter also makes a very apposite point, 'If we tie patriarchy to a feudal parody like Urizen, really a figure of fun [. . .] we have a handy caricature of masculine power onto which we may load our own anxieties as we adopt the belief that revolution will, by some 'necessary' process, lead to a supercession of this patriarchy, that the liberation of the sons will save the 'Daughters of Albion' by some symmetrical process of mechanical linkage', *The Romantic Unconscious* (Hertford: Harvester Wheatsheaf, 1989), p. 99.

167. Aers, ibid., p. 251.

168. Others, of course, do not agree. Robert Manquis, for example, claims that, '*America* leads finally to a vision of peace and love, of sensuous and communal unity', in his article, 'Holy Savagery and Wild Justice: English Romanticism and the Terror', *SiR*, 28, 3 (Fall 1989), 365–95, (p. 388).

169. McCord offers a cyclic reading of the images, 'Blake's Unromantic View', pp. 396–7. David Bindman is rather more sanguine, concluding his account with the claim, 'The design tells in cryptic terms [. . .] of the redemption of the female soul through sexuality, a theme adumbrated in the story of Oothoon', *Blake as an Artist*, (Oxford: Phaidon Press, 1977), p. 79 and this 'parallel' is also noted by Behrendt, 'This Accurs'd Family', p. 44. More useful is David Erdman's, 'America: New Expanses', which deals with how, 'the sexes are out of phase', in *Visionary Forms Dramatic*, ed. by David V. Erdman and John E. Grant (Princeton, NJ: Princeton University Press, 1970), pp. 92–114, (p. 104). He offers some interesting ideas about this and the final plate, although his positive assessment of Orc's fires handicaps him somewhat, pp. 103–6.

170. As S. Foster Damon comments, the last five plates are all pessimistic, *A Blake Dictionary*, Revised ed. (Hanover and London: University Press of New England, 1988, fp. 1969), p. 21.

171. Bloom speaks of 1793 as Blake's 'true *annus mirabilis*', *Blake's Apocalypse*, p. 117, and Bindman elaborates with details of his intense productivity during the years 1793–95, *Blake as an Artist*, p. 72. On the dangers of the period, see Michael Phillips, 'Blake and the Terror', *The Library*, 6th series, 16, 4 (1994), 263–97.

## 5 'Go, Tell the Human Race that Woman's Love is Sin!'

1. Bloom's, 'Commentary', in *The Complete Poetry and Prose of William Blake*, ed. by David V. Erdman (New York: Anchor Press/Doubleday, 1982), p. 903.

2. *The Poems of William Blake*, ed. by W.H. Stevenson (London: Longman, 1971), p. 223. See, too, James E. Swearingen, 'Time and History in Blake's *Europe*', Clio, 20, 2 (1991), 109–21.

3. For Erdman's readings of *Europe* see, *Blake: Prophet Against Empire* (Princeton, NJ: Princeton University Press, 1969, fp. 1954), pp. 201–25; 264–70 and, *The Illuminated Blake* (New York: Anchor Press/Doubleday, 1974), pp. 156–73.

4. Ronald Paulson, 'The Severed Head: The Impact of French Revolutionary Caricatures on England', in *French Caricature and the French Revolution* (Wight Art Gallery, UCLA: The Grunwald Centre for the Graphic Arts, 1988), pp. 55–65, (p. 56). On caricature as a context see Erdman, ibid., and also his, 'Shorter Notes: William Blake's Debt to James Gillray', *Arts Quarterly*, 12 (1949), 165–70. Plus more recently, Nancy Bogan, 'Blake's Debt to Gillray', *American Notes and Queries*, 6 (1967), 35–7 and Stephen C. Behrendt, 'Europe 6: Plundering the Treasury', *BQ*, 21, 3 (Winter 1987–88), 85–94.

5. Erdman, *Prophet*, p. 211; Terry Eagleton, 'The God that Failed', in, *Re-Membering Milton: Essays on Texts and Traditions*, ed. by Mary Nyquist and Margaret W. Ferguson (New York and London: Methuen, 1987), pp. 342–9, (p. 342). See too Hazard Adams, 'Synecdoche and Method', in *Blake and the Argument of Method*, ed. by Dan Miller *et al* (Durham and London: Durham UP, 1987), pp. 41–71, (pp. 64–5).

6. Erdman's claim, for instance, that in *Europe*, 'we are dealing with an orderly sequence of events which can be fitted into the calendar of secular history as soon as we can date some of the minute particulars', is somewhat reductive, 'The Historical Approach', in *William Blake: Modern Critical Views*, ed. by Harold Bloom (New York: Chelsea Publishers, 1985), pp. 19–34, (p. 24). In this context see Jon Mee's critique of Erdman, and his comments about Blake's own 'hostility to allegory', *Dangerous Enthusiasm: William Blake and the Culture of Radicalism in the 1790s* (Oxford: Clarendon Press, 1992), pp. 1–2; 12–14, (p. 12).

7. Butler, 'Telling It Like a Story: The French Revolution as Narrative', *SiR*, 28 (Fall 1989), 345–64, (p. 355). On the subject of British representations and responses, see too: David Punter *et al*, 'Strategies for Representing Revolution', in *1789: Reading, Writing, Revolution* (Essex: University of Essex, 1982), pp. 81–100; 'Romanticism and History', in his *The Romantic Unconscious* (New York: Harvester Wheatsheaf, 1989), pp. 19–67; Stephen C. Behrendt, 'Introduction: History, Mythmaking and the Romantic Artist', in the collection he edited, *History and Myth: Essays on English Romantic Literature* (Detroit: Wayne State University Press, 1992), pp. 13–32; Robert M. Manquis, 'Holy Savagery and Wild Justice: English

Romanticism and the Terror', *SiR*, 28, 3 (Fall 1989), 365–95, (esp. pp. 386–90) and, more generally, Stephen Prickett, *England and the French Revolution* (Macmillan: Basingstoke and London, 1989).

8. Butler, ibid., p. 355.

9. David Bindman offers various insights into Blake's response to the French Revolution. Of particular relevance here is his assessment of the choice of form employed by Blake, whose writings, 'though difficult, allow us to see how a passionate involvement with the issues of revolution could be expressed in forms that are remote from the historical or descriptive. The maintaining of a distance from events allows for the expression of the transcendental significance of revolution: it enables potentially dangerous thoughts to be disguised, *and it also allows a flexibility of response as events unfold – indeed, the very project can redefine itself in the face of the unexpected'* (my emphasis). See his *The Shadow of the Guillotine: Britain and the French Revolution* (London: British Museum Publications, 1989), p. 71.

10. Bindman charts how British revolutionary sympathizers became increasingly uneasy about events in France after 1792, ibid., p. 26 and *passim*, and Ronald Paulson also offers some details of, 'The confusion of response from 1793 onward' in 'The View from England: Stereotypes', in his *Representations of Revolution* (New Haven and London: Yale University Press, 1983), pp. 37–56, (p. 39). See, too: *The French Revolution and Britain in Popular Politics*, ed. by Mark Philp (Cambridge: Cambridge University Press, 1991).

11. The only French female David Erdman discusses in his account of *Europe* is Marie Antoinette, and his assessment of her presence in the text rarely moves beyond stereotypical swipes at her allegedly immoral and tyrannous behaviour. On a more general level, other critics have failed to pursue allusions or intertextual references of a sexual or gendered nature. As recently as 1992, in a section dealing with *Europe* in the context of 'Metamorphosis and Encyclopedic Allusion', Stephen Behrendt ignores all the historical and contemporary discourses which I shall argue are fundamental to an understanding of the work. He comments on Blake's 'eclectic reading list, covering as it does materials from religion, literature, history, Newtonian science, and public political discourse' in a sadly gender-blind way; *Reading William Blake* (London and Basingstoke: Macmillan, 1992), pp. 113–25, (p. 122).

12. Robert Essick, *William Blake's Commercial Book Illustrations* (Oxford: Clarendon Press, 1991), p. 60 and G.E. Bentley Jr. *Blake Books* (Oxford: Clarendon Press, 1977), p. 514, listing No. 418.

13. Essick, ibid., p. 60. David Fuller did recently offer comment on the engraving, but only of the most generally kind, telling us that 'Blake must have had to grit his teeth' whilst he worked on the image, 'Blake as an Illustrator', *Durham University Journal*, ns. LVI, I (Jan. 1993), 115–19, (p. 115).

14. For discussions of Blake's work with Stedman, see James King, *William Blake: His Life* (London: Weidenfeld and Nicolson, 1991),

pp. 88–94 and Richard Price, *Representations of Slavery: John Gabriel Stedman's "Minnesota" Manuscripts* (University of Minnesota: The Associates of the James Ford Bell Library, 1989), pp. 13–21.

15. These plates can be seen in Capt J.G. Stedman, *Narrative, of a Five Years' Expedition, against the Revolted Negroes of Surinam, in Guinea, on the WILD COAST of South America: from the Year 1772, to 1777* (St Paul's Churchyard/Pall Mall, London: Joseph Johnson/ J. Edwards, 1796), 'Flagellation', opposite, Vol. 1, p. 326; 'A Surinam Planter', opposite, Vol. II, p. 56, and, 'Europe Supported by Africa and America', opposite, Vol. II, p. 394. An interesting sidelight on this discussion is provided by Moira Ferguson, *Subject to Others: British Women Writers and Colonial Slavery, 1670–1834* (London: Routledge, 1992) and Clare Midgley, *Women Against Slavery: The British Campaigns, 1780–1870* (London: Routledge, 1992).

16. David Hume quoted by Katherine M. Rogers, 'The View From England', in *French Women and the Age of Enlightenment*, ed. by Samia Spencer *et al* (Bloomington: Indiana University Press, 1984), pp. 357–68, (p. 358–9). James Fordyce also offered this kind of assessment of French women's power, 'In France the women are supreme: they govern all from the court to the cottage; and from their influence the men, at least in the early periods of life, seem to derive their whole system of sentiments, inclinations, and manners', *The Character and Conduct of the Female Sex* (London, the Strand: T. Cadell, 1776), pp. 27–8.

17. Rogers, ibid., notes this about Hume's assessment of French Society, and her whole discussion of English perceptions of French women, both before and during the revolution, is useful.

18. Elizabeth Fox-Genovese, 'Introduction', in *French Women and the Age of Enlightenment*, pp. 1–29, (p. 1); and Madelyn Gutwirth discusses these fears that women were softening and spoiling the social fabric, 'The Representation of Women in the Revolutionary Period: The Goddess of Reason and The Queen of the Night', *Consortium on Revolutionary Europe Proceedings* (1983), pp. 224–41, (p. 226 and *passim*). See, too, Vernon A. Rosario III, 'Phantastical Pollutions: The Public Threat of Private Vice in France', in *Solitary Pleasures*, ed. by him and Paula Bennett (New York and London: Routledge, 1995), pp. 101–32.

19. For a discussion of English stereotypes of the French, see Michael Duffy, 'The Noisie, Empty, Fluttering French: English Images of the French, 1689–1815', *History Today*, 32 (Sept. 1982), 21–6 and, 'Foreign Bugaboos; The French', in his *The English Man and the Foreigner* (Cambridge: Chadwyck-Healey, 1986), pp. 31–9. As Katherine Rogers points out in 'The View from England', the French were largely viewed as an effeminate nation, so general stereotypes fed into and reinforced negative English ideas about French women, pp. 357–9.

20. Much has been written about the alleged 'reign of women' in eighteenth-century France. Gutwirth, 'Queen of the Night'; Fox-Genovese, 'Introduction' and Rogers, ibid., all give examples of male lamen-

tation over this state of affairs as does Barbara Corrado Pope, 'Revolution and Retreat: Upper Class French Women After 1789', in *Women, War and Revolution*, ed. by Carol Berkin *et al* (New York and London: Holman and Meier, 1980), pp. 215–36. Gutwirth also provides a social historical background for this notion in her later article, 'The Engulfed Beloved: Representation of Dead and Dying Women in the Art and Literature of the Revolutionary Era', in *Rebel Daughters: Women and the French Revolution*, ed. by Sara Melzer and Leslie W. Rabine (New York and Oxford: OUP, 1992), pp. 198–227, (pp. 199–201).

21. For a discussion of women's supposed 'sway' in eighteenth-century French politics, see Susan P. Conner, 'Sexual Politics and Citizenship: Women in Eighteenth Century France', *Proceedings of the Tenth Annual Meeting of the Western Society for French History*, 10 (1984), 264–73; 'Women and Politics', in *French Women and the Age of Enlightenment*, pp. 49–63; Joan Landes, 'Women in the Old Regime', in her *Women and the Public Sphere in the Age of the French Revolution* (Ithaca and London: Cornell University Press, 1988), pp. 17–89; Dorinda Outram, 'Le Langage Mâle de la Vertu: Women and the Discourse of the French Revolution' in *The Social History of Language*, ed. by Peter Burke and Roy Porter (Cambridge: CUP, 1987), pp. 120–35, (p. 125) and Jeffrey Merrick, 'Sexual Politics and Public Order in Late Eighteenth Century France: The *Mémoires Secrets* and the Correspondance Secrète', *Journal of the History of Sexuality*, 1 (1990), 68–84.

22. That women were often prostituted in male political games is well illustrated by Jean-Pierre Guicciardi, who notes how numerous husbands offered their wives as replacement mistresses to Louis XV after the death of Mme de Pompadour. See his, 'Between the Licit and the Illicit: the Sexuality of the King', in *'Tis Nature's Fault: Unauthorized Sexuality during the Enlightenment*, ed. by Robert Purks Maccubbin (Cambridge: CUP, 1987), pp. 88–97, (esp p. 92).

23. Barbara Corrado Pope discusses the opportunities open to women in Paris Salons and concludes that the ethos of sociability enabled them to meet and converse with men in a genuinely egalitarian way, 'Revolution and Retreat', *passim*. On this subject, see too, Linda Orr's section, 'Mother/Talk', in her 'Outspoken Women and the Rightful Daughter of the Revolution: Madame de Stael's *Considérations sur la Revolution Française*', in *Rebel Daughters*, pp. 121–36, (pp. 124–7) and Dena Goodman, 'Enlightenment Salons: The Convergence of Female and Philosophic Ambitions', *ECS*, 22, 3 (1989), 329–50.

24. On pornographic accounts of Madame du Barry's life, see Robert Darnton, 'The Forbidden Books of Pre-revolutionary France', in *Rewriting the French Revolution*, ed. by Colin Lucas (Oxford: Clarendon Press, 1991), pp. 1–32, (pp. 26–32) and, more generally, *The Invention of Pornography*, ed. by Lynn Hunt ((New York: Zone Books, 1993).

25. On this scorn of the 'lowly' origins of Louis XV's lovers, especially Mme du Barry, see, 'Between the Licit', pp. 92–3; 96. An observation

Mary Wollstonecraft made in her *An Historical and Moral View of the Origin and Progress of the French Revolution* (1794) in *The Works of Mary Wollstonecraft*, ed. by Janet Todd and Marilyn Butler (London: William Pickering, 1989), 6, pp. 29–30.

26. Quoted by Guicciardi, 'Between the Licit', p. 90.

27. My account of the *libelle* writers is drawn from Robert Darnton's, *The Literary Underground of the Old Regime* (Cambridge, Mass and London: Harvard University Press, 1982), chs 1, 2, 4 and 6. Useful, too, are *Revolution in Print*, ed. by Robert Darnton and Daniel Roche (Berkeley, Los Angeles and London: University of California Press, 1989), Part One; Jeremy Popkin, 'From the Press of the Old Regime to the Press of the Revolution', in his *Revolutionary News: The Press in France, 1789–1799* (Durham and London: Duke University Press, 1989), pp. 16–34 and for a summary of works on this topic, Joan Landes, 'More than Words: The Printing Press and the French Revolution', *ECS*, 25, 1 (1991), 85–98.

28. For an account of this expatriate community, see Peter Wagner, 'French Emigré Writers in London', in his *Eros Revived: Erotica of the Enlightenment in England and America* (London: Secker and Warburg, 1988), pp. 91–100. His whole chapter on 'Anti-Aristocratic Erotica' provides invaluable background information for my entire discussion, pp. 87–112. In this context the following comment from Horace Walpole is also noteworthy, 'Our newspapers are deservedly forbidden in France for impudent scandal on the French Queen. I am always ashamed that such cargoes of abuse should be dispersed all over Europe; and frequently our handsomest women are the themes. What Iroquais must we seem to the rest of the world!'. 'Letter to Mann, Wed 2 Feb, 1785', in *The Yale Edition of Horace Walpole's Correspondence*, ed. by W.S. Lewis (Oxford and New Haven: OUP/Yale University Press, 1965), pp. 555–7), (p. 557).

    For Blake's connection with Chevalier D'Eon, see Marsha Keith Schuchard, 'Blake's "Mr Femality": Freemasonry, Espionage and the Doubled-Sexed', *Studies in Eighteenth Century Culture*, 22, 1 (1992), 51–71.

29. Erdman, *Prophet*, p. 92.

30. Erdman, ibid., p. 90. See, too, David Bindman's speculations in *The Complete Graphic Works of William Blake* (London: Thames and Hudson, 1978), pp. 469–70.

31. Blake's, *An Island in the Moon* (1784) contains plenty of scatological humour and it also – as Erdman notes – demonstrates that Blake had an awareness of the French fashions which were exported to England. See, for example, Miss Gittipin's speech in ch. 8 (E.456–7).

32. For a discussion of the vast influence of French pornography, especially of the political variety, in Britain see, Peter Wagner, *Eros Revived*, pp. 87–112.

33. This was the reply of the Jacobins when a deputation of *citoyennes* from the *second des quatre-Nations* requested the use of their meet-

ing room, quoted in *Women in Revolutionary Paris*, ed. by Darline Gay Levy *et al* (Urbana, Chicago and London: University of Illinois Press, 1979), p. 127.

34. It must be noted, however, that there are significant political nuances within different writer's assessments of women's achievements in the French Revolution.

For the most positive kind of assessment, which centres upon the new concept of popular sovereignty forged by revolutionary women, see the various writings of Darline G. Levy and Harriet Applewhite. Of most relevance here are, 'Women of the Popular Classes in Revolutionary Paris, 1789–1795', in *Women, War and Revolution*, pp. 9–35; 'Women, Democracy and Revolution in Paris, 1789–1793', in *French Women in the Age of Enlightenment*, pp. 64–79; 'Responses to the Political Activism of Women of the People in Revolutionary Paris, 1789–1793', in *Women and the Structure of Society*, ed. by Barbara J. Harris and Jo Anne McNamara (Durham: Duke University Press, 1984), pp. 215–31 and the various essays in the recent collection edited by them, *Women and Politics in the Age of Democratic Revolutions* (Ann Arbor: The University of Michigan Press, 1990).

At the other end of the spectrum is the work of Olwen Hufton who, by paying attention to the fate of women in the provinces, decides that the Revolution was an unequivocal disaster for them. See her, 'Women in Revolution, 1789–1796', *Past and Present*, 53 (1971), 90–108 and also, 'Voilà la Citoyenne', *History Today*, 39 (May 1989), 26–32. Jane Abray also comments on the failure of feminism in the Revolution in her 'Feminism in the French Revolution', *American Historical Review*, 80 (1975), 43–62.

In this discussion I am also indebted to the work of Ruth Graham, 'Loaves and Liberty: Women in the French Revolution', in *Becoming Visible: Women in European History*, ed. by Claudia Koonz (Boston: Houghton Mifflin Company, 1977), pp. 236–54; R.B. Rose, *The Making of the Sans-Culottes* (Manchester: Manchester University Press, 1983); Sian Reynolds, 'Marianne's Citizens?: Women, the Republic and Universal Suffrage in France', in the collection she edited, *Women, State and Revolution* (Brighton: Harvester Press, 1986), pp. 102–22; Hazel Mills, '"Recasting the Pantheon?" Women and the French Revolution', *Renaissance and Modern Studies*, 33 (1989), 89–105; Joan Wallace Scott, 'French Feminists and the Rights of "Man": Olympe de Gouges *Declarations*', *History Workshop Journal*, 28 (Autumn 1989), 1–21 and the essays of Susan Conner already listed above. The most recent collection on Women in the French Revolution, *Rebel Daughters*, edited by Sara Melzer and Leslie M. Rabine, extends these discussions and I draw upon it throughout.

35. See the works listed above, especially Jane Abray's, 'Feminism in the French Revolution' and Joan Wallace Scott, 'French Feminists and the Rights of "Man"'.

36. See Olwen Hufton, *The Limits of Citizenship in the French Revolution* (Toronto: Toronto University Press, 1989) and Joan Landes,

who comments on how 'the Republic was constructed against women, not just without them'. For an elaboration of this, see 'Women in the French Revolution', which is Part II of her *Women and the Public Sphere*, pp. 93–200, (p. 12).

37. Olympe de Gouges, *The Rights of Woman* (London: Pythia Press, 1989, fp. 1792), p. 13. For a discussion of de Gouges' works, including this one, see Joan Wallace Scott, 'French Feminists and the Rights of "Man"'. Helen Maria Williams also expressed doubts about whether women could unequivocally welcome the Revolution. 'The Revolution has been a thing in the eyes of women, of doubtful and sometimes portentous aspect [...] That the almost universality of Frenchmen should have readily embraced, and, notwithstanding all its phases of ominous aspect, should have adhered to the Revolution, is not surprising; the vast majority have been great and substantial gainers. The women, indeed, participate in some of those advantages at second hand; but they may be allowed to entertain certain doubts whether the positive benefits they enjoy from the change, form a sufficient subsidy to tempt them to depart from their neutrality', 'On the State of Women in the French Revolution', in her *Sketches of the State of Manners and Opinions in the French Republic, Towards the Close of the Eighteenth Century. In a Series of Letters* (London: G.G. and J. Robinson, 1801), II, Letter XXVI, pp. 50–51.

38. Both Ruth Graham, 'Loaves and Liberty', pp. 246–7 and Elizabeth Colwill agree that, 'Charlotte Corday's assassination of Jean Paul Marat, 'friend of the people', on 13 July 1793 unleashed a torrent of invective against women as political actors, regardless of political allegiances', 'Just Another *Citoyenne*? Marie Antoinette on Trial, 1790–1793', *History Workshop Journal*, 28 (Autumn 1989), 63–87, (pp. 74–5). This was an injustice bitterly resented by revolutionary women and a deputation of them went to the Convention to point it out: 'Nature has without doubt produced a monster which has deprived us of the friend of the people; but are we answerable for that crime? Was Corday a member of our society?' Reported in the *Universal Magazine* (October 1793) 306.

39. This constellation of female deaths is noted and discussed by Germaine Bree, 'Preface: Perilous Visibilities', in *French Women and the Age of Enlightenment*, pp. ix–xv. See too, Camille Naish, ''Tis Crime and not the Scaffold: Charlotte Corday, Marie Antoinette', in her *Death Comes to the Maiden: Sex and Execution, 1431–1933* (London and New York: Routledge, 1991), pp. 110–32.

40. Kelly, *Women of the French Revolution* (London: Hamish Hamilton, 1987), p. 102.

41. See Dorinda Outram, 'Le Langage mâle de la vertu', p. 132.

42. Quoted by Jane Abray, 'Feminism in the French Revolution', p. 57.

43. Most commentators agree that by mid-1793 all politically active, or indeed just publicly visible, French women were under attack from the revolutionary establishment. See, in particular, Jane Abray,

ibid., p. 57 and *passim* and Barbara Corrado Pope, 'Revolution and Retreat', p. 218 and *passim*. For more general discussions of the events of 1793 see, Mary Jacobus, 'Incorruptible Milk: Breast-feeding and the French Revolution', pp. 54–75, (pp. 61–5) and Darline G. Levy and Harriet B. Applewhite, 'The *Other* Revolution: Women as Actors in the Revolutionary Period', pp. 79–101, (pp. 92–7), both in *Rebel Daughters*.

44. Quoted by Levy *et al*, *Women in Revolutionary Paris*, p. 214.
45. Ibid., p. 215.
46. Ibid., p. 219.
47. Quoted by Levy *et al*, *Women in Revolutionary Paris*, p. 219.
48. Madelyn Gutwirth, 'Queen of the Night', p. 229 and see, too, the second part of her fascinating study, *The Twilight of the Goddesses* (New Brunswick: Rutgers UP, 1992). Lynn Hunt also discusses how the republic rendered women particularly suitable for representing abstract principles by excluding them from public affairs, 'The Political Psychology of Revolutionary Caricatures', in *French Caricature and the French Revolution, 1789–1799*, pp. 33–40, (p. 39).
49. For information about a whole range of these images, see the section entitled, 'Allegories and Emblems', in *French Caricature*, pp. 227–36. Maurice Agultor has asked the most important question about this iconic use of women, 'could it be that over the past millennium a succession of cultures founded upon male dominance has assigned women subsidiary roles as 'objects', and that the allegory is, all in all, no more than an abstract dummy', but sadly his magisterial study does not attempt to answer it. See, *Marianne into Battle: Republican Imagery and Symbolism in France, 1789–1880* (Cambridge: Cambridge University Press, 1981), p. 1. The chapter most relevant to my discussion is, 'Liberty, the Republic and the Goddess, 1789–1830', pp. 11–37, and should be consulted for general information on French iconography in this period.
50. Hunt's arguments can be found in, 'Hercules and the Radical Image in the French Revolution', *Representations*, 1, II (1983), 95–117 and *Politics, Cultures and Class in the French Revolution* (Berkeley, Los Angeles and London: University of California Press, 1986). Of interest, too, is her shorter article on related issues, 'Engraving the Republic: Prints and Propaganda in the French Revolution', *History Today*, 30 (1980), 11–17.
51. Interesting in this context is Joan Landes' discussion of Liberty and of the way in which, 'the revolution marks the point of dramatic shift away from the iconic, visual order of representation of the absolutist public sphere to a new masculine, symbolic, discursive order of writing, the law, speech and its proclamation'. She discusses in illuminating ways the fact that Liberty was *only* a picture, throughout her article, 'Representing the Body Politic: The Paradox of Gender in the Graphic Politics of the French Revolution', in *Rebel Daughters*, pp. 15–37, (p. 31).
52. Olwen Hufton discusses David's, 'macho Republican virtue', 'Voilà la Citoyenne', p. 26 and Madelyn Gutwirth also deals with this

issue by examining the predominance of 'largely feminocentric' rococo art prior to the Revolution and the greater currency gained by Roman themes and forms in the 1780s, 'Queen of the Night', pp. 228–9. Also of interest are the following, which touch upon the homoeroticism latent in these developments: Alex Potts, 'Beautiful Bodies and Dying Heroes: Images of Ideal Manhood in the French Revolution', *History Workshop Journal*, 30 (Autumn 1990), 1–21; Joan Landes, 'Republican Bodies', in her *Women and the Public Sphere*, pp. 152–68; Dorinda Outram, *The Body and the French Revolution: Sex, Class and Political Culture* (New Haven and London: Yale University Press, 1989) and Thomas Crow, 'Revolutionary Activism and the Cult of Male Beauty in the Studio of David', in *Fictions of the French Revolution*, ed. by Bernadette Fort (Evanston: Northwestern University Press, 1991), pp. 55–83. A Blakean look at this context is provided by Stewart Crehan, 'Republican Art', in his *Blake in Context* (Dublin: Gill and Macmillan, 1984), pp. 192–238.

53. See Mona Ozouf, *Festivals and the French Revolution* (Cambridge, Mass and London: Harvard University Press, 1988), esp. pp. 87; 116. Ruth Graham reinforces Ozouf's observation that Rousseau's suckling ideal was everywhere present, 'Loaves and Liberty', p. 250.

54. My account of Robespierre's festival in honour of the supreme being is drawn from Graham, ibid., p. 250. On these festivals, see too Mary Jacobus, 'Incorruptible Milk', pp. 65–71.

55. Marie-Claire Vallois, 'Exotic Femininity and the Rights of Man: *Paul et Virginie* and *Atala*, or the Revolution in Statis', in *Rebel Daughters*, pp. 178–97, (p. 186).

56. On Rousseau's suckling ideal, see Mary Jacobus, 'Incorruptible Milk', pp. 56–61 and Londa Schiebinger, 'Why Mammals are called Mammals: Gender Politics in Eighteenth Century Natural History', *American Historical Review* 98, 2 (April 1993), 382–411, (pp. 408–9).

57. Robert Darnton discusses the serious measures taken to stop the importation of 'libelles' into France in *The Literary Underground*. See, in particular, the numerous references to Vergennes and his desperate efforts to keep these books out of the country.

58. For discussions of this cultural revolution and the return of expatriates to France, see Robert Darnton, 'The High Enlightenment and the Low-Life of Literature', ibid., pp. 1–41 and Peter Wagner, *Eros Revived*, p. 98.

59. Langlois, Claude, 'Counterrevolutionary Iconography', in *French Caricature and the French Revolution*, pp. 41–54, (p. 43) and Peter Wagner, ibid., p. 98. Antoine de Baecque comments on the great increase in pornographic pamphlets published during the early years of the Revolution, in his fascinating study, 'Pamphlets: Libel and Political Mythology', in *Revolution in Print*, pp. 165–76, (p. 167). See, too, his article, 'The "Livres remplis d'horreur": Pornographic Literature and Politics at the Beginning of the French Revolution', in *Erotica and the Enlightenment*, ed. by Peter Wagner (Frankfurt am Main: Peter Lang, 1991), pp. 123–65.

60. The Princess Lamballe's fate was known and widely sympathized with in England. It was reported in English papers, as the editor of Walpole's letters (one of which dealt with this event) notes, 'All the newspapers had reported her murder in gory detail. Horace Walpole's restrained account is essentially accurate', see, *The Yale edition of Horace Walpole's Correspondence*, pp. 218–21, (p. 219).

61. Quoted by Simon Schama, *Citizens – A Chronicle of the French Revolution* (London: Viking/Penguin Group, 1989), p. 800.

62. Quotations from Elizabeth Colwill, 'Just Another *Citoyenne*', p. 63. My account of Marie Antoinette's biography, both mythic and literal, is greatly indebted to the excellent articles by Colwill, Gutwirth, 'Queen of the Night' and Nancy Davenport, 'Maenad, Martyr, Mother: Marie Antoinette Transformed', *Consortium on Revolutionary Europe, Proceedings 1985* (Athens 1986), pp. 66–84. I also draw heavily upon the accounts offered by Simon Schama, Linda Kelly, Susan Conner, Lynn Hunt and Camilla Naish, all listed above.

63. Gutwirth, ibid., p. 231.

64. Davenport, 'Maenad, Martyr, Mother', p. 67.

65. Details of Marie Antoinette's humiliating arrival in France can be found in Nancy Davenport, ibid., p. 66 and Christopher Hibbert, *The French Revolution* (Harmondsworth: Penguin, 1982), p. 21.

66. Quoted by Hibbert, ibid., p. 23.

67. For an account of the 'Diamond Necklace Affair', see Simon Schama, 'Uterine Furies and Dynastic Obstructions', in his *Citizens*, pp. 203–211; Robert Darnton, 'The Forbidden Books' and Rory Browne, 'The Diamond Necklace Affair Revisited: The Rohan Family and Court Politics', *Renaissance and Modern Studies*, 33 (1989), 21–39 – which focuses upon the unfortunate Cardinal's role. This scandal was rehashed for the British public just a couple of years before Blake wrote *Europe* by the publication of the Countess De Valois De La Motte's *Memoirs [. . .] containing a complete Justification of her conduct and an explanation of the intrigues and artifices used against her by her enemies, relative to the Diamond necklace* (London: sold by J. Ridgeway, York Street, St. James, 1789).

68. A statistic noted by Madelyn Gutwirth, 'Queen of the Night', p. 232, although 34 conquests pales into insignificance when we note that pamphleteers and cartoonists of the late 1780s coupled her with the entire French Assembly, a point discussed by Nancy Davenport, 'Maenad, Martyr, Mother', p. 70.

69. See Jean-Pierre Guicciardi for details of some of the more distasteful activities of French male monarchs, many of whom improved their popular standing immensely, 'Between the Licit and the Illicit', *passim*.

70. Simon Schama provides these and other details of the prolific productivity of writers sexually slandering Marie Antoinette, *Citizens*, pp. 221–6 and Nancy Davenport provides a list of titles of just a few of the vast number of works which existed, 'Maenad, Martyr, Mother', p. 71. For a fuller discussion see Peter Wagner, *Eros Revived*, pp. 94–100; Lynn Hunt, 'The Bad Mother', in her *The Family*

*Romance of the French Revolution* (London: Routledge, 1992), pp. 89–123, (pp. 102–14) and Antoine de Baecque, who comments that, 'Marie Antoinette is undoubtedly *the* victim, the scapegoat of the "miry lampoonists" [. . .] The queen never ceases to be a political character, and moves from the erotic world, in which the gallant anecdote serves as decor, in to the pornographic space in which the positions themselves compose a vicious architecture of the body', 'The "Livres remplis d'horreur"', pp. 154–60, (pp. 147; 155).

71. For discussions of how densely visual French political culture was during the Revolution see the essays in *French Caricature*, and the two articles by Tom Gretton, 'Representing the Revolution', *History Today*, 39 (May 1989), 39–44, and 'Picturing the Revolution', in *The Story So Far*, pp. 28–9. Jeremy Popkin also provides a useful review of recent materials in this field, 'Pictures in a Revolution: Recent Publications on Graphic Art in France, 1789–1799', *ECS*, 24, 2 (1990–91), 251–9.

72. For a full account of this presentation of the King and Queen see the section, 'The Royal Family', in *French Caricature*, pp. 178–98.

73. Simon Schama, *Citizens*, p. 206. Hunt also discusses this engraving in 'The Bad Mother', pp. 109–10. See, too, the works of Antoine de Baecque, 'The "Livres remplis d'horreur"' and 'Pamphlets: Libel and Political'.

74. For an illuminating discussion of Hébert's *Père Duchesne*, see Lynn Hunt, 'The Bad Mother', pp. 111–13; 122; Jeremy Popkin, *Revolutionary News*, pp. 16–34 and Elizabeth Colwill, 'Just Another Citizen', *passim*, p. 64. As Popkin comments, 'Hébert put back into his descriptions of its victims the humiliation and cruelty that had been the lot of those put to death under the Old Regime', p. 164.

75. The notion that Marie Antoinette was 'feminizing' government is taken up by most of the writers I've cited – of particular interest are the accounts of Simon Schama, 'Uterine Furies', and Lynn Hunt, 'The Political Psychology', which both discuss the central issue of male psychosexual anxiety. Colwill, 'Just Another *Citoyenne*?', p. 70.

76. Quoted by Colwill, ibid., pp. 66–7.

77. Of related interest here is the concept of 'fuck regeneration', which figures in a number of pamphlets discussed by Antoine de Baecque. The virile sexual practices of revolutionary males were seen to be instrumental in the rejuvenation of the country. See, 'The "Livres remplis d'horreur"', pp. 161–2 and, 'Pamphlets: Libel and Political', p. 173.

78. Quoted by Colwill, 'Just Another *Citoyenne*?', p. 73.

79. Marie Antoinette's contemporaries were well aware that she was on trial as a mother. Madame de Stael, for example, set herself the task of defending the queen in precisely these terms. See Gutwirth, 'Queen of the Night', pp. 232–7 for an account of her efforts. De Stael's *Reflections* on the queen's trial were, incidentally, published anonymously in Britain late in 1793. Another useful account of these two women is offered by Dorinda Outram, 'Words and Flesh: Mme Roland, the Female Body and the Search

for Power', in her *The Body and the French Revolution*, pp. 124–52. As Outram comments, 'The trial of Marie Antoinette was staged virtually as a morality play on the evil impact of women on the body politic, as well as an epitome of monarchical corruption', p. 127. More generally, see Lynn Hunt's excellent psycho-historical study, *The Family Romance of the French Revolution*. The issue of the Queen's trial is focused in her aptly named chapter, 'The Bad Mother', pp. 89–123, see especially, pp. 91–5.

80. Colwill, 'Just Another *Citoyenne*', pp. 78; 81. There is no small amount of irony in the fact that the Rousseauean heroine who triumphed after Marie Antoinette's death was precisely the ideal that the queen had always thought she was aspiring to. See Schama for some details of Marie Antoinette's devotion to Rousseau – which prompted her to, amongst other things, visit his grave at Ermenonville, *Citizens*, pp. 156–7.

81. Quoted by Schama, ibid., p. 800. The American Ambassador, Gouverneur Morris, also testified to Marie Antoinette's composure, 'The Queen was executed the day before yesterday. Insulted during her trial and reviled in her last moments, she behaved with dignity throughout', *The Diaries and Letters of Gouverneur Morris*, ed. by Anne Cary Morris (London: Kegan Paul, Trench & Co. 1889), II, p. 53.

82. Drawn from Marilyn Yalom, 'The King and Queen in the Face of Death: Witnessed by Madame Royale and Rosalie Lamorlière' in her *Blood Sisters: The French Revolution in Women's Memory* (London: Pandora, 1993), pp. 56–73, (pp. 69–70).

83. Revel, 'Marie Antoinette in Her Fictions: The Staging of Hatred', in *Fictions of the French Revolution*, pp. 111–29.

84. An interesting sidelight to this intellectual exchange is provided by David V. Erdman's, *Commerce des Lumières: John Oswald and the British in Paris, 1790–1793* (Columbia: University of Missouri Press, 1986).

85. Each month after September 1792 the *Bon Ton Magazine* carried a feature entitled, 'Epitome of the Times', which reported events in France and their effect in England. As you might expect the Death of Louis XVI was reported in an account that described the Queen's hysteria, XXIV (Feb 1793), 449–51. Also interesting in this context is the first part of the treatise, *Modern Propensities; or, an essay on the art of strangling* (London, 1791).

86. David Bindman, *Shadow of the Guillotine*, pp. 28–9 and Mary Dorothy George, *English Political Caricature* (Oxford: OUP, 1959), I, p. 205.

87. Details from *The Satirical Etchings of James Gillray*, ed. by Draper Hill (New York: Dover Publications, 1976). Especially useful is the introductory discussion, 'Caricature and the Print-Shop', pp. xii–xvii.

88. (?Isaac Cruikshank's) 'Le Roi Esclave Ou les Sujets Rois Female Patriotism' was published on the 31 October 1789 by S.W. Fores. An account of it can be found M.D. George, *Catalogue of Political and Personal Satires* (London: British Museum Publications, 1938),

Vol. VI (1784–1792), no. 7560. W. Dent's, 'Female Furies or Extraordinary Revolution' was published on 18 October 1789. An account
of it can be found in Bindman, *Shadow of the Guillotine*, p. 93.

89. Dorothy George, with supreme understatement, notes, 'It is to be
suspected that the harsh treatment of Marie Antoinette derives from
cruel French caricatures of *L'Autrichienne*', ibid., p. 206.

90. 'The Commercial Treaty; or, John Bull Changing Beef and Pudding for Frogs and Soup Maigre!' was published on 25 November
1786 by Wm Holland. An account of it can be found in George,
*Catalogue*, Vol. VI (1784–1792), no. 6995. 'The Ladies Churchyard'
was published on 22 September 1783 by B. Pownall. An account
of it can be found in M.D. George, *Catalogue*, Vol. V (1771–1783),
no. 6263.

91. W. Dent's, 'Revolution, or Johnny Bull in France' was published
on 25 July 1789. An account of it can be found in Bindman, *Shadow
of the Guillotine*, p. 89.

92. James Gillray, 'The Offering to Liberty' was published on 3 Au-
gust 1789 by J. Aitken. An account of it can be found in George
Vol. VI (1784–1792), no. 7548. Anon., 'La Chute du Despotisme/
The Downfall of Despotism' was published on 14 August 1789 by
Wm Holland. An account of it can also be found in Bindman, *Shadow
of the Guillotine*, p. 89.

93. Ronald Paulson notes that the flight to Varennes was a turning
point for Gillray, who also produced as caricature of the event,
*Representations of Revolution*, pp. 190–95, (p. 190). James Gillray,
'French Democrats Surprising the Royal Runaways' was published
on 27 June 1791 by H. Humphrey. An account of it can be found
in George, Vol. VI (1784–92), no. 7882. Richard Newton, 'An Escape à la Française!' was published on 1st July 1791 by Wm Holland. An account of it can be found in George, Vol. VI (1784–92),
no. 7886.

94. Thomas Rowlandson, 'The Grand Monarch Discovered in a Pot
De Chambre Or The Royal Fugitives Turning Tail', was published
on 28 June 1791 by S.W. Fores. An account of it can be found in
George, Vol. VI (1784–92), no. 7884.

95. William Thomas Fitzgerald, 'Lines On The Murder of the Queen
of France; With Admonition To The Infant King, Louis XVII', in
his *Miscellaneous Poems* (London: W. Bulmer and Sons, 1801),
p. 14. Katherine M. Rogers notes that English fears about French
moral laxity and acceptance of adultery remained constant, 'The
View from England', pp. 357–8.

96. Hannah More, 'Village Politics. Addressed to all the Mechanics,
Journeymen, and Day Labourers in Great Britain, by Will Chip, a
Country Carpenter', in *Burke, Paine, Godwin and the Revolutionary
Controversy*, ed. by Marilyn Butler (Cambridge: CUP, 1984), pp.
180–84, (p. 183).

97. Betty Bennett gives many examples of poems expressing fear that
war/invasion will mean the violation of British women, for example, 'The Farmer and The Labourer' (1794), 'The Soldier' (1795)

and 'Ode to Peace' (1796), in her collection, *British War Poetry in the Age of Romanticism: 1793–1815* (New York and London: Garland Publishing, 1976), pp. 117–19; 135–6; 168–9.

98. Brewer, '"This monstrous tragi-comic scene": British Reactions to the French Revolution', in *Shadow of the Guillotine*, pp. 11–25, (p. 22).

99. David Bindman offers an account and reproductions of 'The Contrast' in *Shadow of the Guillotine*, pp. 118–21. For a discussion of the work, see Neil Hertz, 'Medusa's Head: Male Hysteria Under Political Pressure', *Representations*, 4 (Fall 1983), 27–54. Hertz, however, offers a scanty reading which is largely ahistorical and must be viewed in the light of the comments offered in the same volume by Professor Catherine Gallagher, who notes 'From 1789 to 1870 French Revolutionary violence repeatedly enacted an ambivalent attack on patriarchy. And the emblematic importance of the uncontrolled and luridly sexual woman cannot be separated from that attack. On the one hand the revolutionaries needed to undermine the patriarchal assumptions that buttressed monarchical and aristocratic power. Thus the symbol of liberty who leads is a female. But liberty, in the iconography of the age, often turns into a whore when she threatens the patriarchal family as such. The sexually uncontrolled woman then becomes a threat to all forms of property and established power. Her fierce independence is viewed, even by revolutionaries, as an attack on the Rights of Man [. . .] the fear of Medusa's head can be analyzed as a much more historical and much less hysterical phenomenon than Professor Hertz makes it seem', 'More About Medusa's Head', pp. 55–7, (pp. 56–7). See, too, Robert Hole, 'British Counter-revolutionary Popular Propaganda in the 1790s', in *Britain and Revolutionary France: Conflict, Subversion and Propaganda*, ed. by Colin Jones (Exeter: Exeter University, 1983), pp. 53–69, (esp. pp. 57–63).

100. David Punter, 'The Sex of Revolution', *Criticism* 24, 20 (1982), 201–17. For the account of Coleridge's, 'Happiness' (1791), see pp. 204–5; quotation, p. 205. In this context Ann Yearsley's lines on liberty are interesting,

> Where fancied liberty, with rude Excess,
>   Courts Man from Sober Joy, and lures him on
> To Frantic war, struck by her gaudy Dress,
>   His ardent Soul is in the Chace undone.

> The *Ignis Fatuus* follow'd by the clown,
>   Deceives not more than liberty, her Arms
> Were never round the weary Warrior thrown,
>   He dies a Victim of fallacious Charms.

> Ask, Ye! Where joyous Liberty resorts,
>   In *France*, in *Spain*, or in *Britannia's Vale*?
> O no!—She only with the poor fancy Sports
>   Her richest Dwelling is the passing Gale

Unlike most (especially male) writers of the time, Yearsley refuses to take a patriotic stance, a fact which is doubly intriguing as these lines are drawn from her sympathetic, *Reflections on the Death of Louis XVI* (Bristol, 1793), p. 5.

101. Punter, ibid., p. 205.
102. 'Church and King' can be found in *British War Poetry*, pp. 71–3. Bennett also includes the poem, 'A Word to the Wise', pp. 78–80 which contains the stanza.

> But our Ladies are virtuous, Our Ladies are Fair
> Which is more than they tell us your French Women are;
> They know they are happy, they know they are Free
> And that Liberty's not at the top of a tree. (p. 79)

103. For a discussion of the *Anti-Jacobin Review and Magazine*, see Emily Lorrainède Montluzin, *The Anti-Jacobins 1798–1800 – The Early Contributors to the 'Anti-Jacobin Review'* (Basingstoke: Macmillan Press, 1988). An informative context for this discussion is also offered by Richard Soloway, 'Reform or Ruin: English Moral Thought during the First French Republic', *Review of Politics*, 25, 1 (1963), 110–28.
104. For an account of the transformation of Marie Antoinette see John Brewer, in *Shadow of the Guillotine*, pp. 22–4; and see also the sentimental images discussed and reproduced by Bindman in the same volume, pp. 129–33.
105. For an idea of just how idealized Marie Antoinette had become by the time of her death, see I. Cruikshank, 'The Death of Marie Antoinette Queen of France', which was published on 23rd October by J. Aitken. An account of it can be found in George, *Catalogue*, Vol. VII (1793–1800), no. 8343. I Cruikshank, 'The Martyrdom of Marie Antoinette Queen of France' which was published on 28 October by S.W. Fores. An account can be found in George, *Catalogue*, Vol. VII (1793–1800), no. 8344. (?), 'The Unfortunate Marie Antoinette Queen of France at the Place of Execution, October 16th, 1793', which was published on the 12th December 1793 by John Fairburn. An account can be found in George, *Catalogue*, Vol. VII (1793–1800), no. 8354. See also Bindman, ibid., pp. 150–54 for a selection of sentimental paintings.
106. See David Bindman for a number of prints, by the most famous caricaturists (Cruikshank and Gillray), dealing with Corday's murder of Marat. Many of these do not allude to the circumstances in which Corday assassinated the 'friend of the people', *Shadow of the Guillotine*, pp. 147–9. Other interesting discussions are provided by, Michael Maninan, 'Images and Ideas of Charlotte Corday: Texts and Contexts of an Assassination', *Arts Magazine*, 54, 8 (April 1980), 158–76 and Claudine Mitchell, 'Spectacular Fears and Popular Arts: A View from the Nineteenth Century', in *Reflections of Revolution*, ed. by Alison Yarrington and Kelvin Everest (New York and London: Routledge, 1993), pp. 159–81, especially the section, 'The Angel of Assassination', pp. 170–74.

107. Francis Grose, *A Classical Dictionary of the Vulgar Tongue* (London: S. Hooper, 1788).

108. David Erdman identifies the lines from Milton which Blake's frontispiece refers to, 'When the Almighty "took the golden Compasses" in his hand to circumscribe universe and creatures, "One foot he centred, and the other turn'd"' (*Paradise Lost* VIII 224–8)', *Illuminated Blake*, p. 156. A reference which further underlines the notion of patriarchal power, as Milton's Almighty is first and foremost a father.

109. Erdman, ibid., p. 157.

110. Erdman, ibid., p. 398.

111. Carol P. Kowle, 'Plate III and the Meaning of *Europe*', *BS*, VIII (1987), 89–99.

112. Another more personal poem upon this theme of failure/refusal to ejaculate with sufficient joy is the notebook verse which reads: 'Thou hast a lap full of seed/ And this is a fine country/ Why dost thou not cast thy seed/ And live in it merrily (E.469). Perhaps one answer to this question can be found in the eighteenth-century myth of the 'precious sperm', according to which 'To copulate means *spending* a precious balm of life, a quintessential liquor originating, some thought, from the brain, others from the marrow, or from the "better blood" after ingested food had been duly "concocted"', Paul-Gabriel Bouce, 'Chthonic and Pelagic Metaphorization in Eighteenth Century English Erotica', in *'Tis Nature's Fault*, pp. 202–16, (p. 208).

113. Brenda Webster, *Blake's Prophetic Psychology* (Basingstoke: Macmillan, 1983), p. 189.

114. Bloom, 'Commentary', p. 903 and Carol P. Kowle argues that the poem's tone is, 'so similar to that of *Songs of Innocence*', 'Plate III', p. 95. An intriguing, although equally celebratory, interpretation of this poem is offered by Jon Mee, who speculates about the creature's function as Blake's muse, *Dangerous Enthusiasm*, p. 142 and see the more detailed account, pp. 116–19.

115. This important link with *The Gates of Paradise* is made by Carol P. Kowle, 'Plate III', p. 99.

116. Kowle also suggests that we look at the other Fairy poems Blake wrote, ibid., pp. 98–9. 'A Fairy' and 'A Fairy Skipped' both associate the creature with sexual impishness and (female?) coyness. Swearingen is, then, surely wrong to claim that the fairy is 'essentially gender-neutral though designated by the masculine pronoun', and in much else besides, 'Time and History', p. 118.

117. Erdman, 'Prophet', p. 264.

118. Susan Fox interestingly describes the situation, 'The shadowy female is a wildflower plucked again and again without even the consolation of dying', and in a footnote she also censures the 'Edenic' fairy. See *Poetic Form in Blake's Milton* (Princeton, NJ: Princeton University Press, 1976), p. 10; p. 11, n. 5.

119. This is an exact chime with Thel's question, 'who shall find my place' (*Thel*, 2:12; E.4); and we should note that the shadowy

female's name is already beginning to 'vanish': in *America* she was, 'The shadowy daughter of Urthona' (*America*, 1:1; E.51) now she is simply, 'The nameless shadowy female' (*Europe*, 1:1; E.60).

120. Erdman discusses the historical specificity of these plates, *Prophet*, pp. 201–25 and, *Illuminated*, pp. 159–61, although the context is British, not French, politics.

121. George, *Blake and Freud* (London and Ithaca: Cornell University Press, 1980), p. 160.

122. Butter, P.H., 'Blake's *The French Revolution*', *The Yearbook of English Studies*, 19 (1989), 18–27, (p. 26). The most expansive modern exposition of the 'dominant mother' theory is provided by John Howard, *Infernal Poetics* (London and Toronto: Associated University Presses, 1984), pp. 127–51, (p. 126). Also, Cox, *Love and Logic* (Ann Arbor: The University of Michigan Press, 1992), p. 137.

123. David Erdman offers a whole chapter on 'The Secret Child' which centres upon depicting Orc as the saviour-Christ, coming this time as tiger not lamb, *Prophet*, pp. 264–70.

124. Webster, *Blake's Prophetic Psychology*, p. 130. John Howard comments, 'The "peaceful night" will be for her another kind of joy, the joy of female dominion that will ravage the world of men [. . .]. The mother intends her wishes to supersede the father's joys to which the children tend', *Infernal Poetics*, p. 142. Los, we should note, also underlines that though he has, 'joy'd in the peaceful night' he is still, 'strong Urthona' (*Europe*, 3:10; E.61) – so perhaps Webster need not have worried about his loss of 'adult masculinity'.

125. Harold Bloom outlines his reading and Erdman's thus: '4:1–14 This is all part of a Song of Los, with the sons of Urizen dramatically depicted in it as uttering the lines 3–9. Erdman [. . .] reads it differently, assigning lines 3–9 to the sons of Urizen directly, and lines 1–14 to Enitharmon. This is very possible, but loses the complex irony of Los's dramatic self-deception and his misunderstanding of the new birth.', 'Commentary', p. 904. My own reading converges quite closely with Bloom's, his insistence that Los reacts inappropriately to Orc's birth is of fundamental importance, as is his dispatching of the idea that Enitharmon tyrannizes her son.

126. It is legitimate to read the line, 'joy'd in the peaceful night' as a reference to a sexual union between Los and Enitharmon because joys and joy'd are continually used to denote sexual activity in Blake's poetry; see for example: *Visions*, 6:6; E.49 and *America*, 2:4; E.52.

127. Carole P. Kowle, 'Plate III', p. 92. Northrop Frye makes a distinction between Enitharmon's Orc (who is the 'great selfhood') and Los's Orc (who is the 'universal imagination'), and contends that Enitharmon is hostile to Los's Orc, *Fearful Symmetry* (Princeton, NJ: Princeton University Press, 1974. fp. 1946), p. 264. David Erdman offers the most complete case, with Orc representing everything revolutionary and Enitharmon embodying everything which that revolution must destroy, *Prophet*, *passim*. John Howard also comments that, 'This formidable syndrome of tyranny, as in *America*,

is opposed by the force of freedom, led by Orc', *Infernal Poetics*, p. 131.

128. For Erdman's discussion of various Gillray prints see, *Prophet*, pp. 201–25 and, *Illuminated*, pp. 159–60. His selection is no less speculative than the one which I make, as I hope the following discussion will demonstrate and in some places is a good deal more perverse. He, for example, has very little to say about who the enormous female figure might be who dominates the European skyline of Plate 3 (see, *Illuminated*, pp. 161–2). Another account, also glaringly deficient, is offered by Vincent Carretta, *George III and the Satirists from Hogarth to Byron* (Athens and London: University of Georgia Press, 1990), pp. 220–41.

129. Very few critics have found Marie Antoinette represented in *Europe*. Erdman, as I've already noted, makes some stereotypical swipes and Frye does identify 'the mistress of chivalry', *Fearful Symmetry*, p. 263, but generally no one has considered the queen's presence in the text to be at all important. It should be noted that John Grant and Mary Lynn Johnson do offer the comment that, 'Enitharmon's characterization as charming tyrant bears considerable resemblance to Wollstonecraft's portrait of Marie Antoinette in her *History of the French Revolution* (1793) [sic]', *Blake's Poetry and Designs* (New York and London: W.W. Norton, 1979), p. 122, but more typical is David Bindman's claim that her 'fate seems to have left him unmoved, though it excited widespread sympathy in England', '"My Mind is My Own Church": Blake, Paine and the French Revolution', in *Reflections of Revolution*, pp. 112–33, (pp. 122–3).

130. Erdman, *Prophet*, p. 227.

131. For a discussion of English reactions to beheading, see Ronald Paulson, 'The Severed Head – The Impact of French Revolutionary Caricatures on England', in *French Caricature*, pp. 55–65. See, too, David Punter's article, 'Parts of the Body/Parts of Speech: Some Instances of Dismemberment and Healing', in *Reflections of Revolution*, pp. 10–25, (pp. 15–17; 20–21).

132. M.D. George discusses Fore's model guillotine in *Political Caricature*, I, p. 205.

133. This information about newspaper reports on Marie Antoinette in 1793 comes from Lucyle Werkmeister, *A Newspaper History of England, 1792–1793* (Lincoln: University of Nebraska Press, 1967), pp. 258; 298; 359–60; 412.

134. For some effusive magazine reporting of Marie Antoinette's death see the *Universal Magazine* for late 1793. In October it ran: 'OBSERVATIONS on the TRIAL and EXECUTION of the late unfortunate Louis XVI and on the subsequent situation of the QUEEN and the ROYAL FAMILY in the Temple', pp. 247–56, and 'Execution of the Queen of France', pp. 307–8; in November 'Further PARTICULARS of the TRIAL and EXECUTION of the late unfortunate MARIE ANTOINETTE, Queen of France', pp. 370–74 and in December was still engaged with related themes: reproducing

sections of John Moore's, 'Journal during a Residence in France, Vol. II'. Moore constructed an amazing image of the queen, see his *A View of the Causes and Progress of the French Revolution* (London: G.G. & J. Robinson, 1795), esp. Vol. II which discusses the 'invasion of Versailles', the foiled flight to Varennes and the queen's execution – which to Moore was the 'most wanton, unmanly, and detestable exercise of tyranny, that ever revolted the soul of humanity', II, p. 501. See also his *A Journal During A Residence in France* (London: G.G. & J. Robinson, 1793) which describes with high colour the final interview of Louis XVI and his family, after which, according to Moore, the queen, 'In the bitterness of her soul [. . .] beat her breast and tore her hair; and her screams were heard at intervals, all that night of agony and horror', II, p. 596.

135. Quotation is from Mary Robinson's, *Monody To the Memory of the late Queen of France* (London: T. Spilsbury, 1793), p. 9. Her poem is, in fact, a good deal more admirable than most of the verse produced to commemorate Marie Antoinette's death, as is Ann Yearsley's, *An Elegy on Marie Antoinette, of Austria, Ci-Devant Queen of France* (Bristol, c. 1795). To list all the works which appeared in various magazines would occupy too much space, a taste however can be gained by looking at those reproduced by Betty Bennett, *War Poetry*, and especially, 'Stanzas, Supposed to be written whilst the late QUEEN OF FRANCE, was sleeping, by her attendant in the TEMPLE', pp. 87–9 – an entirely Burkean production which typifies the genre. It appeared in the *Gentleman's Magazine* in October, 1793. The *Gentleman's Magazine* was a major publisher of this kind of verse, which it continued to carry until February 1799, when a 'Sonnet in the Character of the Queen of France' appeared, Lxix, Pt. 1 (Feb. 1799), 149.

136. An example is the *Authentic Trial at large of Marie Antoinette, Late Queen of France, Before the Revolutionary Tribunal [. . .] To which are Prefixed Her Life and a Verbal Copy of Her private examination previous to her public Trial with a supplement containing The particulars of her Execution* (London: Chapman, 1793). This extremely detailed document takes up on various occasions (see for example p. 9), the issue of Marie Antoinette's 'female frailities' and seeks to absolve the queen through the idea that she's suffered enough in the past few years to earn forgiveness for whatever she might have done.

137. One contributor to the *Gentleman's Magazine* was mortified to discover that the, 'infamous publication [. . .] "The Life of the Late Queen of France"' was now circulating in London and in his elegy makes indignant reference to this new work of political pornography on Marie Antoinette, *Gentleman's Magazine*, Lxiv Pt. 2 (Sept. 1794), 841. An example of a 'Church and King' broadside which is topped by a sexually suggestive image of Marie Antoinette is, 'A NEW SONG, On the Cruel Usage of the French Queen' which was produced sometime after the King's death and sometime before the Queen's. It centres on her suffering as a mother and contains

the cheering chorus, 'Pray Death come ease, kind Death come ease me,/ And Free me from the hardships I am doom'd for to bear'.

138. Erdman, *Illuminated*, p. 163.

139. Marilyn Butler provides these, and other, examples of stereotypical radical slurs cast upon Marie Antoinette in *Burke, Paine, Godwin*. I have quoted James Mackintosh, p. 93 and Lord Bryon, p. 241, n. 7, but see, too, the remarks of Joseph Priestley, p. 87.

140. *The Jockey Club* (London: 1792), III. This was the work of Charles Pigott, although it was published anonymously. It contains an entire section on Marie Antoinette, in which her character is comprehensively assassinated, see Vol. III, pp. 66–88. Also of interest in this context is his later, *The Female Jockey Club* (1794), which centres upon the idea of women's power and contains the prefatory warning that the objects of its attack will be harshly treated, as 'miserably impotent and defective must that satire ever prove, which does not strike at *persons*', from unpaginated Preface.

141. Thomas Christie, for example, drew these conclusions from her experiences, 'The Revolution was for her a severe, but it will prove a salutary lesson; and I have little doubt [. . .] that the character of a virtuous wife, and an affectionate mother, confers purer joys than the incense offered to a flattered coquette, or the dissipated pleasures of an intriguing *virago*. And though Mr Burke is very angry that a queen should be thought *only a woman*, it is however an undeniable truth, that the real happiness of a queen, is exactly of the same kind, as that which constitutes the felicity of the humblest female of her dominions', *Letters on the Revolution of France* (London: Joseph Johnson, 1791), I, p. 220.

142. Smith, 'The Emigrants A Poem, in Two Books' (London: T. Cadell, 1793), p. 49.

143. Erdman, *Illuminated*, p. 163.

144. Blake also parodied Burke's famous description of Marie Antoinette, 'The Queen of France just touchd this Globe/ And the Pestilence darted from her robe' (E.500). He was clearly aware of at least the key sections of *Reflections*. On this verse see Erdman, *Prophet*, pp. 184–8.

145. M.D. George lists numerous prints that responded to Burke and just over a third of them make reference to his devotional description of Marie Antoinette, *Catalogue*, Vol. VI, *passim* and especially those listed in 'Index of Persons', p. 1020. There were many reviews of Burke's *Reflections*, with perhaps the most comprehensive appearing in the *Analytical Review* 8 (Nov. 1790), 295–307. It devoted 12 pages to summarizing Burke's work and then offered a number of thoughtful objections, stylistic as well as political. This critique was also continued in the next issue, 8 (Dec. 1790), 408–14.

146. Mary Wollstonecraft, *Vindication of the Rights of Men*, in *The Works*, 5, p. 10. For a discussion of the relationship between the treasury newspapers and Burke's *Reflections*, see Lucyle Werkmeister, *The London Daily Press*, 1772–1792 (Lincoln: University of Nebraska Press, 1963), pp. 19; 335–6.

147. Lucyle Werkmeister, *A Newspaper History*, p. 366. This book also reports on the controversy surrounding Lord George Gordon who had been imprisoned for five years in 1788 for libelling Marie Antoinette. In 1793 there was a second hearing, after which he was returned to prison where he died – reputedly of 'gaol distemper' – on the 1st of November, pp. 228–9. Yet one more incident that may have placed Marie Antoinette on Blake's agenda, for it can be reasonably assumed that he'd have been interested in the fate of the hero of the 'Gordon Riots'.

148. Joan B. Landes discusses Burke's (Sublime and Beautiful?) obsession with these two groups of women, *Women and the Public Sphere*, p. 112.

149. For the full account of Burke on Marie Antoinette, see *Reflections on the Revolution in France* (Harmondsworth: Penguin, 1968), pp. 169–70 and for his description of the women of the people, see p. 165. Horace Walpole defended Burke's account against its critics and commented, 'Had I had Mr Burke's powers, I would have described her in his words. I like 'the swords leaping out of their scabbards' – in short, I am not more charmed with his wit and eloquence, than with his enthusiasm'. He also shared Burke's hostility towards the women of the people, 'All the blessed liberty the French seemed to have gained, is that every man or woman, if *poissardes* are women, may hang whom they please', 'Letter to Lady Ossary', Wed 1 Dec., 1790, *The Yale Edition of Horace Walpole's Correspondence*, Vol. 34, pp. 97–9, (p. 98).

150. Butler discusses Burke's, 'popular tale of "the Revolution epitomized"' in 'Telling it Like a Story', p. 348. So too does Tom Furniss, 'Stripping the Queen: Edmund Burke's Magic Lantern Show', in *Burke and the French Revolution: Bicentennial Essays*, ed. by Steven Blakemore (Athens and London: The University of Athens Press, 1992), p. 80.

151. My interpretation of Burke is indebted to the work of Tom Furniss, ibid.; 'Gender in Revolution: Edmund Burke and Mary Wollstonecraft', in *Revolution in Writing*, ed. by Kelvin Everest (Milton Keynes and Philadelphia: Open University Press, 1991), pp. 65–100 and his 'Nasty Tricks and Tropes: Sexuality and Language in Mary Wollstonecraft's Rights of Woman', *SiR*, 32, 2 (1993), 177–209. Also Ronald Paulson, *Representations of Revolution*; Julie Carson, 'Impositions of Form: Romantic Antitheatricalism and the Case against Particular Women', *ELH*, 60 (1993), 149–79, (pp. 152–4) and, more generally, to Stephen Blakemore, *Burke and the Fall of Language: The French Revolution as Linguistic Event* (Hanover and London: University Press of New England, 1988) and Gary Farnell, 'A "Competition of Discourses" in the French Revolution', *Literature and History*, 2nd ser, 32 (Autumn 1991), 35–53, (esp. pp. 44–8).

152. *Reflections*, p. 171 (all quotations are from this page, unless otherwise stated).

153. Punter, 'The Sex of Revolution', p. 217. On the idea that Burke saw Marie Antoinette as the perfect victim, it is interesting to note

that when he heard reports of her endurance he declared, 'one is interested that beings made for suffering should suffer well', *Reflections*, p. 169.

154. 'Lines on the Murder of the Queen of France; With Admonition To The Infant King, Louis XVII', p. 12.

155. ?H.W., 'Don Dismallo, After An Absence of Sixteen Years, Embracing His Beautiful Vision', was published on 18 November 1790 by Wm Holland. An account of it can be found in George, *Catalogue*, Vol. VI, no. 7679.

156. Isaac Cruikshank, 'The Doctor Indulged with His Favourite Scene', was published on 12 December ?1790 by S.W. Fores. An account can be found in George, *Catalogue*, Vol. VI, no. 7690.

157. My discussion of the dispute between Burke and Wollstonecraft is greatly indebted to the excellent paper by Vivien Jones, 'Narratives of History and Sexuality: Rakes and Progress in Wollstonecraft's *Historical and Moral View*' (University of Leeds, 1989) which was reworked in the essays, 'Women Writing Revolution: Narratives of History and Sexuality in Wollstonecraft and Williams', in *Beyond Romanticism*, ed. by Stephen Copley and John Whale (London and New York: Routledge, 1992), pp. 178–99 and, 'Femininity, Nationalism and Romanticism: The Politics of Gender in the Revolution Controversy', *History of European Ideas*, 16, 1–3 (Jan. 1993), 299–305. Also to the work of Tom Furniss, who comments that 'these textual tensions [. . .] need to be seen in relation to these discourses of the period in which Marie Antoinette's sexuality was abstracted'. Having made this observation Furniss concludes that, 'Burke's text may [. . .] work to establish a kind of complicity with his male radical readers through a shared aggression towards the female emblem of aristocratic society', 'Stripping the Queen', p. 85 and 'Gender in Revolution', p. 80. More generally, see Ronald Paulson, 'Burke, Paine and Wollstonecraft: The Sublime and the Beautiful', in *Representations of Revolution*, pp. 57–87; Harriet Devine Jump, '"The Cool Eye of Observation" Mary Wollstonecraft and the French Revolution', in *Revolution in Writing*, pp. 101–19 and Anne K. Mellor, 'English Women Writers and the French Revolution', in *Rebel Daughters*, pp. 255–72.

158. Wollstonecraft, *A Vindication of the Rights of Men*, in *The Works*, 5, p. 30.

159. Wollstonecraft, *A Moral and Historical View* in *The Works*, 6, p. 205. It is interesting to note that there was quite some dispute about what the Queen was wearing that night, the American ambassador, Gouverneur Morris claimed that, 'The queen [was] obliged to fly from her bed in a shift and petticoat, with her stockings in her hand', *Diaries and Letters*, I, p. 176, whilst *The Times* of 13 October, 1789 contended that, 'The noise was so sudden, that her Majesty ran trembling to the KING'S apartment with only her shift on.' As we noted earlier Blake produced an engraving of this scene, in which the Queen wears rather more garments than are mentioned here.

160. See Jones, 'Narratives of History and Sexuality', p. 6 and *passim* for Wollstonecraft's critique of the 'libertine imagination', especially as embodied in the Duc d'Orléans.

161. Wollstonecraft offered more censure of the French court in numerous pieces she wrote for the *Analytical Review*, including her remarks about, 'that fatal system of *profusion* and *oppression*, which, in the latter part of the reign of Louis XV hurried France to the brink of destruction, and at length brought the affairs of that kingdom to the crisis which gave birth to the present revolution'. In now familiar terms she explained that people had been 'commanded to worship the idol that prostitution has set up', with the lamentable result that 'the sinews of honest industry are strained to pamper the unnatural vices of fastidious sensuality, rendered desperate by satiety', *An Rev*, 12 (1792), reprinted in *The Works*, 7, pp. 415–16, (p. 416).

162. Wollstonecraft, *A Moral and Historical View*, in *The Works*, 6, p. 72 and the other quotation is the title of Chapter 4, *Vindication of the Rights of Woman*. As Butler and Todd comment, 'Marie Antoinette becomes in her revolutionized version another thoroughgoing courtier, an intriguer and a whore; and, as it turns out, rather more of an agent in the crucial events of October 1789 than her husband. Yet the individual woman is not made the villain of the piece. Blame falls on a degenerate system, represented by the mythologized, 'effeminate' court – an image owing much to the pornographic scandal-culture emanating from France in the last decades of the ancient regime', 'Introduction', *The Works*, 1, p. 18.

163. Enitharmon's speech perhaps contains a defensive strategy as a response to the threat of the Sons of Urizen to, 'Seize all the spirits of life and bind/ Their warbling joys to our loud strings' (*Europe*, 4:3–4; E.62).

164. Erdman, *Illuminated*, pp. 163–4, and, *Prophet*, pp. 201–25; 264–70. Erdman is expansive on this point elsewhere, commenting that, 'In an all too esoteric irony Blake has replaced the ugly figure of the queen as sin with two innocent-looking and angel-winged women [. . .] for that was how Queen Charlotte and Queen Marie-Antoinette were pictured to the "youth of England" who must fight in the wars they caused', 'Debt to James Gillray', p. 166.

165. Frye, *Fearful Symmetry*, p. 354 and Cox, *Love and Logic*, p. 137.

166. For more useful readings of Enitharmon's behaviour, see David Aers, 'William Blake and the Dialectics of Sex', *ELH*, 44 (1977), 500–14; David Fuller, *Blake's Heroic Argument* (London: Croom Helm, 1988), pp. 70–71 and K.D. Everest, 'Thel's Dilemma', *Essays in Criticism*, 37, 3 (1987), 193–208, (pp. 196–7).

167. Mary Wollstonecraft in *Vindication of the Rights of Woman*, quotes with censure a couple of extracts from Rousseau's manifesto of female manipulativeness, 'The violence of his desires depends on her charms; it is by means of these she should urge him to the exertion of those powers which nature hath given him. The most successful method of exciting them, is, to render such exertion

necessary by resistance; as, in that case, self-love is added to desire and the one triumphs in the victory which the other is obliged
to acquire. Hence arise the various modes of attack and defence
between the sexes; the boldness of one sex and the timidity of the
other; and, in a word, that bashfulness and modesty with which
nature hath armed the weak in order to subdue the strong [. . .]
Would you have your husband constantly at your feet, keep him
at some distance from your person. *You will long maintain the authority in love, if you know how to render your favours rare and valuable.* It is thus you may employ even the arts of coquetry in the
service of virtue', p. 136; 188 (my emphasis).

168. Wollstonecraft, ibid., p. 89.
169. See David Erdman, *Illuminated*, p. 169.
170. This suggests that Harold Bloom is seriously misguided when he
claims, 'This is the song of triumph of the Female Will, with its
cult of chastity [. . .] and its alliance with the dream of a remote
heaven [. . .] Enitharmon sends her sons, the primal artists, to in-
struct the human race in her deceptions. Rintrah and Palamabron
ought respectively to prophesy and civilise, but instead their functions are subverted by their emanations, Ocalythron, a goddess
of jealousy, and Elynittria, a goddess of chastity', 'Commentary',
p. 904. John Howard elaborates these claims: 'The demons
themselves are female dominated. Ocalythron and Elynittria are
the female forces behind kingship and priesthood', *Infernal Poetics*,
p. 142.
171. Webster, *Blake's Prophetic Psychology*, p. 139.
172. Frye, *Fearful Symmetry*, p. 263; and S. Foster Damon offers the most
succinct reading of this passage as a depiction of women's triumph in Christian culture, *Blake Dictionary*, pp. 131–2.
173. Again see *Prophet*, pp. 201–25; 264–9.
174. For a discussion of spectres see Diana Hume George, *Blake and
Freud*, pp. 158–65, where she very usefully notes that, 'The spectre
is the only pure "male" principle in Blake's mythology, and it is
altogether negative', p. 159.
175. Frye, *Fearful Symmetry*, p. 263.
176. For more recent, and rather tortured, accounts of the gendered
narrative/narratives of the poem see, Swearingen, 'Time and Space'
and Cox, *Love and Logic*, pp. 132–43.
177. John Howard focuses upon Enitharmon's choice of style, but as-
sesses it in negative ways, 'Blake's skill in dramatic expression
reveals the quality of Enitharmon's delusive character [. . .] As she
subtly caresses and represses in her delicately chosen words, we
hear the voice of disdainful nonchalance about anything but her
own purposes' – all Enitharmon's speeches to her children are
thereafter interpreted in the light of this alleged egotism, *Infernal
Poetics*, pp. 144–6, (p. 144).
178. The relevant passages are *Thel*, 3:22–3, 25–30; 4:1–6; E.5 and *Visions*, 5:26–7; 6:6–17; E.49. For associations of patriarchy with solitude, see *The Book of Urizen*, Plates 3 and 4 (E.71–72).

179. Damon, *Dictionary*, p. 124 and Cox, *Love and Logic*, p. 139. Bloom concurs that Enitharmon and her daughters are a pestilential choir in this 'obscure paean of Female triumph, 'Commentary', p. 905.

180. Much more needs to be said about Blake's belief in the regenerative power of maternal love. From the mothers of *Songs of Innocence* through to Jerusalem in Blake's final epic an ethos of female care struggles to redeem a world which is, largely, being ruined by men. Dominating mothers do, of course, also figure but what I am questioning here is the critical identification of such characters when they are present only in a highly ambivalent form.

181. Critics continue to pit Enitharmon against Oothoon, whilst ignoring the protective aspect of the mother's advice and refusing to acknowledge the grave consequences of giving up women's secrecy. Stephen Behrendt, for instance, has continued this strategy in his comment that, 'The indomitable spirit of Oothoon constitutes a radical counter-text to the divisive, delusive dogma of Enitharmon, who explicitly chastises her by name in Europe', *Reading William Blake* (London and Basingstoke: Macmillan, 1992), p. 112.

182. We should note that Enitharmon delivers her infamous 'reactionary' Woman's Love is Sin speech only *after* she's descended down into the red 'revolutionary' light of Orc (*Europe*, 4:17–18; E.62) – this surely upsets any straight 'radical' reading of the episode?.

183. Most recently Edward Larrissy insisted on the complicity of Enitharmon and Urizen, 'The poem itself purports to show how the fixer and freezer of energies has been able to pose as God, with the help of Enitharmon', *William Blake* (Oxford: Basil Blackwell, 1985), p. 91.

184. Butter, 'Blake's *The French Revolution*', p. 26.

185. Aers, 'William Blake and the Dialectic of Sex', p. 508.

186. Brenda Webster offers a useful account of the final plate, where she notes that, 'if this is a rescue of females, it is also a reassertion of male power over them', *Blake's Prophetic Psychology*, p. 142.

187. For opposed assessments of these lines, see David Aers, who asserts that they 'perpetuate the same macho model of revolution and sex: revolution is a cosmic fuck', 'Representations of Revolution: From *The French Revolution* to *The Four Zoas*', in *Blake and the Argument of Method*, ed. by Dan Miller *et al.* (Durham and London: Duke University Press, 1987), pp. 244–70, (p. 357, n. 18). And Jon Mee, who claims 'The orthodox climax of history, the intervention of the judgemental deity, is replaced by a cosmic act of copulation [. . .] Moreover, the vision of cosmic copulation is strikingly different from the configurations of revolution and sexuality presented in the Preludium to *America*. There the daughter of Urizen was violated by male desire in a moment when liberated passion turns into patriarchal oppression [. . .] At the close of *The Song of Los* the liberated womb is [. . .] involved in the process of its emancipation. The 'hollow womb' actively 'clasps the solid stem', *Dangerous Enthusiasm*, pp. 143–4.

188. William Hodges, *Travels in India, during the Years 1780, 1781, 1782,*

*1783* 2nd ed. (London: J. Edwards, 1794), pp. 33–4. Relevant in this context are, Harriet Guest, 'The Great Distinction: Figures of the Exotic in the Work of William Hodges', in *New Feminist Discourses*, ed. by Isobel Armstrong (New York and London: Routledge, 1992), pp. 296–341; *Exoticism and the Enlightenment*, ed. by G.S. Rousseau and Roy Porter (Manchester: Manchester University Press, 1990); *Women's Orients: English Women and the Middle East, 1718–1918*, ed. by Billie Melman (Basingstoke: Macmillan, 1992), pp. 59–76; 77–98 and Andrew Parker *et al.*, *Nationalisms and Sexualities* (New York: Routledge, 1992).

## 6  Conclusion

1. Bakhtin, 'Toward a Methodology for the Human Sciences', in *Speech Genres and Other Late Essays*, ed. by Caryl Emerson and Michael Holquist (Austin, Texas: University of Texas Press, 1986), p. 170.
2. It should be noted, however, that unpublished doctoral dissertations offer a vital lifeline and alternative tradition of scholarship. Anyone interested in the issues I discuss should get hold of the micro-film versions of these works (sadly space does not permit me to offer a bibliography of this sizeable corpus).
3. Feminist writers have also effectively avoided the dangers described by Steven E. Cole, 'Evading Politics: The Poverty of Historicizing Romanticism', *SiR*, 34, 1 (Spring 1995), 29–50.
4. I am thinking here about the paperback edition of *Eighteenth Century Women Poets: An Oxford Anthology*, ed. by Roger Lonsdale (Oxford and New York: Oxford University Press, 1990) and *Women Romantic Poets 1785–1832: An Anthology*, ed. by Jennifer Breen (London: J.M. Dent, 1992). Another exciting development is 'Project Electra', which aims to provide an extensive electronic database for scholars of British literature and women's studies in the period 1785–1815. For information about the project, see Kathryn Sutherland, 'Challenging Assumptions: Women Writers, The Literary Canon and New Technology', *Bulletin of the John Rylands University Library of Manchester*, 74, 3 (Autumn 1992), 109–20, (esp. 114–20). See, too, *British Women Poets 1660–1800: An Anthology*, ed. by Joyce Fullard (New York: Whitson Publishing Company, 1990) and J.R. de J. Jackson, *Romantic Poetry by Women: A Bibliography, 1770–1835* (Oxford: Clarendon Press, 1993).
5. See the collections, *At the Limits of Romanticism*, ed. by Mary A. Favret and Nicola J. Watson (Bloomington and Indianapolis: Indiana UP, 1994) and *Re-visioning Romanticism: British Women Writers, 1776–1837*, ed. by Carol Shiner Wilson and Joel Haefner (Philadelphia: University of Pennsylvania Press, 1994). As the editors of the second volume note 'a whole corpus of ignored work remains to be mapped' (p. 5). Some new works still cling onto the idea that we are simply seeing Romanticism 'proving its power to renew itself', Duncan Wu (ed.) *Romanticism An Anthology* (Oxford: Blackwells, 1994) and also his *Romanticism: A Critical Reader* (Oxford: Blackwell's,

1995) but more noteworthy are the following: Anne K. Mellor, *Romanticism and Gender* (New York and London: Routledge, 1993); *New Romanticisms*, ed. by David L. Clark and Donald C. Goellnicht (Buffalo: University of Toronto Press, 1994); Stuart Curran, 'The I Altered', in *Romanticism and Feminism*, ed. by Anne K. Mellor (Bloomington and Indianapolis: Indiana University Press, 1988), pp. 185–207; Donna Landry, *The Muses of Resistance: Labouring-Class Women's Poetry in Britain, 1739–1796* (Cambridge: CUP, 1990) and Marlon B. Ross, *The Contours of Masculine Desire: Romanticism and the Rise of Women's Poetry* (New York and Oxford: OUP, 1989). The publication of the journal *Women's Writing: The Elizabethan to Victorian Period*, edited by Janet Todd and begun in 1994, will also help to change our perceptions.

6. 'Ozymandias', in *Shelley: Poetical Works*, ed. by Thomas Hutchinson (Oxford and New York: OUP, 1986), p. 550.

7. Donna Landry comments on this, 'peculiar sense of belatedness [. . .] like other forms of critical theory, feminism has only just arrived on the professional and scholarly agendas of eighteenth century specialists'. She also offers some warnings about this arrival, for she feels that, 'feminism is being fetished as a marketable commodity within eighteenth century studies. And, like other forms of critical study, feminism has been commodified before it could become truly institutionalised or realise its most radical effects', 'Commodity Feminism', in *The Profession of Eighteenth Century Literature*, ed. by Leopold Damrosch (Wisconsin: University of Wisconsin Press, 1992), pp. 154–74, (p. 154).

   On the second point see, for example, Claire Goldberg Moses, '"Equality" and "Difference" in Historical Perspective: A Comparative Examination of the Feminisms of the French Revolutionaries and Utopian Socialists', in *Rebel Daughters: Women and the French Revolution*, ed. by Sara Melzer and Leslie Rabine (New York and Oxford: OUP, 1992), pp. 231–54, (especially, 'Deconstructing the "Equality-versus-Difference" Debate', pp. 246–9); Karen Offen, 'Defining Feminism: A Comparative Historical Approach', *Signs*, 14, 1 (Autumn 1988), 119–57 and *Feminists Theorize the Political*, ed. by Joan W. Scott and Judith Butler (London: Routledge, 1992).

8. Scott, '"A Women Who Has Only Paradoxes to Offer": Olympe de Gouges Claims for the Rights of Women', in *Rebel Daughters*, pp. 102–20, (p. 106).

9. I made this case in my chapter on *Thel*, but it is interesting to note E.B. Bentley's comment about the way she was treated during her search for a copy of *The Ladies New and Polite Pocket Memorandumbook*: 'Many librarians are amused by my searches and others try to remind me that this is a search for very "ephemeral stuff"', 'Blake's Elusive Ladies', *BQ*, 26, 1 (Summer 1992), 30–33, (p. 32).

10. Bakhtin, *Discourse in the Poetry and Discourse in the Novel*, in *The Dialogic Imagination*, ed. by Michael Holquist (Austin, Texas: University of Texas Press, 1981), p. 276.

11. Bakhtin, ibid., p. 293.

12. The question of when a recognizable lesbian identity came into being is still hotly contested, but much more research is needed before we can except the arguments about eighteenth-century variants offered by Terry Castle, *The Apparitional Lesbian* (New York: Columbia University Press, 1993), pp. 8–10 and *passim*.

13. It is worth thinking about Blake's formal experiments in the light of Bakhtin's idea that, 'every genre has its methods and means of seeing and conceptualizing reality [. . .] One might say that human consciousness possesses a series of inner genres for seeing and conceptualizing reality. A given consciousness is richer or poorer in genres, depending on its ideological environment. Literature occupies an important place in this ideological environment. As [. . .] the genres of literature enrich our inner speech with the devices for the awareness and conceptualization of reality', *The Formal Method in Literary Scholarship, a critical introduction to sociological poetics* (Baltimore: Johns Hopkins University Press, 1978), pp. 133–4.

14. A volume which usefully demonstrates this is, *History, Gender and Eighteenth Century Literature*, ed. by Beth Fawkes Tobin (Athens and London: University of Georgia Press, 1994), especially 'Introduction: Feminist Historical Criticism', pp. 1–13.

15. Glen E. Brewster, 'Blake and the Metaphor of Marriage', *Nineteenth Century Contexts*, 16, 1 (1992), 64–89, (p. 71).

16. In a review of the Erdman/Magno edition of *The Four Zoas* manuscript Martin Bidney commented that, 'The biggest surprise the volume offers is its disclosure of the intensity of Blake's sexual preoccupations', *SiR*, 29, 2 (Summer 1990), pp. 317–23, (p. 321). As I say, so *much* remains to be done.

17. I would suggest that the following passages could be golden threads for the interested interpreter: *The Four Zoas*, 43:1–22; E.328–9/*Milton*, 22:4–14; E.116–17 and Plate 47 (*Illuminated*, E.263)/*Jerusalem*, 19, 20: 40–41 (E.164–6).

# Select Bibliography

This is a *very* select bibliography. It lists only general studies of Blake which have some kind of 'feminist' orientation. References for criticism of particular works are contained in the footnotes of each relevant chapter. The index directs readers to specific critics, historical figures and events, authors, issues and so forth. Those wishing to consult a more detailed bibliography are directed to my thesis, 'Historicizing Blake in 'A Land of Men and Women Too'' (1993), housed at Oxford Brookes University library and available on microfilm from the British Library, London.

Ackland, Michael. 'The Embattled Sexes: Blake's Debt to Wollstonecraft in *The Four Zoas*', BQ, 16, 3 (Winter 1982–83), 172–83.

Aers, David. 'William Blake and the Dialectic of Sex', *ELH*, 44 (1977), 137–44.

——. 'Blake: Sex, Society and Ideology', in *Romanticism and Ideology*, ed. by David Aers *et al.* (London: Routledge and Kegan Paul, 1981), pp. 27–43.

Ault, Donald. 'Where's Poppa? or, The Defeminization of Blake's "Little Black Boy"', in *Out of Bounds: Male Writers and Gendered Criticism* , ed. by Laura Claridge and Elizabeth Langland (Amherst: The University of Massachusetts Press, 1990), pp. 75–91.

Billingheimer, Rachel. 'The Female in Blake and Yeats', *CEA Critic*, 48, 4/49, 1 (1986), 137–44.

Bohnsack, Marilyn. 'William Blake and the Social Construct of Female Metaphors' (University of Miami, 1988).

Brogan, Howard O. 'Blake on Woman: Oothoon to Jerusalem', *CEA Critic*, 48, 4/49, 1 (1986), 125–36.

Chayes, Irene. 'The Presence of Cupid and Psyche', in *Blake's Visionary Forms Dramatic*, ed. by David V. Erdman and John E. Grant (Princeton, NJ: Princeton University Press, 1970), pp. 214–43.

Clark, Steve. 'Blake and Female Reason', in his *Sordid Images: The Poetry of Masculine Desire* (New York and London: Routledge, 1994), pp. 138–87.

Comer, John. 'Lawrence and Blake', in *D.H. Lawrence and Tradition*, ed. by Jeffrey Meyers (Amherst, MA: University of Massachusetts Press, 1985), pp. 9–20.

Derderian, Nancy Cebula. 'Against the Patriarchal Pomp: A Study of the Feminine Principle in the Poetry of William Blake' (University of Buffalo at New York, 1974).

Di Salvo, Jackie. 'Blake Encountering Milton: Politics and the Family in *Paradise Lost* and *The Four Zoas*', in *Milton and the Line of Vision*, ed. by Joseph Wittreich (Wisconsin and London: Wisconsin University Press, 1975), pp. 143–84.

—— 'The Politics of the Family', in *War of Titans: Blake's Critique of Milton and the Politics of Religion* (Pittsburgh: University of Pittsburgh Press, 1984), pp. 311–64.

Essick, Robert N. 'William Blake's "Female Will" and Its Biographical Context, *SEL*, 31 (1991), 615–30.

Ferber, Michael. 'Nature and the Female', in *The Social Vision of William Blake* (Princeton, NJ: Princeton University Press, 1985), pp. 89–115.

Fox, Susan. 'The Female as Metaphor in the Poetry of William Blake', *Critical Inquiry*, 3 (Spring 1977), 507–19.

Freed, Eugenie R. *"A Portion of His Life": William Blake's Miltonic Vision of Woman* (London and Toronto: Associated University Presses, 1994).

Fulbright, James Stephen. 'William Blake and the Emancipation of Women' (University of Missouri, Columbia, 1973).

George, Diana Hume. *Blake and Freud* (Ithaca: Cornell University Press, 1980).

Greco, Norma A. 'Mother Figures in Blake's *Songs of Innocence* and The Female Will', *Romanticism Past and Present*, 10, 1 (Winter 1986), 1–15.

Gutschera, Deborah A. '"A Shape of Brightness": The Role of Women in the Romantic Epic', *PQ*, 66, 1 (Winter 1987), 87–108.

Haffar, Dana K. 'The "Women" in Blake's Early Writings and the "Females" of the Prophecies' (Oxford University, 1984).

Haigney, Catherine. 'Vala's Garden in Night the Ninth: Paradise Regained or Woman Bound?', *BQ*, 20, 4 (Spring 1987), 116–24.

Haigwood, Laura Ellen. 'Eve's Daughters: The Subversive Feminine in Blake and Wordsworth' (University of California, Santa Cruz, 1984).

Hoeveler, Diane Long. *Romantic Androgyny: The Woman Within* (Philadelphia: The Pennsylvania UP, 1990).

Hood, Margaret. 'The Pleasant Charge: William Blake's Multiple Roles for Women' (University of Adelaide, 1987).

Langland, Elizabeth. 'Blake's Feminist Revision of Literary Tradition in "The Sick Rose"', in *Critical Paths: Blake and the Argument of Method*, ed. by Dan Miller, Mark Bracher and Donald Ault (Durham and London: Duke University Press, 1987), pp. 225–43.

Lee, Judith. 'Ways of Their Own: The Emanations of Blake's Vala', *ELH*, 50 (1983), 131–53.

Lussier, Mark. 'Mirror and Vortex: Blake and Lacan' (Texas A&M University, 1989).

McClenahan, Catherine. 'No Face like the Human Divine?: Women and Gender in Blake's *Pickering Manuscript*', in *Spirits of Fire: English Romantic Writers and Contemporary Historical Methods*, ed. by G.A. Rosso and Daniel Watkins (London and Toronto: Associated University Presses, 1990), pp. 189–207.

Mellor, Anne K. 'Blake's Portrayal of Women', *BQ*, 16, 3 (Winter 1982–83), 148–55.

——. 'Blake's *Songs of Innocence and of Experience*: A Feminist Perspective', *Nineteenth Century Poetry*, II (1988), 1–17.

Murphy, Kathleen Middleton. '"All the Lovely Sex": Blake and the Woman Question', in *Sparks of Fire: Blake in a New Age*, ed. by James Bogan and Fred Goss (Richmond, Cal: North Atlantic Books, 1982), pp. 272–5.

Ostriker, Alicia. 'Desire Gratified and Ungratified: William Blake and Sexuality', *BQ*, 16, 3 (Winter 1982–83), 156–65.

Punter, David. 'Blake, Trauma and the Female', *New Literary History*, 15, 3 (1984), 475–90.

——. 'The Sign of Blake', *Criticism*, 26 (1985), 313–34.

——. *The Romantic Unconscious: A Study in Narcissism and Patriarchy* (Hemel Hempstead: Harvester Wheatsheaf, 1989).

Schotz, Myra Glazer. 'For the Sexes: Blake's Hermaphrodite in Lady Chatterley's Lover', *Bucknell Review*, 24, 1 (1978), 17–26.

——. 'Why the Sons of God Want the Daughters of Men: On William Blake and D.H. Lawrence', in *William Blake and the Moderns*, ed. by Robert J. Bertholf and Annette S. Levitt (Albany: State University Press of New York, 1982), pp. 164–85.

Schuchard, Marsha Keith. 'Blake's Healing Trio: Magnetism, Medicine and Mania', *BQ*, 23, 1 (Summer 1989), 20–32.

——. 'The Secret History of Blake's Swedenborg Society', *BQ*, 26, 2 (Fall 1992), 40–51.

——. 'Blake's "Mr Femality": Freemasonry, Espionage and the Double Sexed', *Studies in Eighteenth-century Culture*, 22, 1 (1992), 51–71.

Sorensen, Peter J. 'The Pistis Sophia: The Fall and Redemption of Blake's Female Characters' in his *William Blake's Recreation of Gnostic Myth* (New York and Salzburg: Edwin Mellen Press, 1995), pp. 37–58.

Stepto, Michele. 'Blake, Urizen and the Feminine: The Development of a Poetic Logic' (University of Massachusetts, 1978).

Storch, Margaret. 'Blake and Women: "Nature's Cruel Holiness"', *American Imago*, 38 (1981), 221–46.

——. '"The Spectrous Fiend Cast Out": Blake's Crisis at Felpham', *MLQ*, 44 (1983), 115–35.

——. *Sons and Adversaries: Women in William Blake and D.H. Lawrence* (Knoxville: The University of Tennessee Press, 1990).

Sturrock, June. 'Blake and the Women of the Bible', *Journal of Literature and Theology*, 6, 1 (March 1992), 23–32.

Tayler, Irene. 'The Woman Scaly', *Midwestern Modern Languages Association Bulletin*, 6 (1973), 74–87.

Verma, K.D. 'The Woman Figure in Blake and the Idea of Shaka in Indian Thought', *Comparative Literary Studies*, 27, 3 (1990), 193–210.

Waxler, Robert Phillip. 'William Blake: The Sexual Dynamics of the Early Illuminated Works' (State University of New York at Stony Brook, 1976).

Webster, Brenda. *Blake's Prophetic Psychology* (London and Basingstoke: Macmillan, 1983).

——. 'Blake, Women and Sexuality', in *Critical Paths: Blake and the Argument of Method*, ed. by Dan Miller, Mark Bracher and Donald Ault (Durham and London: Duke University Press, 1987), pp. 204–24.

Webster, Sarah McKim. 'Circumscription and the Female in the Early Romantics', *PQ*, 61, 17 (Winter 1982), 51–68.

White, Elizabeth. 'Woman's Triumph: A Study of the Changing Symbolic Values of the Female in the Works of William Blake' (University of Washington, 1972).

# Index